The Gun Digest Book of FIREARMS ASSEMBLY/ DISASSEMBLY

Part III
Rimfire Rifles, Revised
by J.B. Wood

DBI BOOKS, INC.

Editorial Staff:

Editor
Harold A. Murtz
Editorial Production Associate
John Duoba
Production Assistant
Jamie L. Puffpaff
Electronic Publishing Manager
Nancy J. Mellem
Electronic Publishing Associate
Robert M. Fuentes
Editorial Assistant
Holly J. Porter
Cover Photography
John Hanusin
Managing Editor
Pamela J. Johnson
Publisher
Sheldon L. Factor

This book is dedicated to Rolan Bennett, Bill Book, Chick Evans, Jim Edlin, Paul James, and the times that used to be.

Acknowledgements

My thanks to these people, who helped to make this book possible:

John S. Yarger, John A. Yarger, James W. Yarger, and Larry McClarney of Lock & Load Gun Shop, Glenn Lancaster, Al Paulsen, Thomas M. Brown, James W. Wood, A. D. Jenkins, Ron Fine of Mossberg, Jack Sharry of Harrington & Richardson, Stanley Hopper of Family Sporting Goods, Carl Bonnell and Jessie Smith of Sportsman's Corner, Gene Wilson, Joe Burton, John Cole of Daisy Manufacturing, Ernie Barriage of Lakefield Arms; Paul Thompson of Browning, Bill Wohl of Remington, Larry Larson of Armscor Precision, Jerry Stern of Action Arms, Rich Krieg of Federal Engineering, Mike Miller of Calico, Merv Chapman of Feather Industries, George Kellgren of Grendel, Rick Krouse of Kintrek, Charles T. Hartigan, Harold A. Murtz, Daniel A. Murtz, Pamela Johnson, Major Terah Flaherty, Philip M. Shannon, Gene Bruce, Jesse Eckels, Charles E. Minton, and Mary Alice Casey.

Arms and Armour Press, London, G.B., exclusive licensees and distributor in Britain and Europe; Nigeria; So. Africa and Zimbabwe; India and Pakistan. Lothian Books, Takapuna, N.Z., exclusive distributor in New Zealand.

ISBN 0-87349-152-1
Library of Congress Catalog Card # 79-54271

Table of Contents

Introduction

Every gunsmith is familiar with what might be called the "sack-of-parts" syndrome. Customers frequently arrive with guns totally or partially disassembled, in all manner of containers. I have seen them in cigar boxes, paper sacks, plastic bags, glass jars, and once in an aluminum vase, the type used to put flowers on graves. In most cases, the reason for the complete takedown was "cleaning," and the unfortunate owner then couldn't remember the proper position of all those small parts and springs.

If the owner had the manual or instruction sheet supplied with each new gun, it was often of little help, as most of these go only as far as simple field-stripping. For some of the older guns, the manuals are scarce collector items, and are not readily obtainable. With some imported guns, the direct-translation sheets are amusing to read, but nearly useless as a guide. Good, clear instructions on total takedown and reassembly were obviously needed, and this is the idea behind this series of books. Volumes I and II cover pistols and revolvers, and the next two books in the series cover centerfire rifles and shotguns.

In complete disassembly and reassembly, there are some points that may require the special tools and skills of the gunsmith. A very knowledgeable amateur can usually manage it, but he must have some mechanical aptitude. This book is intended for both the average gun person and the professional, and for this reason even the simpler operations are described and shown in detail.

Some of the tools required are of a type not readily available at the local hardware store, so I am including a section on tools, and giving the sources from which they may be obtained.

In the takedown of any gun, there are a few general rules which apply. A light tap with a plastic mallet may sometimes be necessary to free a tight assembly, but no extreme force should be used. Always wear safety glasses to protect the eyes from parts expelled by compressed springs. Do not disassemble a gun outdoors, over tall grass, or indoors, over a shag rug. Before you start, read the instructions through, all the way, at least once.

I assume that my readers are sufficiently intelligent not to work on a loaded gun, so I will not begin each set of instructions by repeating that the gun must be entirely unloaded. I'll say it once, right here: *Before you begin the disassembly of any gun, be sure that all cartridges are removed.* Don't trust the feed and ejection systems—make a thorough visual inspection. Some tube-magazine types can "hide" a round in the mechanism.

An important addition to the back of this book is a comprehensive index and cross-reference list, linking all of the rifles covered here to guns of similar or identical pattern. When these are included in the count, the instructions in this revised edition can be used for the takedown and reassembly of hundreds of rifles.

The *Gun Digest Book of Exploded Long Gun Drawings,* also available from DBI Books, Inc., is an excellent companion to this book, showing parts relationships and factory parts numbers for 488 guns.

J.B. Wood
Raintree House
Corydon, Kentucky
January, 1994

A Note on Reassembly

Most of the rifles covered in this book can be reassembled by simply reversing the order of disassembly, carefully replacing the parts in the same manner they were removed. In a few instances, special instructions are required, and these are listed with each gun under "Reassembly Tips." In certain cases, reassembly photos are also provided.

If there are no special instructions or photos with a particular gun, you may assume that it can just be reassembled in reverse order. During disassembly, note the relationship of all parts and springs, and lay them out on the workbench in the order they were removed. By following this procedure you should have no difficulty.

TOOLS

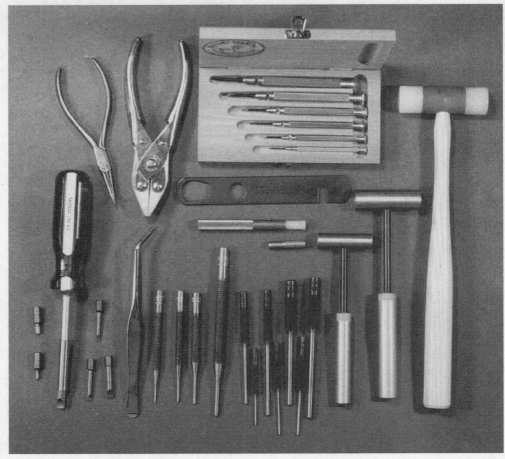

Countless firearms, old and new, bear the marks, burrs and gouges that are the result of using the wrong tools for taking them apart. In the interest of preventing this sort of thing, I am including here a group of tools that are the best types for the disassembly of rifles. Except for the few shop-made tools for special purposes, all of those shown here are available from one of these three sources.

Brownells, Inc.
Route 2, Box 1
Montezuma, Iowa 50171

B-Square Company
P.O. Box 11281
Fort Worth, Texas 76109

Williams Gun Sight Company
7389 Lapeer Road
Davison, Michigan 48423

General Instructions:

Screwdrivers: Always be sure the blade of the screwdriver **exactly** fits the slot in the screw head, both in thickness and in width. If you don't have one that fits, grind or file the tip until it does. You may ruin a few screwdrivers but better them than the screws on a fine rifle.

Slave pins: There are several references in this book to slave pins, and some non-gunsmith readers may not be familiar with the term. A slave pin is simply a short length of rod stock (in some cases, a section of a nail will do) which is used to keep two parts, or a part and a spring, together during reassembly. The slave pin must be very slightly smaller in diameter than the hole in the part, so it will push out easily as the original pin is driven in to retain the part. When making a slave pin, its length should be slightly less than the width of the part in which it is being used, and the ends of the pin should be rounded or beveled.

Sights: Nearly all dovetail-mounted sights are drifted out toward the right, using a nylon, aluminum, or brass drift punch.

1. The tiniest of these fine German instrument screwdrivers from Brownells is too small for most gun work, but you'll see the rest of them used frequently throughout the book. There are many tight places where these will come in handy.

2. When a larger screwdriver is needed, this set from Brownells covers a wide range of blade sizes and also has Phillips- and Allen-type inserts. The tips are held in place by a strong magnet, yet are easily changed. These tips are very hard. With enough force you might manage to break one, but they'll never bend.

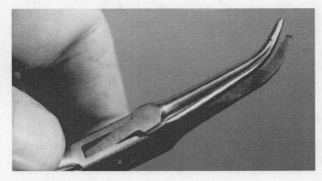

3. You should have at least one good pair of bent sharp-nosed pliers. These, from Brownells, have a box joint and smooth inner faces to help prevent marring.

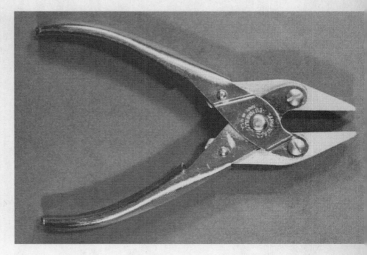

4. For heavier gripping, these Bernard parallel-jaw pliers from Brownells have smooth-faced jaw-pieces of un-hardened steel to prevent marring of parts.

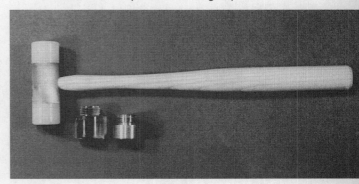

5. For situations where a non-marring rap is needed, this hammer from Brownells is ideal. It is shown with nylon faces on the head, but other faces of plastic and brass are also available. All are easily replaceable.

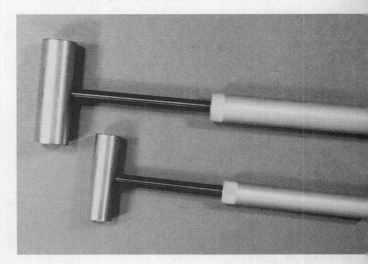

6. For drifting out pins, these small all-metal hammers from B-Square are the best I've seen. Two sizes (weights) are available and they're well worth the modest cost.

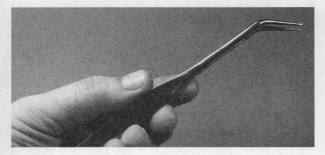

7. For situations where reach and accessibility are beyond the capabilities of sharp-nosed pliers, a pair of large sharp-nosed forceps (tweezers) will be invaluable.

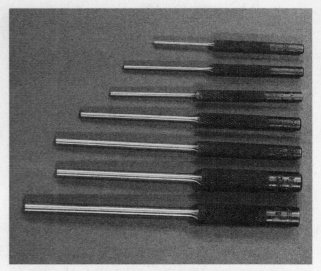

8. One of the most-used tools in my shop is this nylon-tipped drift punch, shown with an optional brass tip in place on the handle. It has a steel pin inside the nylon tip for strength. From Brownells, and absolutely essential.

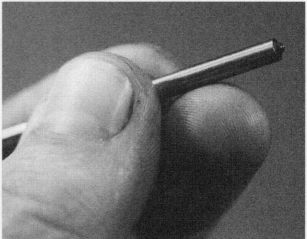

10. These punches by Mayhew are designed specifically for roll pins and have a projection at the center of the tip to fit the hollow center of a roll pin, driving it out without deformation of the ends. From Brownells.

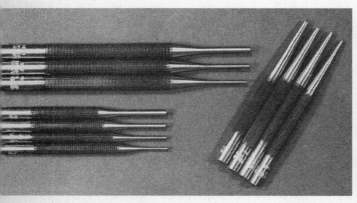

9. A good set of drift punches will prevent a lot of marred pins. These, from Brownells, are made by Mayhew. The tapered punches at the right are for starting pins, the others for pushing them through. Two sizes are available—4 inches or 6 inches.

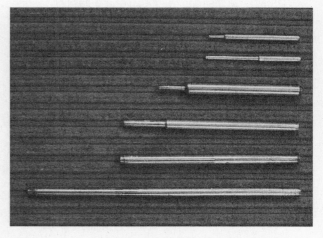

11. Some of the necessary tools are easily made in the shop. These non-marring drift punches were made from three sizes of welder's brazing rod.

12. From Brownells, this wrench is specifically designed for use on the barrel nut on the Winchester 150/250 and 190/290 series.

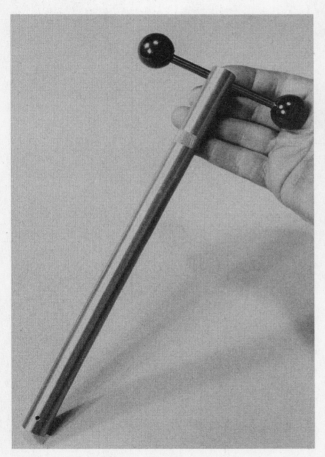

13. The B-Square stock bolt tool automatically centers in the access hole at the rear of the stock, and its wide cross-piece easily "finds" the screw slot. The T-handle gives good leverage.

14. This is the end of the B-Square general stock bolt tool, showing the replaceable cross-piece which contacts the screw slot.

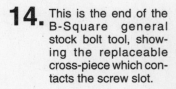

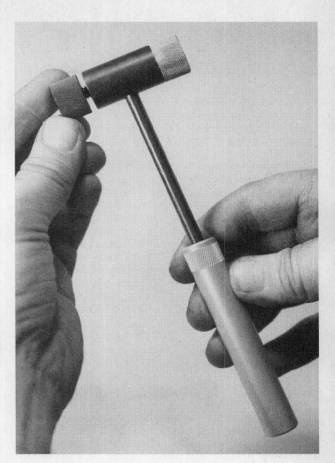

15. This excellent new hammer from B-Square is the same size and weight as the larger of the two hammers shown elsewhere in the tool section, and has an additional feature—knurled replaceable striking faces, in your choice of brass or steel.

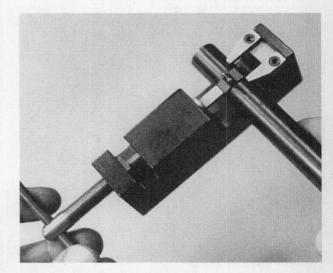

16. When dovetail-mounted sights are not super-tight, this "Sight-Pusher" will move them out or into place gently, without the marring which can occur with the hammer-and-drift method. From Williams.

Inner Magazine Tube Disassembly:

With very few exceptions, the disassembly of the inner magazine tube is the same for most rifles having this type of magazine system. The knurled knob at the end of the tube is retained by a cross pin, with one or both ends of the cross pin protruding to lock the tube in the gun. Most of the pins are driven out toward the non-protruding (or smooth) side. The tube should be supported in a V-block or a slightly opened bench vise during this operation, to avoid deformation of the thin walls of the tube. When the pin is out, the knob can be removed from the end of the tube, and this will release the magazine spring and follower. In some cases, the spring will be slightly compressed, so take care that it doesn't get away, and ease it out. In those cases where the cross pin protrudes on both sides, the pin will be slightly tapered. These should be driven out toward the larger end of the pin. Some box-type magazines can be disassembled, but most of them are of staked construction, and in normal disassembly should not be taken apart.

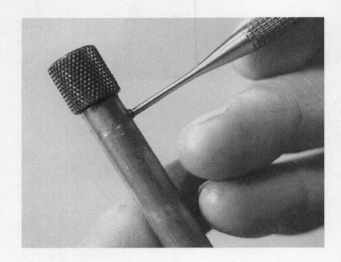

A Note On Coin-Slotted Screws

Many action takedown screws and main stock retaining screws have slots designed for use with a coin, the theory being that a shooter in the field might not have a large screwdriver at hand, but would be likely to have pocket change. The slots in these screws are wider than normal, and the floor of the slots will be curved, to match the curve of a coin edge. It is possible, and advisable, for the gunsmith or advanced amateur to alter a large shop screwdriver to exactly fit these screws. In general, though, the following advice applies: *Do not use an ordinary, unaltered large screwdriver on coin-slotted screws.* To pre-silence the protests of my fellow numismatists, I will add that a piece of ordinary worn pocket change should be used, not a 1938 Proof nickel.

AP-74 (E.M.F.)

Data:	EMF Model AP-74
Origin:	Italy
Manufacturer:	Armi Jäger, Torino, for EMF Co. Inc.
Cartridge:	22 Long Rifle
Magazine capacity:	15 rounds
Overall length:	$38^1/_2$ inches
Barrel length:	20 inches
Weight:	$6^1/_2$ pounds

Designed to be a 22 caliber counterpart to the Colt AR-15 and U.S. M-16, the Model AP-74 is also very similar internally—without the gas system and bolt locking, of course. The gun is a little lighter, but has the same balance and handling qualities as the centerfire version. As those who have trained with the military rifle will be quick to note, the takedown also has many similarities.

Disassembly:

1. Remove the magazine, and cycle the action to cock the internal hammer. Set the safety in the on-safe position. Push out the large cross-pin in the upper rear of the grip frame.

2. Tip the rear of the receiver upward, and pull back the charging handle to pull the bolt out of the rear of the receiver, and remove the bolt.

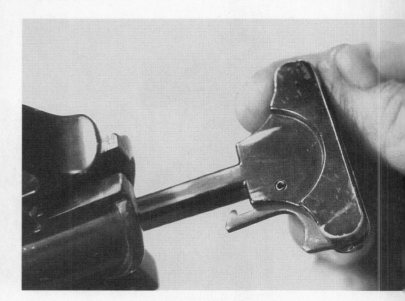

3. Move the charging handle downward, out of its track in the top of the receiver, and remove it toward the rear. Drifting out the vertical roll pin in the left lobe of the handle will allow removal of the lock lever and its spring.

4. The charging handle lug on top of the bolt is screw-slotted and threaded into the bolt, and is also the retainer for the firing pin. Restrain the firing pin, and unscrew and remove the lug.

5. Release the firing pin and remove it toward the rear. The firing pin return spring may stay in its tunnel, and can be shaken out or extracted with a bent paper clip.

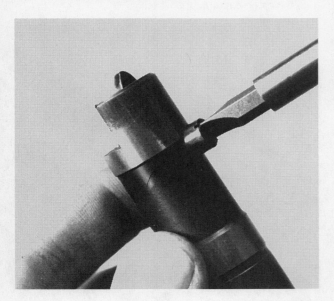

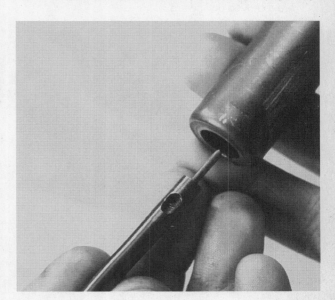

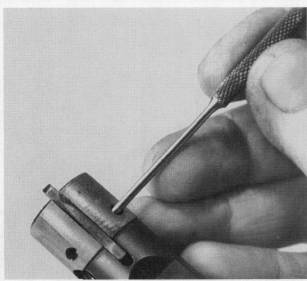

6. The extractor and its coil spring are retained on the right side of the bolt by a vertical roll pin, and when the pin is drifted out, the extractor and its spring are removed toward the right.

7. Remove the cap screw from the barrel and receiver hinge, and push out the hinge pin toward the opposite side. If the screw is tight, use a second screwdriver to stabilize the slotted head of the hinge pin while taking out the cap screw. Separate the barrel and receiver unit from the grip frame.

8. The bolt latch, located on the left side of the receiver at the lower edge, is retained by a cross pin. The pin is drifted out toward the left by inserting a drift punch through the ejection port, and the latch and its spring are removed downward.

9. The hinge pin for the ejection port cover is staked at both ends, and driving it out would damage the loops on the receiver. In normal takedown, the cover and its spring should be left in place. If removal is absolutely necessary, cut or file the spread edges at one end of the hinge pin, and push it out.

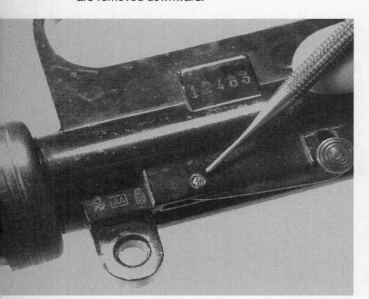

10. Two vertical Allen screws on the underside retain the front sight. Backing out these screws will allow the front sight to be moved forward, and the two sides of the forend can be taken off.

11. Remove the cross-screw on the left side of the ejector/hammer stop, and take off the part upward.

12. Turn the safety to the off-safe position, restrain the hammer, and pull the trigger. Ease the hammer down. Removal of the ejector/hammer stop will allow the hammer to go further forward than its normal position, partially relieving the tension of the hammer spring. Drift out the hammer pivot pin toward the right, and remove the hammer and hammer spring upward.

13. The hammer spring is easily detached from its studs on the side of the hammer.

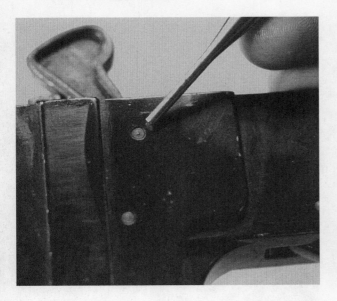

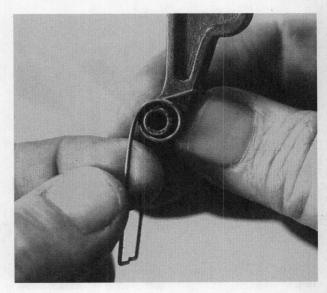

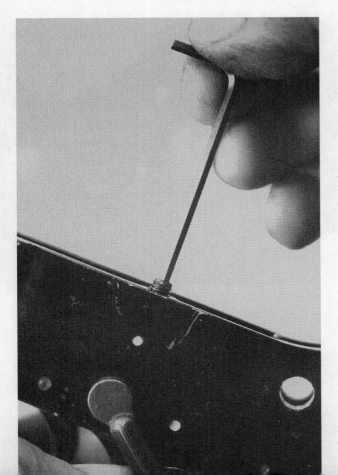

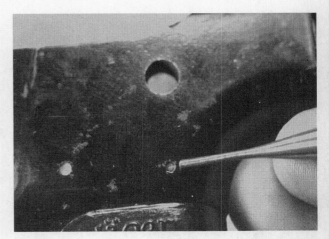

15. Drift out the small pin at the rear of the grip frame, just above the handle, to release the expansion spring at the rear of the trigger.

14. Use an Allen wrench to remove the screw in the left frame wall, and take out the safety plunger and spring upward. Remove the safety toward the left.

16. Drift out the trigger cross pin toward the right.

17. Push the sear forward and hold it there while removing the trigger assembly upward. When the trigger is clear, allow the sear to snap over to the rear, partially relieving the tension of its spring. If necessary, drifting out the cross pin will separate the disconnector from the trigger.

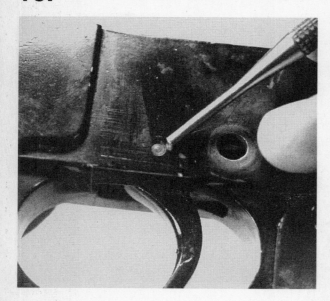

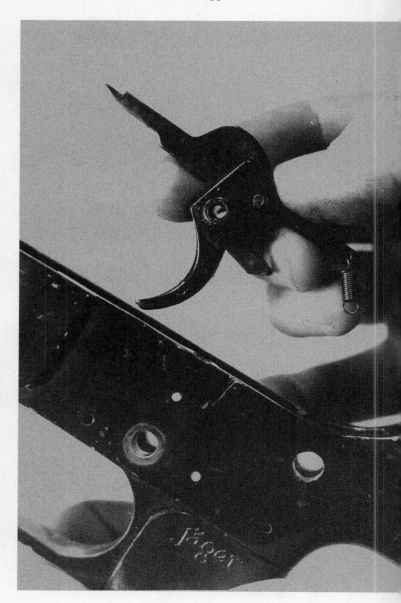

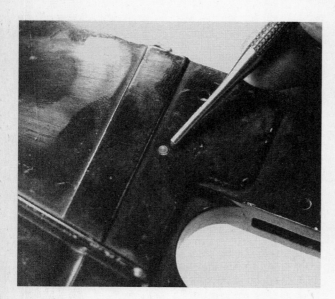

18. Drifting out the sear cross pin toward the right will release the sear and its spring for removal upward. **Caution:** *The sear spring is quite powerful. Restrain the sear and ease it out.*

19. The magazine release button, located on the right side at the lower rear of the magazine housing, is screw-slotted and is threaded into the catch block on the opposite side. Unscrew the button, take it off toward the right, along with the spring, and remove the catch block toward the left.

20. The grip handle is retained by a screw angled upward into the lower frame, accessible through the bottom of the handle. Remove the handle downward.

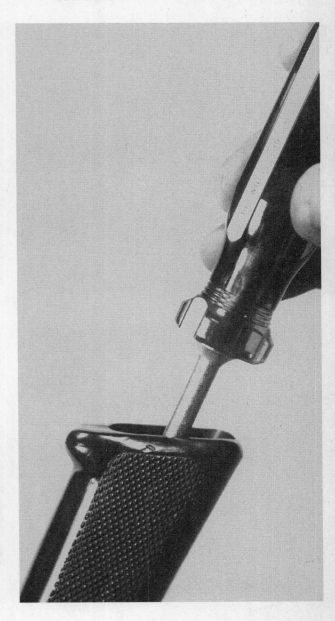

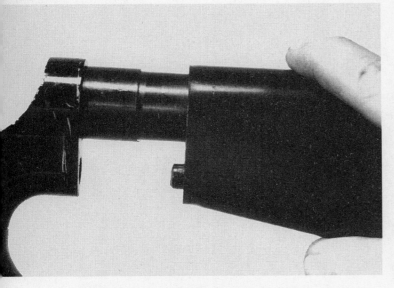

21. Remove the large and small Phillips screws at the rear of the buttstock, and take off the buttplate toward the rear. Slide the buttstock off toward the rear.

23. Turn the upper buttplate screw back into the nylon bushing at the rear of the spring housing, and using the screw and a screwdriver push the bushing inward, then rotate it one quarter turn toward the right (clockwise, rear view). **Caution:** *Grip the rear bushing firmly, and ease it out slowly, as this powerful spring is partially compressed, even when at rest.*

22. Unscrew the spring housing from the rear of the frame, and remove it.

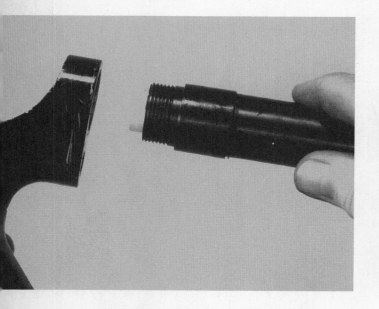

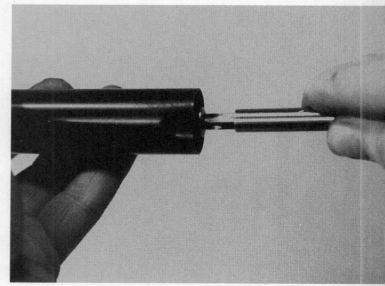

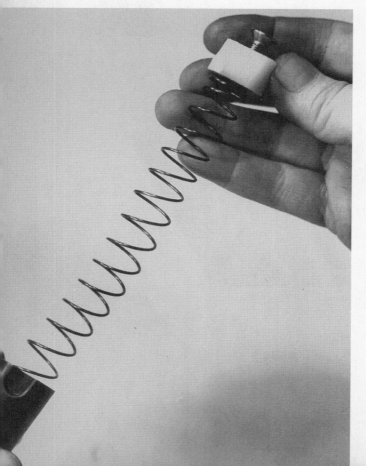

24. Remove the rear bushing and recoil spring toward the rear.

25. Move the spring guide and follower to the rear, and rotate these parts until their lugs are aligned to clear the detent depressions at the rear of the tube. Remove the guide and follower toward the rear.

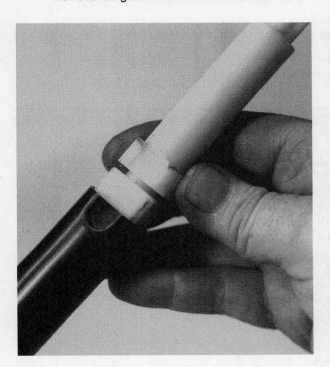

Reassembly Tips:

1. When replacing the firing pin in the bolt, be sure the firing pin is oriented so its retaining recess is toward the top of the bolt, to accept the nose of the retainer.

When replacing the trigger and disconnector assembly, push the small rear spring pin halfway across, and hook the rear loop of the expansion spring onto it. Then, drive the pin into place. Lift the sear and insert the front of the disconnector arm into the vertical slot in the sear. Allow the sear to hold the trigger and disconnector in place while the trigger is positioned for insertion of its cross pin.

When replacing the cocking handle and bolt assembly, the cocking handle must be inserted first, and moved up into its track before insertion of the bolt. Note that the ejection port cover must be open as the bolt is inserted.

Armscor
Model 20P

Similar/Identical Pattern Guns
The same basic assembly/disassembly steps for the Armscor Model 20P also apply to the following guns:

Armscor Model 20C   **Armscor Model 2000SC**
Armscor Model 50S   **Armscor Model 2000**

Data:	Armscor Model 20P
Origin:	Philippines
Manufacturer:	Arms Corp. of the Philippines
Cartridge:	22 Long Rifle
Magazine capacity:	15 rounds
Overall length:	$39^3/_4$ inches
Barrel length:	21 inches
Weight:	$6^1/_2$ pounds

The Model 20P is the current and slightly redesigned version of earlier 22 semi-autos that were made in the Philippines by the Squires Bingham company. These are well-made guns, but there are several points in complete takedown that may be problems for the non-professional. These are noted in the instructions. The Models 20C, 2000SC, 2000, and 50S differ only in stock details and accessories.

Disassembly:

1. Pull the trigger to drop the striker to fired position, and remove the magazine. Loosen the stock mounting bolt and pull it out until it stops.

2. Move the action straight up out of the stock.

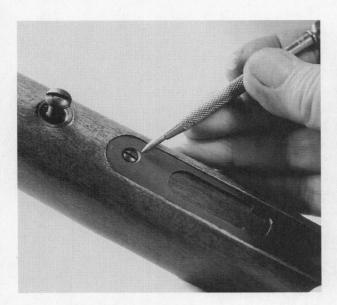

3. The trigger guard unit and the buttplate are each retained on the stock by two wood screws. The stock mounting bolt can be removed by continuing to turn it counterclockwise.

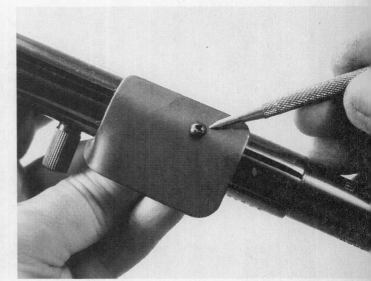

4. Remove the small Phillips-type retaining screw and take off the case deflector.

5. Back out or remove the small Phillips-type screw on the underside of the receiver at the rear.

6. Unscrew and remove the receiver end cap. **Caution:** *Springs are under tension, so control the cap.*

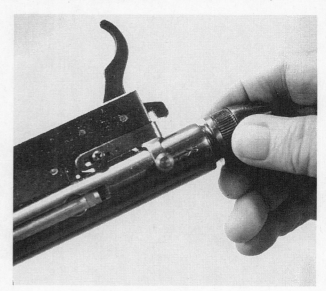

7. Easing the spring tension, remove the end cap, striker spring, recoil spring and their attendant sleeves and guides, toward the rear. If these elements are not being taken out for repair or replacement, it would be well to keep them in original order for reinstallation.

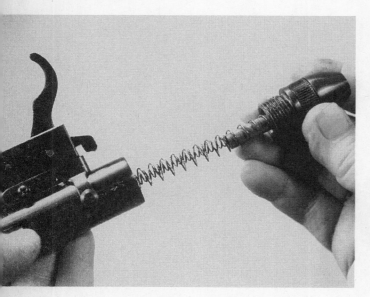

8. Point the barrel upward and retract the bolt handle fully to the rear. While exerting slight outward pressure on the bolt handle, push the striker (firing pin) forward until its exit cut aligns with the bolt handle. The bolt handle can then be removed toward the right.

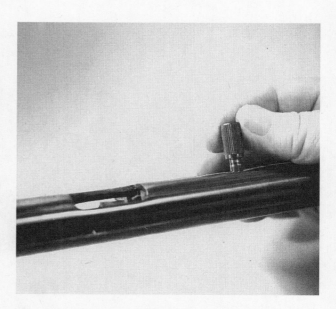

9. Pull the trigger to free the bolt and remove the bolt assembly toward the rear.

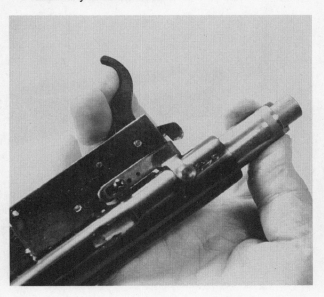

10. The striker (firing pin) is easily removed from the top of the bolt.

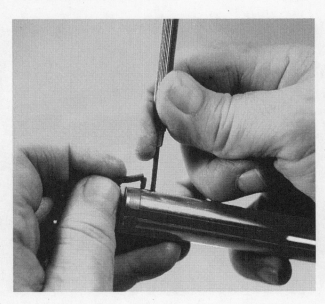

11. Insert a small tool between the extractor and its plunger, and depress the plunger toward the rear. Lift out the extractor. **Caution:** *Control the plunger and the compressed spring, and ease them out.*

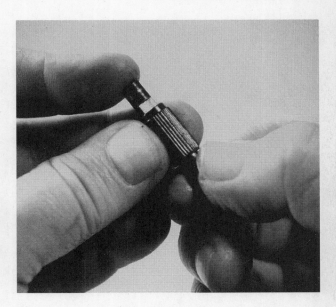

12. The bolt handle has a knurled sleeve that is pushed in to lock the bolt open. This can be removed by pushing it toward the inner tip of the handle shaft. **Caution:** *The tension ball bearing and spring will be released, so control them.* The ball is on the same side of the shaft as the striker recess.

13. Remove the small Phillips-type screw that retains the safety catch on the right side of the trigger group.

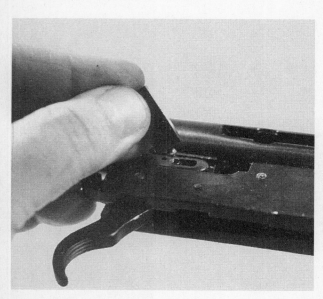

14. Hold a fingertip over the rectangular opening in the safety, and move the safety toward the rear until the detent ball jumps out against the fingertip.

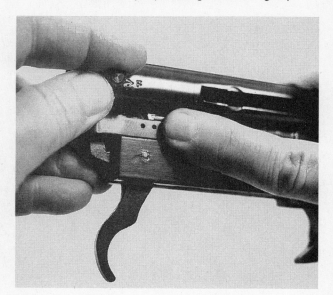

15. Use a magnet or a magnetized tool to remove the detent ball, and take out the spring.

16. Remove the safety catch toward the rear.

17. Drift out the trigger stop cross pin toward the right.

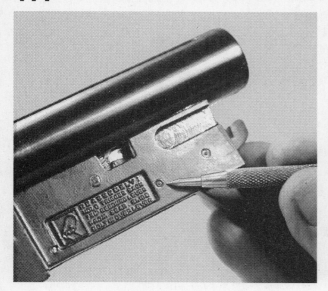

18. Drift out the trigger cross pin toward the right.

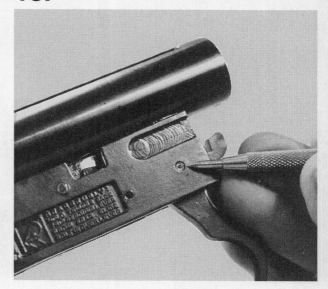

19. Move the trigger assembly downward and toward the rear for removal.

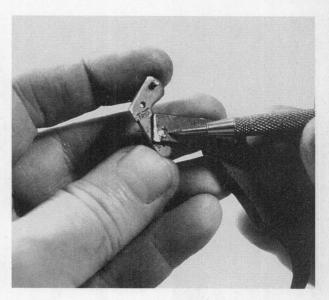

20. The sear trip, or "rebound lever," to use the factory term, is pivoted and retained on the trigger by a cross pin. In normal takedown, this is best left in place. If it is removed, the small ball bearing and spring that power the trip will be released. **Caution:** *Control these parts.*

21. Remove the trigger spring and plunger from inside the housing at the rear.

22. Remove the rear housing retaining screw, located inside the housing, just forward of the trigger spring. Take care that the washer isn't lost.

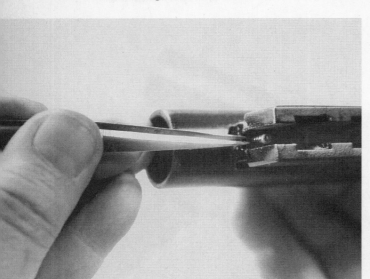

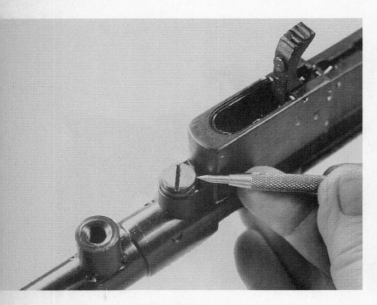

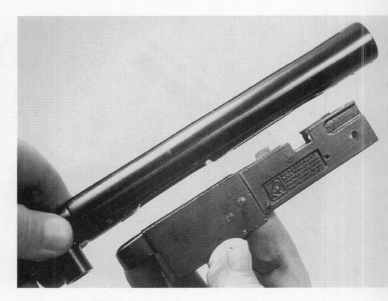

23. Remove the large retaining screw at the front of the housing, along with its lock washer.

24. Remove the trigger group housing from the action.

25. Because the trigger housing is made of alloy, and the parts are steel, further disassembly should be done only if repairs are necessary. We will show the sequence here, without actual removal of the pins and parts. To remove the magazine catch, first drift out the stop pin.

26. Drift out the magazine catch pivot pin toward the right. **Caution:** *Insert a shop cloth in the magazine well to catch the released spring.*

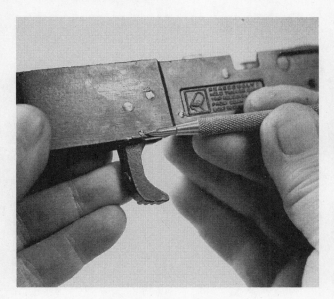

27. Drift out the sear stop pin. Restrain the sear as the drift is removed and ease it upward.

28. Drift out the sear spring retaining pin, and remove the sear spring downward.

29. Drift out the sear pivot pin and remove the sear upward. Again, note that while we have shown the sequence here, the parts are still in place.

30. The stock mounting stud can be drifted out of its dovetail if necessary. However, note that it is factory-staked in place. In normal takedown, it is not removed.

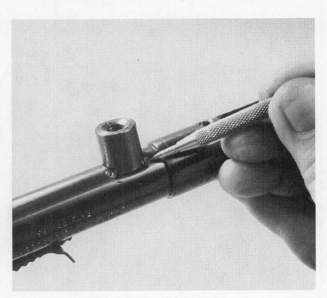

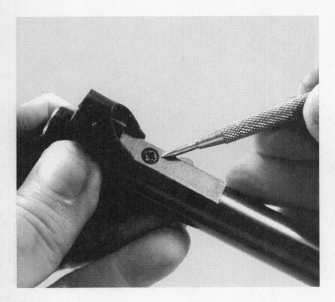

31. The front sight is retained by a small Phillips-type screw. The rear sight is a dovetail mount, and it is drifted out toward the right.

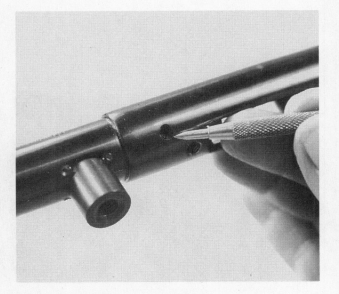

32. The barrel is retained by a large cross pin. In normal takedown, the barrel is not removed.

Reassembly Tips:

1. When installing the cross pins in the trigger housing, remember that they have splined heads and must be inserted from right to left. Be sure the trigger spring plunger engages its shelf at the rear of the trigger before the pin is installed.

2. When replacing the bolt, remember that the striker must be positioned for insertion of the bolt handle. As the bolt is moved forward, insert a small drift in the hole in the sear trip, and tip it to the rear to disengage it from the sear. Directions for this are also embossed on the left side of the housing.

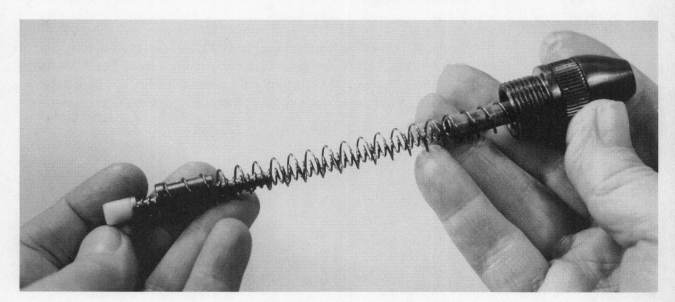

3. If the recoil and striker spring assemblies have been taken apart, here is a view of the proper arrangement for reassembly.

BRNO
Model ZKM 452

Similar/Identical Pattern Guns
The same basic assembly/disassembly steps for the BRNO Model ZKM 452 also apply to the following gun:
BRNO Model ZKM 452D

Data:	BRNO Model ZKM 452
Origin:	Czechoslovakia
Manufacturer:	Zavody Presneho Strajirenstvi, Uhersky Brod
Cartridge:	22 Long Rifle
Magazine capacity:	5 rounds
Overall length:	$43^{1}/_{2}$ inches
Barrel length:	23.6 inches
Weight:	6.9 pounds

The ZKM-452 was introduced in 1992, and this high-quality rifle is imported from Czechoslovakia by Action Arms. There is also a Deluxe version, which differs only in stock quality and added checkering. A synthetic stock is also offered as a lower-priced option.

Disassembly:

1. Remove the magazine. Hold the trigger to the rear, open the bolt, and remove the bolt toward the rear.

2. Remove the front stock mounting bolt.

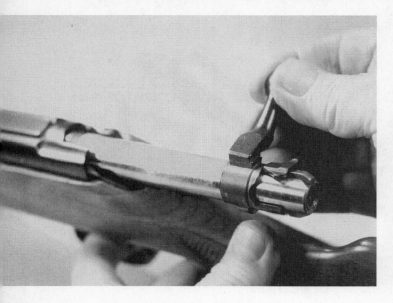

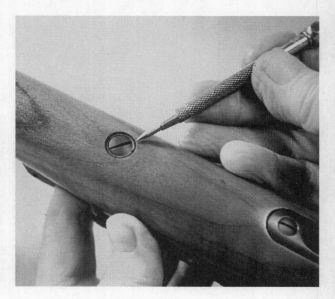

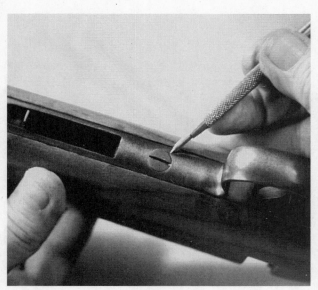

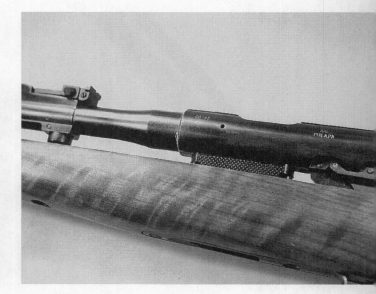

3. Remove the rear stock mounting bolt, located between the trigger guard and magazine well.

4. Remove the action from the stock.

5. The stock buttplate and the trigger guard unit are retained on the stock by two wood screws.

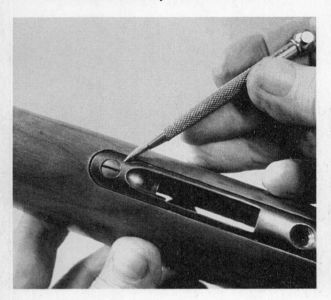

6. Push out the trigger pin toward either side. Restrain the trigger, as the spring is under tension.

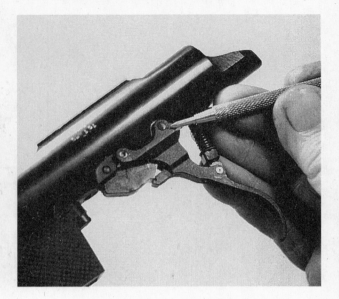

7. Ease the trigger downward. It is not taken off at this time, as it is still retained by its sear-contact cross pin. That cross pin, and the one that pivots and retains the spring guide, are riveted in place, and routine removal is not advisable. The trigger spring and the adjustment lock-washer can be removed from the guide at this point. Take care that the small washer isn't lost.

8. Restrain the sear, and push out the sear cross pin. **Caution:** *The sear spring is powerful, and there is a small ball bearing between the spring and the receiver. Control it and ease it out.* Considering the reassembly difficulty, this system is probably best left in place unless removal is necessary for repair or refinishing.

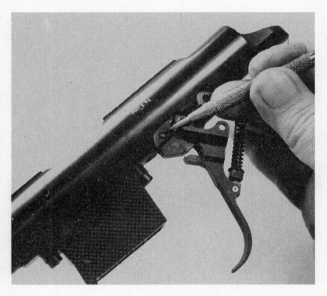

9. Remove the sear and trigger assembly downward. After removal, the parts are easily separated.

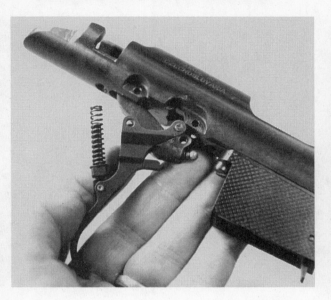

10. The magazine catch and its spring are pivoted and retained by a cross pin. **Caution:** *Control the catch and its spring as the pin is drifted out.* The magazine housing is retained on the receiver by two screws, at front and rear.

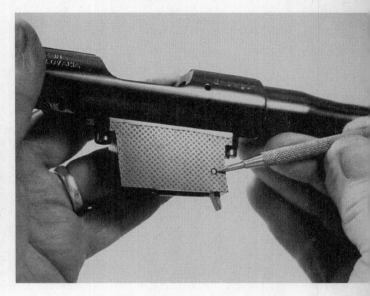

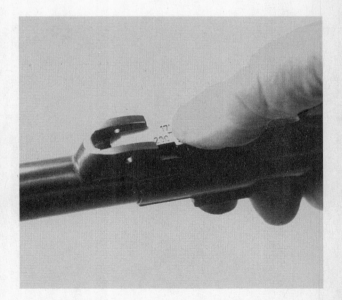

11. The front sight hood can be sprung outward slightly and slid forward out of its tracks. Backing out the front sight elevation adjustment screw will allow the sight blade to be slid down and forward for removal.

12. The rear sight is retained Mauser-style. Push down at the front and slide it toward the rear for removal. There is no cross pin.

13. To remove the twin extractors, insert a tool and pry the end of the saddle-spring outward, just enough to clear its retaining shelf. As the spring is removed, control it. The extractors are then lifted out of their recesses.

14. With the bolt held securely, use a tool to push the combined striker and firing pin toward the rear, and turn the bolt handle, allowing the striker to move forward to fired position.

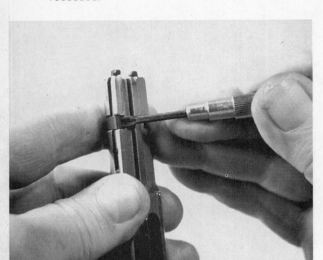

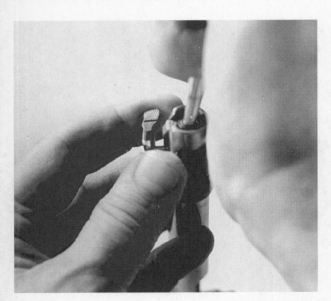

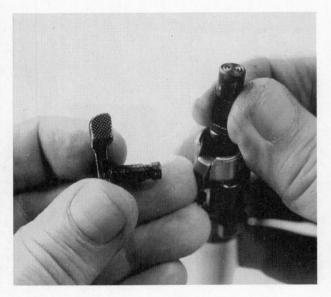

15. Grip the front part of the bolt in a padded vise, and use a tool to depress the safety retainer until the safety can be lifted out. **Caution:** *Control the retainer.*

16. Easing the spring tension, remove the safety and the retaining plunger.

17 Remove the striker assembly toward the rear. The spring is easily removed from inside the striker.

18. Remove the bolt handle toward the rear.

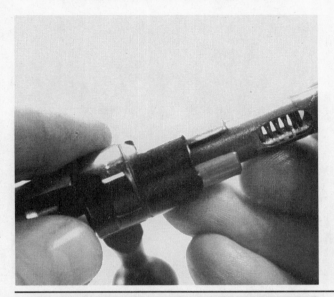

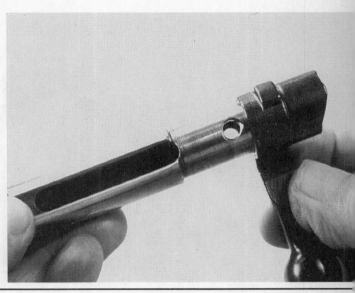

Reassembly Tips:

1. When replacing the sear and trigger assembly, temporarily install the rear stock-mounting bolt in order to supply a compression surface for the sear ball bearing and spring, as shown. Remember to hook the forward trigger cross pin over the sear. Temporarily insert the bolt body to stop the sear inside the receiver. When the ball and spring are compressed, insert a small drift to hold the sear for insertion of the sear cross pin. This is a difficult operation. Keep a shop cloth or apron around the receiver to arrest the ball if it slips.

2. Be sure the trigger spring adjustment washer is installed in the proper orientation, with the locking dimples downward toward the adjustment nut, as shown. Remember that the upper end of the guide must enter its hole in the receiver before the trigger cross pin is reinserted.

3. When replacing the striker assembly in the bolt, remember that the angled lug goes at the bottom to contact the like surface on the bolt handle, as shown.

4. When the safety and its retaining plunger are installed, it will be necessary to again use a padded vise to hold the front of the bolt. Be sure the plunger is oriented as shown, and that the safety is straight across as it is inserted.

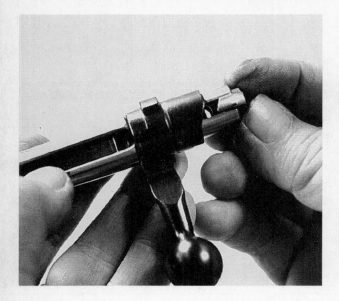

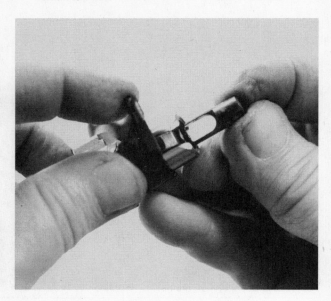

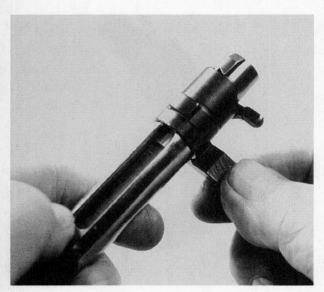

5. Before the bolt can be reinserted in the receiver, the striker must be re-cocked. Hold the front part of the bolt firmly, and turn the handle until the locking lug is at the bottom, as shown.

Browning A-Bolt 22

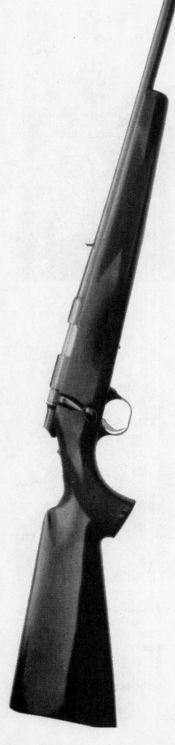

Similar/Identical Pattern Guns
The same basic assembly/disassembly steps for the Browning A-Bolt 22 also apply to the following gun:
Browning A-Bolt 22 Gold Medallion

Data:	Browning A-Bolt 22
Origin:	Japan
Manufacturer:	Miroku
Cartridge:	22 Long Rifle
Magazine capacity:	5 rounds
Overall length:	40¼ inches
Barrel length:	22 inches
Weight:	5 pounds 9 ounces

The Browning A-Bolt in 22 LR and 22 WMR is also offered in a Gold Medallion version that differs only in fancy stock wood and other embellishments. The standard rifle was introduced in 1986, but fewer than 150 were made in that year. The deluxe model was first made in 1988, and the 22 WMR version in 1989. Among the high-class 22 bolt actions, the A-Bolt ranks as one of the best.

Disassembly:

1. Remove the magazine, open the bolt, and depress the bolt latch. Remove the bolt toward the rear.

2. Remove the stock mounting bolt, located just forward of the magazine well.

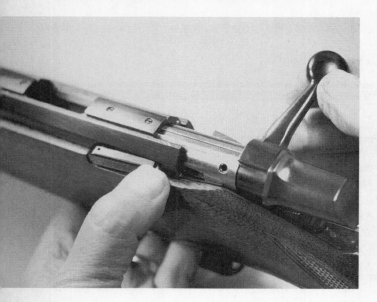

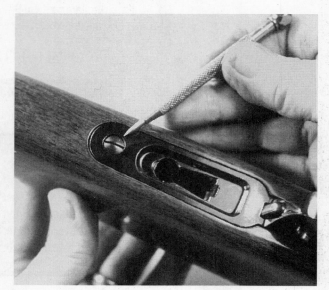

3. Remove the rear stock mounting bolt, located at the rear of the trigger guard unit.

4. Remove the trigger guard assembly downward. The magazine catch and its spring, located in the guard forward of the trigger, are best left in place in normal takedown. If removal is necessary for repair, insert a drift or rod through the loop at the rear of the catch, and draw it back until its side wings align with the exit cuts; then lift it out. Control the spring.

5. Remove the action from the stock, upward.

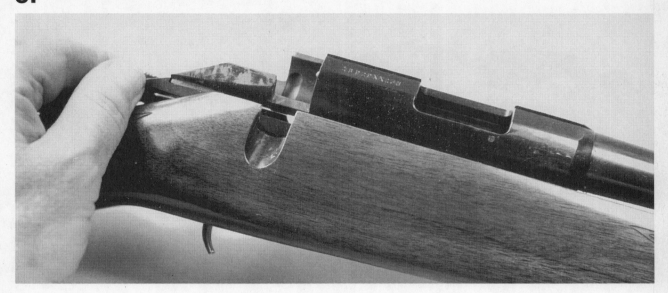

6. Drift out the roll pin at the front of the trigger housing.

7. Use an 8mm socket to remove the mounting bolt at the rear of the trigger housing. Take care that the lock washer is not lost.

8. Remove the trigger housing downward.

9. The bolt latch can be removed from the left side of the receiver by backing out its retaining and pivot screw. Restrain the latch as the screw is taken out, and ease it off. Remove the spring. In the front of the latch, a vertical roll pin retains the bolt stop/guide pin.

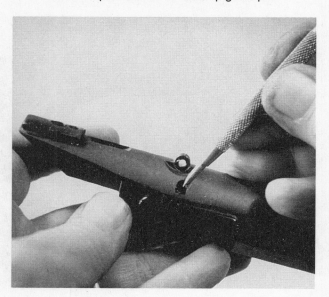

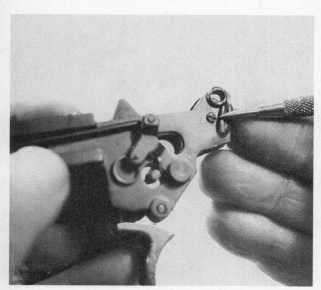

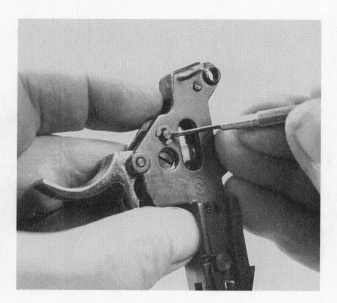

10. Because several of the parts in the trigger group are set or staked at the factory, disassembly of this system should be reserved for repair purposes. The sear pivot, for example, is riveted on both sides, and it is not routinely removable.

11. If necessary, the safety system can be removed. First, pry off the C-clip on the left side of the housing. Control it during removal, as it will snap off when freed.

12. Control the torsion spring, and remove the safety toward the right.

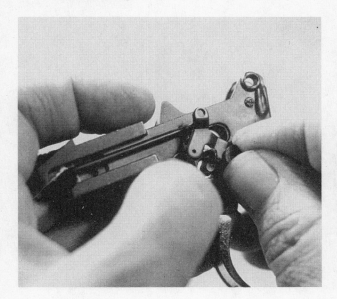

13. Remove the safety spring.

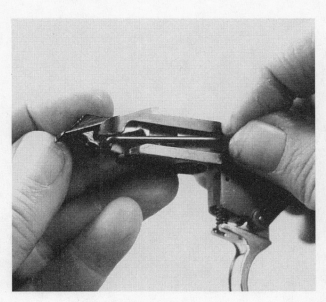

14. Move the connecting rod and the safety button out toward the rear.

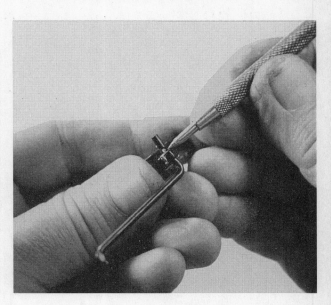

15. The connecting rod is staked on the left side of the button, and these parts are not routinely separated.

16. Unhook the safety-lever spring at the rear to release its tension.

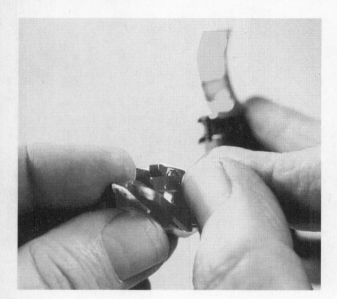

17. Insert a drift in the access hole on the right side, and drift out the safety-lever post toward the left. Remove the lever and spring.

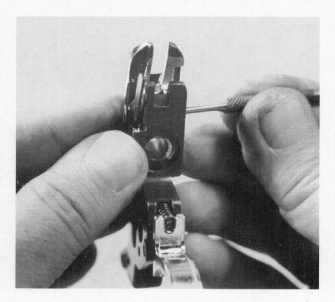

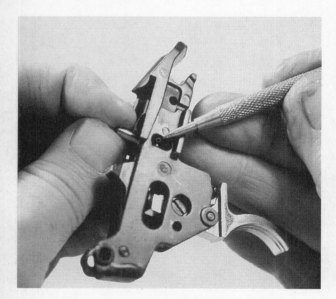

18. In order to remove the safety bolt lock pin, it is necessary to grip its side roll pin with pliers and pull it out. The lock pin is then taken out upward. Damage to the roll pin is likely, so this should not be done in normal takedown.

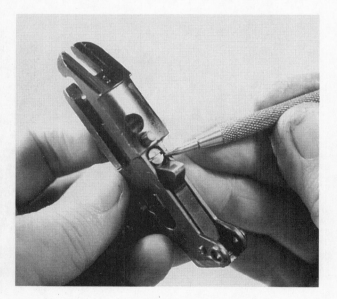

19. While the sear is not routinely removed, its spring is accessible by removal of the sear limit screw. However, this screw is factory set for proper engagement of the sear contact stud in the top of the trigger. If the screw is disturbed, it must be reset.

20. If the trigger has to be removed for repair, the first step is to unscrew and take out the safety post, shown here.

21. After the safety post is removed, drift out the trigger pin and take out the trigger and its spring downward. The sear contact stud in the top of the trigger is a separate part. In normal takedown, this system is best left undisturbed.

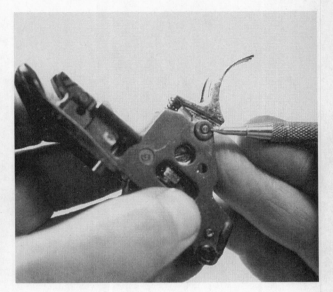

22. To remove the extractor, insert a small tool to depress the plunger and spring toward the rear, and lift out the extractor. **Caution:** *Keep the plunger and spring under control and ease them out.*

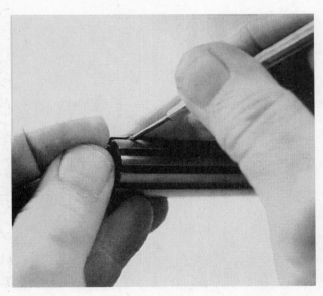

23. The combination ejector and firing pin can be removed by drifting out this roll pin, but the plunger and spring may be difficult to remove without further disassembly of the bolt. It can be done, though, if only this part needs to be replaced in repair. The forward roll pin is a guide only, and it does not have to be removed.

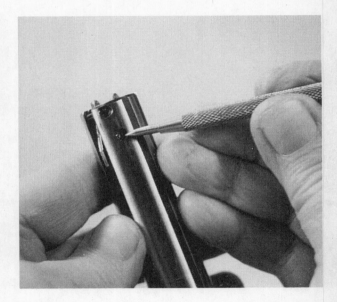

24. Hold the bolt firmly at the front, and turn the handle to lower the striker to fired position, as shown.

25. Restrain the bolt end piece and use an Allen wrench to remove the bolt sleeve retaining screw. **Caution:** *Even in fired mode, the striker spring has some compression, so control the end piece.*

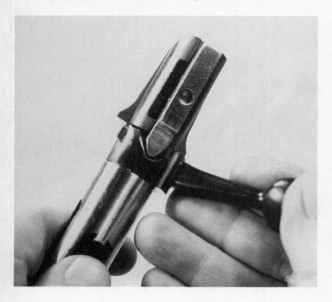

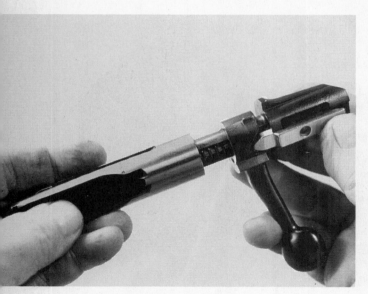

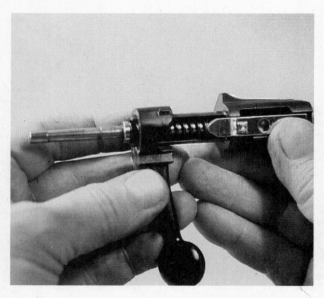

26. Remove the end piece and striker assembly toward the rear.

27. Remove the bolt handle toward the front.

28. With the front of the striker against a firm surface, such as a workbench edge, tip the striker and spring assembly downward, out of the bolt end piece.

29. The striker, its spring, and the collar at the rear can be separated from the cocking piece by drifting out the roll cross pin. **Caution:** *The captive spring is still under tension. Except for repair, this system should be left intact.*

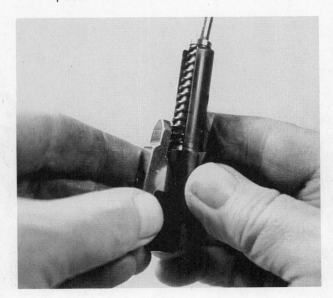

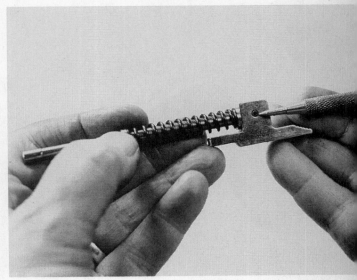

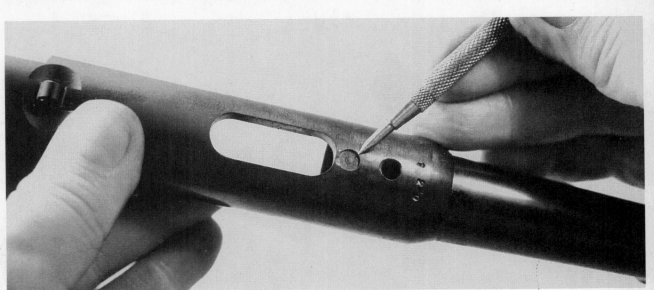

30. The cartridge guide is a separate part, driven into a well in the underside of the receiver. If it is damaged and must be replaced, it can be driven out downward. Replacement requires precise positioning. In normal takedown, even for refinishing, it is best left in place.

Reassembly Tips:

1. When installing the striker assembly in the bolt end piece, place the spring collar against the shoulders in the end piece, and push the assembly back and inward to snap it into place.

2. When replacing the Allen screw, be sure the screw hole is precisely aligned before turning the screw into place.

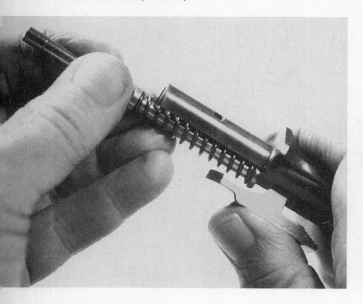

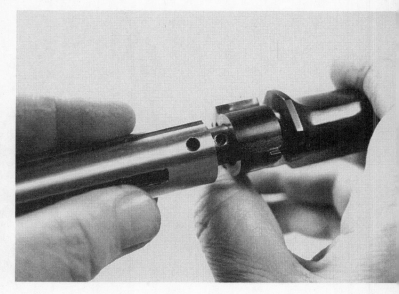

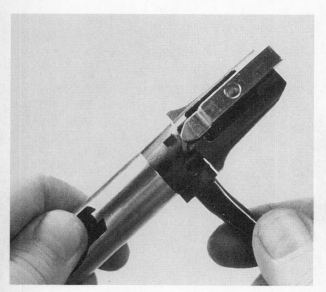

3. Before the bolt can be put back into the receiver, the striker must be in cocked position. Grip the front of the bolt firmly in a shop cloth or a padded vise, and turn the handle until the lug is in the position shown.

4. When installing the safety-lever, be sure its front fork engages the bolt lock side pin, as shown. After the post is drifted into place, remember to rehook the spring under the lever at the rear.

Browning Model BL-22

Similar/Identical Pattern Guns
The same basic assembly/disassembly steps for the Browning BL-22 also apply to the following gun:
Browning BL-22 Grade II

Data:	Browning BL-22
Origin:	Japan
Manufacturer:	Made in Japan by Miroku for Browning Arms, Morgan, Utah
Cartridge:	22 Short, Long, or Long Rifle
Magazine capacity:	22 Short, 17 Long, 15 Long Rifle
Overall length:	36³/₄ inches
Barrel length:	20 inches
Weight:	5 pounds

Browning's neat little lever-action 22 has been made by Miroku of Tokyo for around 25 years, and it will probably be around for many years to come. It is unique among currently-made 22-caliber lever actions in having the trigger mounted in the lever, rather than in the receiver. It also has a very short lever arc that allows operation of the action without removing the hand from the wrist of the stock. For the nonprofessional, some elements of the takedown and reassembly can be rather difficult.

Disassembly:

1. Remove the inner magazine tube, and set the hammer on its safety step. Partially open the action. Take out the large cross-screw at the rear of the receiver.

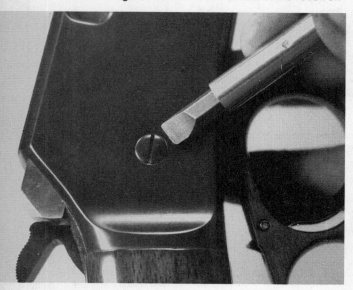

2. Move the sub-frame and buttstock assembly straight out toward the rear. Move it slowly, and insert a fingertip through the ejection port to restrain the ejector, as it will be released as the front of the bolt clears it.

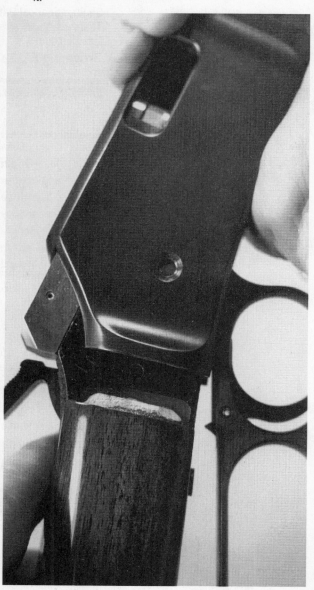

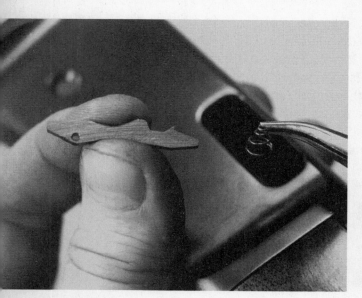

3. Remove the ejector spring from its recess in the left inner wall of the receiver. Move the ejector downward off its fixed pivot post, and take it out.

4. Tip the bolt upward at the rear, and move it a short distance toward the front.

5. Bring the rear of the bolt back down parallel with the top of the sub-frame, then lift the bolt off upward.

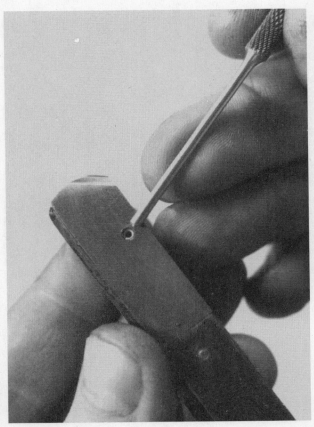

6. The firing pin and its return spring are retained in the bolt by a roll cross pin. Drift out the pin, and remove the firing pin and spring toward the rear.

7. The bolt cover plate on the right side is taken off by prying it gently outward at the rear, equally at the top and bottom, until it snaps off its fixed mounting pin.

8. Insert a screwdriver blade between the extractor and its plunger, depress the plunger, and remove the extractor from its recess in the bolt. **Caution:** *Take care that the screwdriver doesn't slip, and ease out the plunger and spring.*

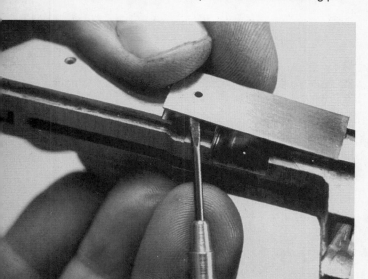

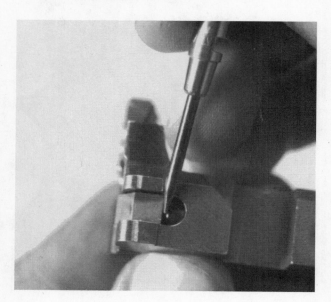

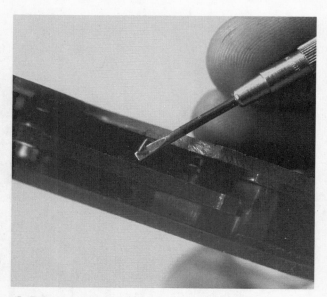

9. Depress the carrier, and remove the locking block from the lever link toward the left.

10. Unhook the carrier spring and allow its front arm to swing upward, relieving its tension.

11. Drift out the carrier pivot pin toward the right, and remove the carrier and its spring upward.

12. Removal of the carrier pin will also release the hammer stop block, and it can now be removed upward.

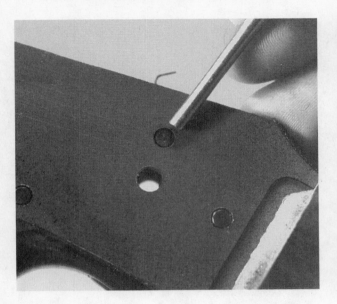

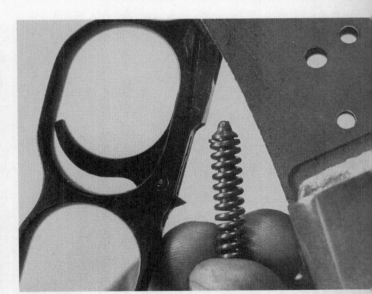

13. Restrain the hammer, pull the trigger, and ease the hammer down beyond its normal forward position, relieving the tension of its spring. Drift out the hammer pivot pin toward the right, and remove the hammer and its attached spring guide upward. The guide pin is staked in place, and should not be removed in normal takedown.

14. Open the lever, and remove the mainspring and its lower guide downward.

15. Drift out the lever link pivot pin.

16. Removal of the pin will allow the lever to be pivoted downward beyond its normal position, and the link can then be removed toward the right.

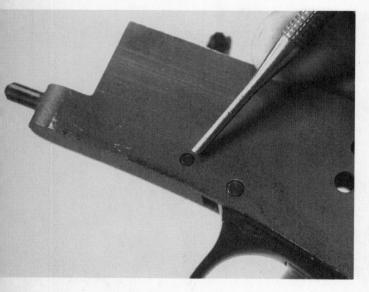

17. Drift out the lever pivot pin, and remove the lever downward.

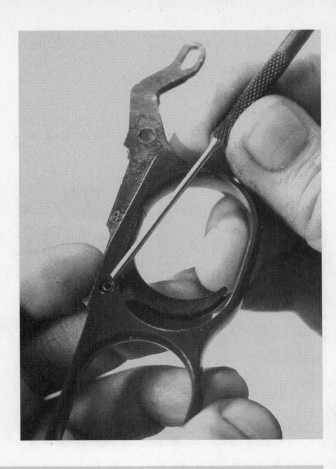

18. Drift out the roll cross pin at the rear of the trigger, restrain the sear link, and remove the link and its spring upward.

19. Drift out the trigger cross pin and remove the trigger and its spring upward.

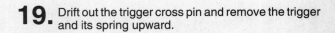

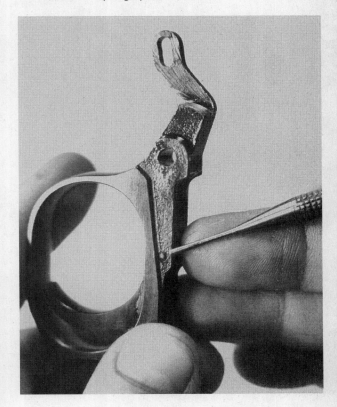

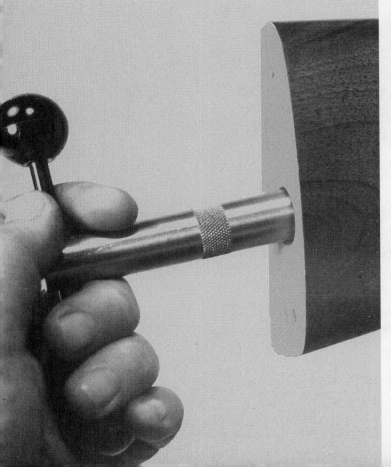

20. Remove the buttplate, and use a B-Square stock tool or a long screwdriver to remove the stock bolt. Take off the stock toward the rear.

21. Push out the cross pin that retains the sear, and remove the sear and its spring downward.

22. Remove the cross-screw in the front barrel band.

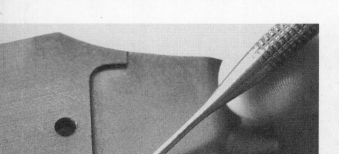

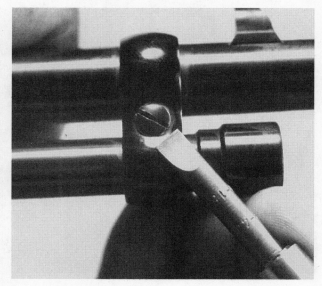

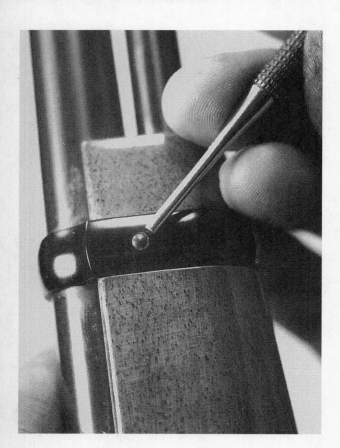

23. Drift out the cross pin in the rear barrel band, and slide the band off the forend toward the front. Remove the outer magazine tube toward the front, and take off the forend downward. The front barrel band can be removed only after the front sight is drifted out of its dovetail.

Reassembly Tips:

1. After the sear is installed, flip it over and insert the spring, then rotate it back into position, and insert a tool from the top to nudge the spring onto its plate inside the frame.

2. After the hammer is installed, tip its spring guide upward, and fit the spring and lower guide onto it.

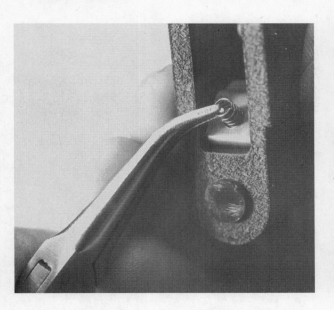

3. Swing the mainspring assembly downward, with the lever in closed position. Pull the trigger to release the hammer, and tip it forward beyond its normal lowered position. Snap the nose of the lower spring guide into its recess on the lever. Open the lever, and insert a fingertip to support the underside of the spring while slowly cocking the hammer. **Caution:** *If solid resistance is felt, stop and be sure that the spring is being kept straight (it will tend to bow downward).*

4. When replacing the locking block on the lever link, note that its side projection must be at the right rear, as shown.

5. Grip the ejector spring with forceps or sharp-nosed pliers for insertion. The same procedure can be used for the ejector. When the spring and ejector are in place, insert a fingertip through the ejection port to hold them while sliding the bolt and sub-frame back in.

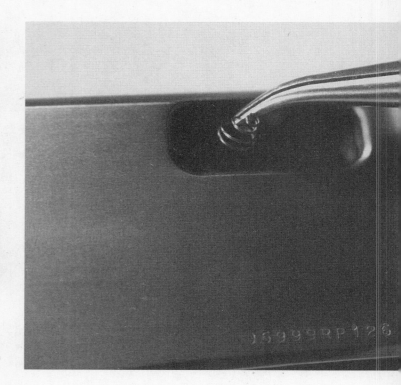

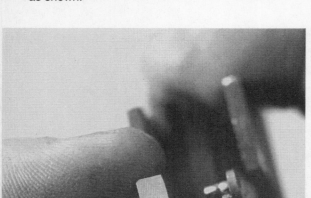

6. When replacing the carrier and lever link, be sure the pointed front arm of the lever link lies on *top* of the carrier guide pin.

Browning Semi-Auto 22

Similar/Identical Pattern Guns
The same basic assembly/disassembly steps for the Browning Semi-Auto 22 also apply to the following guns:

Browning Standard Auto Grade II   **Norinco 22 ATD**
Browning Standard Auto Grade III   **Remington Model 24**
Browning Standard Auto Grade VI   **Remington Model 241**

Data:	Browning Semi-Auto 22
Origin:	Belgium
Manufacturer:	Browning Arms Company, Morgan, Utah
	(Made for Browning by FN in Belgium)
Cartridge:	22 Long Rifle
Magazine capacity:	11 rounds
Overall length:	37 inches
Barrel length:	$19^{1}/_{4}$ inches
Weight:	$4^{3}/_{4}$ pounds

This neat little semi-auto rifle was first produced in 1914 by Fabrique Nationale in Belgium, and in 1922 the production rights for the U.S. were leased to the Remington company. It was made by them as the Model 24 and Model 241 until 1951. In 1956, an altered version of the original gun was introduced by Browning, and it is still in production. Through all of this time, some 65 years, the internal mechanism has been essentially unchanged. In recent years, the gun has been neatly copied by Norinco of China as the Model 22 ATD. Among all of the different variations, there are minor differences in the extractor and cartridge guide systems, but the instructions will still apply.

Disassembly:

1. The takedown latch is located on the underside of the forend, at its rear edge. Push the latch forward into its recess in the forend.

2. Retract the bolt slightly, and turn the barrel assembly clockwise (rear view) until it stops. Then, remove the barrel assembly toward the front.

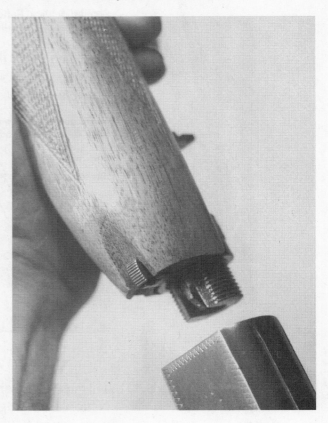

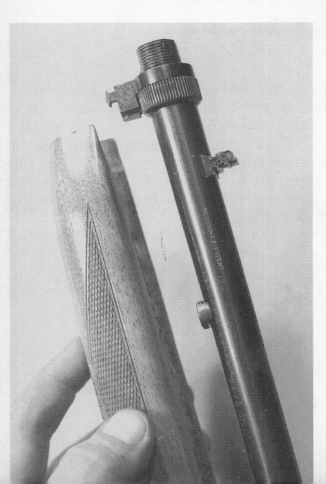

3. Remove the screw on the underside of the forend, and take off the forend downward.

4. Slide the takedown latch forward out of its base at the rear of the barrel. **Caution:** *Two plunger-and-spring assemblies will be released, and must be restrained to prevent loss.* The first will be the positioning plunger and spring at the rear of the latch, and the second will be the wedge-shaped plunger under the latch which bears on the barrel adjustment nut serrations. Ease both of these out, and take care that these small parts aren't lost.

5. Remove the takedown latch base ring toward the rear. Unscrew the knurled barrel adjustment nut and remove it toward the rear.

7. Pull the trigger to release the striker into the bolt, then move the front of the bolt upward out of the guard unit and ease it off forward. **Caution:** *Both the bolt spring and the striker spring are under some tension, so take care that they don't get away.* Remove the springs and their guides from the rear of the bolt.

6. Insert a finger through the trigger guard, place the thumb on the bolt handle, and retract the bolt to the rear while exerting forward pressure on the guard. The trigger group and bolt assembly can now be moved forward together and removed downward.

8. Remove the striker from the rear of the bolt.

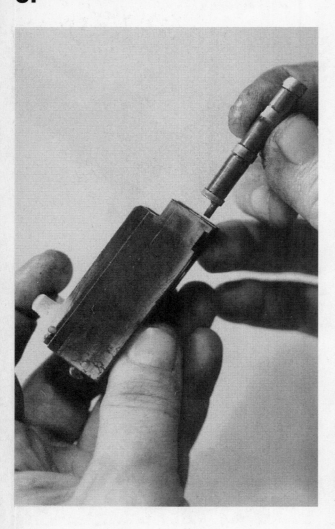

9. Drifting out the cross pin at the lower front of the bolt will release the extractor retainer and allow removal of the extractor and its spring downward.

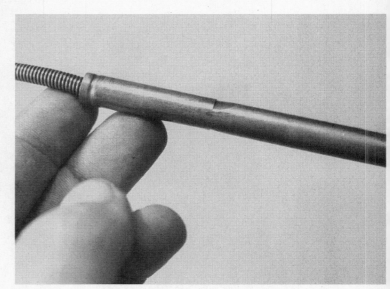

10. To remove the inner magazine tube, pull it out until it stops, then turn it 180 degrees to clear its side steps from the detents in the outer tube and take it out toward the rear.

11. Drifting out the locking cross pin at the head of the inner magazine tube will allow removal of the handle piece, spring, feed cable, and follower.

12. Use a very wide screwdriver or a special shop-made tool to remove the nut at the rear of the buttstock, and its lock washer, and take off the stock toward the rear. The outer magazine tube can now be unscrewed from the rear of the receiver. **Caution:** *Avoid gripping the tube too tightly and deforming it.*

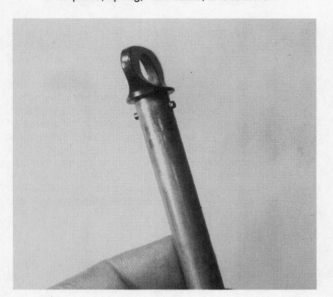

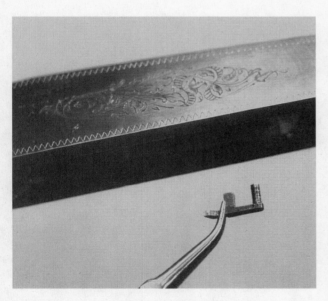

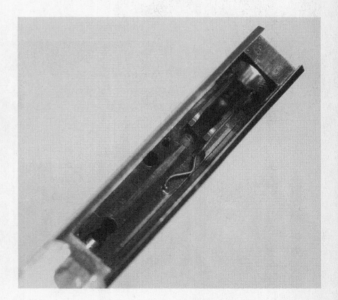

13. Swing the cartridge stop toward the inside wall of the receiver to clear its inner arm and lift it out of its pivot-hole in the roof of the receiver. It should be noted that on older guns that have seen a lot of use, the cartridge stop may fall out when the bolt and trigger assembly are removed, so be sure it isn't missed and lost.

14. Removal of the cartridge guide spring in the top front of the receiver will release the cartridge guide to be taken out toward the front. To remove the spring, use a small tool to pry its rear loop from beneath its flange in the receiver.

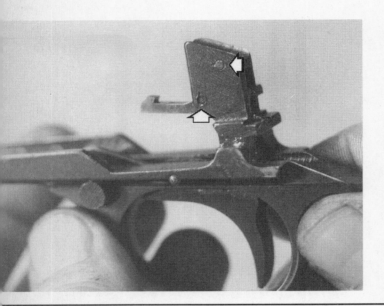

15. Drifting out the small cross pin (upper arrow) at the top of the vertical trigger group extension will release the sear spring and plunger for removal upward. Drifting out the sear pivot pin (lower arrow) will allow the sear to be taken out toward the front. The trigger and disconnector pivot on the same pin, and are removed as a unit, along with the disconnector spring. The disconnector can be separated from the trigger by drifting out the short pin that mounts it in the trigger. To remove the safety, use a small screwdriver to depress the plunger and spring inside, at the center, under the safety, and move the safety out toward the right. **Caution:** *Control the compressed spring and plunger and ease them out.*

Reassembly Tips:

1. When replacing the striker in the bolt, note that the striker has a guide lug on its left side that mates with a track inside the bolt.

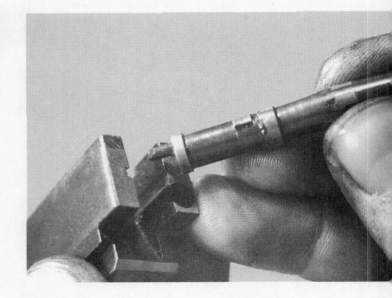

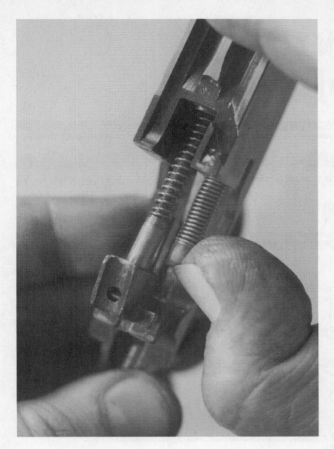

2. When replacing the bolt in the trigger group, carefully compress the recoil spring on its guide, then use a fingertip to hold the spring and guide in place on the bolt while fitting the bolt into place, inserting the tip of the striker spring guide into its hole in the vertical extension. Then, fit the rear bracket of the bolt spring guide onto its lug on the extension. **Caution:** *While the bolt spring is compressed, keep it aimed away from your eyes, in case the finger should slip.*

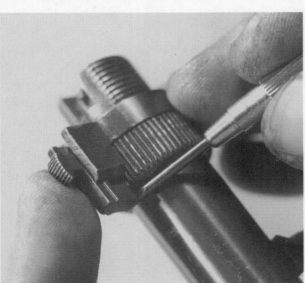

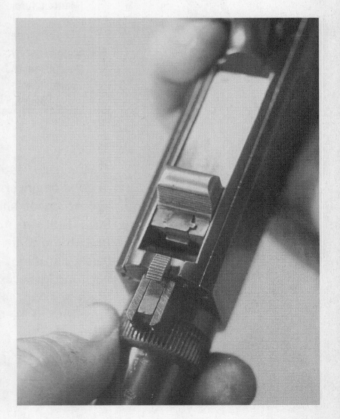

3. When reassembling the takedown latch system, be sure the small wedge-tipped plunger on the underside of the latch is oriented so the wedge tip aligns with the serrations on the adjustment nut. Use a small screwdriver to depress the two plungers alternately as the latch is moved into place.

4. To readjust the barrel nut, install the barrel on the gun before replacing the forend, lock the takedown latch in place, and turn the knurled adjustment nut until the ring is snug against the receiver. Then, reinstall the forend.

Browning T-Bolt

Similar/Identical Pattern Guns

The same basic assembly/disassembly steps for the Browning T-Bolt also apply to the following gun:

Browning T-2 T-Bolt

Data:	Browning T-Bolt
Origin:	Belgium
Manufacturer:	Fabrique Nationale, Herstal (for Browning Arms Company, Morgan, Utah)
Cartridge:	22 Long Rifle
Magazine capacity:	5 rounds
Overall length:	$39^1/_4$ inches
Barrel length:	22 inches
Weight:	$5^1/_2$ pounds

The unusual "straight pull" bolt of this fine little gun is a masterpiece of good engineering, and works beautifully. Unfortunately, the average American shooter has never been fond of unusual actions, and the T-Bolt was imported for less than ten years, from 1965 to 1973. In addition to the plain T-1 model, a T-2 was offered, with 24-inch barrel and fancy stock. The gun was also available in a left-hand version. An accessory single-shot adapter would allow the use of 22 Short or Long, as well as Long Rifle. Except for the reversal of some directions in the left-hand model, the instructions will apply to all of them.

Disassembly:

1. Remove the magazine, and remove the main stock mounting screw, on the underside just forward of the magazine well. Separate the action from the stock.

2. Removal of the wood screw at the rear of the trigger guard unit will allow the guard to be taken off downward.

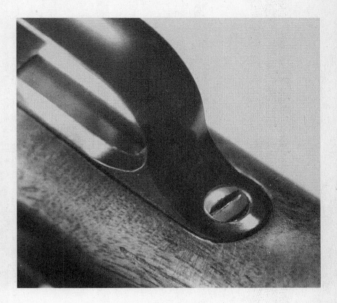

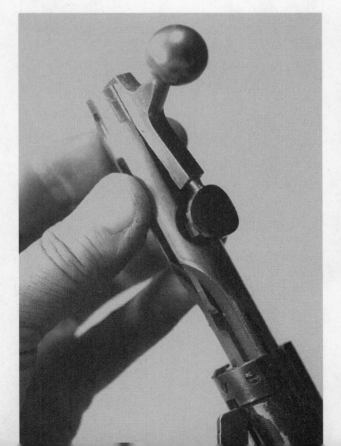

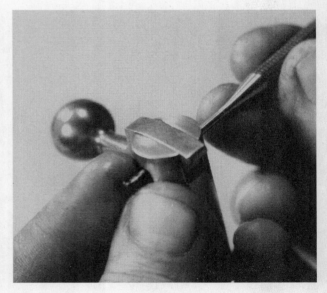

4. With the bolt handle in the closed (locked) position, push the vertical pin at the rear of the bolt upward, and remove it.

3. To remove the bolt, hold the trigger to the rear, and move the bolt out the rear of the receiver.

5. Remove the bolt handle toward the rear.

6. Remove the striker spring and its plunger toward the rear.

7. Turn the locking block ("cross-bolt") slightly to raise the firing pin out of its inside shoulder, and remove the locking block toward the right.

8. Remove the firing pin from its channel in the top of the bolt.

9. The twin extractors are retained by two vertical roll pins at the front of the bolt. Use a roll pin punch to drift out the pins, and remove the extractors from each side, along with the single transverse coil spring that powers both.

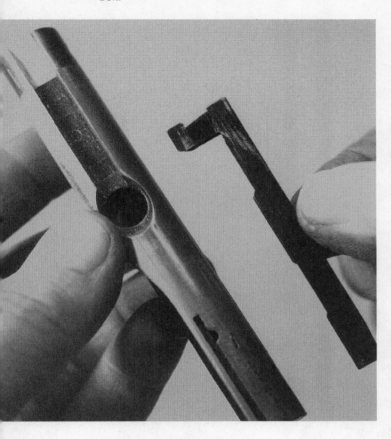

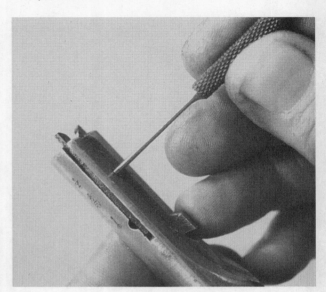

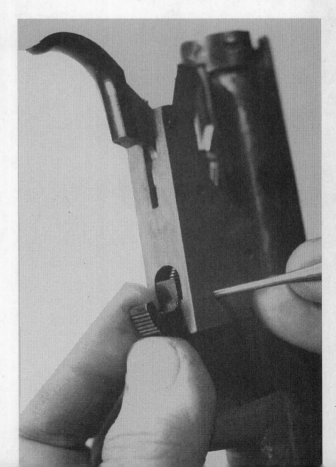

10. Push out the magazine catch cross pin, and remove the magazine catch and its coil spring downward.

11. Removal of the magazine catch will give access to the magazine housing screw, which is taken out downward.

12. Remove the magazine housing downward.

13. Push out the cross pin at the top of the magazine housing, and remove the sear upward and toward the front.

14. Note the relationship of the trigger and its spring before removal, to aid in reassembly. Push out the cross pin at the lower rear of the magazine housing, and remove the trigger and its spring toward the rear and downward. Take care that the trigger spring isn't lost. Restrain it, and ease it out.

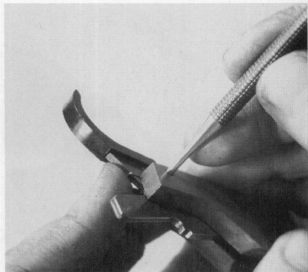

15. The trigger stop pin can also be drifted out, but can be left in place, as it retains no part.

16. The ejector is easily pushed from its slot in the underside of the receiver for removal.

17. Removal of the two screws in the outer band of the safety catch at the rear of the receiver will allow the catch to be taken off. **Caution:** *Removal of the safety will release the safety positioning plunger and spring, so restrain them and ease them out.*

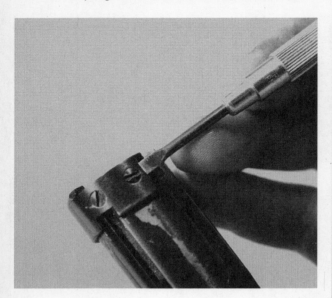

Reassembly Tips:

1. When replacing the ejector in its slot in the underside of the receiver, be sure its vertical face is toward the front, and its angled end toward the rear, as shown.

2. When replacing the trigger and its spring, taking out the trigger stop pin will make this operation easier. Insert the cross pin from the right, just far enough to hold the spring in position, then put in the trigger, and move the cross pin the rest of the way across. Be sure the front arm of the spring is against its shoulder or shelf inside the housing.

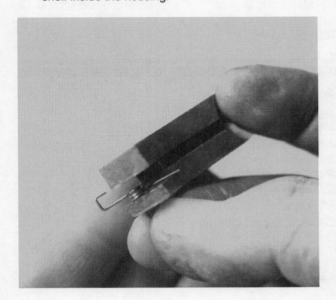

3. When replacing the locking cross bolt in the body of the bolt, note that the face with the deep cut and hole must be oriented toward the rear, and install the locking bolt before the firing pin is returned to its channel.

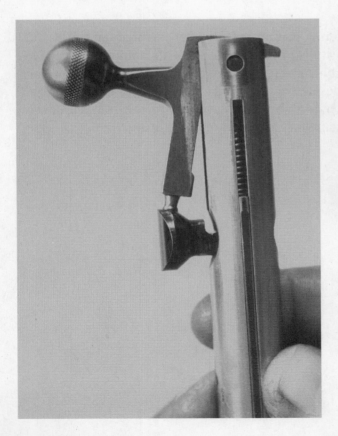

4. When replacing the bolt handle, be sure its front projection enters the hole in the rear face of the locking bolt, and note that the handle must be in the unlocked position, as shown, when the bolt is inserted into the receiver.

Calico
M-100

Similar/Identical Pattern Guns
The same basic assembly/disassembly steps for the Calico Model 100 also apply to the following gun:
Calico M-105 Sporter

Data:	Calico M-100
Origin:	United States
Manufacturer:	California Instrument Co. Bakersfield, California
Cartridge:	22 Long Rifle
Magazine capacity:	100 rounds
Overall length:	35.8 inches (stock extended) 29.8 inches (stock folded)
Barrel length:	16.1 inches
Weight:	4.2 pounds

In 1986, the California Instrument Company startled the world of 22 rimfire rifles by bringing out a semi-auto with a unique helical-feed magazine that had a capacity of 100 rounds. This was not the only innovation—the design has many nice little touches of engineering. The M-105 Sporter, with a wood stock and forend, was introduced in 1989. It is the same mechanically, and the instructions will apply.

Disassembly:

1. Remove the magazine and open the stock. Cycle the action to cock the hammer, and set the safety in on-safe position. It is not necessary to take off the folding stock for further disassembly, but if removal is required, drift the stock retaining pin out upward. The stock can then be slid off toward the rear.

2. The stock latch can be removed by drifting out the roll cross pin. If this is done, the coil spring and the magazine ejector plunger can then be taken out.

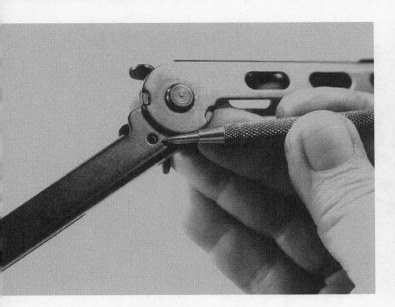

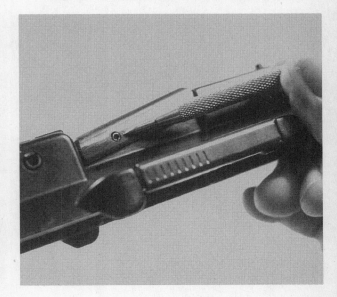

3. The stock release lever and its coil spring can be removed by drifting out this roll cross pin. The other stock components are riveted in place, and routine removal is not advisable.

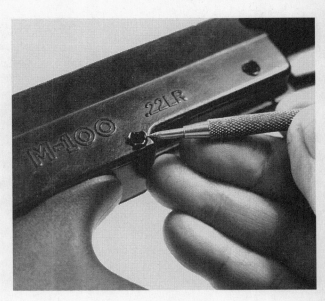

4. The lower receiver is retained by two hollow cross pins at the rear, and a hinge post at the front. The cross pins are flared on one side and must be pushed out in that direction—in this case, toward the left.

5. Drift or push out the rear cross pin.

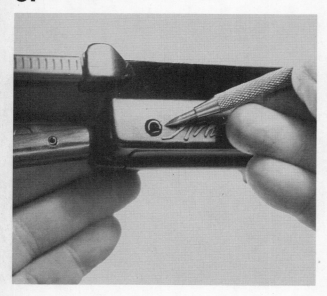

6. Drift out the other cross pin.

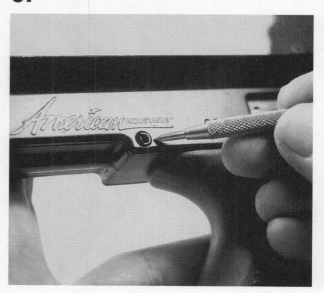

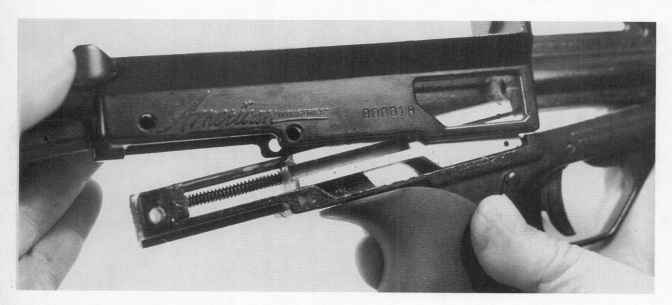

7. Draw the bolt back slightly to clear the extractor from its recess in the barrel, and keeping the bolt snugged against the lower receiver, pivot the upper receiver upward.

8. Remove the bolt assembly from the top of the lower receiver. Take care that the plastic buffer at the rear is not lost.

9. Remove the ejector from its recess in the top of the bolt.

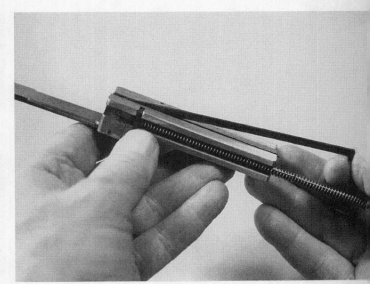

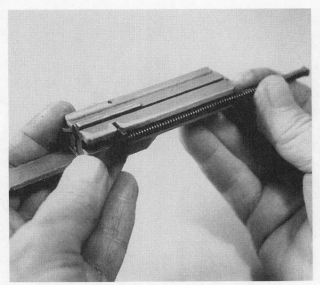

10. Remove the recoil spring assembly from the side of the bolt. This unit is staked at the ends, and routine disassembly is not advisable.

11. Drift out the cross pin at the lower front of the bolt.

12. Remove the cocking handle plate toward the front. Take care that the firing pin return spring is not lost.

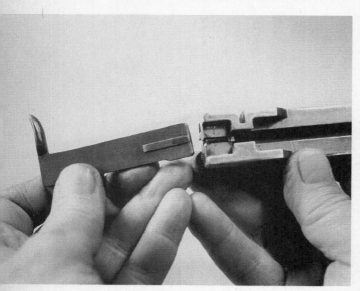

13. Remove the firing pin return spring.

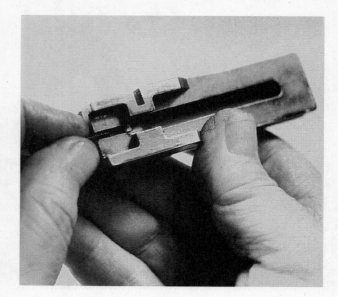

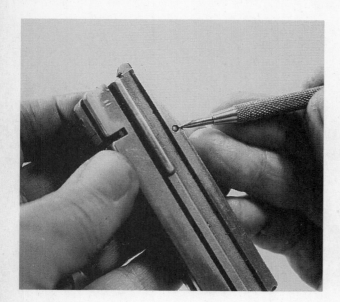

14. Drift out the extractor pin downward. Note that this pin is angled toward the center of the bolt, not straight downward. Control the extractor and its spring.

15. Remove the extractor from its recess.

16. Remove the extractor spring from its well in the bolt.

17. Tip the firing pin out of its recess. The cross pin is staked in place, and it is not removed in normal takedown.

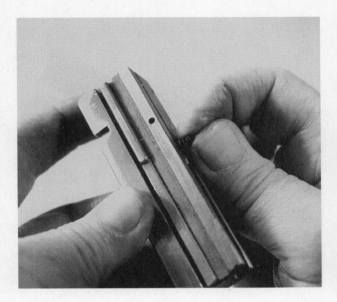

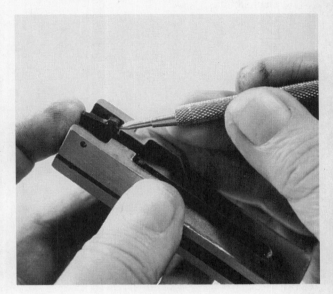

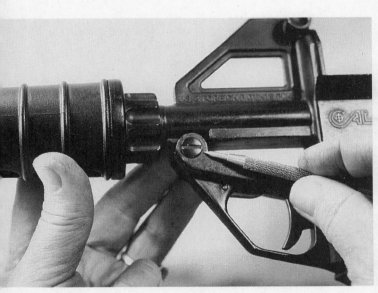

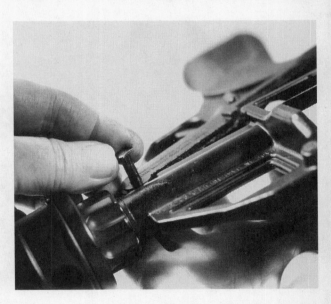

18. For easier access to the parts in the lower receiver, you may wish to separate it from the upper receiver. To remove the pivot shaft, use a properly-fitted screwdriver to take off the cap screw. It will be necessary to hold the head of the shaft on the other side. Grip it with non-marring pliers, or, as I did, just press it against the wooden edge of a workbench. The finish is easily marred, so work with care.

19. Push out the pivot shaft and separate the upper and lower receivers.

20. Drifting out the cross pin at the front of the sight unit will allow this assembly to be pushed off toward the front. If this is done, take care that the positioning key, in a recess on top of the barrel, isn't lost. If necessary, the flanged nut at the rear of the forend can be unscrewed for removal of the barrel. There is also a positioning key at the barrel flange, at the rear. In normal takedown, this entire system is best left in place. The factory suggests that it not be dismounted.

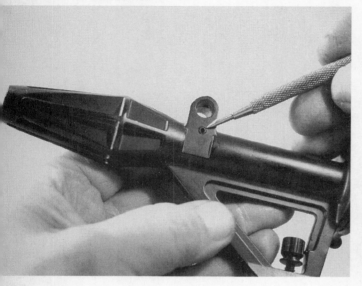

21. The twin magazine catches and their coil springs are pivoted and retained by vertical roll pins.

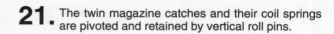
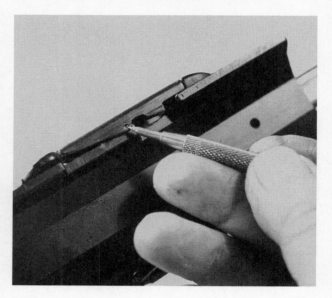

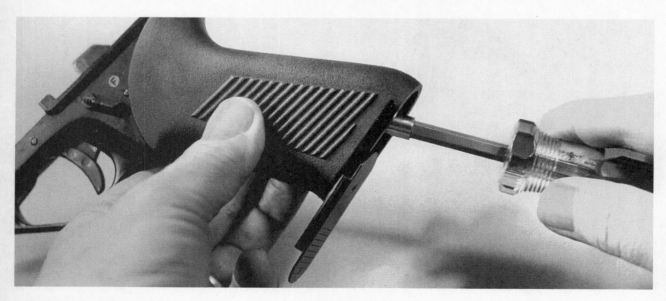

22. Slide open the pistol grip cap and use a screwdriver to remove the mounting screw.

23. Remove the pistol grip from the lower receiver.

24. Move the safety to off-safe position, restrain the hammer, pull the trigger, and ease the hammer down to fired position. Restrain the hammer and drift out the hammer pivot pin.

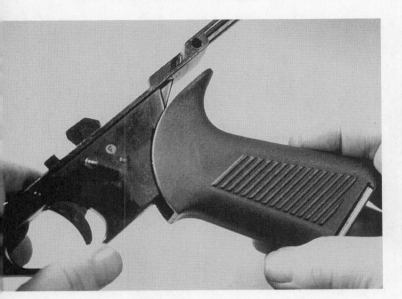

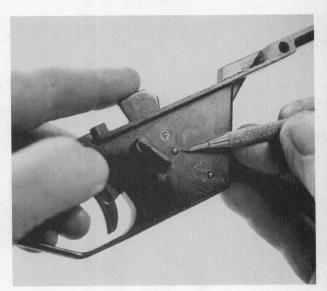

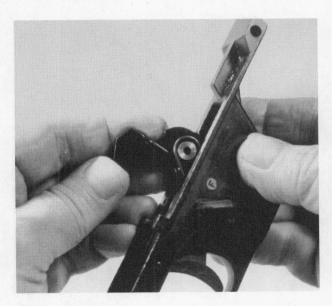

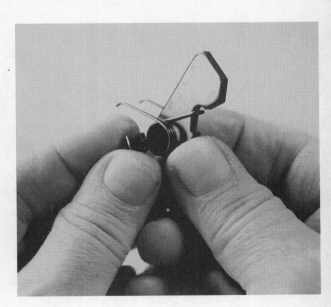

25. Remove the hammer and its spring assembly.

26. The bushings are easily removed from the hammer.

27. Further disassembly of the trigger group is not advisable because of possible damage and the difficulty of reassembly. However, in repair situations, it may be necessary to take out certain parts, so we will show the sequence without removal. The safety-levers are retained on each side by internal C-clips. When these are turned to position and pried off upward, the levers can be removed, along with the center shaft and the safety block.

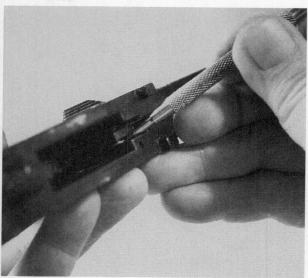

28. Drifting out this cross pin will release the bolt hold-open and its coil spring for removal.

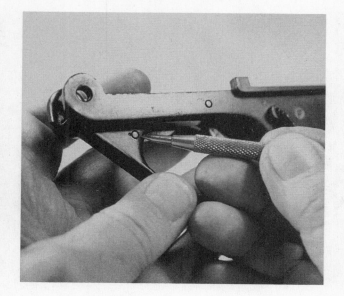

29. Drifting out the trigger cross pin will allow the trigger to be moved forward and turned down into the guard opening for removal.

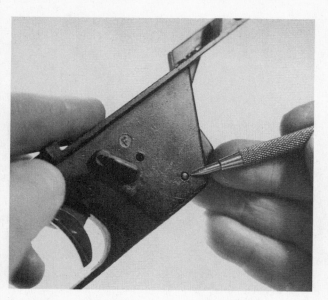

30. Drifting out this cross pin will release the sear assembly for removal. **Caution:** *The primary and secondary sears and their coil and torsion springs will be released, so control them. A slave pin and much patience will be necessary for reinstallation. In normal takedown, this system is definitely best left in place.*

31. By sliding off the upper and lower ribbon clamps, it is possible to disassemble the magazine. The winder assembly, however, should not be taken apart. If a magazine malfunctions, it is best to return it to Calico for service.

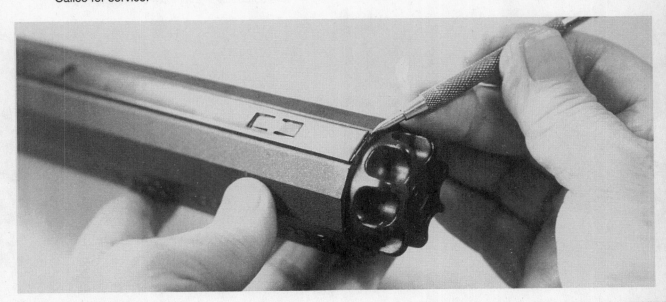

Reassembly Tips:

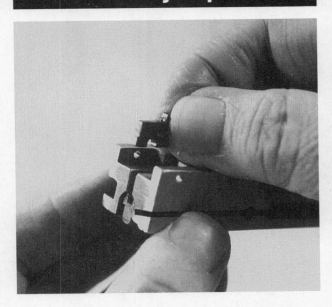

1. When installing the firing pin in the bolt, be sure it is oriented properly, as shown.

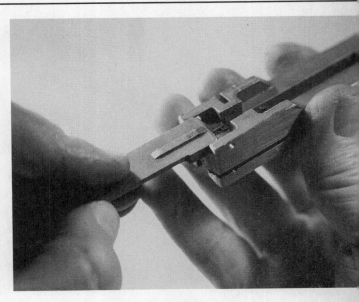

2. When attaching the bolt handle plate, be sure its rear lug engages the firing pin return spring.

3. When the bolt assembly is put back into the lower receiver, be sure the buffer is oriented properly to engage the tail of the ejector and the rear tip of the recoil spring unit.

4. As the bolt is installed, be sure the ejector is hooked into its recess at the rear, and push it forward as the upper receiver is tipped back into place. Also, draw the bolt back slightly to clear the extractor.

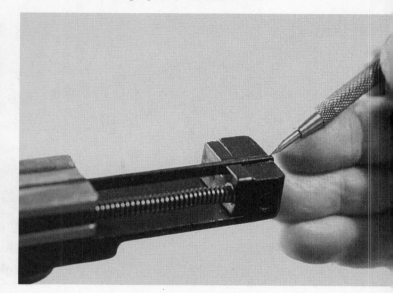

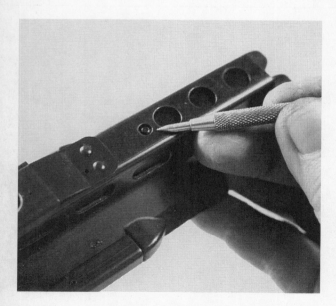

5. If the stock has been removed, drift the retaining pin down until its tip is level with the exterior of the stock piece, as shown.

Charter AR-7 Explorer

Data:	Charter AR-7 Explorer
Origin:	United States
Manufacturer:	Charter Arms Corp. Stratford, Connecticut
Cartridge:	22 Long Rifle
Magazine capacity:	8 rounds
Overall length:	35 inches
Barrel length:	16 inches
Weight:	2$\frac{1}{2}$ pounds

In 1959, Armalite, Incorporated of Costa Mesa, California, introduced the AR-7 Explorer, and this little semi-auto carbine instantly became popular with backpackers, fishermen, pilots, and everyone who might eventually be faced with a survival situation. The barrel, receiver, and magazine can be stowed inside the hollow plastic stock, and with the rubber buttplate/cover in place, the whole thing will even float. From 1973 to 1990, the AR-7 was made by Charter Arms. From 1992 to the present, it has been produced by Survival Arms, Incorporated. It remains essentially unchanged from the original guns made by Armalite.

Disassembly:

1. The stock retaining bolt is accessible in a recess at the bottom of the pistol grip portion of the stock, and its head has a raised center piece that is easily grasped with finger and thumb. Turn the bolt counter-clockwise until the stock is released from the receiver, and remove the stock down and toward the rear.

2. The barrel is retained by a knurled collar which is threaded onto the front of the receiver. Turn the collar counterclockwise (front view) until it is free of the receiver, and remove the barrel toward the front. Note the guide or key on top of the barrel, which mates with a slot in the top of the receiver extension.

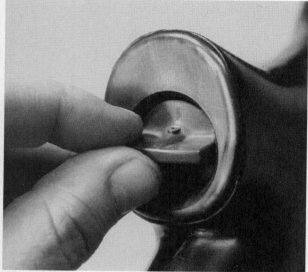

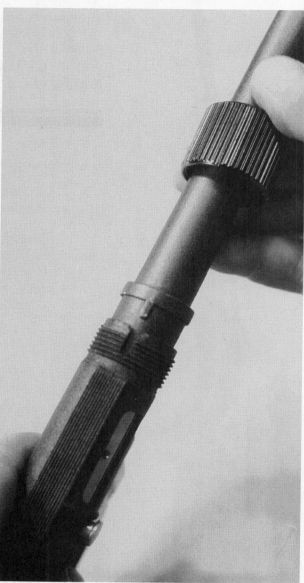

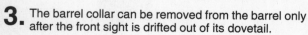

3. The barrel collar can be removed from the barrel only after the front sight is drifted out of its dovetail.

4. Be sure hammer is at rest (in the fired position) and remove the large screw on the left side which retains the sideplate.

Remove the sideplate toward the left. Proceed cautiously, as the left end of the hammer pivot rests in a small hole in the sideplate. If the plate is tight, it may have to be nudged from inside the magazine well and pried gently at the lower rear.

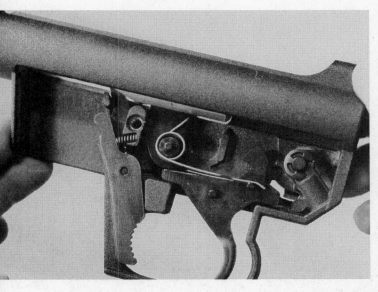

5. After the plate is removed, take note of the relationship of the internal parts before taking them out.

6. Restrain the magazine catch spring to prevent its loss, and remove the catch and spring toward the left.

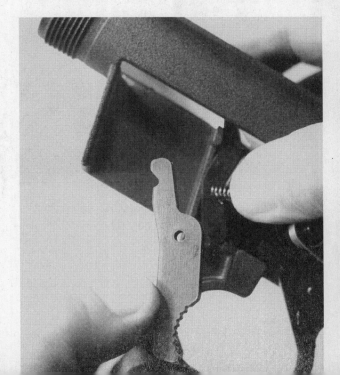

7. Disengage the outside (left) rear arm of the mainspring from its groove in the bearing pin at the rear of the trigger, and swing the spring arm down and forward to relieve its tension.

8. With a small screwdriver, lift the inside (right) rear arm of the mainspring from its groove in the pin at the rear of the trigger, and remove the pin toward the left.

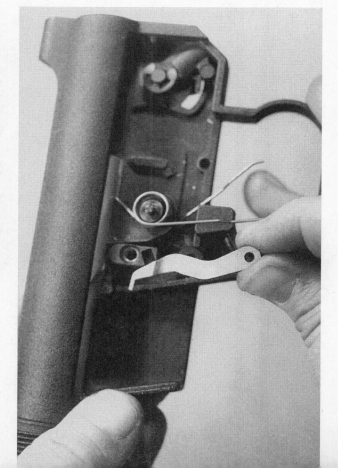

9. Remove the trigger and its pivot pin toward the left.

10. Remove the magazine catch pivot pin toward the left to release the ejector for removal downward.

11. Tip the hammer toward the rear and remove the hammer, spring and pivot assembly toward the left. The spring is easily detached from the hammer. In normal disassembly, the pivot should not be removed from the hammer.

12. Depress the bolt very slightly to align the bolt handle with the enlarged portion of its track in the receiver, and remove the handle toward the right.

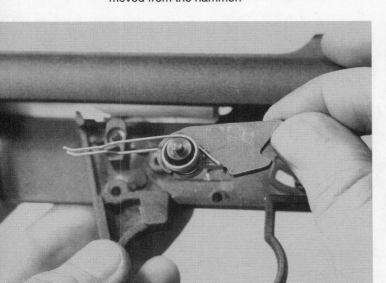

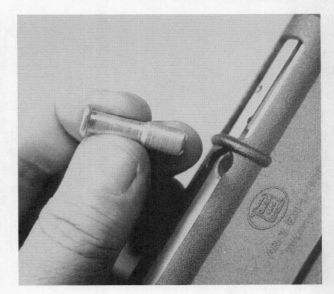

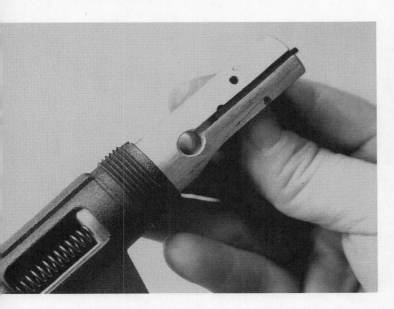

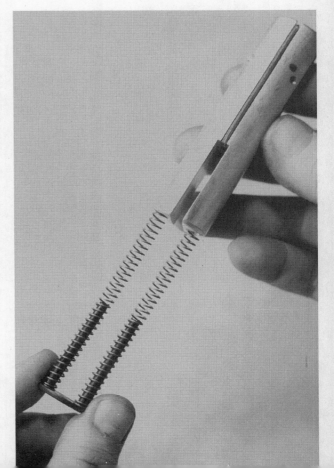

13. Remove the bolt, along with its twin springs and spring guide unit, toward the front.

14. Remove the springs and spring guide unit from the rear of the bolt.

15. Drifting out a horizontal roll pin will release the firing pin for removal from the top of the bolt.

16. Drifting out a vertical roll pin (arrow) on the right side of the bolt will release the extractor and its spring for removal toward the right.

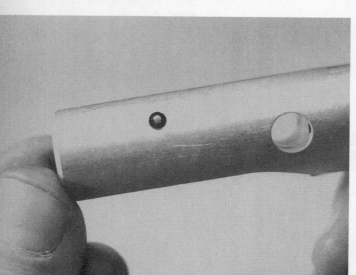

17. The safety is retained by a spring C-clip inside the receiver. After removal of the clip, the safety is removed toward the right.

18. Backing out the screw at the rear of the receiver will release the rear sight for removal.

Reassembly Tips:

When replacing the bolt and bolt spring assembly in the receiver, be sure the two springs are completely seated on the guide, and that the guide is horizontally oriented so the springs will not kink.

Before replacing the trigger in the receiver, swing the inside arm of the mainspring up to the rear and rest it on the inside of the receiver. When the trigger is in place, use a small screwdriver to lift the inner arm of the spring while inserting the spring base pin. Be sure the tip of the spring engages the groove in the pin.

1. When replacing the rear sight, note that the position of the sight plate is adjustable, and any change will affect the point of impact.

2. When replacing the sideplate, be sure the small tip of the hammer pivot is aligned with its hole in the sideplate.

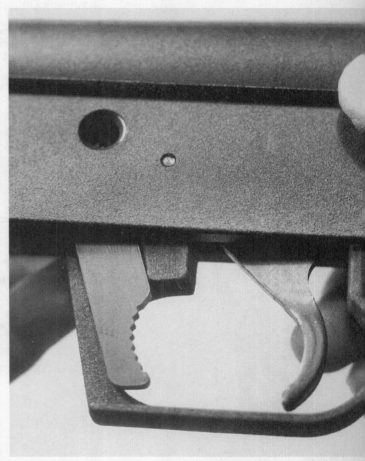

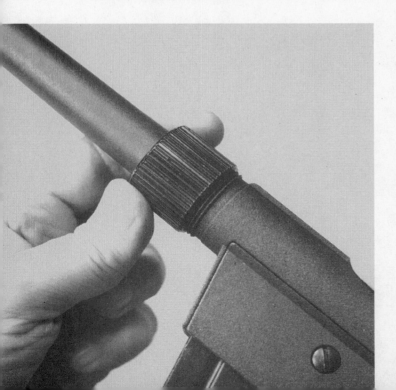

3. When replacing the barrel, be sure the guide key on the top of the barrel enters its slot in the front of the receiver. Tighten the barrel collar firmly, by hand, but do not over-tighten, as both collar and receiver are made of alloy.

Chipmunk

Similar/Identical Pattern Guns
The same basic assembly/disassembly steps for the Chipmunk also apply to the following gun:
Chipmunk Deluxe

Data:	Chipmunk
Origin:	United States
Manufacturer:	Oregon Arms, Inc. Medford, Oregon
Cartridge:	22 Long Rifle
Overall length:	30 inches
Barrel length:	$16^{1}/_{8}$ inches
Weight:	$2^{1}/_{2}$ pounds

This elegant little rifle was designed for young shooters, but it has also seen some use by backpackers, campers and others who value its small size and reliable mechanism. First made by the Chipmunk Manufacturing Company from 1982 to 1988, the gun is now produced by Oregon Arms. The instructions can be applied to both the early and current production rifles.

Disassembly:

1. Hold the trigger to the rear, open the bolt, and remove the bolt toward the rear.

2. Remove the stock mounting bolt, located on the underside, just forward of the trigger guard. Remove the action from the stock, straight upward. The fitting is often tight, so use care, and apply equal pressure at each end.

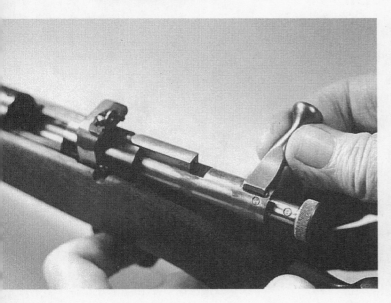

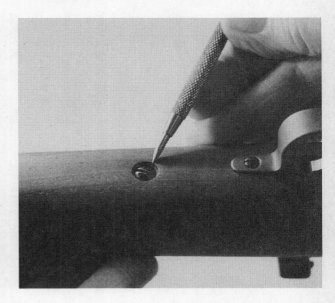

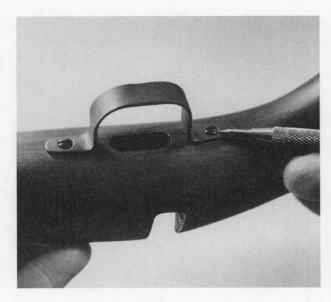

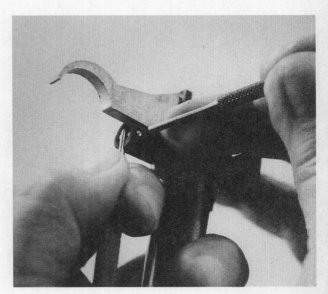

3. The trigger guard and the stock buttplate are each retained by two wood screws.

4. The cross pin that retains the combination sear and trigger spring is rebated at each end. To remove it, depress it upward with a tool or fingertip until its larger central portion is aligned with the exit hole on either side. Then, push it out. **Caution:** *The spring is under tension, so control it.*

5. Remove the spring from its recess.

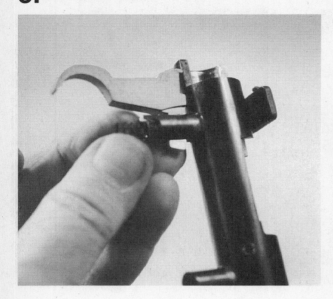

6. Remove the trigger downward.

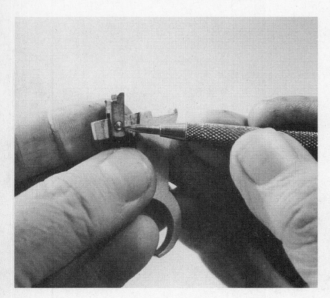

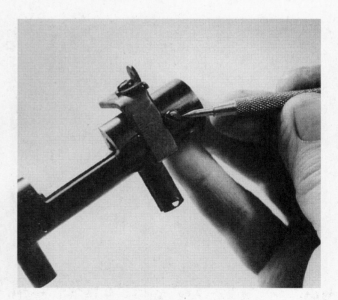

7. Pushing out the cross pin will allow the sear to be separated from the trigger.

8. The elevation adjustment screw also retains the rear sight on the receiver. The windage adjustment screw retains the aperture on the sight base.

9. A cross pin retains the barrel in the receiver. In normal takedown, this is not disturbed. If removal is necessary, drift out the pin and use a hardwood block to drive the receiver off the barrel. Note that the cross pin is a roll pin, so use a roll pin punch to avoid deformation.

10. With a tool or a strong thumbnail, depress the extractor plunger and remove the extractor toward the side. **Caution:** *Control the strong spring and plunger.*

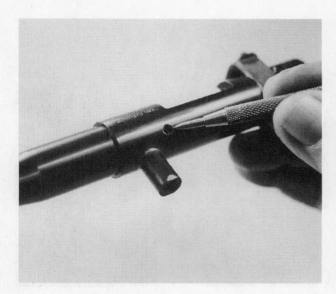

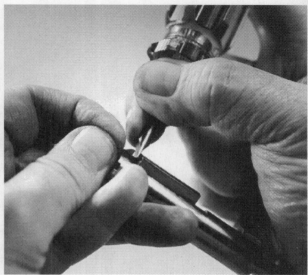

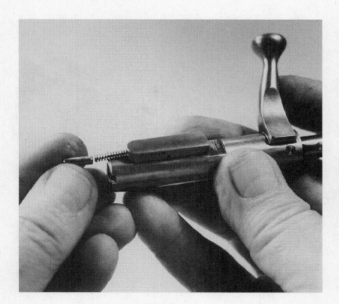

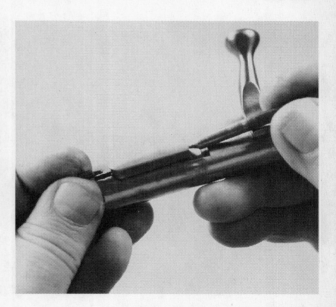

11. Remove the extractor plunger and spring.

12. Use a small tool to nudge the bolt detent plunger forward, into the extractor spring tunnel, and take the plunger out toward the front.

13. Drift out the cross pin that retains the cocking knob. When the drift is withdrawn, control the knob, as it is under tension of the rebound spring.

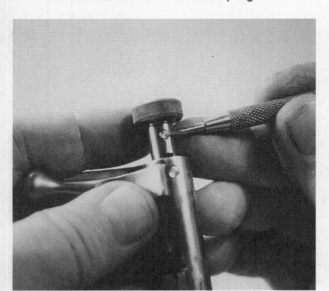

14. Remove the cocking knob and rebound spring toward the rear. The spring is easily removed from inside the knob shaft.

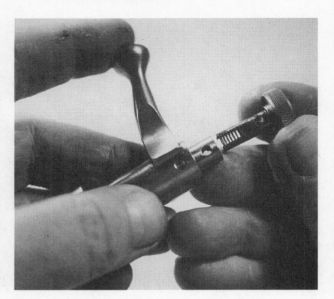

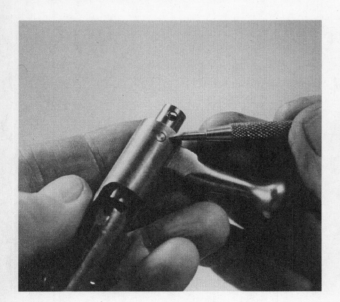

15. Drift out the striker retaining pin upward. Avoid canting the pin after it clears one wall of the bolt. **Caution:** *Control the striker spring as the drift is withdrawn.*

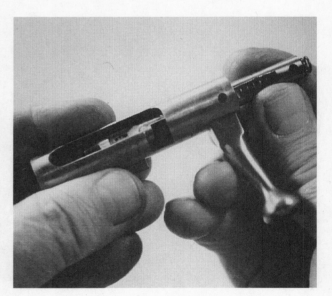

16. Remove the striker and spring toward the rear. The spring is easily removed from inside the striker.

Reassembly Tips:

1. When installing the striker retaining pin, insert a tool at the rear to slightly compress the striker spring, keeping it forward of the pin.

2. When installing the bolt detent plunger, note that its smaller tip goes toward the rear.

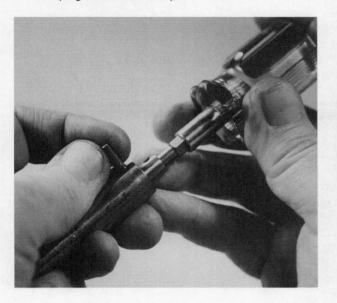

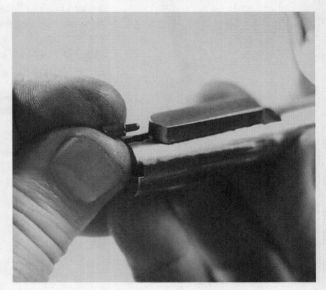

3. If the sear has been removed from the trigger, be sure it is reinstalled as shown, with its step toward the front.

Daisy
Model 2202

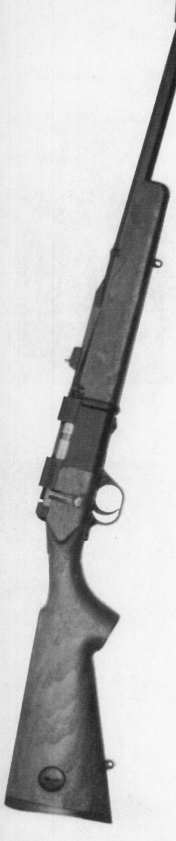

Similar/Identical Pattern Guns
The same basic assembly/disassembly steps for the Daisy Model 2202 also apply to the following guns:

Daisy Model 2201   Daisy Model 2211
Daisy Model 2212

Data:	Daisy Model 2202
Origin:	United States
Manufacturer:	Daisy Manufacturing Rogers, Arkansas
Cartridge:	22 Long Rifle
Magazine capacity:	10 rounds
Overall length:	$34\frac{1}{2}$ inches
Barrel length:	19 inches
Weight:	5 pounds

Marketed under the trade name Legacy, the Model 2202 was introduced in 1988. There was also an identical gun with walnut stock and forend, the Model 2212. The single shot guns of the same design, the Model 2201 and Model 2211, have the same firing mechanism. All four versions were discontinued in 1990. They were neat little guns, and I wish they had stayed in production.

Disassembly:

1. Open the bolt and pull it back until it stops. Put the safety in on-safe position. Depress and hold the button at the rear of the trigger guard.

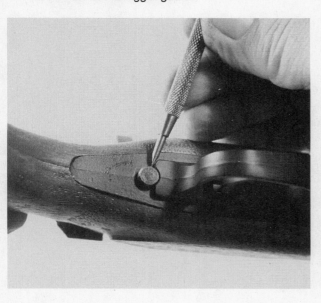

2. Move the trigger guard unit toward the rear, and take it out downward.

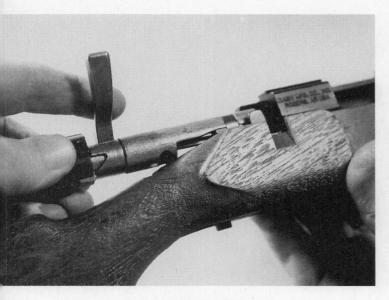

3. Remove the bolt toward the rear.

4. Operate the latch and push the magazine downward out of the receiver.

5. A special barrel nut wrench was supplied with each gun. In the absence of the wrench, a drift of the proper size can be inserted in the holes in the nut to turn it. Unscrew the barrel nut, turning it toward the right (rear view). As the nut is turned, stabilize the forend, keeping it straight.

6. After the forend extensions have cleared the collar of the receiver, the rear portion of the gun can be turned to unscrew it from the nut, and the parts can be separated.

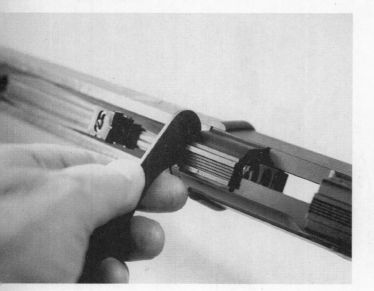

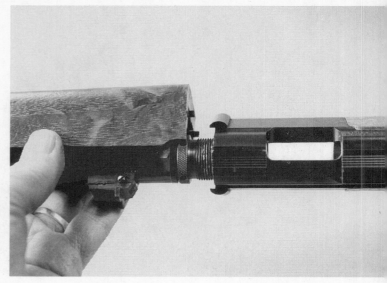

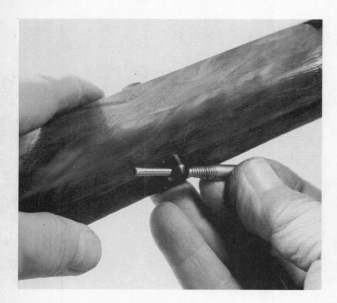

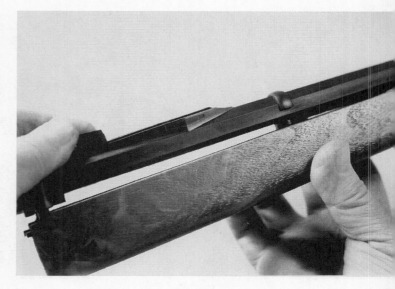

7. To remove the forend from the barrel, insert a drift through the hole in the sling stud and unscrew it, as shown.

8. Remove the forend downward. Further takedown of the barrel assembly is not advisable.

9. To remove the buttstock from the receiver, you must unscrew the button that controls the adjustable buttplate and take out the latch and the buttplate extension. This will give access to the internal stock retaining bolt. As some damage to the button is inevitable, this should be done only if absolutely necessary.

10. The bolt end piece is retained by an inner spring ring and routine disassembly is not recommended.

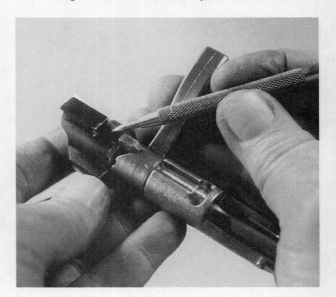

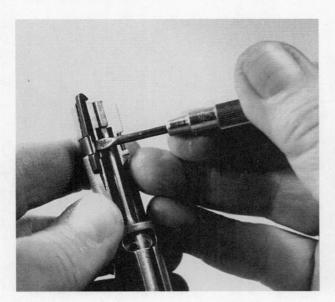

11. To remove the extractor, use a tool to pry the band-type spring until its hook clears the shelf. **Caution:** *Control the spring band.*

12. Remove the Phillips-type screws on the right side of the trigger housing.

13. Carefully lift off the plate.

14. Restrain the trigger and its spring and carefully lift out the sear. Control the sear spring.

15. Remove the sear lever.

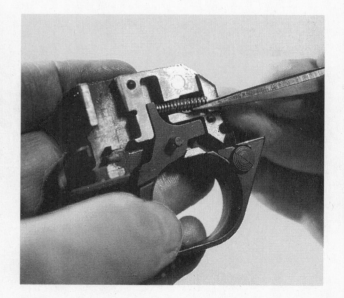

16. Taking care to control it, carefully pry the trigger spring out of its recess and remove it.

17. Lift the trigger off its pivot post.

18. Push the safety button out toward the right. **Caution:** *The positioning ball and spring will be released at the top as they clear, so control them.*

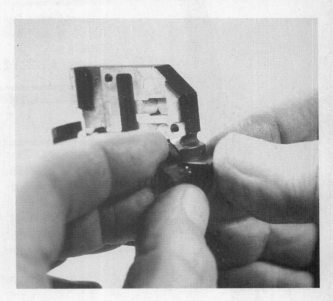

Reassembly Tips:

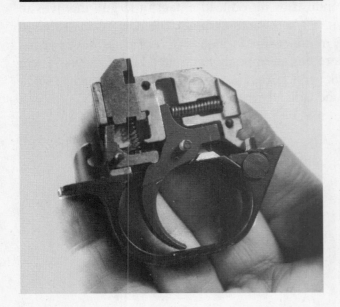

1. The trigger group components are shown here in proper order before replacement of the sideplate.

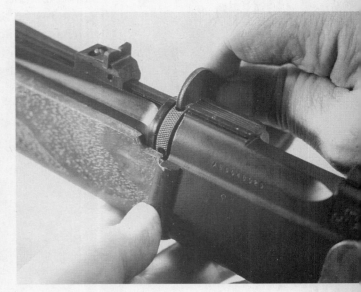

2. When tightening the barrel nut, be sure the forend is kept in alignment to properly enter the flange at the front of the receiver.

Feather
AT-22

Data:	Feather AT-22
Origin:	United States
Manufacturer:	Feather Industries Boulder, Colorado
Cartridge:	22 Long Rifle
Magazine capacity:	20 rounds
Overall length:	35 inches (stock extended) 26 inches (stock stored)
Barrel length:	17 inches
Weight:	$3^{1}/_{4}$ pounds

In 1986, Feather Industries introduced a neat little gun that was to become my favorite 22 semi-auto carbine. The design was so good that it has had only minor cosmetic changes over the past seven years. The gun shown here has an optional ventilated barrel sleeve. There is also a fixed-stock version, the F2. Except for the difference in stock attachment, it is mechanically the same.

Disassembly:

1. Remove the magazine, and pull the trigger to drop the striker to fired position. Unscrew the barrel collar at the front of the receiver, and remove the barrel toward the front.

2. The cartridge guide above the chamber and its coil spring are retained by a roll-type cross pin.

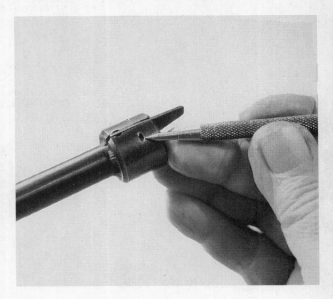

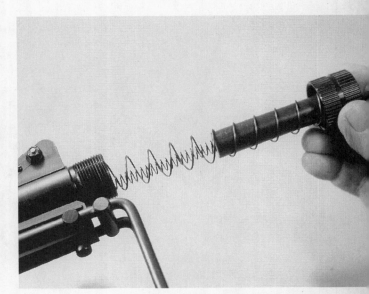

3. Unscrew the knob at the rear of the receiver. **Caution:** *Control the knob, as the recoil and striker springs will be released.*

4. Ease the spring tension slowly. Remove the knob, the guide, and the striker spring toward the rear.

5. Remove the recoil spring and its guide toward the rear.

6. Move the bolt toward the rear until the handle aligns with the exit cut in its track, and take out the bolt handle toward the right.

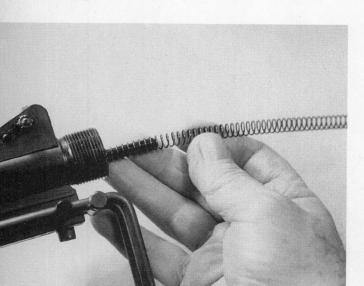

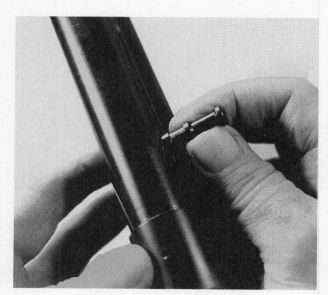

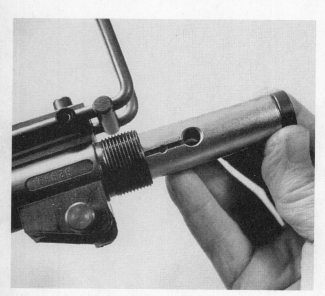

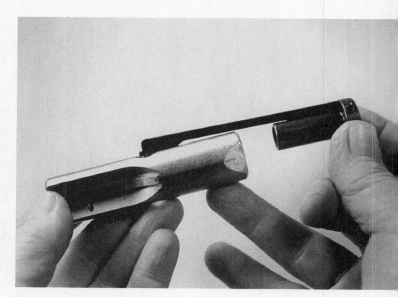

7. Use a tool to push the bolt assembly toward the rear, and remove the bolt assembly.

8. Move the striker assembly rearward out of the bolt. When its central guide clears, it can be lifted off.

9. The firing pin is attached to the striker unit by a roll-type cross pin. The cross pin is factory-staked on both sides, and it should be removed only for repair purposes.

10. The extractor and its coil spring are retained in the bolt by a vertical roll pin that is best drifted out upward. The pin is lightly staked in place and should be removed only for repair.

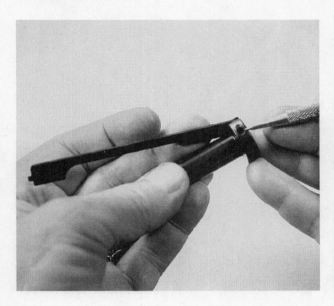

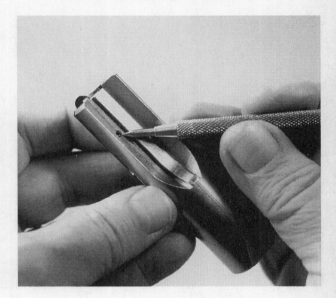

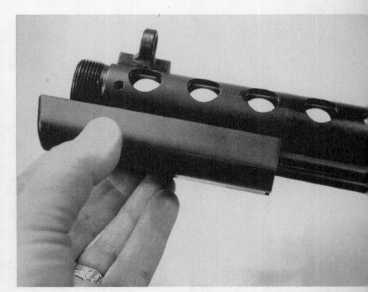

11. The forend is retained by a single Allen screw.

12. If the stock is in stored position, take off the forend toward the front.

13. If the stock is to be removed, drift the roll pin in its right shaft out toward the right. The stock can then be removed toward the rear.

14. Remove the large Allen screw at the front of the lower receiver.

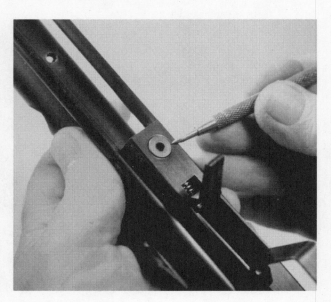

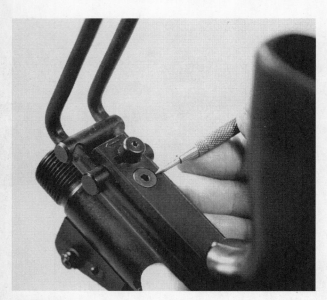

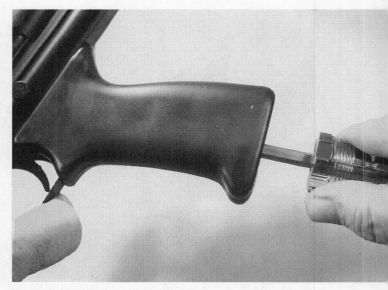

15. Remove the large Allen screw at the rear of the lower receiver.

16. With a larger Allen bit, remove the screw inside the pistol grip. Note that there are two washers on this screw. Take care that they are kept in order and not lost.

17. Remove the pistol grip downward.

18. Remove the middle Allen screw in the lower receiver.

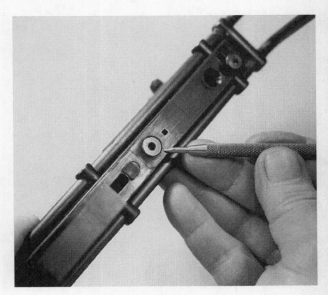

19. Remove the lower receiver downward.

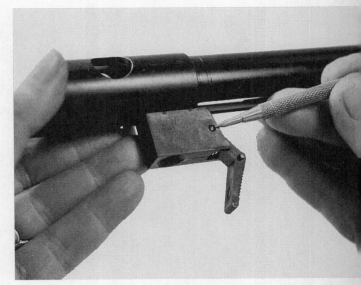

20. The magazine catch is pivoted and retained by a cross pin. Control the catch and its coil spring as the pin is removed.

21. The front and rear sights are retained on the receiver by two Allen screws in each location. For access to the rear screw in the rear sight, the aperture must be removed from the sight.

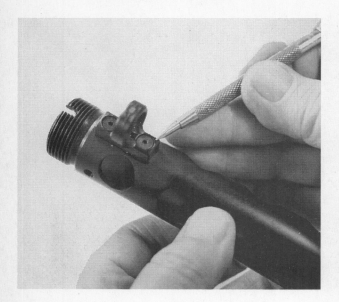

22. Inside the rear of the lower receiver are two polymer spacer blocks, through which the mounting screws pass. Remove these and keep them in the correct order and orientation as they are not interchangeable.

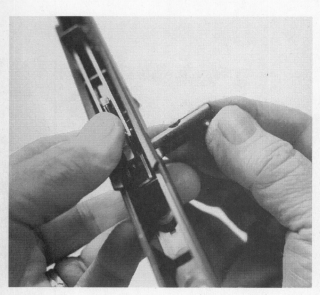

23. The lower receiver parts should not be removed unless necessary for repair. If the trigger system is to be removed, first drift out the stock retaining pin (see step 13), and remove the stock toward the rear. Push out the front stock cross pin.

24. With the safety in off-safe position (forward), carefully move the trigger group sub-frame slightly upward and forward, taking the tip of the trigger through the recess in the safety cross-piece.

25. Put the safety back in on-safe position, tilt the sub-frame as shown, and remove it upward.

26. The safety detent spring, mounted on the left tip of the trigger cross pin, will be freed as the sub-frame is removed. Retrieve the spring from inside the sub-frame.

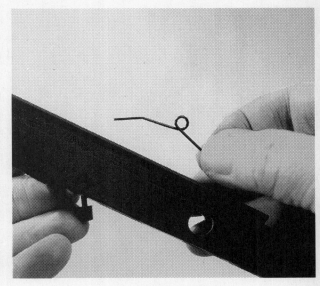

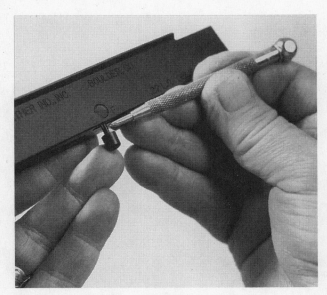

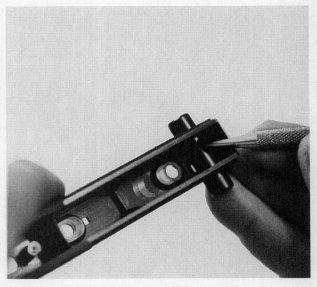

27. In most cases, the safety is best left in place. If it must be removed, its handle pin is drifted out of the cross-piece, downward. The cross-piece is then easily removed.

28. If the rear stock cross pin is to be removed, the pin in its release knob must be drifted out downward. **Caution:** *Control the plunger and spring.*

29. The forward pin in the trigger group is the trigger stop pin. It retains no part, and is easily removed.

30. Push the trigger forward and push out the trigger cross pin toward either side.

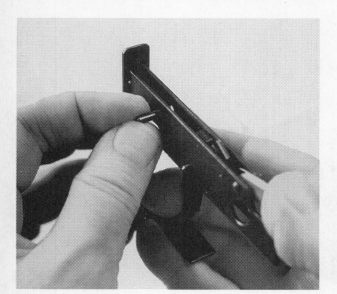

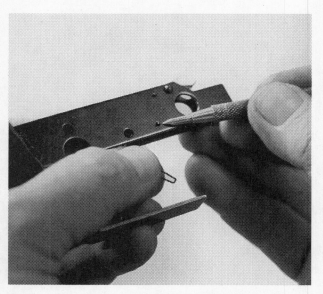

31. Remove the trigger and disconnector assembly upward. This is more easily done by depressing the disconnector slightly at the rear, and moving the trigger forward. A cross pin retains the disconnector on the trigger.

32. Unhook the combination trigger and disconnector spring from its lock hole in the left side of the sub-frame and remove it.

33. Tip the sear upward, and push out the sear cross pin.

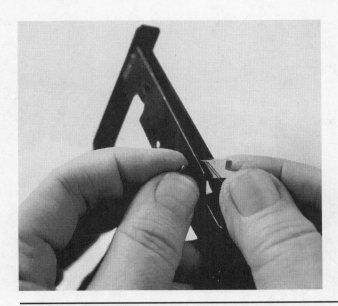

34. Remove the sear upward. The sear spring is easily detached from its lock holes on each side.

Reassembly Tips:

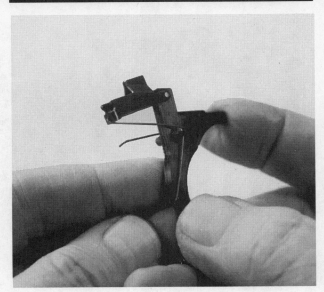

1. When installing the trigger and disconnector system, remember to re-hook the spring in its lock hole. The long rear arm of the spring must be hooked into a notch beneath the rear tip of the disconnector, as shown. The parts are assembled here for purposes of illustration, as they would be in the sub-frame.

2. The safety detent spring is shown here in the proper orientation, as it should be when it is installed in the sub-frame.

3. As the trigger system is put back into the sub-frame, tip the disconnector upward and use it to position the trigger, as shown.

4. Be sure the two spacer blocks are installed in the proper order, as shown.

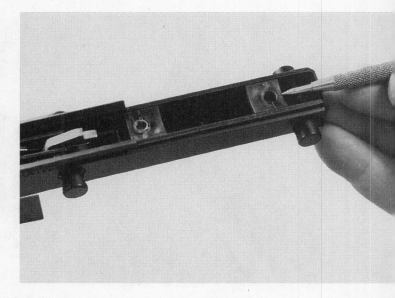

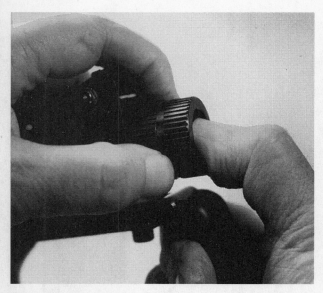

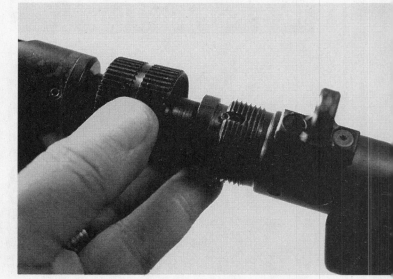

5. As the rear receiver end cap is turned into place, be sure the striker is in the fired position. In the last few turns, depress the button at the center of the knob to be sure the guide seats properly.

6. As the barrel assembly is put back into place, retract the bolt slightly. Note that the barrel has a positioning stud that must enter a slot at the front of the receiver.

Federal Engineering XC220

Data:	Federal Engineering XC220
Origin:	United States
Manufacturer:	Federal Engineering Corp. Bensenville, Illinois
Cartridge:	22 Long Rifle
Magazine capacity:	30 rounds
Overall length:	34$\frac{1}{2}$ inches
Barrel length:	16$\frac{1}{2}$ inches
Weight:	7$\frac{1}{4}$ pounds

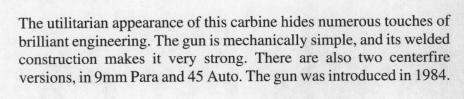

The utilitarian appearance of this carbine hides numerous touches of brilliant engineering. The gun is mechanically simple, and its welded construction makes it very strong. There are also two centerfire versions, in 9mm Para and 45 Auto. The gun was introduced in 1984.

Disassembly:

1. Remove the magazine and pull the trigger to drop the hammer to fired position. Unscrew the knurled collar at the rear of the receiver and take off the buttstock toward the rear.

2. Unscrew the ventilated barrel sleeve and take out the barrel toward the front.

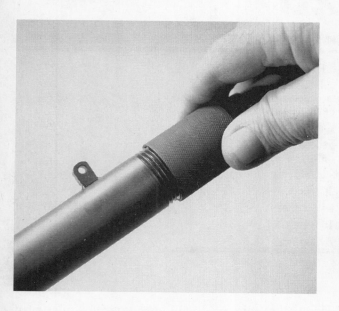

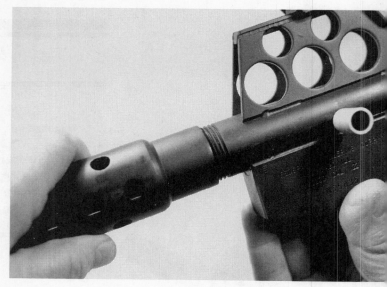

3. Push the bolt slightly to the rear to align the bolt handle with its exit opening in the track. Remove the bolt handle toward the left.

4. Nudge the bolt forward, and remove the bolt and recoil spring assembly toward the front. The recoil spring is easily removable from the guide. The guide rod, however, is not routinely removed from the bolt.

5. Insert a small tool to push the extractor plunger toward the rear and lift out the extractor. **Caution:** *Control the plunger and spring, and ease them out.*

6. The firing pin and its return spring are retained in the bolt by an Allen screw. Control the firing pin as the screw is backed out, and ease the firing pin and spring out toward the rear.

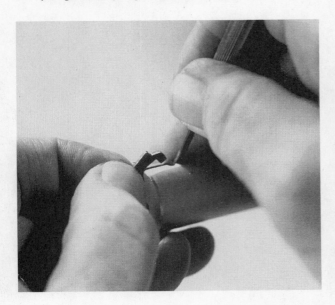

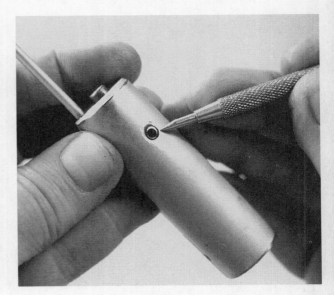

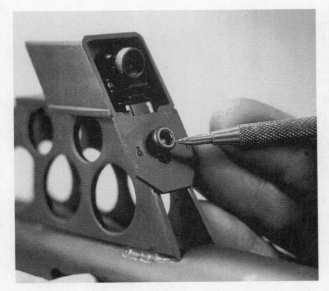

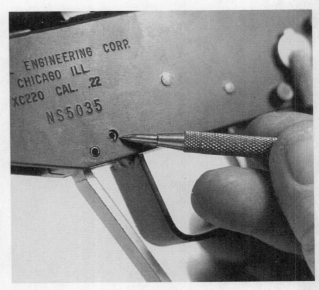

7. The rear sight hood is retained on the base by an Allen screw. Removal of the hood will give access for removal or adjustment of the rear sight.

8. With a roll-pin drift, remove the forward guard plate cross pin.

9. Drift out the rear guard plate cross pin.

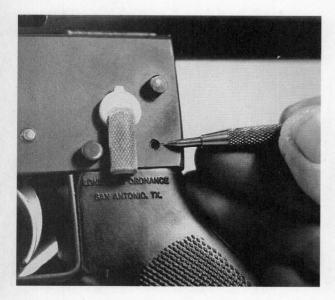

10. Remove the guard plate assembly downward. If removal of the pistol grip is necessary, take out the Allen screw and plate inside the grip.

11. Drift out the magazine catch cross pin.

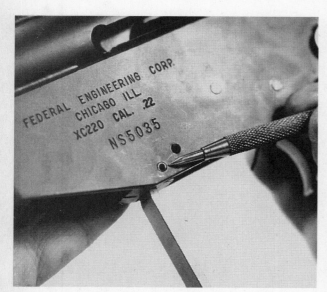

12. Remove the magazine catch and its spring downward. The spring is easily detached from its post on the back of the catch.

14. Remove the trigger downward. The secondary sear will be released internally as the trigger is taken out, and the tension of the hammer spring will be relieved as its rear arms rest on the trigger cross-piece. The trigger spring is easily unhooked from the trigger, and the sear spring can be removed from its recess at the rear.

13. Restrain the trigger and push out the trigger cross pin toward either side.

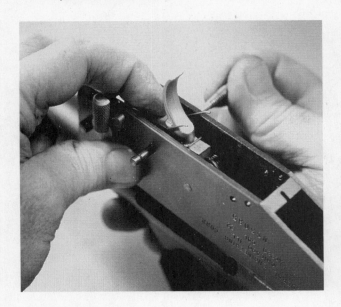

15. Retrieve the secondary sear from inside the receiver.

16. Push out the hammer cross pin.

17. Remove the hammer and hammer spring downward. The spring is easily detached from the hammer. The cross pin latch spring, located inside the hammer, is not routinely removed.

18. An Allen screw retains the safety spring and plunger at the rear of the receiver on the right side.

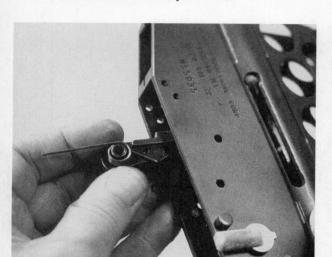

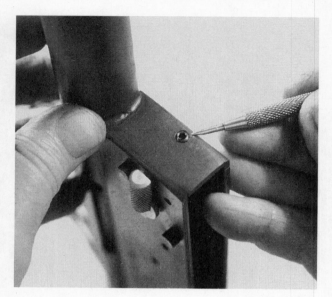

19. Remove the screw and take out the spring and plunger toward the rear.

20. Remove the safety-lever toward the left.

Reassembly Tips:

1. When installing the safety plunger and spring, avoid over-tightening. Try the safety as the screw is turned into place. The head should be about level with the surface of the receiver.

2. A slave pin will be necessary for installation of the trigger assembly, as shown. As the pin is reinserted, it will be necessary to depress each rear arm of the hammer spring to clear it.

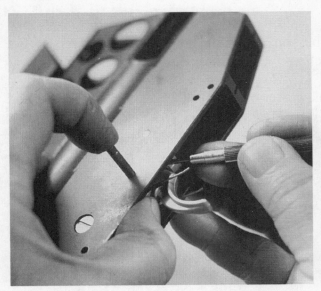

3. As the trigger assembly is moved into place, be sure the safety is in off-safe position. The tool shown is depressing one arm of the hammer spring. Be sure the slave pin is nearly the same size as the trigger pin to avoid problems with passage through the secondary sear.

4. As the guard plate and grip are put back into place, note that the fork at the upper front of the plate must engage the spring and guide of the magazine catch. The parts are shown here outside the receiver, for illustration.

F.I.E.
Model 122

Similar/Identical Pattern Guns
The same basic assembly/disassembly steps for the F.I.E. Model 122 also apply to the following gun:
Magtech MT-22C

Data:	F.I.E. Model 122
Origin:	Brazil
Manufacturer:	CBC, Santo Andre, Brazil
Cartridge:	22 Long Rifle
Magazine capacity:	6 and 10 rounds
Overall length:	39 inches
Barrel length:	21 inches
Weight:	$5^3/_4$ pounds

While this rifle has an external resemblance to some earlier Remington bolt actions, it is mechanically very different. It was imported by the F.I.E. Corporation from 1986 to 1990. In 1991, importation was taken over by Magtech Recreational Products, and it was marketed as their Model MT-22C. Disassembly is fairly easy, but reassembly has some points that could be difficult for the amateur.

Disassembly:

1. Remove the magazine. Open the bolt, hold the trigger back, and remove the bolt toward the rear.

2. Remove the screw at the front of the trigger and magazine plate.

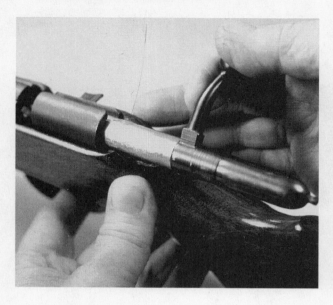

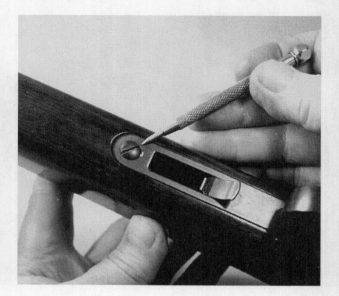

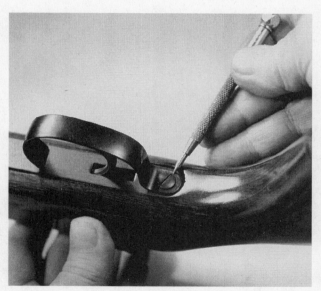

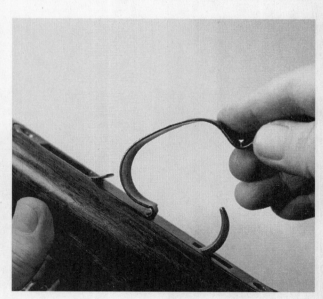

3. Remove the screw at the rear of the trigger and magazine plate.

4. Tip the trigger guard forward and remove it.

5. Tip the trigger and magazine plate outward at the rear and remove it.

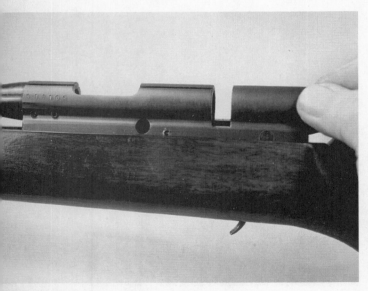

6. Remove the action from the stock.

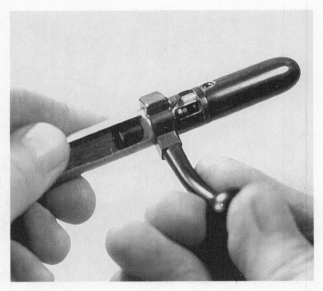

7. Grip the forward portion of the bolt firmly and turn the bolt to lower the striker to fired position, as shown.

8. With a tool, lift the loop of the bolt sleeve retainer up to the position shown.

9. Turn the bolt sleeve, or end piece, clockwise (rear view) to feed the retainer out of the lock opening, as shown. **Caution:** *Keep forward pressure on the end piece, as the striker spring is under some tension, even in uncocked position.*

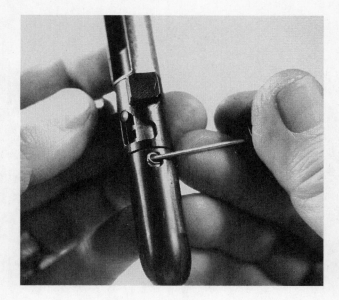

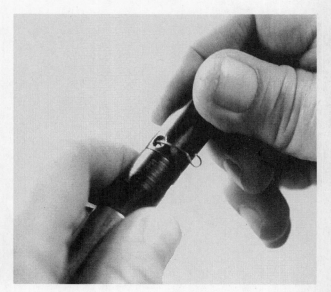

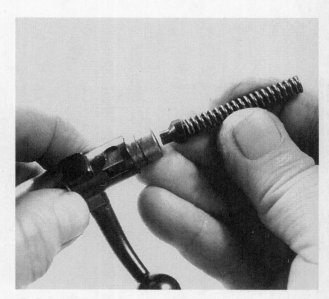

10. When the end of the retainer is cleared, remove it. Ease the spring tension and take off the end piece toward the rear.

11. Remove the striker spring and guide toward the rear.

12. Insert a tool in the access hole in the bolt handle collar and push out the striker cam pin.

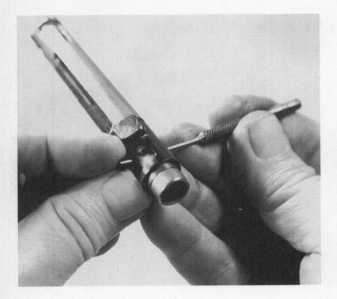

13. Remove the bolt handle toward the rear.

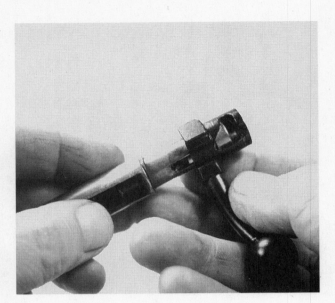

14. Remove the bolt handle washer toward the rear.

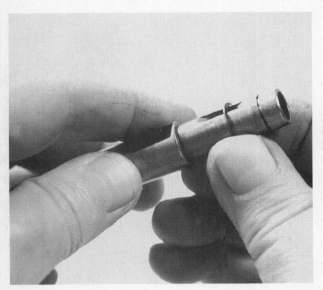

15. Remove the striker/firing pin toward the rear.

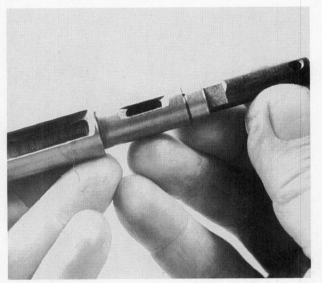

16. To remove the extractors, insert a tool under the edge of the saddle spring and pry it outward. **Caution:** *Control the spring. When the extractors are removed from their recesses, keep them separate and in order, as each must be put back on its proper side.*

17. Remove the screw that retains the safety-lever. **Caution:** *The safety positioning plunger and its spring will be released as the lever is taken off, so control them.*

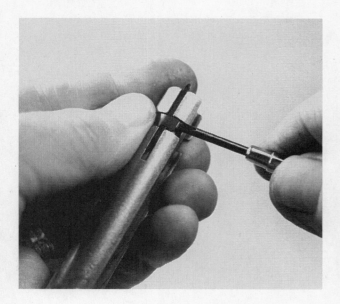

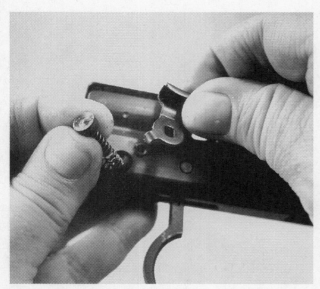

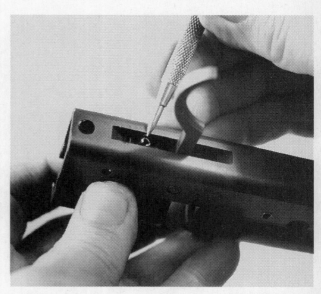

18. Remove the positioning plunger and its spring.

19. Before the safety cross-piece can be removed, the roll pin that engages the disconnector slide must be drifted out downward, from inside the receiver.

20. Push out the safety cross-piece toward the left.

21. Push out the trigger cross pin.

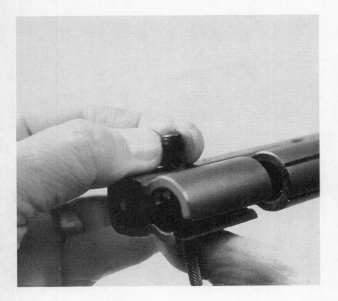

22. Move the trigger inward and toward the rear for removal, along with the disconnector slide.

23. Use a tool to nudge the trigger spring rearward for removal.

24. Use a roll pin drift to remove the cross pin at the center of the receiver.

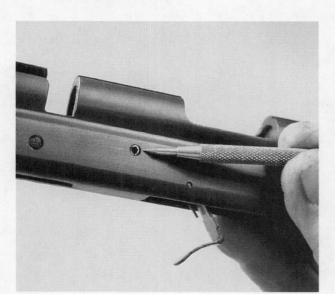

25. As the drift is removed, exert rearward pressure on the magazine catch as it bears on the insert block.

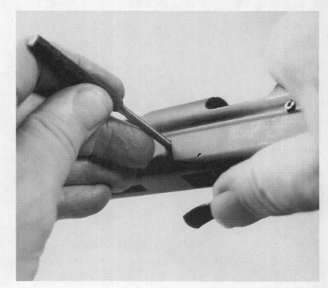

26. With the receiver inverted, move the insert or sub-frame out toward the rear.

27. Push out the upper cross pin and remove the sear.

28. Push out the lower cross pin and remove the sear prop lever.

29. Removal of this screw will allow the ejector to be taken off. There is also an access hole in the receiver, and the ejector can be removed and replaced without taking out the sub-frame. If the ejector is removed, note for reinstallation that its square corner must be at upper front.

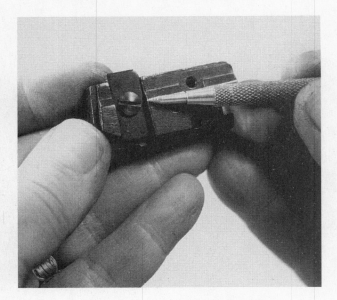

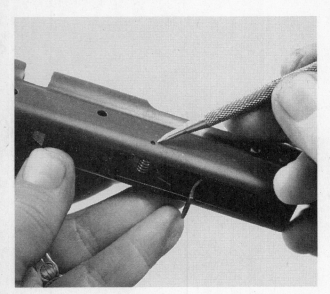

30. Removal of the sub-frame insert will have eased the tension of the magazine catch spring. The catch and spring may be removed by drifting out this cross pin.

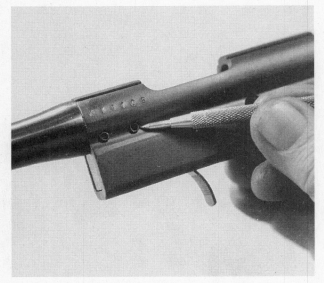

31. Two cross pins retain the barrel and the front insert block in the receiver. In normal takedown, these are best left in place. The rear sight is retained by two Phillips-type screws, and the dovetail-mounted front sight is drifted out toward the right.

Reassembly Tips:

1. When the trigger, disconnector slide and spring are reinstalled, they must be arranged as shown here before the cross pin is reinserted. The parts are shown outside for purposes of illustration. They must be put into the receiver separately. Note that the forward cross-piece of the disconnector slide must engage the notch in the sear prop.

2. When installing the safety cross-piece, depress the rear arms of the trigger spring on each side, to bear under the cross-piece.

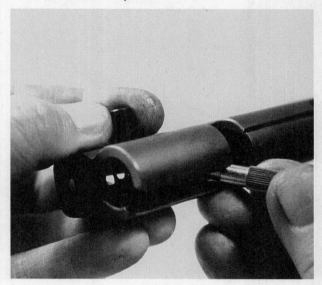

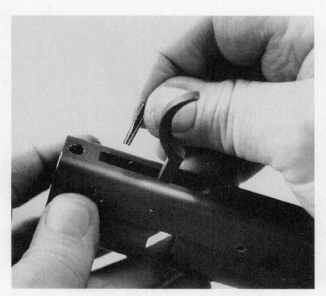

3. Note that the end of the safety connector roll pin that enters the safety cross-piece is a smaller diameter. When in place, the lower end of the roll pin should be even with the underside of the receiver.

4. When installing the striker cam pin, note that the longer, nonrebated end must be outward, as shown.

5. There is a tiny hole in the bolt body to accept the hooked end of the end piece retainer. The end piece is pushed into place against the spring tension, aligning the lock opening with this hole, and the tip of the retainer is inserted.

6. After the retainer tip is in place, turn the end piece counterclockwise (rear view) to feed the retainer back into its internal groove.

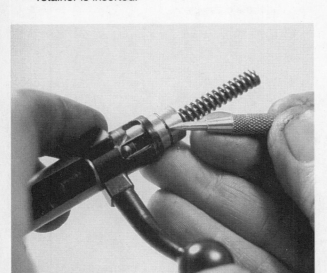

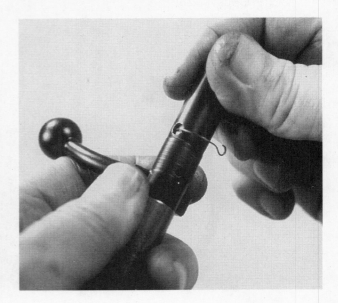

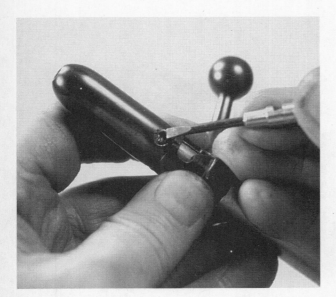

7. When the loop of the retainer is aligned with the lock hole, use a tool to push it down into place.

8. Before the bolt is put back into the receiver, it must be recocked. Hold the front portion of the bolt firmly in a shop cloth or a padded vise, and turn the bolt handle until the striker is in the position shown.

Grendel R-31

Data:	Grendel R-31
Origin:	United States
Manufacturer:	Grendel, Incorporated Rockledge, Florida
Cartridge:	22 WMR
Magazine capacity:	30 rounds
Overall length:	31 inches (stock extended) 24 inches (stock stored)
Barrel length:	16 inches
Weight:	4 pounds

Introduced in 1991, the carbine version of the Grendel P-31 pistol has a longer barrel and a storable buttstock. Available in 22 WMR only, it is perhaps the ultimate "survival"-type carbine. There are some elements of takedown and reassembly that could be very difficult for the non-professional.

Disassembly:

1. Cycle the action to cock the internal hammer. Set the safety in on-safe position and remove the magazine. Open the stock to its extended position. Unscrew the barrel retaining collar.

2. Move the left sidepiece forward and lift it off.

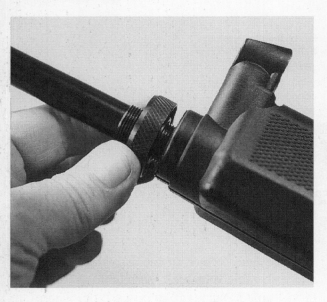

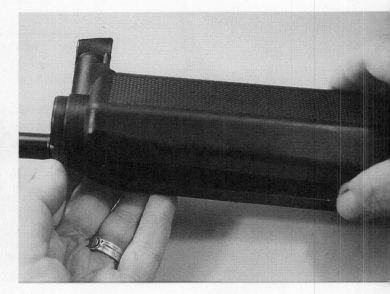

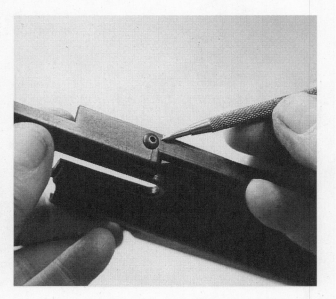

3. Move the right sidepiece forward and lift it off. Note that it must be moved far enough to clear the cocking handle.

4. The Phillips-type screws in the top of each sidepiece are bearing screws that lock into a recess in the receiver, and they are not to be removed.

5. Using the serrated wings provided, push the recoil spring assembly forward until it is clear of the rear vertical plate of the receiver. **Caution:** *Keep the unit under control.*

6. Tip the assembly out toward either side and remove it. Ease the spring tension slowly.

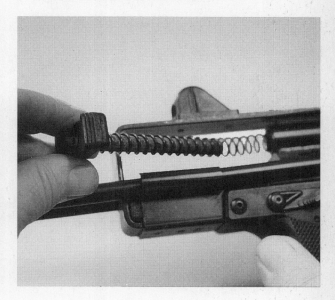

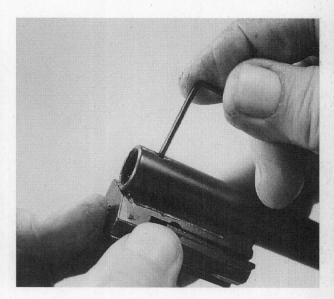

7. Move the bolt assembly all the way to the rear, and tip the bolt handle downward. Remove the bolt assembly toward the right.

8. Use an Allen wrench to back out the screw which retains the firing pin and its spring. **Caution:** *The return spring is quite strong, so keep the firing pin under control.*

9. Ease the spring tension carefully and remove the firing pin and its spring toward the rear.

10. The extractor pin is drifted out toward the left and upward, at an angle. Restrain the extractor and spring and ease them out.

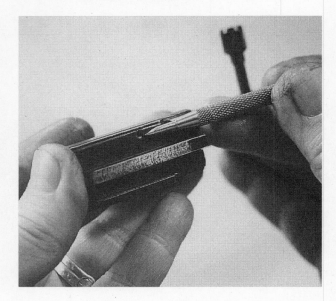

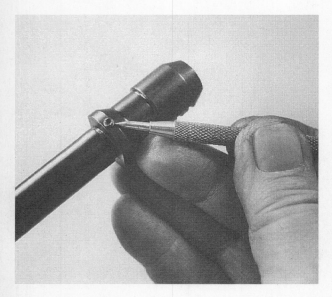

11. If removal of the muzzle brake is necessary, it is locked by an Allen screw on the underside. After the screw is backed out, the brake can be unscrewed from the muzzle. This will also allow the barrel collar to be taken off.

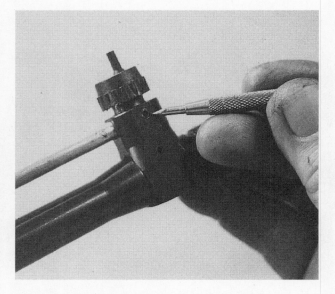

12. The adjustable front sight can be unscrewed from its base, and the detent plunger and its spring can be lifted out. If removal of the bolt guide rod is necessary, it is retained by this roll pin.

13. The lower roll pin retains the base for the sight and guide rod on the barrel.

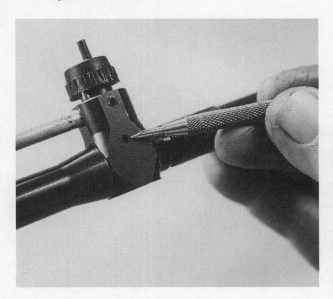

14. Use an Allen wrench to remove the screw in the inside floor of the receiver at the rear.

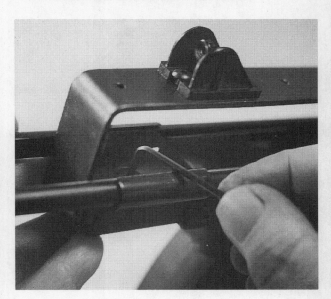

15. Move the stock mounting plate upward and forward, detach it from the stock, and remove the stock toward the rear.

16. Remove the nylon screw spacer from inside the receiver.

17. Remove the stock support piece from the rear of the receiver.

18. Move the safety to off-safe, and restrain the hammer with a fingertip. Pull the trigger, and ease the hammer over forward until it is resting against the ejector. Use an Allen wrench to remove the screw from the left safety-lever.

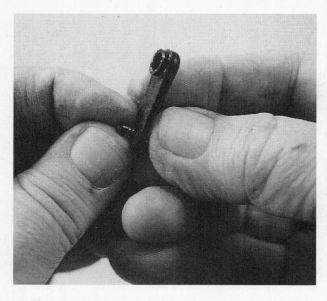

19. Remove the safety-lever toward the left. **Caution:** *Take care that the small detent plunger is not lost.*

20. The plunger and spring are easily removed from inside the lever.

21. Repeat this operation with the right safety-lever.

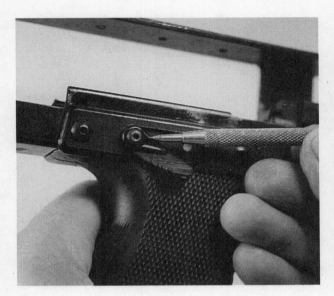

22. Restrain the hammer and push out the safety cross-piece, which is also the hammer pivot.

23. Remove the hammer and hammer spring assembly. The bushing and spring are easily removed from inside the hammer.

24. Remove the internal safety-lever from inside the receiver, on the right side.

25. Remove the hammer spacer from inside the receiver, on the left side.

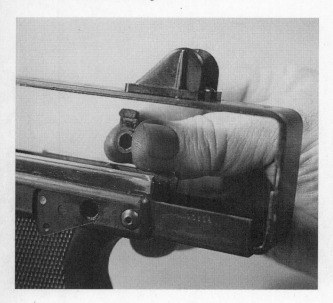

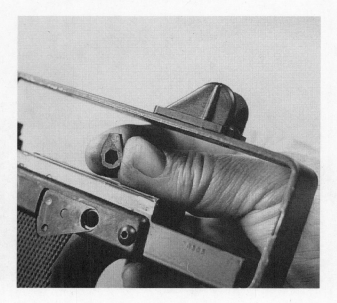

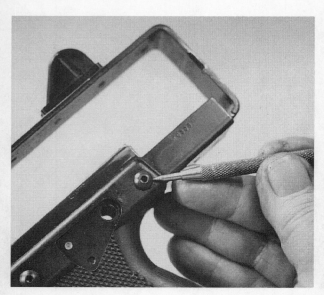

26. Remove the Allen screw on the left side at the rear of the grip frame.

27. Remove the Allen screw on the right side at the rear of the grip frame.

28. Remove the center screws on both sides of the grip frame. Note that there is an internal nut on each of these screws, and these will have to be held with a small wrench.

29. Remove the front screws on both sides of the grip frame. Note that these, also, have internal nuts. Insert a screwdriver to hold them. Also note that the right screw is longer, and its nut holds the stock latch spring.

30. Remove the grip frame and the stock latch spring.

31. Unhook the right arm of the magazine catch spring from its recess inside the grip frame and take out the spring upward.

32. Move the magazine catch toward the left until its right end clears the opening in the grip frame. Turn it as shown, and move it inward for removal. The roll-type stop pin in the catch is not removed in normal takedown.

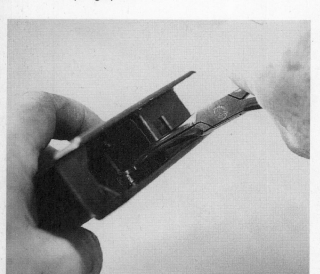

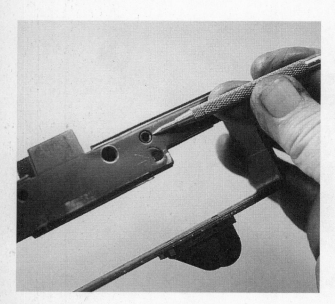

33. If removal of the sear and its torsion-coil spring is necessary, push out the sear pivot. **Caution:** *The spring will be released, so control it.*

34. The spring that powers the trigger bar can be seen here, protruding below the receiver. To remove it, insert a tool to unhook its upper arm from the bar, then move the loop of the spring inward, toward the center, for removal.

35. In normal takedown, the barrel is not removed. If this is necessary, drifting out this cross pin will release the barrel for removal toward the front. This will also release the barrel sleeve and the stock latch.

36. Drifting out this cross pin will allow the trigger to be taken out downward. **Caution:** *The trigger spring will be released.* The trigger bar is turned upward to follow the trigger out.

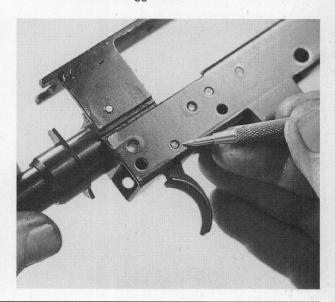

Reassembly Tips:

1. Use slim pliers to position the nut for the right front grip frame screw. Start it, but do not tighten it at this point.

2. Fit the long loop of the stock latch spring onto the right front screw. Use a tool to hold it in place, and tighten the screw, with the nut retaining the spring.

3. If the hammer spring has been removed, be sure the spring and bushing are replaced so the arm of the spring enters the recess on the hammer, as shown.

4. A slave pin will be necessary to stabilize the spring and bushing in the hammer for reassembly.

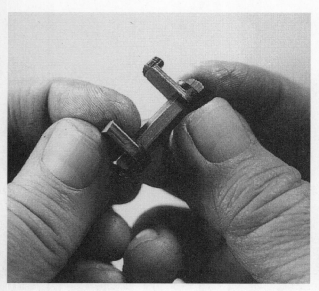

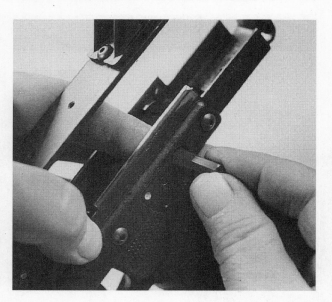

5. When the safety cross-piece/hammer pivot is in the receiver, the internal safety-lever and the spacer must be in the relative positions shown. For illustration, they are assembled here, outside.

6. Because the rear arm of the hammer spring bears on the right side, the cross-piece is best inserted from the left, as shown. Start it through the spacer, then insert the hammer, tipped over forward, and align it for entry of the cross-piece.

7. After the internal safety-lever is installed, move it back into on-safe position. Then, install the external safety-levers in on-safe position.

8. If the firing pin has been removed, check the free movement of the firing pin as the Allen screw is tightened. If it binds the firing pin, back it off until the pin moves freely.

9. As the bolt assembly is reinstalled, it must be depressed downward to properly engage the rails, working against the tension of the hammer spring. This is easily done by using a large screwdriver at the top, as shown.

Harrington & Richardson Model 700

Similar/Identical Pattern Guns

The same basic assembly/disassembly steps for the Harrington & Richardson Model 700 also apply to the following gun:

Harrington & Richardson Model 700 Deluxe

Data:	Harrington & Richardson Model 700
Origin:	United States
Manufacturer:	Harrington & Richardson Gardner, Massachusetts
Cartridge:	22 WMR
Magazine capacity:	5 or 10 rounds
Overall length:	$42^1/_2$ inches
Barrel length:	22 inches
Weight:	$6^1/_2$ pounds

There had been earlier attempts to make a semi-auto rifle in 22 WMR—Kodiak in the U.S., Landmann in Germany—but they were not successful. Then, in 1977, two fine rifles in this chambering were introduced. One was the Heckler & Koch Model 300; the other was the Harrington & Richardson Model 700. Beautifully engineered and elegantly styled, the Model 700 was made from 1977 until the original H&R company ceased operations at the end of 1985.

Disassembly:

1. Remove the magazine and pull the trigger to drop the striker to fired position. Back out the two screws in the magazine plate (they are captive in the plate).

2. Remove the plate and the attached screws.

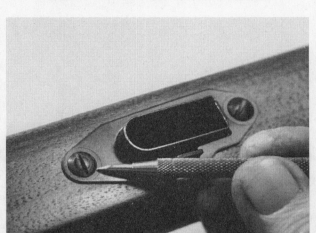

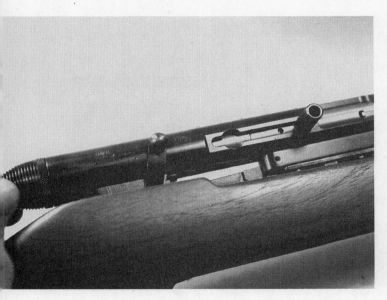

3. Remove the action from the stock.

4. The trigger guard and the stock buttplate are retained on the stock by two Phillips-type screws in each location.

5. Unscrew the receiver end piece. **Caution:** *Even in fired mode, the striker spring retains some tension.*

6. Remove the end piece toward the rear. In normal takedown, the nylon buffer is not removed from the end piece.

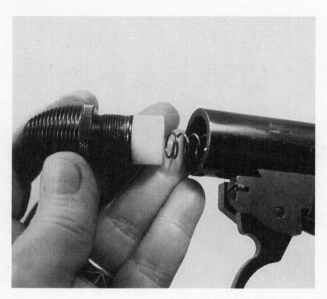

7. Remove the striker spring toward the rear.

8. Cycle the bolt to nudge the striker toward the rear. Pull the trigger and remove the striker toward the rear.

9. Use a ⁵/₈-inch wrench to remove the large nuts at the front and rear of the magazine housing.

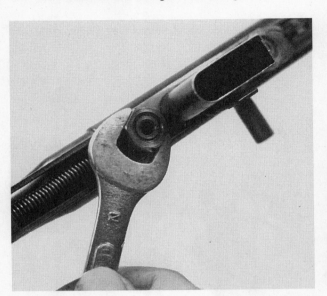

10. Remove the magazine housing. Take care that the two lock washers are not lost.

11. The magazine catch pivot is factory staked at one end. For removal, it would have to be cut off and a new pivot made. If this system is taken off, the coil catch spring will be released.

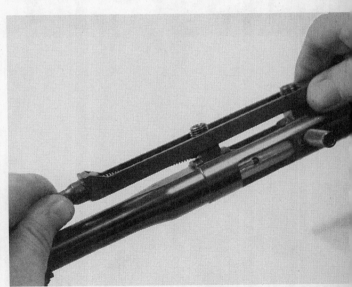

12. Lift the recoil spring assembly equally at front and rear and use a shop cloth (not shown) over the spring to arrest it as it is released. An alternative method is to draw the assembly back until the small holes in the spring housing and guide are aligned, and insert a sharp tool to trap the spring (see Reassembly Step 3). **Caution:** *Either way, keep control of the spring.* The spring housing at the front of the unit can be unscrewed from the harness and the bolt contact block can be removed by drifting out its roll-type cross pin. In normal takedown, this is not done.

13. Move the bolt back until the handle aligns with the exit opening in its track and give the handle a half-turn. Pull the handle out toward the right.

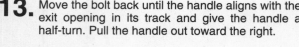

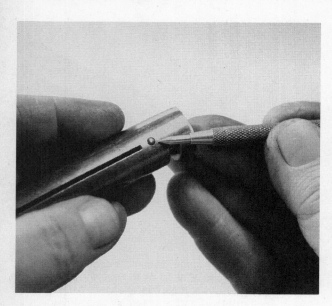

14. Pull the trigger and remove the bolt toward the rear.

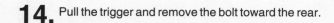

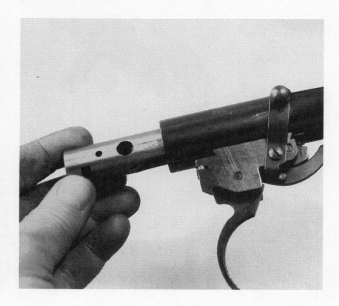

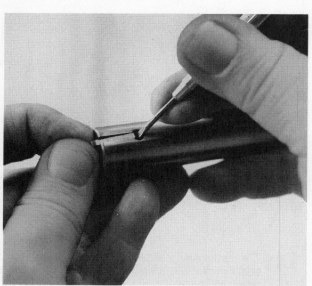

15. Restrain the firing pin, drift out this cross pin and remove the firing pin and its return spring toward the rear.

16. Insert a small tool between the extractor and its plunger and lever the plunger toward the rear. Lift out the extractor and remove the plunger, spring and bolt handle detent plunger toward the front. **Caution:** *Control the spring.*

17. While the recoil spring assembly is off the action, do not attempt to move the safety to on-safe position or it could be damaged. Remove the safety-lever screw and take off the safety-lever toward the right.

18. Restrain the trigger and push out the trigger pivot pin. **Caution:** *Two small plunger-and-spring systems are mounted in the trigger, so control them.*

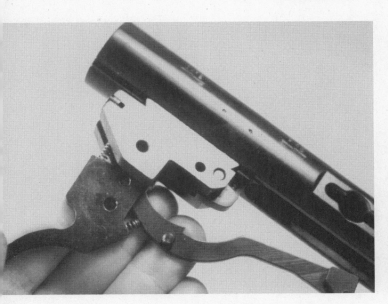

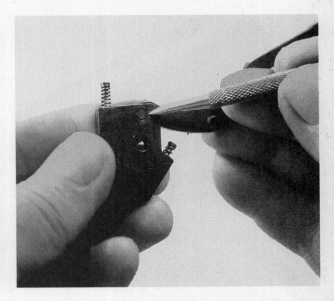

19. Remove the trigger and disconnector assembly downward.

20. Push out the disconnector pivot and detach the disconnector from the trigger. The trigger and disconnector springs and plungers are easily removed from their wells in the trigger.

21. The trip block on the front of the disconnector has a riveted pivot, and this part and its coil spring should be removed only for repair.

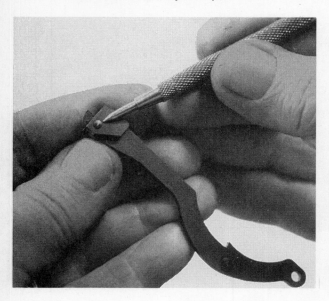

22. Restrain the sear and push out the sear cross pin. **Caution:** *The spring is under tension.*

23. Remove the sear and its spring downward.

24. The screw at the rear of the trigger housing is the trigger adjustment screw. It is pre-set by the factory, and should not be disturbed.

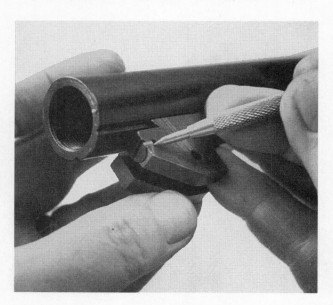

Reassembly Tips:

1. When installing the bolt handle, note that there is a small lock-recess at one point in its circumference. After the handle is pushed into place, turn it until this recess engages the detent plunger.

2. The recoil spring housing and the spring guide have holes to allow trapping of the recoil spring.

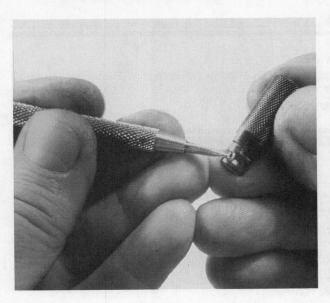

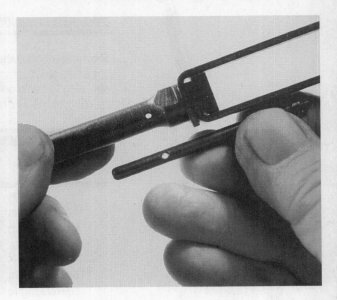

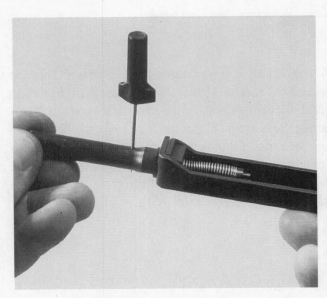

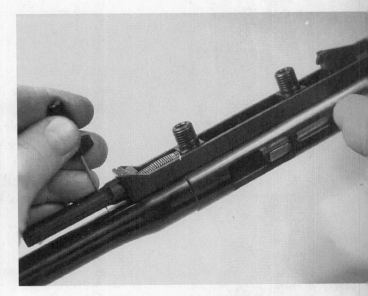

3. With the spring compressed and the holes aligned, a sharp tool is used to trap the recoil spring, as shown.

4. After the system is in place, with the rear lug engaging the bolt, draw the bolt back until the tip of the recoil spring guide enters its recess in the frame. The tool can then be taken out to release the spring.

Harrington & Richardson Model 750

Similar/Identical Pattern Guns
The same basic assembly/disassembly steps for the Harrington & Richardson Model 750 also apply to the following gun:
Harrington & Richardson Model 751

Data:	Harrington & Richardson Model 750
Origin:	United States
Manufacturer:	Harrington & Richardson Gardner, Massachusetts
Cartridge:	22 Short, Long, or Long Rifle
Overall length:	39 inches
Barrel length:	22 inches
Weight:	5 pounds

Introduced in 1954, the Model 750 was named the "Pioneer" like the Model 765 which preceded it. The Model 750 is a good, solid single shot rifle. As a general rule, single shot bolt-action rifles are mechanically very simple, since there are no cartridge feed systems. Each one, though, has a firing mechanism that is unique to its particular manufacturer. There are certain general similarities, however, and the Model 750 H&R is a typical representative of the type. The instructions can also be used for the H&R Model 751.

Disassembly:

1. Back out the large screw on the underside of the stock, forward of the trigger guard, and separate the action from the stock.

2. To remove the bolt, open it and move it toward the rear. Pull the trigger, hold it back, and press the lower lobe of the sear to tip it downward, holding it down while removing the bolt toward the rear.

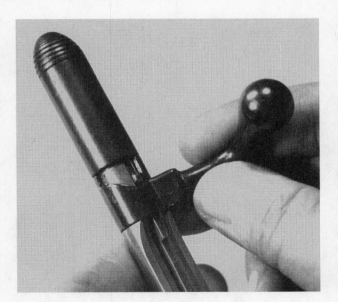

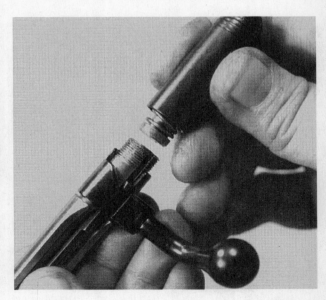

3. Grip the forward portion of the bolt in a padded vise and turn the bolt handle to allow the striker to move forward to the fired position. The photo shows the striker in the forward position, with the tension of its spring partially relieved.

4. With the front portion of the bolt still gripped in the padded vise, unscrew the domed rear end piece. **Caution:** *The striker spring is quite powerful and has considerable tension, even when at rest. Hold the end piece firmly, control it, and ease the spring tension off slowly.*

5. Remove the striker spring and its guide from the bolt end piece.

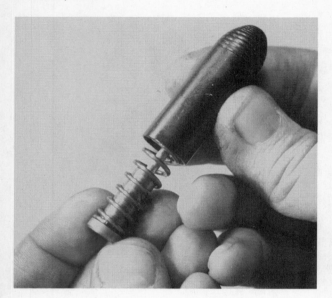

6. Move the bolt handle sleeve off toward the rear, taking with it the striker/firing pin unit.

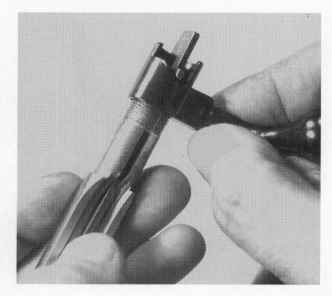

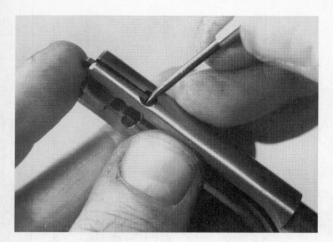

7. To remove the twin extractors, use a small screwdriver to depress the extractor spring plungers, and lift the extractors out of their recesses on each side. **Caution:** *Take care to keep the depressed plungers under control, as the springs can propel them quite a distance if they are released suddenly.* Keep the springs with their respective extractors, as they are not interchangeable.

8. Remove the spring clip on the left side of the trigger housing from the end of the trigger pivot and take out the pivot pin toward the right.

9. As the pivot pin is removed, restrain the trigger against the tension of its spring, and take it off downward. The safety-lever will also be released for removal toward the right. The trigger spring and its plunger are easily removed from their well in the upper rear of the trigger.

10. Remove the spring clip from the left end of the sear pivot and push the pivot pin out toward the right. This will allow removal of the sear and its spring downward, and the safety bar and its spring toward the right. The sear spring is easily removed from its well in the top rear of the sear.

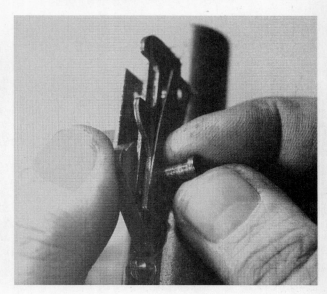

11. The cartridge guide platform with its integral ejector is retained inside the receiver by a screw on the underside, just forward of the trigger housing.

12. The barrel is retained in the receiver by a cross pin, but removal is not recommended in normal disassembly.

Reassembly Tips:

1. When replacing the safety positioning spring, note that the dimple at its center must have its convex side inward, to bear on the recesses in the safety bar.

2. When replacing the safety-lever, be sure the lower turned-in portion of the lever engages its opening in the safety bar.

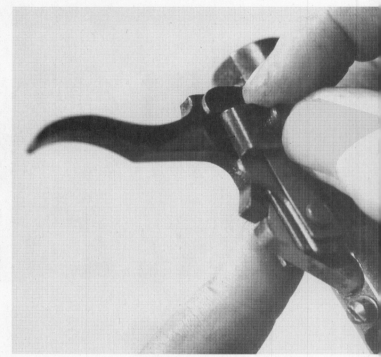

3. When replacing the spring clips on the sear and trigger pins, be sure the pins are turned fully toward the left, so the clips will engage their grooves in the heads of the pins.

5. Replacement of the rear end piece of the bolt, working against the tension of the striker spring, will require that the front portion of the bolt be gripped in a padded vise. Be sure the bolt handle is turned so the striker is in fired position. Be very careful not to cross-thread the end piece. When the end piece is in place, the bolt must be in cocked condition for reinsertion in the receiver. With the bolt still in the padded vise, turn the bolt handle to recock the striker. The photo shows the striker in the cocked position.

4. When replacing the striker/firing pin unit in the bolt, insert it only as far as shown, then install the bolt handle sleeve, and let it carry the striker into the bolt.

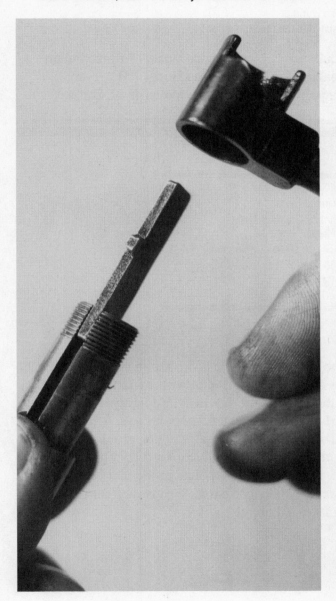

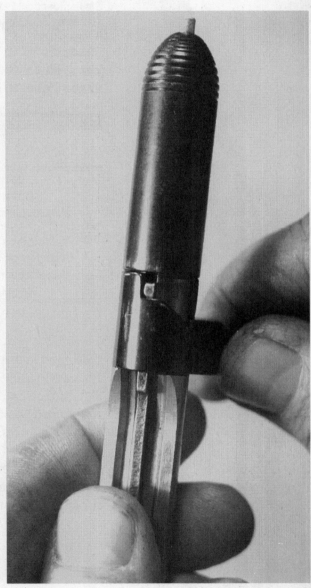

Ithaca Model 49

Similar/Identical Pattern Guns

The same basic assembly/disassembly steps for the Ithaca Model 49 also apply to the following guns:

Ithaca Model 49 Youth
Ithaca Model 49 Deluxe
Ithaca Model 49 Magnum

Ithaca Model 49 Presentation
Ithaca Model 49R
Ithaca Model 49 St. Louis

Data:	Ithaca Model 49
Origin:	United States
Manufacturer:	Ithaca Gun Company Ithaca, New York
Cartridges:	22 Long Rifle, 22 Magnum (WMR)
Overall length:	35 inches
Barrel length:	18 inches
Weight:	$5^{1}/_{2}$ pounds

Designed to resemble a western-style lever-action repeating rifle, the Ithaca Model 49 is actually a single shot with a Martini-type action. The "magazine tube" below the barrel is a dummy. The gun was introduced in 1961, and soon became popular as a "first gun" for young shooters. To accommodate the younger group, Ithaca produced a version with a shorter-than-standard stock. While the Model 49 is a simple gun, there are several points in the takedown where a wrong move can result in damaged parts. The instructions can be used for all of the variants listed above.

Disassembly:

1. Take out the screw at the bottom of the barrel band and remove the barrel band toward the front.

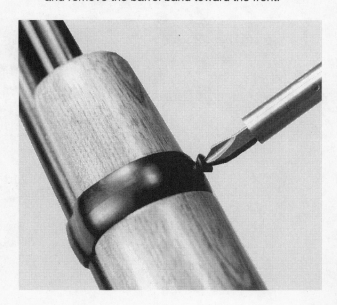

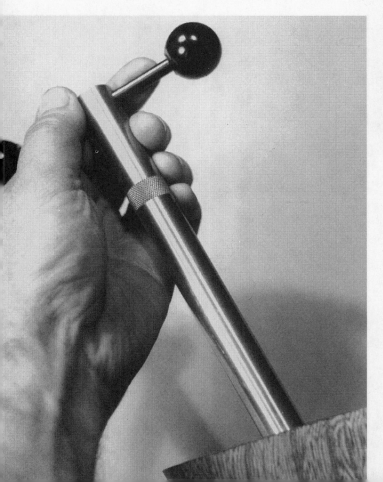

2. Drift out the small cross pin in the magazine tube loop (arrow), and slide the dummy magazine forward. Remove the forend downward and slide the tube out of the loop toward the rear. Take care not to lose the small plastic cap at the end of the tube. It is a friction fit, and may come out as the tube is removed.

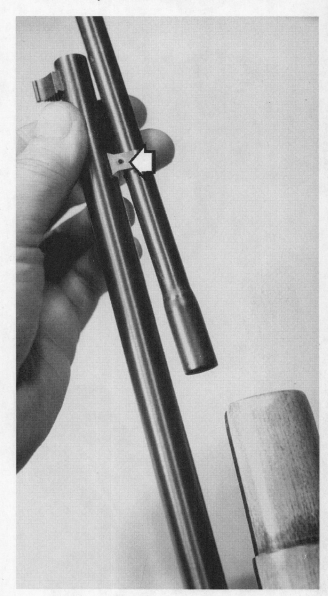

3. Take off the buttplate and use a B-Square stock tool, a 3/8-inch socket wrench, or a long screwdriver to remove the stock mounting bolt. Take off the stock toward the rear. Grip the stock mounting stud firmly with leather-padded pliers and unscrew it from the rear of the receiver. Take out the hammer spring toward the rear, and take care not to lose the lock washer on the neck of the stud.

4. Drift out the lever pivot pin (arrow) toward the right. It should be noted that on all late production guns, the cross pins are knurled on the right side and must be taken out in that direction. On some very early guns, certain pins may have the knurled end on the left side. If you have an older gun, it would be best to check the heads of the pins before removal.

5. Remove the lever downward, and remove the trigger spring and plunger from the back of the lever base.

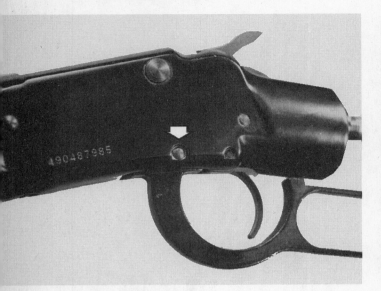

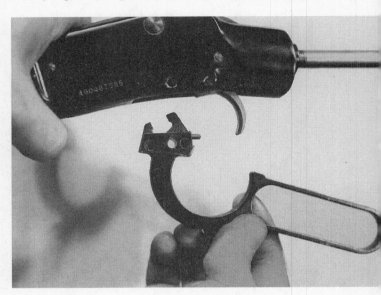

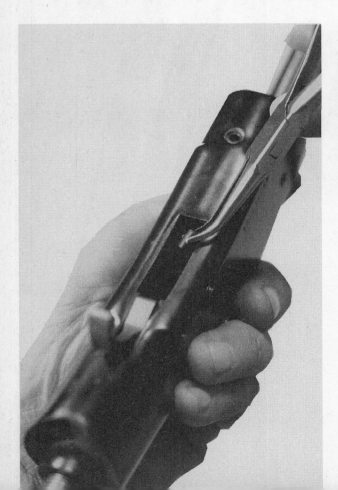

7. When the spring and both plungers are removed from the breechblock pivot, the pivot can easily be pushed out toward either side. It should be noted, though, that any attempt to remove the pivot with the upper plunger still in place can result in damage to the pivot, receiver and plunger.

6. Remove the bolt spring plunger, bolt spring and bolt pivot lock plunger from the hole in the bottom of the lower lobe of the bolt. The lower plunger and the spring should come out easily. If the upper plunger is reluctant to come out, hold the gun right-side up, and move the large bolt pivot gently from side to side. If this fails, give the receiver a few light taps with a plastic mallet.

8. Remove the breechblock (bolt) from the top of the receiver. Restrain the firing pin spring on the left side to prevent its escape, as it is held in place only by the inside wall of the receiver.

9. The firing pin, return spring and lock pin are shown in their proper positions, before disassembly.

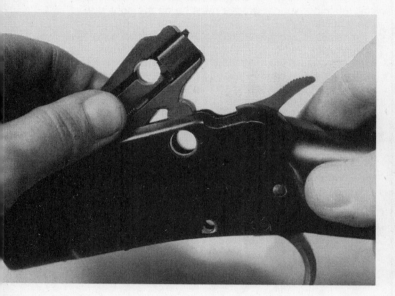

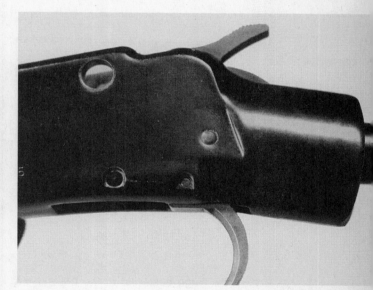

10. Remove the spring, lock pin and firing pin toward the left.

11. Drift out the hammer and trigger pivot pins toward the right. Remove the hammer and hammer spring strut toward the top, and the trigger from the bottom.

Reassembly Tips:

12. Use an Allen wrench of the proper size to remove the ejector trip spring screw from the bottom front of the receiver and take out the spring and plunger.

When replacing the breechblock pivot, remember that the retaining plunger groove must be on the right side of the receiver.

When replacing the retaining plunger in the bottom of the breechblock, remember that the shorter plunger with the flat ends goes in first. The longer plunger with one rounded end goes at the bottom, with the rounded end downward. As the plungers and spring are installed, move the breechblock pivot slightly from side to side, to ensure that the top plunger enters its groove.

Keep the gun inverted while installing the lever to avoid losing the spring and plungers from their hole in the breechblock.

Remember to reinsert all cross pins from right to left, because the knurled ends will have slightly expanded the holes on the right side.

When replacing the dummy magazine tube, be sure the groove for the cross pin is at the top and aligned with the hole in the hanger loop before driving in the pin.

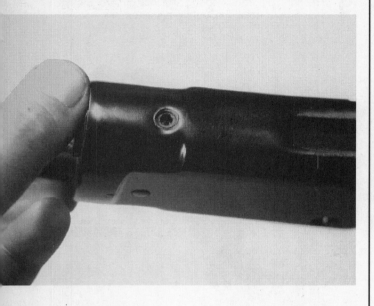

13. Drift out the large cross pin at the front of the receiver toward the right. Depress the ejector trip to ensure that it is disengaged from the ejector, and remove the ejector and its spring toward the rear. The large cross pin also retains the barrel. Drift out the smaller cross pin toward the right to release the ejector trip, and use a large hardwood dowel or some other non-marring tool to prevent damage while driving the barrel out forward. The ejector trip can then be removed from inside the receiver.

Kimber Model 82

Similar/Identical Pattern Guns
The same basic assembly/disassembly steps for the Kimber Model 82 also apply to the following guns:

Kimber Model 82 Gov't. Target	**Kimber Model 82 America**
Kimber Model 82 All Amer. Match	**Kimber Model 82 Super**
Kimber Model 82 Sporter	**Kimber Model 82B**
Kimber Model 82 Varminter	**Kimber Model 82A Gov't.**
Kimber Model 82 Deluxe	**Kimber Model 82 Mini-Classic**
Kimber Model 82 Custom Classic	**Kimber Model 82 Hunter Grade**
Kimber Model 82 Hornet	**Kimber Model 82 Classic**

Data:	Kimber Model 82
Origin:	United States
Manufacturer:	Kimber of Oregon, Inc.
	Clackamas, Oregon
Cartridge:	22 Long Rifle
Magazine capacity:	5 rounds
Overall length:	41 inches
Barrel length:	24 inches
Weight:	$6^{1}/_{4}$ pounds

Quality and price were both notably high, and the Kimber rifle lasted for about eleven years, from 1980 to 1991. Now, treasured by both shooters and collectors, the original Kimber guns have become difficult to find. The Model 82 was made in several grades and styles, but all were mechanically essentially the same.

Disassembly:

1. Remove the magazine. Hold the trigger to the rear, open the bolt and remove the bolt toward the rear.

2. Remove the large screw in front of the magazine opening.

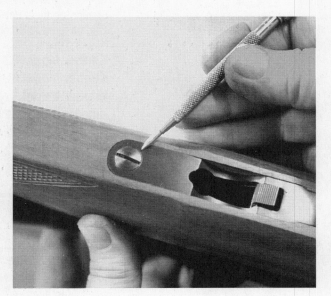

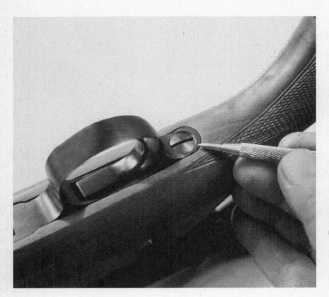

3. Remove the large screw behind the trigger guard. Keep the two screws in order, as they are not interchangeable.

4. Remove the action from the stock.

5. Remove the trigger guard unit from the stock.

6. Hold the front of the bolt firmly with a shop cloth and turn the handle to lower the striker to fired position, as shown.

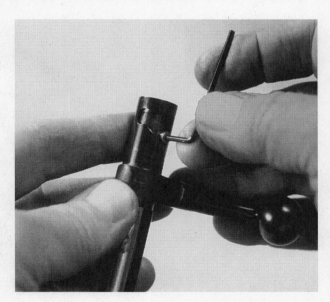

7. Use an Allen wrench to remove the cocking stud from the striker.

8. Remove the bolt handle unit toward the rear.

9. Insert a tool at the rear to arrest the striker spring and push out the retaining cross pin. **Caution:** *Control the spring.*

10. Remove the striker spring toward the rear.

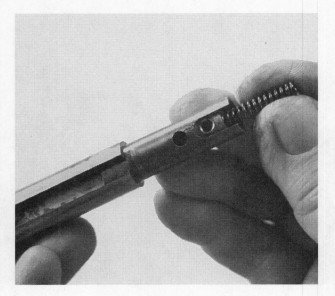

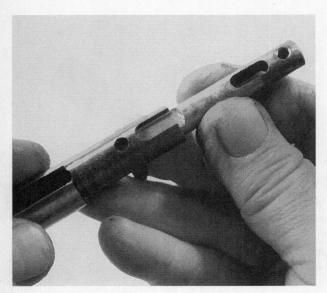

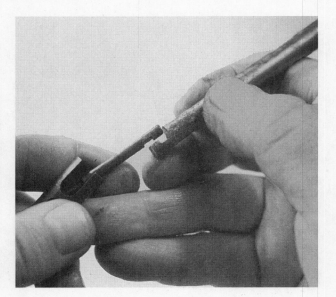

11. Remove the striker toward the rear.

12. As the striker emerges, the firing pin will be released from its hook at the front of the striker.

13. Carefully pry the narrow left arm of the saddle-type spring from its engagement with the left extractor. Control the spring as it is taken off.

14. The extractors are now easily lifted out of their recesses in the bolt. Keep them in order, as they are not interchangeable.

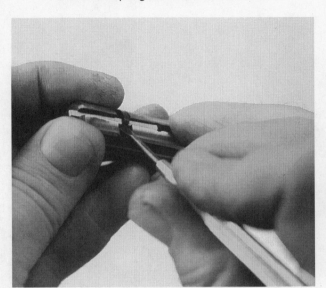

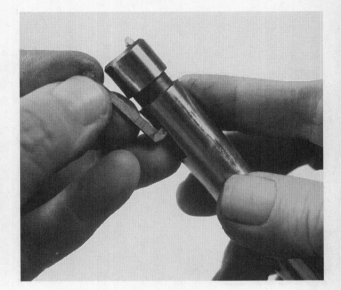

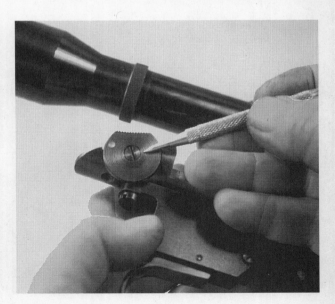

15. Grip the shaft of the safety positioning spring guide and move it downward to disengage its upper tip from the recess in the safety disc. Keep control of the guide and spring and swing them out toward the rear for removal.

16. The safety disc need not be removed for further disassembly. However, if it is to be taken off, its pivot screw is the retainer.

17. Remove the vertical screw at the front of the trigger and magazine housing. Take care that the lock washer is not lost.

18. Remove the screw and lock washer at the rear of the housing.

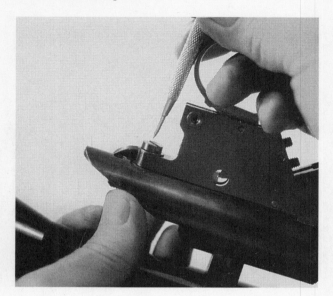

19. Restrain the magazine catch and push out the cross pin.

20. Remove the magazine catch and its spring downward.

21. Remove the center housing screw and its lock washer.

22. Remove the trigger and magazine housing downward.

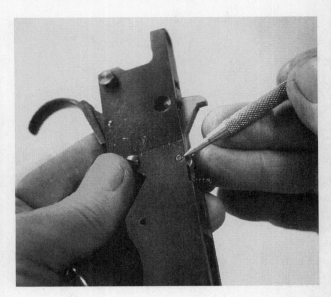

23. The ejector is released internally with removal of the center screw. Retrieve it from inside the action.

24. The sear spring is easily removed from its well in the front of the sear. Drifting out this cross pin will allow removal of the sear upward.

25. Except for repair, removal of the trigger is not advisable, as the original adjustments will be cancelled. However, if it is necessary, the first step is to back out the cinch screw that locks the adjustment screws.

26. The next step is to remove the trigger spring adjustment screw and the spring. The upper screw is the over-travel stop and it can be left in place.

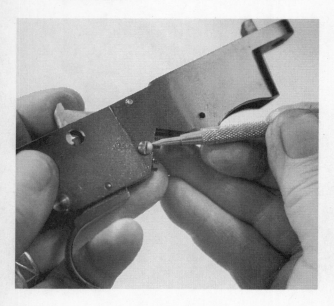

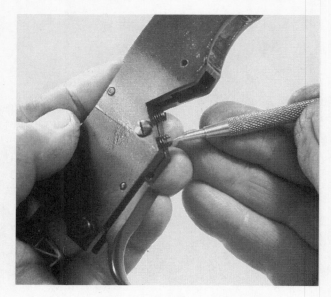

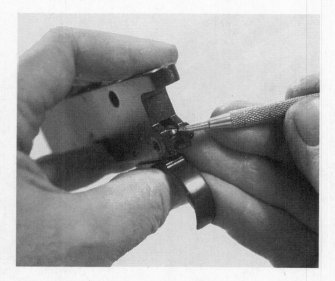

27. If the previous steps have been done, drift out the trigger cross pin and remove the trigger downward.

28. To remove the safety cross-piece, the adjustment screw must first be backed out. Here, again, it is best left in place in normal takedown. If the screw is removed, it will have to be carefully reset for proper bearing on the trigger. Also at the rear of the receiver (not shown) is the bolt handle detent plunger and spring, retained by a small pin in the right side of the receiver. The pin is drifted inward to release the plunger and spring. In normal takedown, leave it in place.

Reassembly Tips:

1. When the ejector is reinstalled, it must be oriented as shown, with the ejector projection at left front. Use a fingertip inside the receiver to hold it in place as the screw is inserted. Before this is done, it is best to put the trigger and magazine housing in place with the front and rear screws.

2. Use a screwdriver blade the same width as the diameter of the striker spring to compress the spring for insertion of the retaining cross pin. This is more easily done with the front part of the bolt in a well-padded vise.

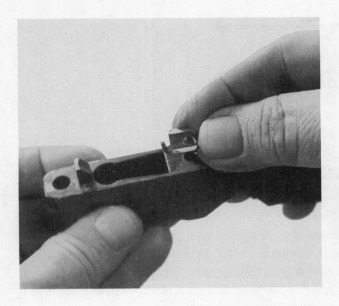

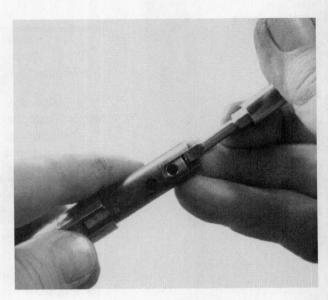

3. Before the bolt can be reinserted in the receiver, the striker must be in cocked position, as shown. Hold the front of the bolt in a shop cloth (or in a padded vise), and turn the handle to recock the striker.

Kintrek KBP-1

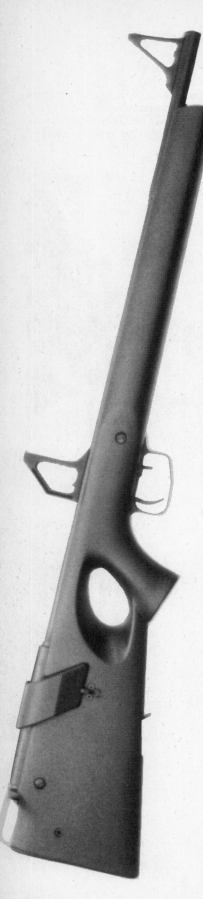

Data:	Kintrek KBP-1
Origin:	United States
Manufacturer:	Kintrek, Incorporated Owensboro, Kentucky
Cartridge:	22 Long Rifle
Magazine capacity:	17 rounds
Overall length:	$31^1/_2$ inches
Barrel length:	25 inches
Weight:	$5^1/_2$ pounds

This excellent carbine was designed around 1985 by Rick Krouse, and I examined the prototype in 1987. Production began in 1991, and lasted for only about a year. Apparently, there were not enough shooters who liked the "bull-pup" design to keep it going. This is a pity, because it is a beautifully engineered gun.

Disassembly:

1. Remove the magazine and cycle the action to cock the internal hammer. Set the safety in on-safe position. Open the ejection port cover and remove the screw on the right side, just above the front of the trigger guard.

2. Remove the screw at the rear, between the port cover and the buttplate.

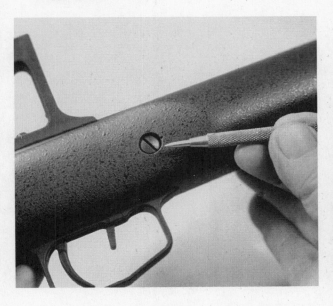

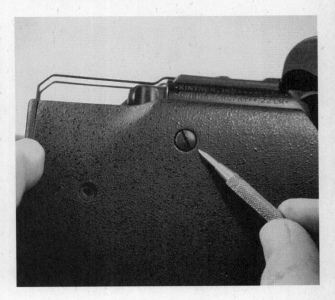

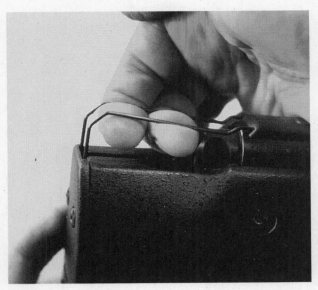

3. Pull the cocking piece guard upward slightly at the rear, just enough to snap it out of engagement with its detent.

4. Lift the action straight up out of the stock.

5. The ejection port cover latch and its coil spring are retained by two screws that require a square bit. In normal takedown, leave this system in place.

6. Three square-bit screws retain the buttplate.

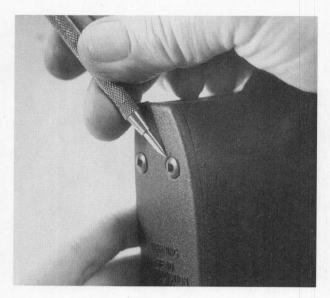

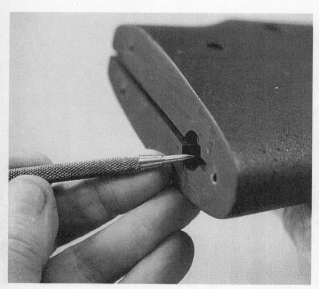

7. Removal of the buttplate will give access to the recoil spring lever, the recoil spring and its plunger. If this system is to be taken out, it will be necessary to depress and restrain the recoil spring plunger with a tool, at the point shown.

8. With the plunger slightly depressed, remove the square-bit screw that pivots and retains the recoil spring lever. **Caution:** *Control the spring.*

9. Maintain pressure on the plunger and remove the recoil spring lever.

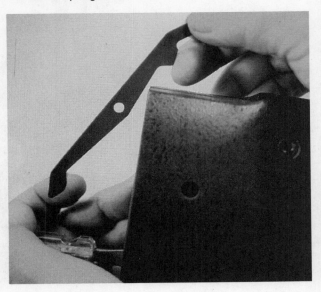

10. Ease the spring tension slowly and remove the plunger and spring toward the rear.

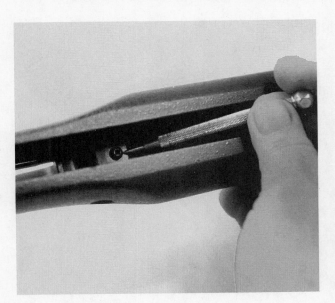

11. The trigger guard is retained on the inside of the stock by two Phillips-type screws. When these are taken out, the guard is removed upward.

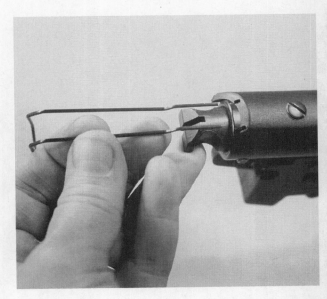

12. Pull the cocking piece guard straight out toward the rear.

13. Push out the bolt stop pin toward either side.

14. Pull the firing system housing downward at the rear, as shown.

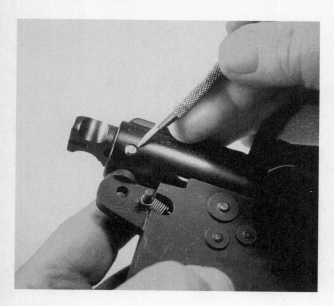

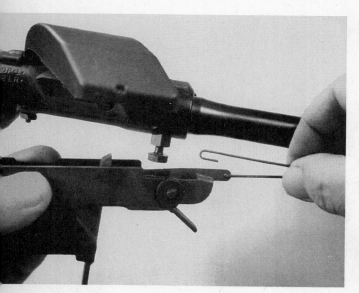

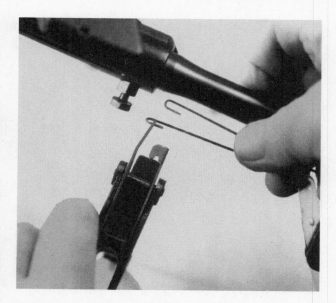

15. Move the system slightly forward and unhook the trigger rod from the trigger bar/disconnector.

16. Turn the housing and unhook the grip safety rod.

17. Unhook the large end of the grip safety rod from the top of the grip safety. If necessary, the cross pin can be pushed out to free the grip safety for removal.

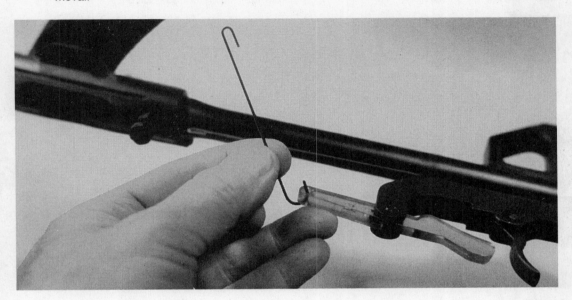

18. Remove the bolt toward the rear.

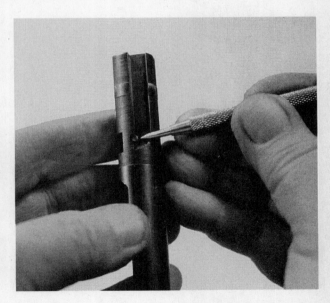

19. The firing pin and its return spring are retained by a cross pin in the bolt. Restrain the firing pin and drift out the cross pin toward the right. Remove the firing pin and spring toward the rear.

20. To remove the extractor, insert a small tool between the extractor and its plunger and push the plunger toward the rear. Lift out the extractor, and ease the plunger and spring out toward the front. **Caution:** *Control the plunger and spring.*

21. The firing system has steel cross pins in a polymer housing, and disassembly should be done only for repair purposes. Without removing the parts, we will show the sequence here. First, pull forward on the grip safety bar, restrain the hammer and pull forward on the trigger bar/disconnector. Ease the hammer down to fired position.

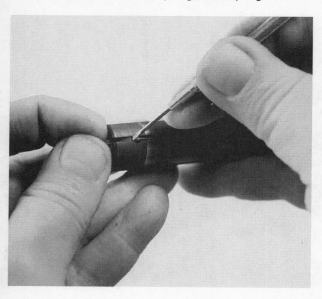

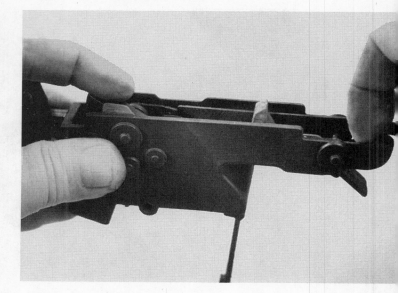

22. With the hammer at rest, pushing out this cross pin will allow removal of the hammer upward. By tipping the hammer further forward, the hammer strut and captive spring can be taken out, without removal of the hammer.

23. Unhook the grip safety spring from its post at the bottom of the housing.

24. Drifting out the cross pin at the front of the housing will free the forward portions of the trigger bar and grip safety bar. Each is still retained at the rear.

25. The cross pin that retains the grip safety bar at the rear must be drifted out toward the right. A spacer washer will be freed inside the unit as the pin is removed. The grip safety bar can then be moved forward and is taken out upward, along with its attached expansion-type spring.

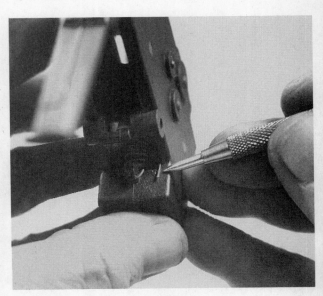

26. Unhook the trigger bar spring from its post at the rear and remove the trigger bar upward with its attached spring.

27. Note that the long arm of the sear spring bears on the lower edge of the housing, and that it must be installed this way during reassembly.

28. Drifting out this cross pin will allow removal of the sear and its spring. **Caution:** *Control the spring.* Again, all parts are still in place here. The sequence has been shown for repair-disassembly purposes.

29. The trigger group is retained by two Allen screws, one visible here. As with the firing system housing, the trigger group has steel pins in a polymer housing, and it should be taken apart only for repair.

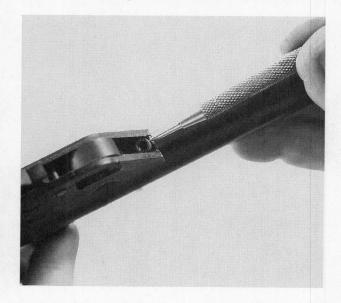

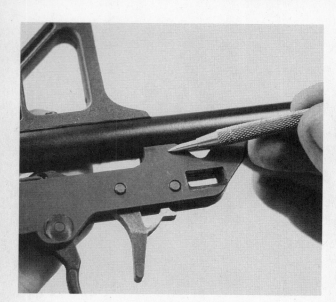

30. The other Allen screw is inside the group, at this location. For access, the safety detent pin and safety-lever pin will have to be removed. With the group removed, drifting out the trigger pin will release the trigger and trigger rod for removal.

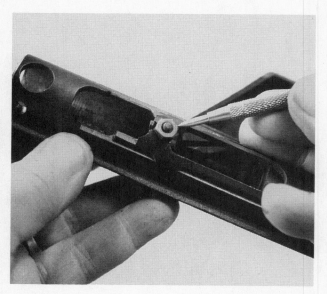

31. The combination ejector and bolt guide is retained on the underside of the receiver by a hex-nut. The part is moved inward for removal.

32. Removal of the two large screws on top will allow the cheekpiece and ejection port cover to be taken off upward.

33. Lift off the case deflector.

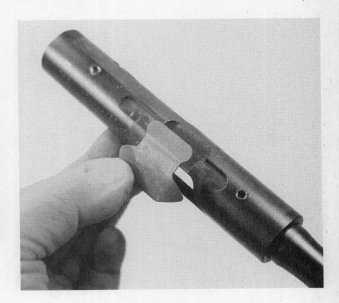

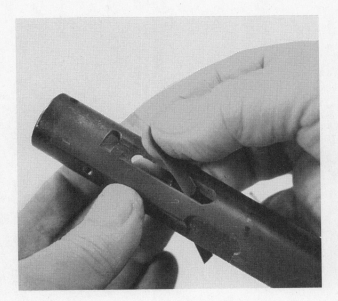

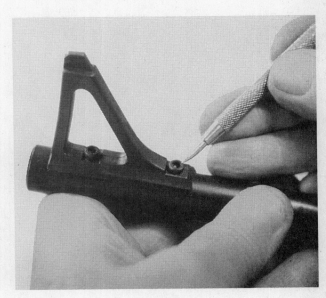

34. The sweep is now easily detached and can be removed toward the left.

35. The front and rear sights are each retained by two Allen-type screws. The rear sight leaf is adjusted and retained by two Phillips-type screws.

Reassembly Tips:

1. When installing the sweep, be sure its rear tip engages the recess, as shown, and that its front end protrudes from the ejection port.

2. Re-hook the trigger rod and grip safety rod to their bars in the firing system before the system housing is swung back upward into place. The proper arrangement is shown.

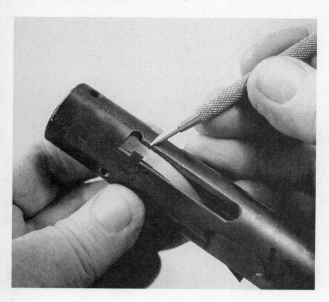

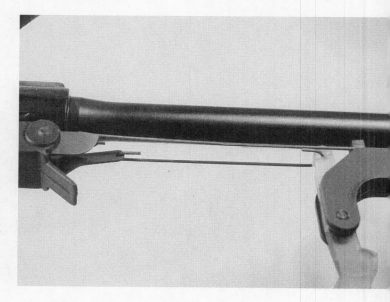

3. When the firing system is in place, remember to reinstall the bolt cross pin before the action is put back into the stock. Also, when the action is in place, remember to push the cocking piece guard back down into locked position.

Krico
Model 304

Similar/Identical Pattern Guns
The same basic assembly/disassembly steps for the Krico Model 304 also apply to the following guns:

Krico Model 302

Krico Model 352

Krico Model 302E

Krico Model 352E

Krico Model 302 DRC

Data:	Krico Model 304
Origin:	Germany
Manufacturer:	Kriegeskorte GmbH Stuttgart
Cartridge:	22 Long Rifle
Magazine capacity:	5 rounds
Overall length:	$38\frac{1}{2}$ inches
Barrel length:	20 inches
Weight:	6.2 pounds

The Krico brand rifles by Kriegeskorte of Stuttgart have always been of consistently high quality. In the past, they have been imported into the U.S. by several companies, and their present importer is Mandall's of Scottsdale, Arizona. The Model 304, shown here, is essentially a Model 302 with a full Mannlicher-style stock and a shorter barrel. Both models were made from 1982 to 1984.

Disassembly:

1. Remove the magazine and open the bolt. Pull the bolt stop outward and remove the bolt toward the rear.

2. Grip the front portion of the bolt firmly and turn the handle to lower the striker to fired position.

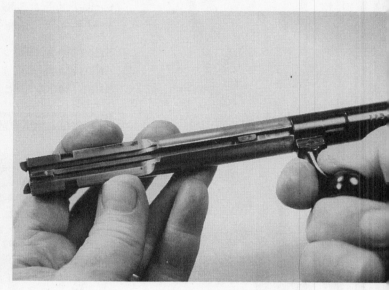

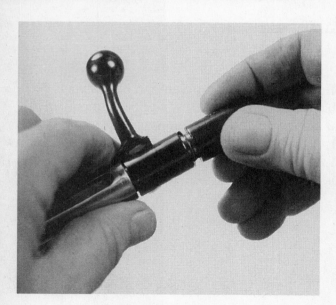

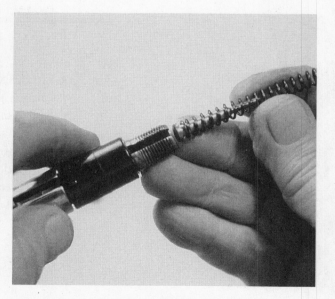

3. Grip the bolt end piece in a leather-padded vise and turn the bolt body (not the handle) to begin unscrewing the end piece. After it is "broken loose," it can be unscrewed by hand. **Caution:** *The striker spring still has some tension, so control the end piece as it is removed.*

4. Remove the striker spring and guide toward the rear.

5. Remove the lock washer toward the rear.

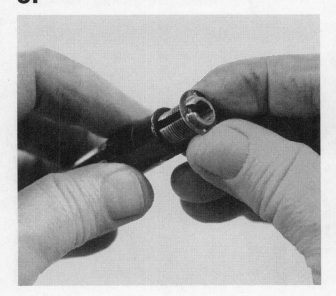

6. Remove the bolt handle toward the rear.

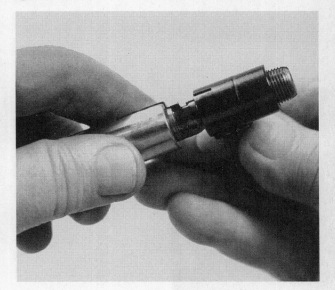

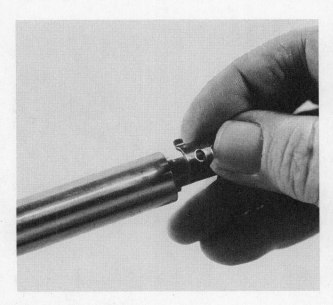

7. Remove the cocking cam piece.

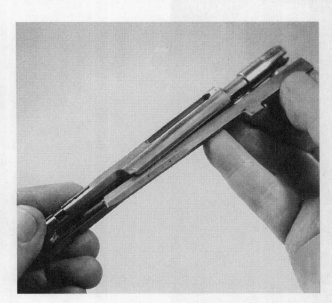

8. Remove the striker (firing pin) from the bolt.

9. To remove the extractors, insert a tool to pry the saddle-type spring off the extractor on either side. Control the spring as it is taken off. The extractors can then be lifted out of their recesses on each side. Keep them in order for replacement, as they are not interchangeable.

10. The nosecap of the stock is normally removed before the action is taken out in most guns having a full Mannlicher-style stock. In the Krico, however, this is not done. The screw indicated enters a free nut, and removal is not possible at this time.

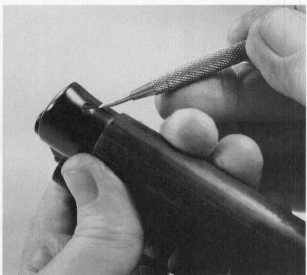

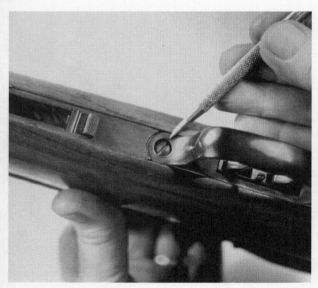

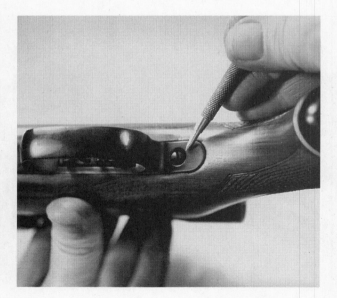

11. Remove the screw in front of the trigger guard.

12. Remove the screw behind the trigger guard.

13. Remove the trigger guard.

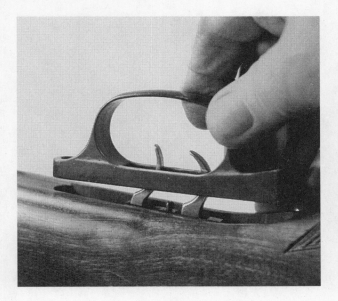

14. Back out the screw in front of the magazine well. This is a captive screw and will stay with the escutcheon in the stock.

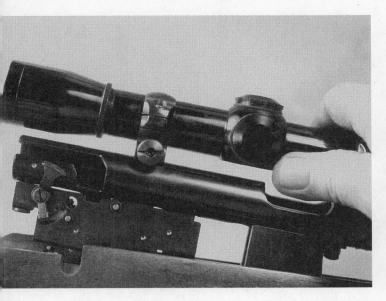

15. Lift the action at the rear and remove it rearward and upward.

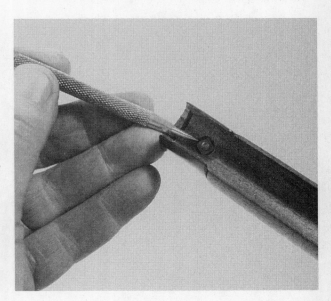

16. If necessary, the nosecap can be removed from the stock by immobilizing the inside nut and taking out the screw shown in step 10.

17. Remove the screw at the front of the magazine housing. Because of the slant of the housing, an angle-tipped screwdriver should be used. Remove the magazine housing.

18. Remove the cartridge guide.

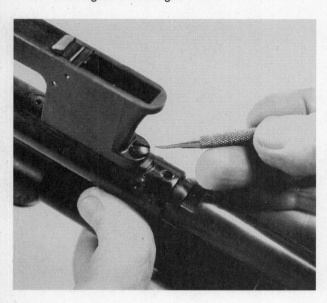

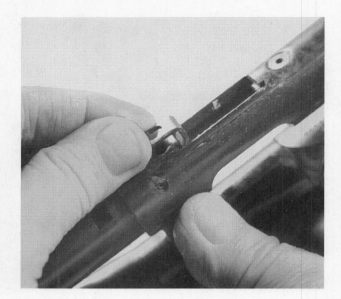

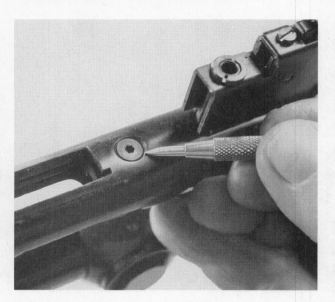

19. Pushing out this cross pin in the magazine housing will allow removal of the magazine catch and its spring. Control the spring.

20. The combination bolt guide and ejector is retained by an Allen-type screw. In normal takedown, it is best left in place.

21. Removal of the trigger housing will require a twin-point tool, made to fit the recesses in the cap nuts at front and rear.

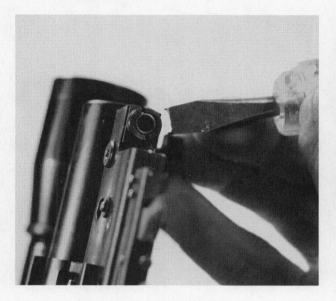

22. Remove the bolt stop by pushing its retaining clip off the post. Control the clip as it is freed from the post.

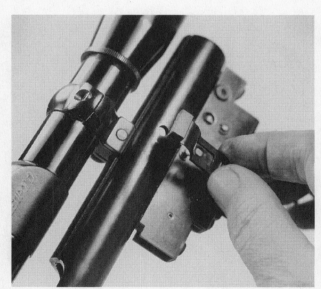

23. Remove the bolt stop toward the left.

24. Remove the trigger group downward.

25. The principal spring-bearing cross pins in the trigger group are riveted in place, and routine removal is not possible. The set-trigger system is in the same category. If necessary for repair, some of the main parts can be removed, and we will show the sequence here, without removal of the parts. The safety-lever and its detent ball and spring can be taken off by removing this screw. Take care that the detent ball isn't lost.

26. The sear can be removed by taking off this C-clip and pushing out its cross pin. Restrain the sear and ease off the spring tension.

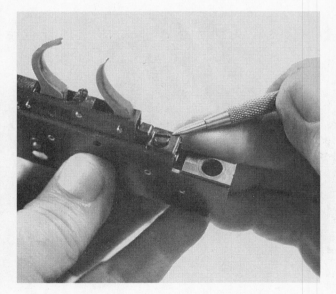

27. The sear trip can be removed in the same way. Control the spring.

28. The spring for the main (firing) trigger is removable by taking out the screw that retains its housing.

Reassembly Tips:

1. When installing the cocking piece, or cam, note that it must engage the angle of the lug on the striker, as shown.

2. As the bolt handle is installed, be sure the flange of the cocking cam enters its slot in the handle sleeve. Also, note that the lock washer at the rear must have its raised locking projections toward the end piece.

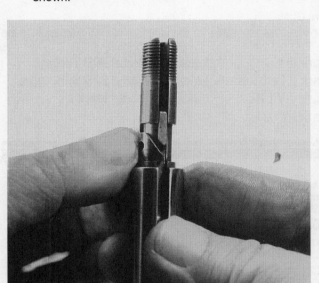

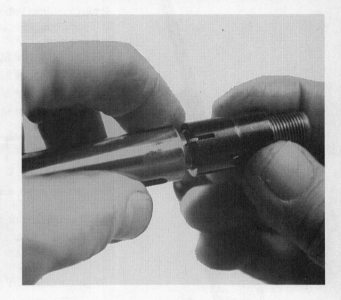

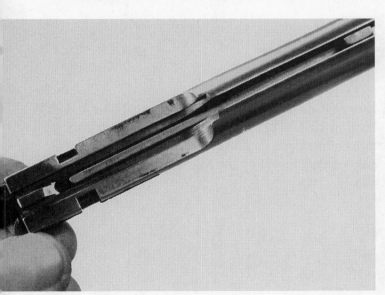

3. Before the bolt can be put back into the receiver, it must be recocked, with the striker in the position shown. Grip the front of the bolt lightly in a padded vise and turn the handle to cock it.

4. If the extractors have been removed, be sure they are put back with the beaked one on the right and the bevelled one on the left, as shown.

Lakefield
Mark II

Similar/Identical Pattern Guns

The same basic assembly/disassembly steps for the Lakefield Mark II also apply to the following guns:

Lakefield Model Mark II-Y   **Lakefield Model 90B Target**
Lakefield Model Mark II Left-Hand   **Lakefield Model 92S Silhouette**
Lakefield Model Mark II-Y LH   **Lakefield Model Mark I**
Lakefield Model Mark I-Y

Data:	Lakefield Mark II
Origin:	Canada
Manufacturer:	Lakefield Arms, Ltd.
	Lakefield, Ontario
Cartridge:	22 Long Rifle
Magazine capacity:	10 rounds
Overall length:	39½ inches
Barrel length:	20½ inches
Weight:	5½ pounds

A medium-priced and well-made gun from Canada, the Lakefield Mark II was introduced in 1990. There is also a single-shot version, the Mark I, and a smaller-dimension youth version of that one. Except for the magazine system being absent on the Mark I, mechanically it is essentially the same.

Disassembly:

1. Remove the magazine and hold the trigger to the rear. Remove the bolt from the action.

2. Push the cocking lug off its step to lower the striker to fired position.

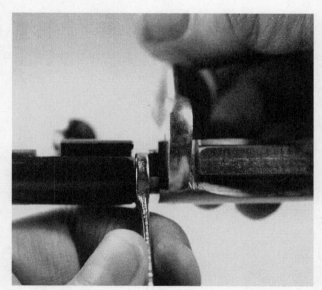

3. Grip the cocking lug in a bench vise, and pull the front portion of the bolt forward to expose the striker spring retaining nut. The nut takes a $\frac{5}{16}$-inch wrench. On the bolt body, a $\frac{9}{16}$-inch wrench can be used.

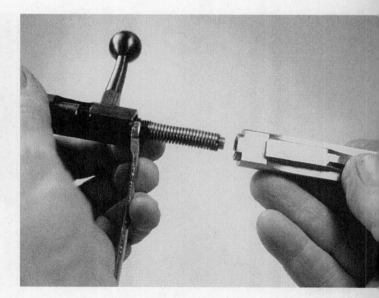

4. After the nut is "broken loose," the front portion of the bolt can be unscrewed from the nut by hand.

5. Remove the wrench to allow the nut to snap rearward, partially relieving the tension of the striker spring. Pull the spring back from the front end of the guide, and pry off the C-clip retainer. **Caution:** *The striker spring is powerful, so use care and control it.* The best way to compress the spring for this operation is to make a small tool from scrap steel, as shown, and use a bench vise to hold it for compression.

6. After the C-clip is removed, ease the spring tension slowly and remove the striker spring toward the front.

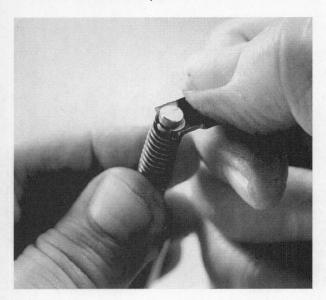

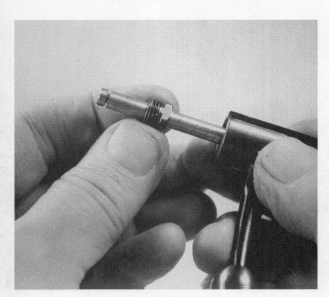

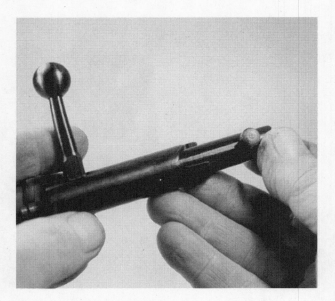

7. Remove the retaining nut toward the front.

8. Remove the striker assembly toward the rear.

9. The spring guide rod and the cocking lug are retained on the striker head by roll-type cross pins.

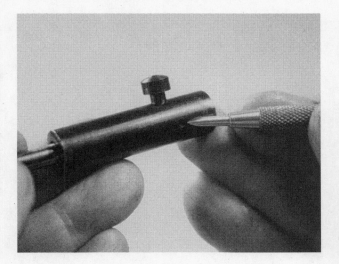

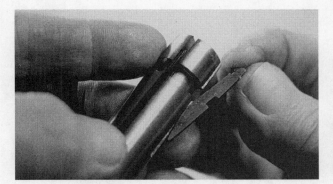

11. Lift the extractors out of their recesses. Keep them in order, as they are not interchangeable.

12. The extractor spring also retains the firing pin, and it can now be removed from its recess in the top of the bolt.

10. Insert a tool at the edge of the saddle-type extractor spring and pry it outward, just enough to clear. Control the spring and remove it.

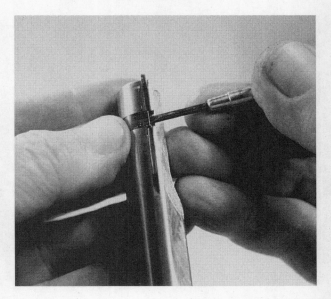

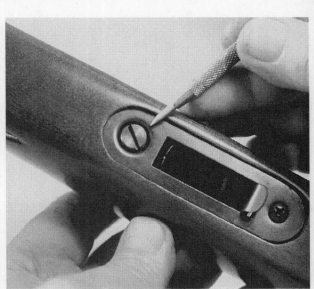

13. Remove the stock mounting screw and take the action out of the stock. The trigger guard, guard plate, magazine plate and the stock buttplate are each retained on the stock by Phillips-type wood screws.

14. Remove the two screws between the magazine housing and the trigger housing. Take care that the lock washers are not lost.

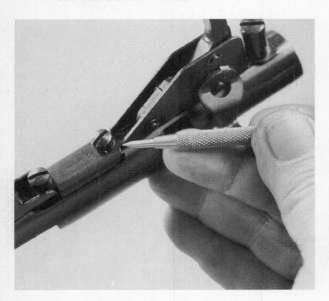

15. Remove the screw-slotted stock mounting post.

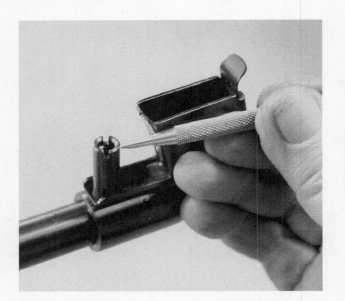

16. Move the magazine housing forward and take it off.

17. Move the magazine catch inward for removal.

18. Move the ejector and bolt guide rearward and tip it outward for removal.

19. Remove the screw-slotted post at the rear of the trigger housing, and remove the housing from the receiver.

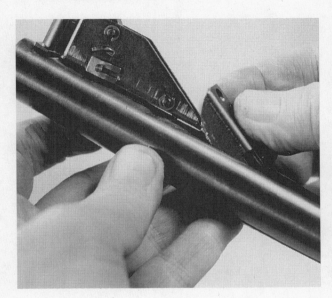

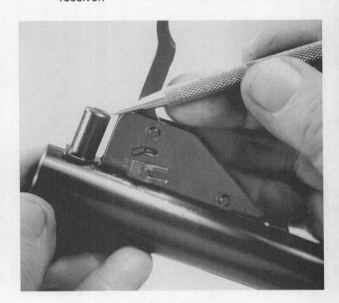

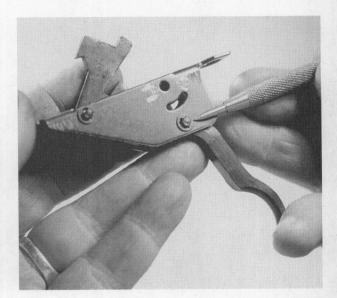

20. Removal of this spring-clip will allow the safety-lever to be taken off toward the right. Control the spring clip. Note that the pivot is separate from the safety-lever.

21. With the safety removed, the trigger and sear are allowed to pivot beyond their normal arcs, and the tension of the sear spring will be relieved. Removal of the C-clips on the cross pins will allow removal of the trigger, sear and sear spring from the housing.

Reassembly Tips:

1. If the sear and its spring have been removed, note that in reassembly the closed loop of the spring goes to the rear, as shown.

2. A large screwdriver bit and a small hammer will make replacement of the safety retainer easier, as shown.

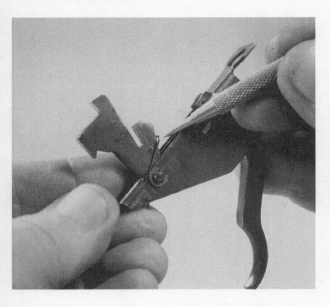

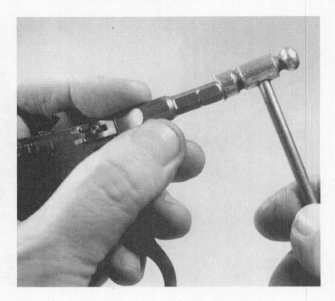

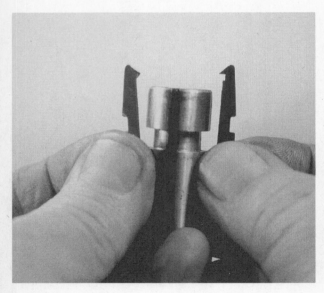

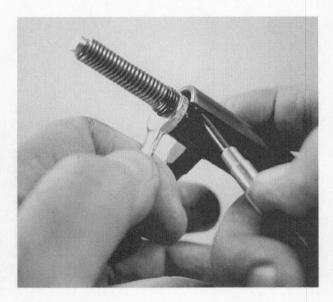

3. If the extractors have been removed, be sure the beaked one is installed on the right, and the bevelled one on the left.

4. The bench vise will have to be used again, as in disassembly, for installation of the striker spring retaining nut. After the C-clip has been installed, pry the nut forward and attach the $5/16$-inch wrench to hold it in position for attachment of the bolt body. Remember that the bolt must be recocked before it is put back into the receiver.

Marlin
Model 39A

Similar/Identical Pattern Guns

The same basic assembly/disassembly steps for the Marlin Model 39A also apply to the following guns:

Marlin Model 39	**Marlin Model 1892**
Marlin Model 39TDS	**Marlin Model 1897**
Marlin Model 39AS	**Marlin Model 39A 90th Anniv.**
Marlin Model 39A Mountie	**Marlin Model 39M Mountie**
Marlin Model 39 Carbine	**Marlin Model 39A Octagon**
Marlin Model 39D	**Marlin Model 39M Octagon**
Marlin Model 39M	**Marlin Golden 39M Carbine**
Marlin Model 39M Golden Carbine	**Marlin Model 39A-DL**
Marlin Model 39 Century LTD	**Marlin 39A Article II**
Marlin Model 39M Article II	

Data:	Marlin Model 39A
Origin:	United States
Manufacturer:	Marlin Firearms North Haven, Connecticut
Cartridge:	22 Short, Long or Long Rifle
Magazine capacity:	26 Short, 21 Long, 19 Long Rifle
Overall length:	40 inches
Barrel length:	24 inches
Weight:	$6^{1}/_{2}$ pounds

When the Marlin Company introduced the first lever-action, repeating 22 rimfire rifle in 1891, it had one particularly notable feature: It was the first repeating 22 rifle that would feed Short, Long and Long Rifle cartridges interchangeably. The basic gun was slightly redesigned in 1897, 1922 and 1938, finally arriving at the excellent Model 39A that is so popular today. Except for slight manufacturing changes—such as the use of modern round-wire springs—the internal mechanism is basically unchanged from the original 1891 version. With the exception of a shorter barrel and carbine-style, straight-gripped stock, the Mountie model is mechanically identical. The instructions can be used for all of the variants listed above.

Disassembly:

1. Use a coin to start the large, knurled takedown screw on the right side of the receiver. Then use your fingers to back it out until its threads are free. An internal shoulder will keep the screw from coming completely out.

2. Set the hammer on the safety step and bump the left side of the stock with the heel of your hand to force the stock and receiver plate toward the right. Separate the stock and its attached parts from the front portion of the gun.

3. Slide the breechblock (bolt) toward the rear until its lower projection stops against the shoulder of the receiver, and then remove the bolt toward the right side of the frame.

4. The firing pin is easily lifted from the top of the breech-block.

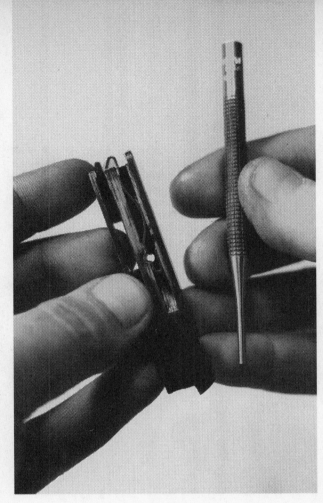

5. Insert a drift punch of the proper size through the small hole in the underside of the breechblock and push the extractor upward and out of its recess in the top of the bolt.

6. The ejector housing is retained on the inside of the receiver by two screws which enter from the outside left of the receiver, near the top. Back out the two screws and remove the ejector assembly toward the right. The ejector spring will be released by removal of the housing, and drifting out a vertical pin will free the ejector for removal. In normal takedown, the ejector lock rivet is not removed. The cartridge stop (arrow), located below the ejector and toward the front, is retained by a single screw which also enters from the outside left of the receiver. Back out this screw and remove the stop and its spacer block toward the right.

7. The cartridge guide spring, located just above the chamber, is retained by a screw which enters from the top of the receiver. This is the larger screw near the front scope mount screw. The cartridge guide spring is removed downward.

8. Drifting out the small cross pin in the magazine tube hanger will allow removal of the outer magazine tube toward the front. If the inner magazine tube is to be taken apart, drifting out the cross pin which also locks the tube in place will allow removal of the knurled end piece, spring and follower. There is some risk of damage to the thin tube, and in normal takedown the inner tube should be left assembled.

9. Removal of the two screws in the forend cap will allow it to be taken off forward, and the forend cap base can then be driven out of its dovetail toward the right side. When doing this, take care not to damage the screw holes. The forend can now be moved slightly forward and taken off downward.

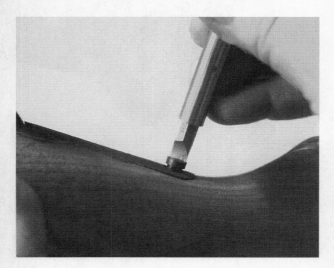

10. Take out the stock mounting bolt—the large screw at the rear tip of the upper tang. The stock can now be removed toward the rear. If the fitting is very tight, it may be necessary to bump the front of the comb with the heel of your hand or a soft rubber hammer.

11. The firing mechanism is shown in proper order, prior to disassembly. Note the relationship of all parts, to aid in reassembly.

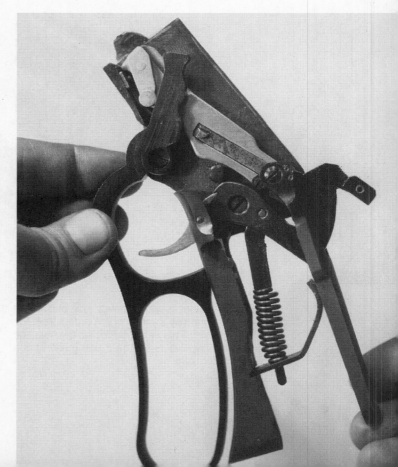

12. Grip the upper part of the hammer spring base with pliers and slide it out toward either side, moving its lower end out of its slot in the lower tang. The hammer, of course, must be at rest (in fired position). Remove the base and the spring toward the rear.

13. Take out the hammer pivot screw and remove the hammer from the top of the frame. During this operation, it will be necessary to tilt the attached hammer strut slightly to one side or the other to clear. Proceed carefully, and use no force.

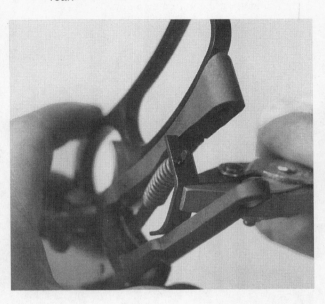

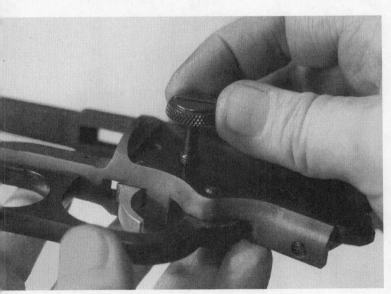

14. Move the takedown screw over until its threads engage the threads in the right side of the receiver, and unscrew it toward the right side for removal.

15. Remove the small screw on the underside of the frame, just forward of the lever, and take out the lever spring from inside the frame.

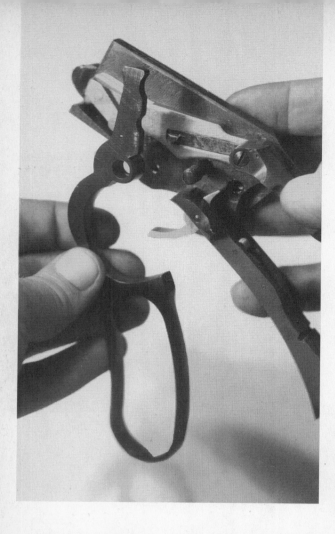

16. Take out the lever pivot screw and remove the lever toward the left.

17. Take out the carrier pivot screw and remove the carrier assembly toward the front. Taking out the carrier rocker screw will allow removal of the rocker and its spring from the carrier.

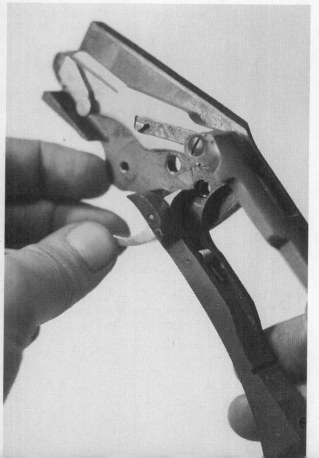

18. Drift out the trigger pin toward the right, and remove the trigger downward. Drift out the trigger spring pin and remove the trigger spring from inside the frame.

Reassembly Tips:

1. When replacing the hammer spring and its base, be sure the hammer is at rest and insert a lower corner of the base into its slot in the lower tang. Then tip the upper part downward and slip it under the upper tang, moving it inward into place.

2. When rejoining the front and rear parts of the gun, be sure the breechblock is all the way forward, the hammer is at full cock or on the safety step, and take care that the front tongue of the sideplate (arrow) is properly engaged with its mating recess in the main frame.

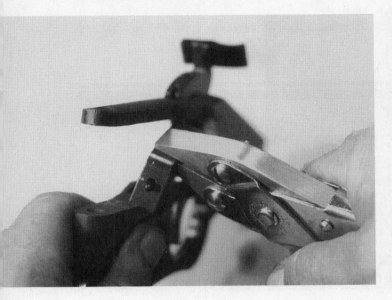

Avoid over-tightening the small screw which holds the cartridge guide spring above the chamber, or the spring may crack. This advice also applies to the cartridge stop screw. Both should be firm and snug, but use no excessive force.

When replacing the extractor in the top of the breechblock, start its rear portion into the recess; then flex the front portion slightly for proper alignment and push it into place.

Marlin Model 57

Similar/Identical Pattern Guns

The same basic assembly/disassembly steps for the Marlin Model 57 also apply to the following guns:

Marlin Model 57M   **Marlin Model 56**

Data:	Marlin Model 57
Origin:	United States
Manufacturer:	Marlin Firearms Company North Haven, Connecticut
Cartridge:	22 Short, Long or Long Rifle
Magazine capacity:	27 Short, 21 Long, 19 Long Rifle
Overall length:	42$\frac{3}{4}$ inches
Barrel length:	24 inches
Weight:	6 pounds

In 1955, Marlin introduced a new internal hammer lever-action rifle with an accelerated short-lever movement, the box-magazine Model 56. Three years later, they added the gun covered here, the tube magazine Model 57, and a 22 WMR chambering, the Model 57M. Except for the different feed systems, these three guns are mechanically the same, and the instructions will apply to any of them. The Model 56 and Model 57 were discontinued in 1964 and 1965 respectively, and the Model 57M in 1969.

Disassembly:

1. Remove the inner magazine tube. Back out the large screw on the underside of the stock, forward of the lever plate.

2. Open the lever and remove the larger of the two screws at the rear of the lever plate. Move the action upward and then forward out of the stock.

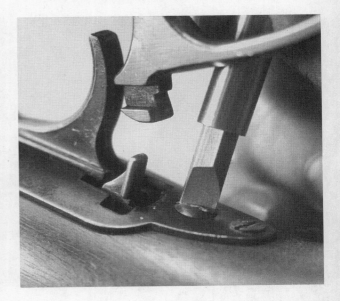

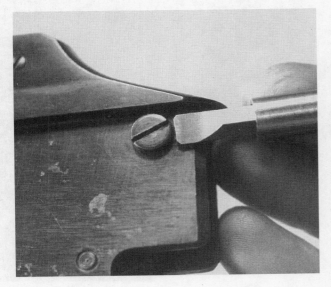

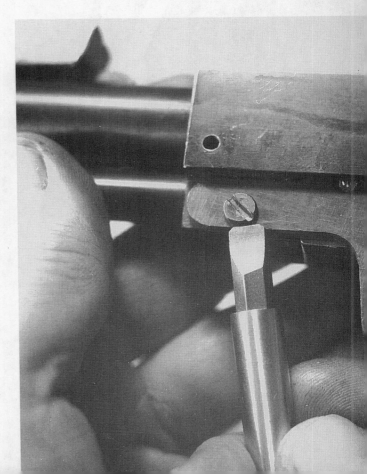

3. Remove the cap screw on the cross-post at the rear of the sub-frame. It may be necessary to use another screwdriver to stabilize the screw-slotted cross-post on the opposite side. After the cap screw is removed, push out the cross-post.

4. Remove the two small screws on each side, at the front of the sub-frame.

5. With the lever opened, remove the sub-frame downward.

6. Drift out the lever link pin, in the lower rear section of the bolt, and remove the bolt upward. If the pin is as originally installed, it should be drifted out toward the right. Take care not to lose the small bolt cam roller, which will be released as the pin is taken out.

7. Restrain the hammer, pull the trigger and ease the hammer down to fired position. Remove the sideplate screw on the right side of the sub-frame.

8. The sideplate can now be removed toward the right. If the plate is very tight, pry it gently at several points until it is free and carefully lift it off.

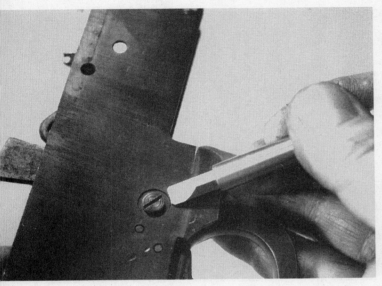

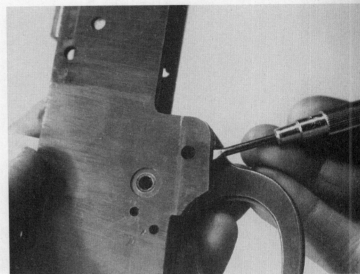

9. Taking care not to disturb the other parts, unhook the upper arm of the carrier spring from the carrier, slowly release its tension, and remove the spring from its post toward the right.

10. Detach the upper arm of the hammer spring from its groove at the back of the hammer and slowly release its tension, allowing it to swing over toward the front and downward. Remove the spring from its post toward the right. **Caution:** *This spring is quite strong, and if it slips can cause injury, so proceed carefully.*

11. Move the safety catch off its two posts and take it off toward the right.

12. Use a small screwdriver to detach the sear spring from the rear of the sear and allow it to swing downward, relieving its tension.

13. Remove the sear toward the right.

14. Remove the hammer toward the right.

15. With the lever opened, use sharp-nosed pliers to remove the front arm of the trigger block spring from the trigger limit pin and remove the spring toward the right.

16. Remove the spacer sleeve and the trigger block toward the right. It will be necessary to push the lever latch slightly upward to free the trigger block.

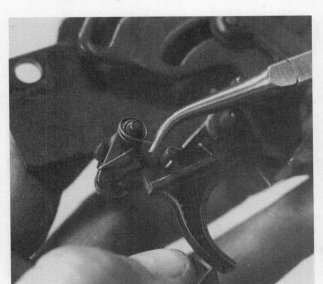

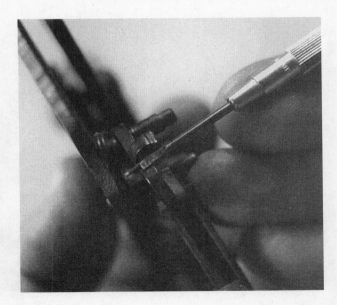

17. Disengage the lever latch spring from the back of the lever latch and allow the spring arm to swing forward, releasing its tension.

18. Remove the lever latch toward the right.

19. Disengage the trigger spring from the top of the trigger, swing it inward, and allow it to swing downward, releasing its tension. Keep fingertips out of the way!

20. Remove the trigger toward the right. The lever latch spring and the combination sear and trigger spring can now be removed from their posts toward the right.

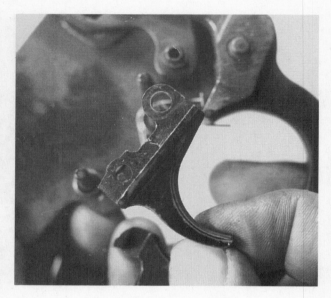

21. Move the lever and lever cam plate off their posts toward the right. The cam plate may be tight and will have to be worked and pried gently off.

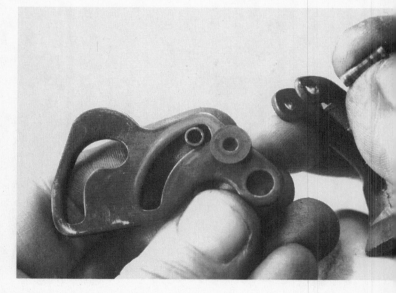

22. The lever cam plate can be separated from the lever by drifting out the connecting pin. The cam roller and the washer-like hammer cocking roller will also be released, so take care that they aren't lost.

23. Remove the C-clip on the inside tip of the carrier pivot and take out the carrier pivot toward the left.

24. Remove the carrier toward the rear.

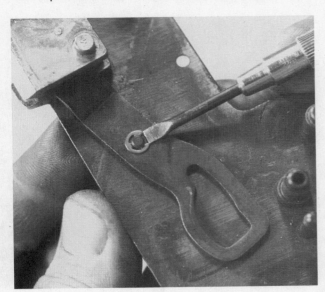

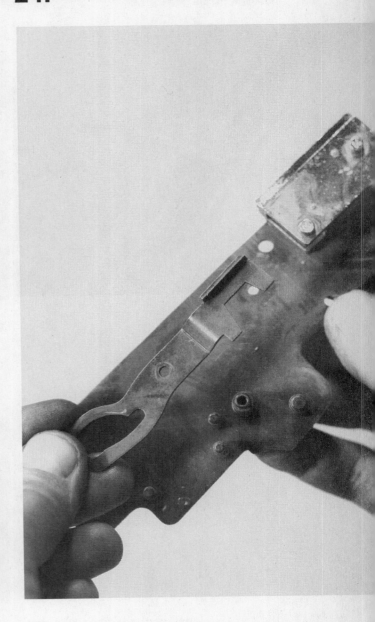

25. Remove the cartridge feed throat toward the right. If necessary, the two sides of the feed throat can be separated.

26. Drifting out the cross pin in the magazine tube hanger loop will allow removal of the magazine tube toward the front.

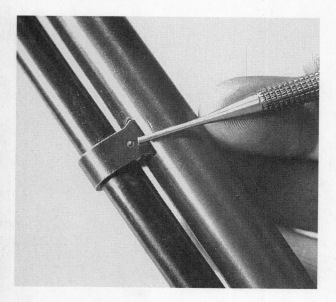

27. The barrel is retained in the receiver by a single cross pin. After removal of the pin, grip the barrel in a padded vise and use a non-marring tool to drive the receiver off toward the rear.

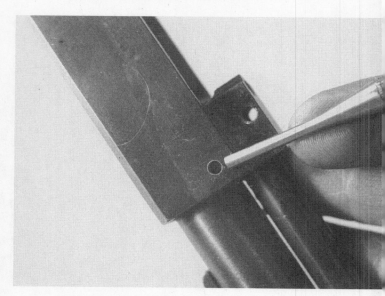

28. The firing pin is retained in the bolt by a small rectangular block, and the block is held in place by two cross pins. Drifting these out will release the block and allow removal of the firing pin toward the rear.

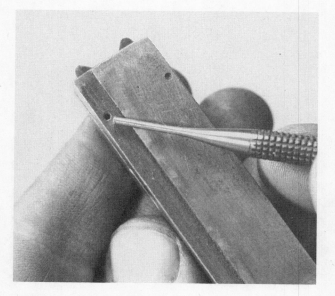

29. The twin extractors are retained by two vertical pins near the front of the bolt. After these are drifted out, the extractors and their coil springs are taken off toward each side.

Reassembly Tips:

1. This photo shows the internal parts of the sub-frame in proper order. The safety is not in place, to allow a view of the other parts.

2. This photo shows the safety catch in place and in the on-safe position. Note that the spring arm at its lower edge goes *below* the stop pin.

3. When replacing the bolt on the lever cam plate, remember that the bolt cam roller must be put back in its track on the plate, and the pin must pass through.

When replacing the sub-frame on the underside of the receiver, the action must be partially opened.

Marlin Model 80

Similar/Identical Pattern Guns
The same basic assembly/disassembly steps for the Marlin Model 80 also apply to the following guns:

Marlin Model 80C

Marlin Model 80E

Marlin Model 80DL

Marlin Model 80G

Data:	Marlin Model 80
Origin:	United States
Manufacturer:	Marlin Firearms Company North Haven, Connecticut
Cartridge:	22 Long Rifle
Magazine capacity:	8 rounds
Overall length:	43 inches
Barrel length:	24 inches
Weight:	6½ pounds

During my early shooting days I owned a Marlin Model 80, and for many youngsters of that time period who wanted a low-priced bolt action it was the rifle of choice. The gun was offered in several sub-models featuring various options in sights and sling loops. A counterpart tube-magazine rifle, the Model 81, has the same mechanical features, except for the magazine and feed system. The Model 80 was made from 1934 to 1971, when it was replaced in the Marlin line by the Model 780.

Disassembly:

1. Remove the magazine. Open the bolt and hold the trigger to the rear while sliding the bolt out the rear of the receiver. The safety must be in off-safe position, of course.

2. Drift out the cross pin in the bolt, just to the rear of the front section.

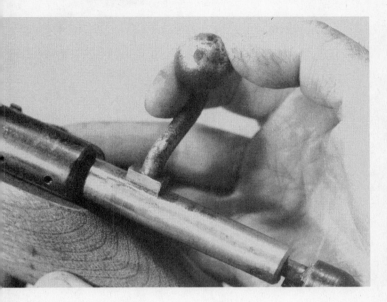

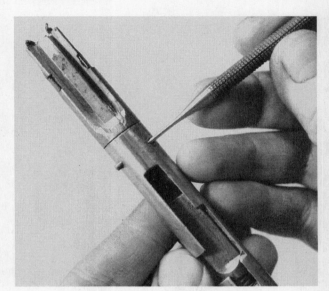

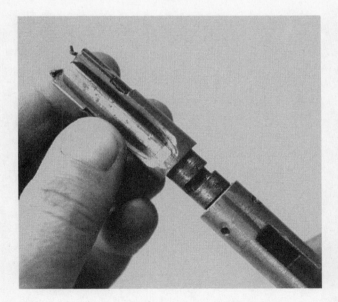

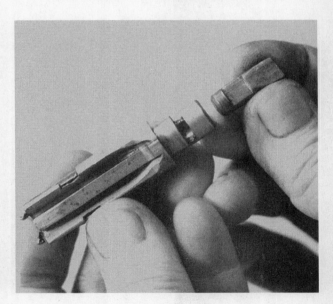

3. Remove the front section of the bolt toward the front.

4. Remove the rear firing pin from the front section.

5. Tap the front section to shake out the front firing pin and its return spring, and remove them toward the rear.

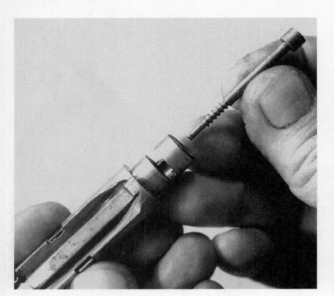

6. Insert a very small screwdriver from the front under the left extractor arm, and lever it outward and over toward the right to remove the twin extractor unit. Be sure to lift it only enough to clear, to avoid deformation or breakage.

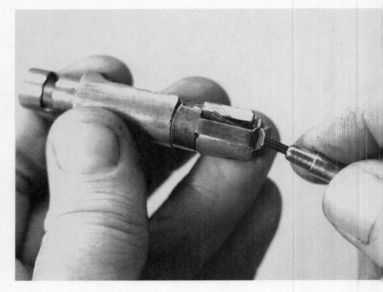

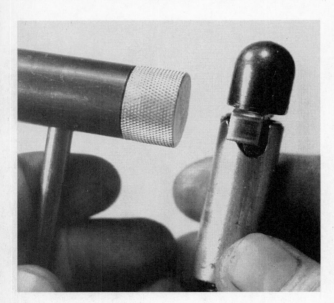

7. Tap the cocking lug pin on the striker knob toward the side, out of its detent notch at the rear of the bolt, to allow the striker to go forward, partially relieving its spring tension. When the striker is forward, it will be in the position shown.

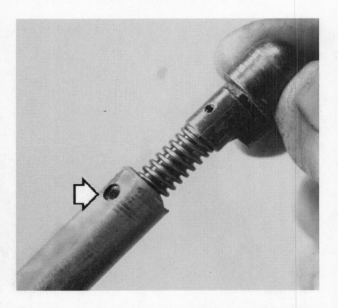

8. Remove the small screw (arrow indicates hole) on the side of the bolt near its rear edge. Remove the striker assembly toward the rear.

9. Grip the forward portion of the striker firmly in a vise, and while keeping pressure on the striker knob, drift out the small cross pin. **Caution:** *The striker spring is under tension, so control it and release the pressure slowly.* Remove the striker knob, sleeve ring and striker spring toward the rear.

10. Back out the main stock mounting screw, located on the underside at the rear edge of the magazine plate, and separate the action from the stock.

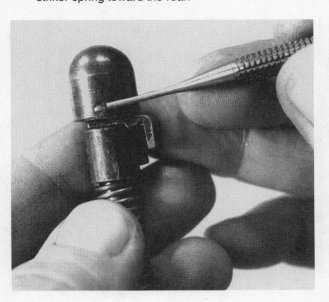

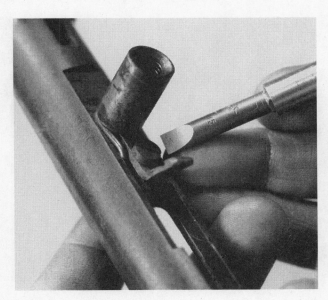

11. The magazine catch hook is retained on the underside of the receiver by a single screw, and is taken off downward.

12. The safety and its positioning spring are retained on the right rear of the receiver by two post screws, and both are removed toward the right.

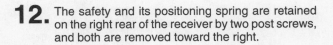

13. The trigger is mounted on a post below the receiver by a cross pin. When the cross pin is drifted out, the trigger and its spring will be released downward. The spring is under some tension, so control the trigger during removal. As the pin is drifted out, be sure the mounting post is well-supported, to avoid deformation or breakage.

14. After the trigger is removed, the sear pin can be drifted out and the sear and its spring removed downward. The same cautions as in the preceding step should be applied.

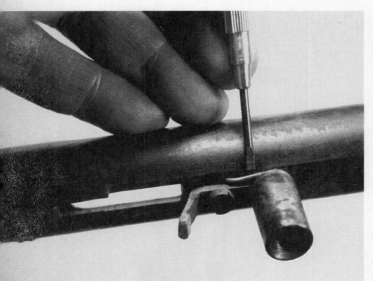

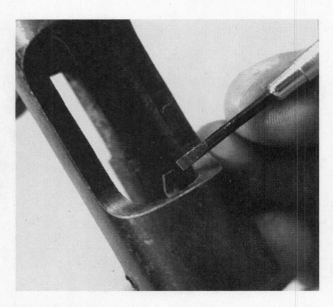

15. The ejector, a part made of round spring-wire, is held in place by the stock screw base, which is threaded into the underside of the receiver. Grip the base firmly with non-marring pliers and unscrew it to release the ejector.

16. Removal of the cartridge guide above the chamber requires removal of the barrel.

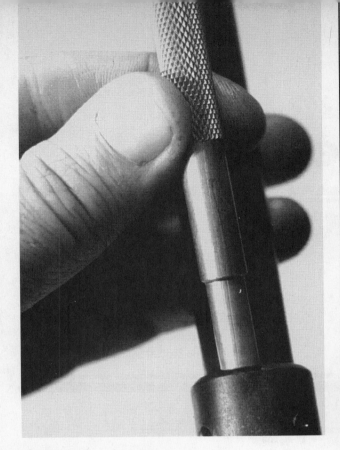

17. A cross pin retains the barrel in the receiver. If the barrel is very tight in the receiver, grip the barrel in a padded vise and use a non-marring drift punch to drive the receiver off the barrel toward the rear. When the barrel is out, the cartridge guide can be lifted from its recess at the top rear of the barrel.

Reassembly Tips:

1. When replacing the striker assembly in the bolt, be sure the threaded hole in the retaining sleeve is aligned with the screw recess in the side of the bolt, and insert a small screwdriver to cam the sleeve into position for insertion of the screw. In this operation, a third hand would be helpful.

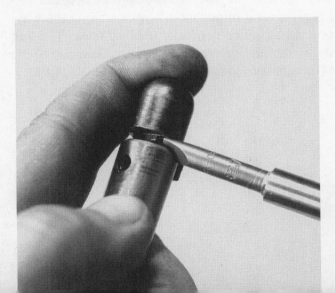

2. When replacing the front section of the bolt, note that the cross-groove in the tail piece and the groove in the rear firing pin must be oriented for passage of the retaining cross pin.

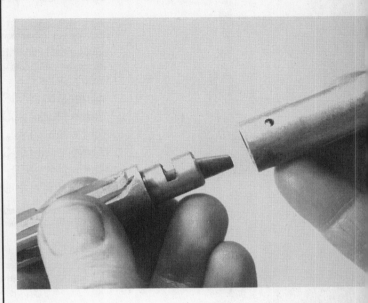

3. Before the reassembled bolt can be reinserted in the receiver, the striker must be recocked. Grip the front section of the bolt in a vise, and turn the bolt handle counterclockwise (rear view) until the cocking lug is in the position shown.

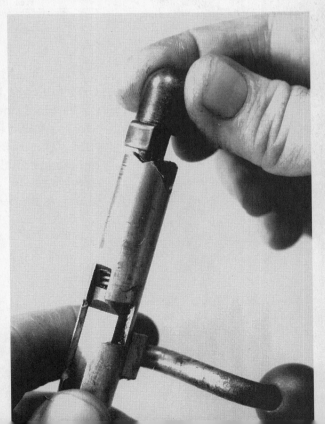

Marlin Model 99M1

Similar/Identical Pattern Guns

The same basic assembly/disassembly steps for the Marlin Model 99M1 also apply to the following guns:

Marlin Model 99C	**Marlin Model 989M1**
Marlin Model 99DL	**Marlin Model 989M2**
Marlin Model 99	**Marlin Model 989G**
Marlin Model 99G	**Marlin Model 989MC**
Marlin Model 49	**Marlin Model 995**
Marlin Model 49DL	**Marlin Model 990L**

Data:	Marlin Model 99M1
Origin:	United States
Manufacturer:	Marlin Firearms North Haven, Connecticut
Cartridge:	22 Long Rifle
Magazine capacity:	18 rounds in rifle, 9 in carbine
Overall length:	Rifle—42 inches, Carbine—37 inches
Barrel length:	Rifle—22 inches, Carbine—18 inches
Weight:	Rifle—5$\frac{1}{2}$ pounds, Carbine—4$\frac{1}{2}$ pounds

The original Model 99 semi-auto was introduced in 1959 and was soon followed by several sub-models—the 99DL, 99C and 99M1, the carbine shown here. The same basic action was later used in the Model 49 and its sub-models, the 989 and the current 990 and 995 rifles. There have been several minor modifications along the way, but the instructions can be applied generally to all of these. The gun is available in both tubular and box magazine types. The gun in the photos is the 99M1 tubular version.

Disassembly:

1. Remove the barrel band retaining screw, located on the right side of the barrel band, and take off the band toward the front. Remove the inner magazine tube.

2. Remove the two screws at the top rear of the handguard and take off the handguard piece.

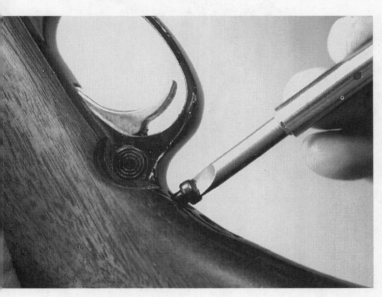

3. Remove the screw on the underside at the rear of the trigger guard—the screw nearest the guard. Remove the main stock mounting screw, located on the underside just forward of the trigger guard, and lift the action out of the stock.

4. Removal of the screws at each end of the trigger guard will allow the guard to be taken off downward. The rear screw is a wood screw, and the front screw has a flat internal nut-plate which may have to be stabilized during removal. The trigger and its spring are retained in the guard unit by a cross pin. Note the position of the spring before removal of the pin, to aid reassembly.

5. Remove the cap screw and screw-slotted post at the rear of the sub-frame below the receiver. If this assembly is very tight, it may require two opposed screwdrivers to immobilize the post while the screw is taken out.

6. Remove the two opposed screws at the front of the sub-frame below the receiver.

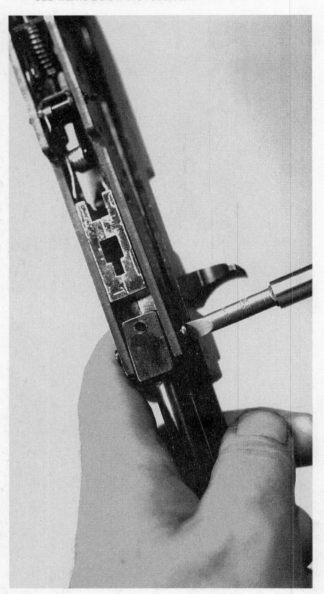

7. Remove the sub-frame downward.

8. Before disassembling the sub-frame, note the relationship of all parts and springs, to aid reassembly. Lower the hammer to the fired position, easing it down. Unhook the right arm of the carrier spring from its resting place on the carrier and ease it downward, relieving its tension. Remove the C-clips from the tips of the hammer/carrier pivot and the sear pivot on the **right** side only, taking care that the small clips are not lost. Depending on its tightness, it may also be necessary to remove the cross pin at the rear of the sub-frame which retains the recoil buffer. Remove the right sideplate of the sub-frame toward the right. This will allow disassembly of all the internal mechanism parts except the disconnector, which is mounted on the left sideplate on a post retained by a C-clip on the left side.

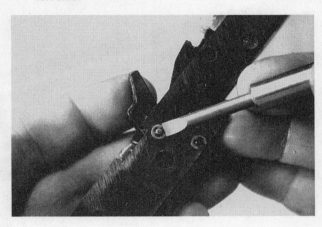

9. Invert the gun and retract the bolt far enough so that a finger or tool can be inserted in front of it. Lift the front of the bolt away from the inside top of the receiver and remove the bolt handle from the ejection port. Continue to lift the bolt, until its front will clear the underside of the receiver, and take out the bolt, bolt spring and follower. **Caution:** *The spring will be compressed. Control it, and ease its tension slowly.*

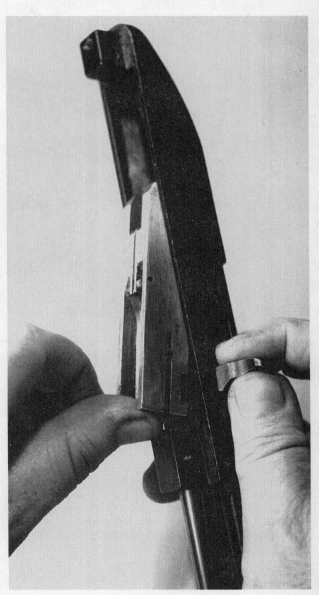

10. The firing pin is retained in the bolt by a cross pin at the lower edge of the bolt. Note that there is also a small roller on the cross pin (arrow), on the right side of the bolt, and take care that this roller isn't lost. When the pin is out, the firing pin can be removed toward the rear.

11. The extractors are retained by vertical pins on each side of the bolt, and these are driven out toward the top. The extractors and their small coil springs are then removed toward each side. **Note:** Keep each spring with its extractor because the springs are not of equal tension. The stronger spring must be put back on the right side.

12. Drifting out the small cross pin in the magazine tube hanger will allow removal of the outer magazine tube toward the front. The hanger can then be driven out of its dovetail cut toward the right. The front sight is retained by a single Allen screw in its top, just to the rear of the sight blade. After the screw is backed out, the sight is removed toward the front. After its large positioning screw on the right side is loosened, the rear sight can be slid off the scope rail in either direction.

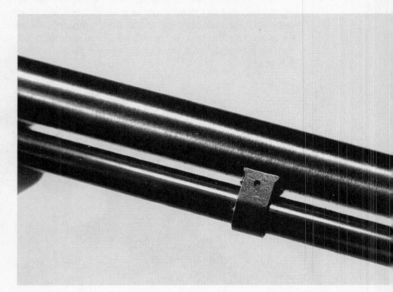

Reassembly Tips:

When replacing the sub-frame in the receiver, be sure the hammer is cocked. There will be some tension from the carrier spring as the sub-frame is pushed into place. Insert the rear screw-post first; then start the two front screws. Do not tighten the screws until all three are in position and started.

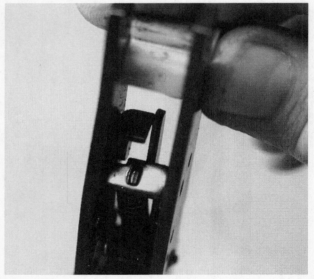

1. When replacing the hammer spring baseplate in the sub-frame, note that there is a notch in one corner of the plate. This must go on the left side at the top, to clear the rear portion of the disconnector.

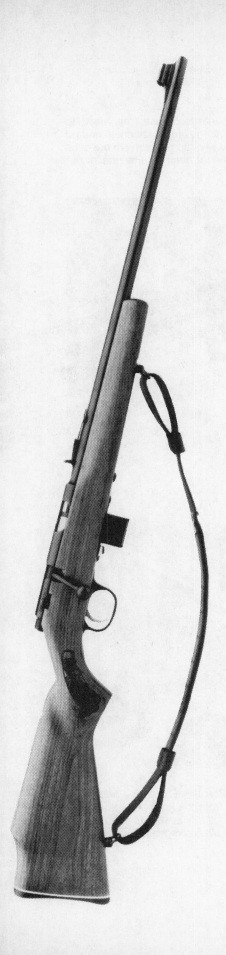

Marlin Model 782

Similar/Identical Pattern Guns
The same basic assembly/disassembly steps for the Marlin Model 782 also apply to the following guns:

Marlin Model 780   **Marlin Model 781**
Marlin Model 783

Data:	Marlin Model 782
Origin:	United States
Manufacturer:	Marlin Firearms Company North Haven, Connecticut
Cartridge:	22 WMR
Magazine capacity:	7 rounds
Overall length:	41 inches
Barrel length:	22 inches
Weight:	6 pounds

The Marlin 780 series is comprised of four guns with identical firing systems, the only difference being in the chamberings and the magazines. The Model 780 and 782 are detachable box magazine guns, chambered for regular 22 and 22 WMR, respectively. The Model 781 and 783 have the same chamberings, with tubular magazine systems. Except for the magazines, takedown and reassembly instructions can be applied to any of the guns in the group. The Model 782 was made from 1971 to 1988.

Disassembly:

1. Remove the magazine. Open the bolt and hold the trigger pulled to the rear while removing the bolt from the rear of the receiver.

2. Turn the end piece counterclockwise (rear view) to drop the striker forward to the fired position. If the end piece can't be turned easily, tap the cam pin out of its engagement with its detent notch at the rear of the bolt.

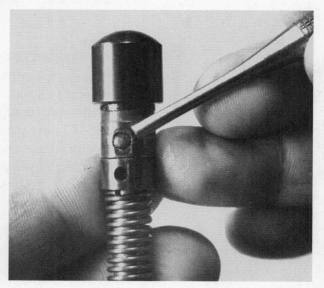

3. Remove the small screw on the side of the bolt near the rear edge. Remove the striker assembly toward the rear.

4. Grip the front of the striker firmly in a vise and drive out the striker cam pin from the knob. **Caution:** *Restrain the knob, as the striker sleeve and knob will be forced off when the cam pin is removed. Control them, and ease them off.*

5. Drift out the bolt retaining cross pin.

6. Remove the bolt head toward the front.

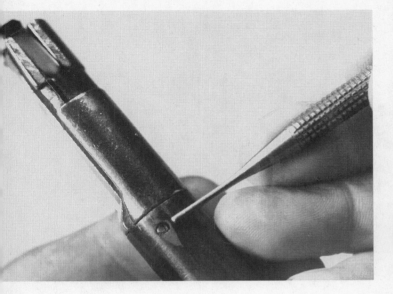

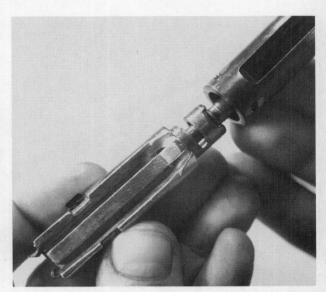

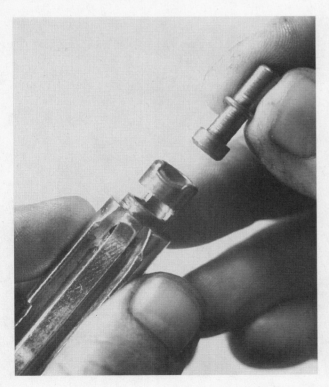

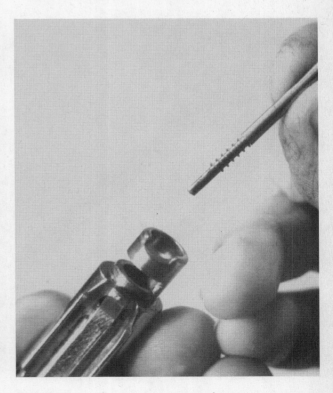

7. Remove the rear firing pin from the bolt head.

8. Remove the front firing pin and its return spring from the bolt head.

9. Insert a small screwdriver under the left extractor and lift it out of its recess just enough to clear. Turn the screwdriver to lever the extractor clip off the bolt.

10. Back out the stock mounting bolt, on the underside forward of the magazine plate, and remove the action from the stock. Removal of the small vertical screws at each end of the trigger guard and magazine plate will allow the guard and plate to be taken off downward.

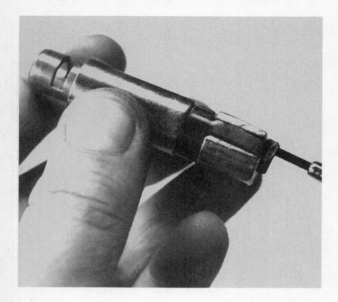

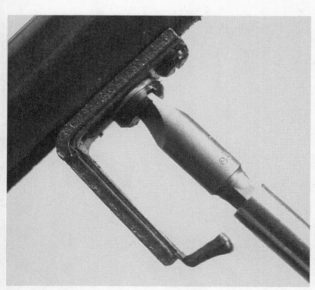

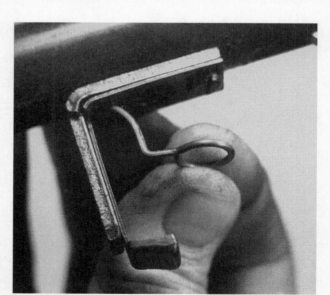

11. Remove the large vertical screw on the underside of the receiver, just to the rear of the magazine guide bar and catch.

12. Remove the ejector downward and toward the rear.

14. Remove the trigger and its spring downward.

13. Remove the smaller screw, at the rear of the magazine guide bar and catch base. Remove the guide bar and magazine catch downward. Drift out the trigger cross pin, taking care that the trigger post is well supported.

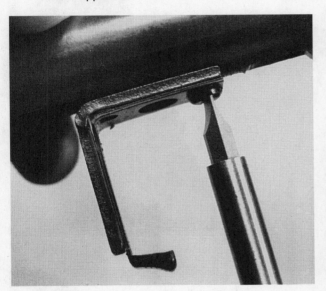

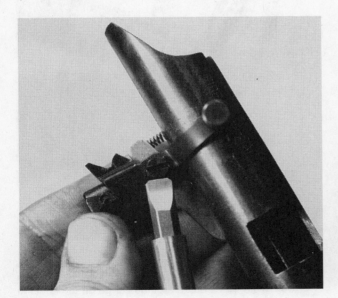

15. Restrain the sear and remove the screw on the right side of the receiver. Remove the safety-lever toward the right.

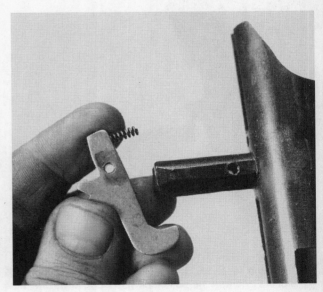

16. Remove the sear and its spring downward.

Reassembly Tips:

1. When replacing the bolt head, note that it must be oriented with the retaining cut aligned for insertion of the cross pin. Also, the rear firing pin must be pushed forward as the pin is inserted.

2. When replacing the striker assembly, be sure the screw hole in the striker sleeve is at the top, aligned with the screw recess in the bolt body.

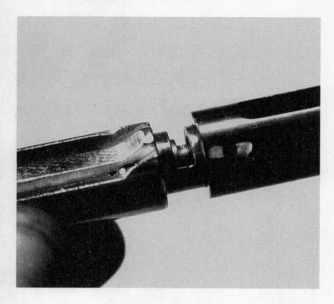

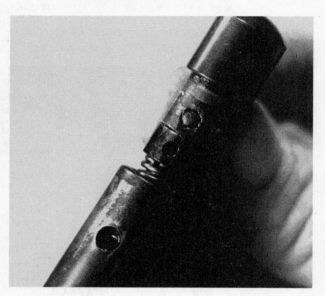

3. The striker must be cocked before the bolt is put back into the receiver. Grip the cam pin with non-marring pliers and turn the bolt clockwise (rear view) until the cam pin engages its notch at the rear of the bolt.

4. Before inserting the bolt, turn the bolt head so its underside aligns with the opening in the bottom of the bolt. Note that there is a guide flange on the left side of the extractor which must mate with a small groove inside the left wall of the receiver.

Mauser DSM 1934

Similar/Identical Pattern Guns
The same basic assembly/disassembly steps for the Mauser Model DSM 1934 also apply to the following guns:

Navy Arms TU-KKW   **Navy Arms TU-33/40**
Navy Arms TU-KKW Sniper

Data:	Mauser Deutsches Sportmodell 1934
Origin:	Germany
Manufacturer:	Mauser Werke, Oberndorf (and others, on contract)
Cartridge:	22 Long Rifle
Overall length:	$43^3/_4$ inches
Barrel length:	26 inches
Weight:	$7^1/_2$ pounds

Designed in 1934 as a training rifle for the Hitler Youth and the regular army, these fine little rifles were usually marked "Deutsches Sportmodell," in retrospect a wry comment on the Nazis' idea of "sport." The guns are of typical excellent pre-war German quality in both materials and workmanship, and are highly prized by shooters and collectors. Their single shot action is a miniature variation of the Mauser 98 military system, and the takedown is thus quite similar. The gun shown in the photos has been sporterized and lacks the forward extension of the stock and the front barrel band, but is otherwise mechanically unaltered. The Navy Arms TU-KKW, TU-33/40 and TU-KKW Sniper are imported from China, and the instructions will generally apply.

Disassembly:

1. Cycle the bolt to cock the striker and turn the safety-lever up to the vertical position. Open the bolt and move it toward the rear, while holding the bolt stop, at the left rear of the receiver, pulled outward. Remove the bolt from the rear of the receiver.

2. Taking care not to trip the safety-lever, unscrew the bolt sleeve, turning it counterclockwise (rear view). Remove the bolt sleeve and striker assembly toward the rear.

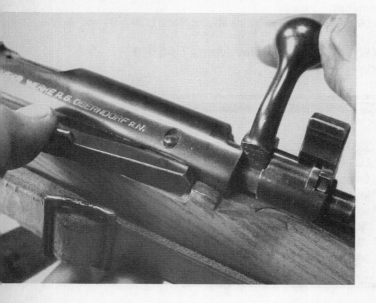

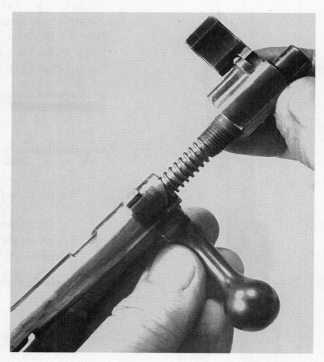

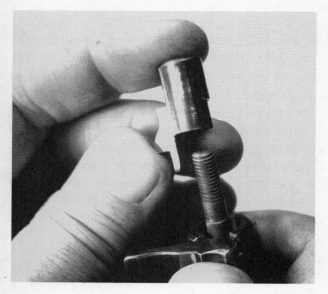

3. If the disassembly bushing is still in the sides of the buttstock, insert the firing pin in the hole at its center. If not, grip the firing pin in a vise, taking care to exert no side pressure. Holding firmly to the bolt sleeve to control the striker spring, turn the safety-lever back to the off-safe position, and push the sleeve toward the front until its rear edge clears the front of the cocking lug on the striker head. With the sleeve held firmly down (forward), unscrew the striker head piece counterclockwise (rear view) and remove it toward the rear. **Caution:** *Keep a firm grip on the bolt sleeve, as the striker spring is fully compressed.*

4. Slowly release the spring tension, allowing the bolt sleeve to move off the striker shaft, and take off the sleeve and striker spring.

5. Turn the safety-lever all the way over to the full-safe position and remove it toward the rear.

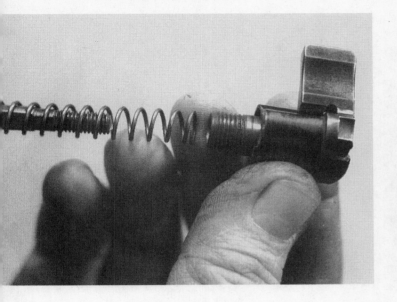

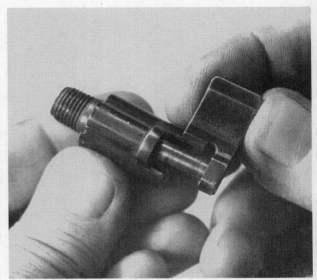

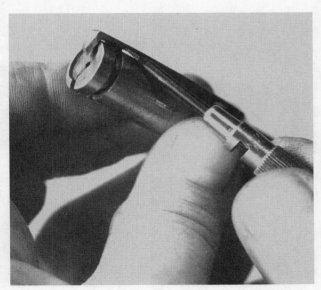

6. Insert a small screwdriver to lift the front of the extractor, just enough for its underlug to clear the groove at the front of the bolt, and slide the extractor off toward the front. Be sure to lift it only enough to clear, and no further, or it may break.

7. If the gun has a sling, unhook it from its post on the buttstock and remove it. Drive out the cross pins that retain the front and rear barrel bands, and take off the bands toward the front.

8. Move the upper handguard wood forward; then remove it upward. Take care not to lose the metal handguard tip at the rear, just forward of the rear sight.

9. Remove the two vertical screws on the underside of the stock, at the front and rear of the trigger guard. Take off the trigger guard downward and remove the action from the stock.

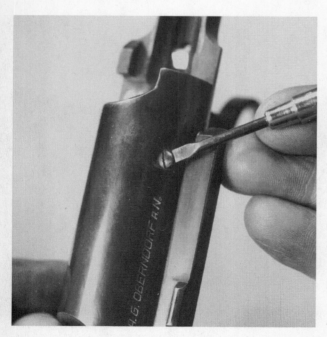

10. Remove the vertical screw at the left rear of the receiver, the pivot and retaining screw for the bolt stop. Slight inward pressure on the stop will ease removal of the screw.

11. Take off the bolt stop assembly toward the left, and take care that the small coil spring isn't lost.

12. The ejector is mounted in the bolt stop by a hollow pivot sleeve, and should be left in place unless removal is necessary for repair. If it must be removed, turn a drift punch or a piece of drill rod to the exact diameter of the sleeve and drive it out very carefully. The small coil ejector spring is mounted inside the bolt stop, under the ejector.

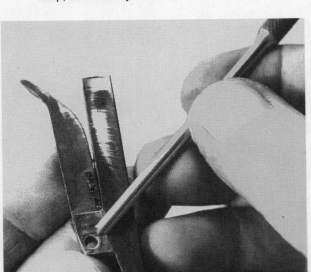

13. The sear/trigger assembly is mounted on the underside of the receiver by a cross pin, and after the pin is drifted out it is removed downward, along with the sear spring. Drifting out the trigger pin will allow separation of the trigger from the sear.

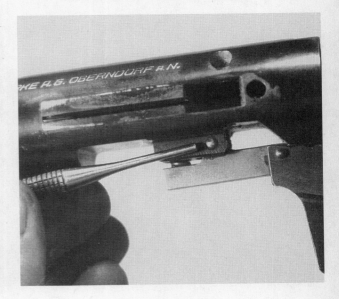

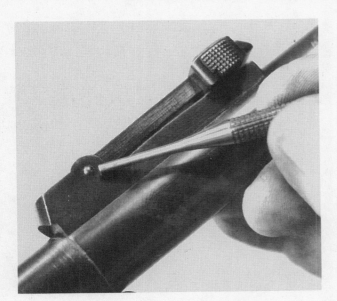

14. The rear sight is retained on its base by a cross pin. After the sight is removed, the elevation slide can be moved forward and off the sight.

Reassembly Tips:

1. When replacing the screws on the underside, at the front and rear of the trigger guard, note that the longer screw goes at the rear of the guard.

2. When replacing the sleeve and striker assembly, note that there is a flat on one side of the striker shaft, and this must be oriented to mate with the flat in the sleeve tunnel. Also note that the safety-lever must be in its midway or vertical position when the sleeve and striker assembly are turned back into the bolt.

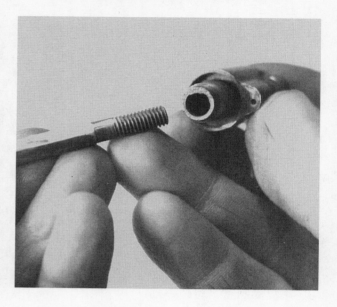

Mauser Ms420B

Data:	Mauser Ms420B
Origin:	Germany
Manufacturer:	Mauser Werke, Oberndorf
Cartridge:	22 Long Rifle
Magazine capacity:	5 rounds
Overall length:	45¼ inches
Barrel length:	26¾ inches
Weight:	7½ pounds

Around 1935, the Mauser factory redesigned their Model 420 22-caliber rifle to be more like the classic military rifle, the Model 98. The single shot training version, the DSM34, was even stocked like the Model 98. The Ms420B, however, was a commercial sporting gun. It was made from 1935 to around 1940, and today is prized by both shooters and collectors.

Disassembly:

1. Remove the magazine and operate the bolt to cock the striker. Set the safety in vertical on-safe position. Open the bolt, pull the bolt stop lever outward, and remove the bolt toward the rear.

2. Taking care that the safety-lever is not moved from its position, unscrew the striker assembly from the body of the bolt and remove it.

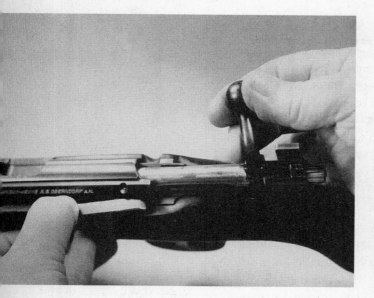

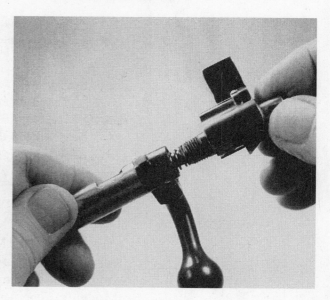

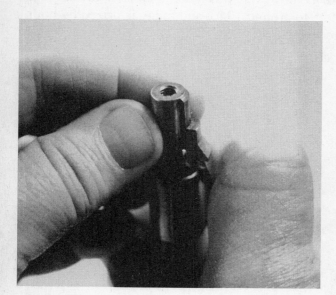

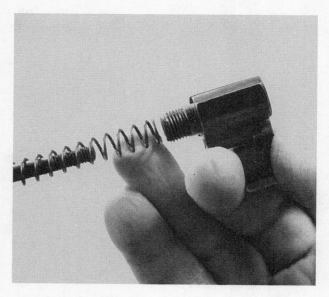

3. Rest the firing pin point on a firm surface and push the end piece down, compressing the striker spring, until the sear lug on the striker head clears the end piece. Unscrew the striker head and remove it. **Caution:** *Keep the striker spring under control.*

4. Ease the spring tension slowly, and take off the end piece and the striker spring.

5. Turn the safety-lever all the way to the right and remove it toward the rear.

6. Exerting pressure on both ends, turn the extractor until it is aligned with the bolt handle base. Use a tool to pry it very slightly outward, just enough for the forward lug to clear the recess, and push it off toward the front.

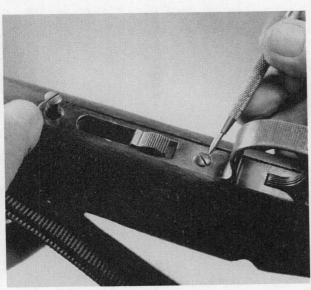

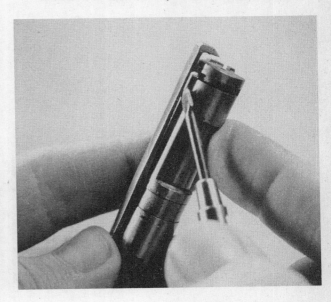

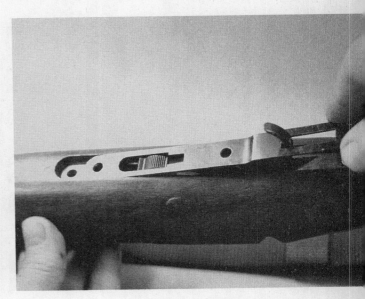

7. Remove the screw at the front of the magazine opening. Remove the wood screw behind the magazine catch. Remove the screw behind the trigger guard.

8. Remove the trigger guard from the stock. Lift the magazine plate slightly, move it rearward to clear the catch, and take it off downward.

9. Remove the magazine housing downward.

10. Drifting out this cross pin will allow removal of the magazine catch and its spring from the housing.

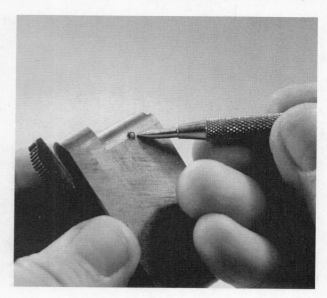

11. Unscrew the front sling loop and remove it, and take the action out of the stock.

12. Move the sling loop base rearward in its dovetailed track until it aligns with the exit opening, and remove it.

13. Restrain the sear, and push out the sear cross pin.
Caution: *This is a strong spring.*

14. Ease the spring tension slowly, and remove the trigger and sear assembly downward.

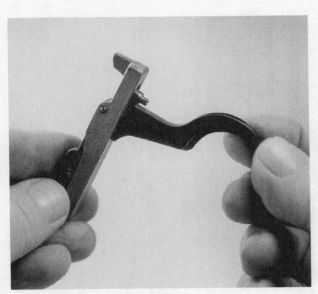

15. The trigger and sear can be separated by drifting out the cross pin. The trigger adjustment screw can be removed by turning it clockwise and backing it out upward. In normal takedown, it is best left in place.

16. Remove the vertical screw at the left rear of the receiver, and take off the bolt stop and ejector assembly toward the left. The bolt stop spring will also be freed for removal.

17. The ejector is mounted in the bolt stop on a hollow pivot pin. If this is to be removed, use a drift with a diameter almost exactly the same as the diameter of the pin, or it may be damaged. Removal of the ejector will free the ejector spring, located in a recess in the bolt stop.

18. To remove the rear sight, press it down at the front and slide it out toward the rear. The flat spring is easily removed from its slot under the sight, and the adjustment slide can then be moved off toward the front. The front sight can be taken off toward the front by depressing the button forward of the blade. The base ramp is not removable.

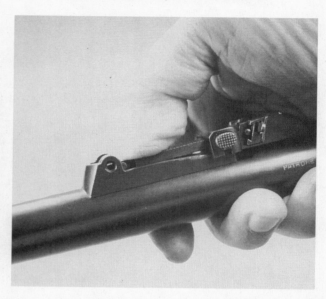

Reassembly Tips:

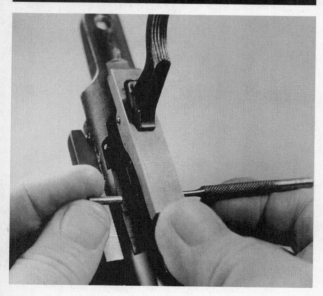

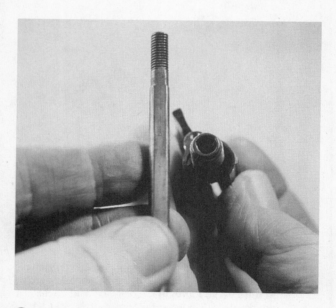

1. When installing the sear, press it into place and insert a drift to align it for insertion of the cross pin.

2. When reassembling the striker assembly, note that one side of the striker shaft is flat, and it must mate with a like surface inside the end piece.

Mitchell AK-22

Similar/Identical Pattern Guns
The same basic assembly/disassembly steps for the Mitchell AK-22 also apply to the following gun:
AP-80

Data:	Mitchell AK-22
Origin:	Italy
Manufacturer:	Armi Jäger, Turin
Cartridge:	22 Long Rifle
Magazine capacity:	20 rounds
Overall length:	36 inches
Barrel length:	18 inches
Weight:	6½ pounds

An excellent 22 rimfire copy of the famed Russian AK-47 carbine, the Mitchell AK-22 was introduced in 1985. In 1988 it was also offered in 22 WMR chambering. The AK-22 designation was used by the U.S. importer, Mitchell Arms. In Europe, Armi Jäger calls it the AP-80.

Disassembly:

1. Remove the magazine and cycle the action to cock the internal hammer. Depress the button at the rear of the receiver, and lift the receiver cover at the rear.

2. Remove the receiver cover, upward and toward the rear.

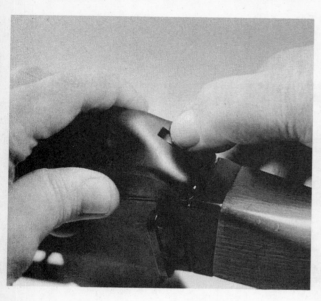

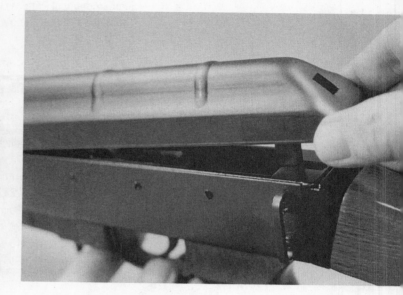

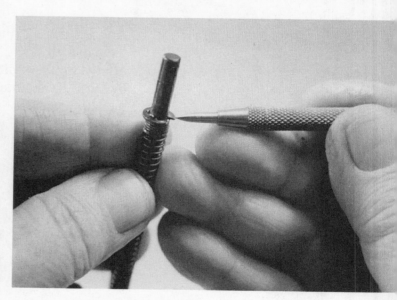

3. Move the recoil spring end piece forward to disengage it from the spring base, and move it to the side. **Caution:** *Keep the spring system under control.* Ease the tension slowly, and remove the spring assembly toward the rear.

4. If removal of the spring from the guide is necessary, pull the spring away from the C-clip and remove the C-clip from the rod. **Caution:** *Control the spring.*

5. Tip the recoil spring base forward, and remove it upward.

6. Move the bolt all the way to the rear, and lift it off upward.

7. Restrain the firing pin, and drift out the roll-type cross pin at the rear of the bolt. The pin does not have to be removed, just drifted far enough to free the firing pin.

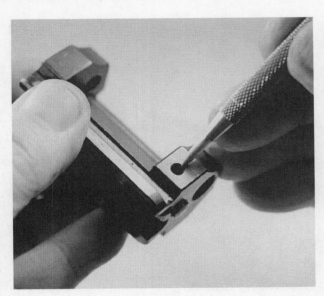

8. Remove the firing pin and its return spring.

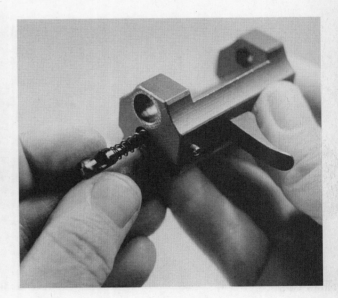

9. Insert a small tool to push the extractor plunger toward the rear, and lift out the extractor. **Caution:** *Control the plunger and spring.*

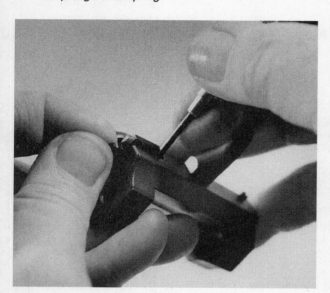

10. Ease the spring tension slowly, and remove the plunger and spring toward the front.

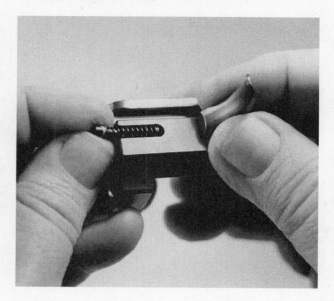

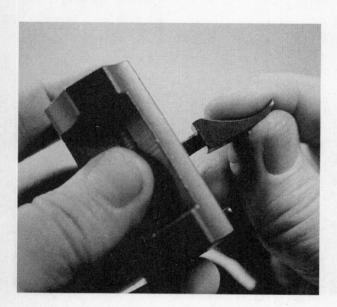

11. Rap the front of the bolt on a non-marring surface to move the retaining plunger forward, and take off the bolt handle toward the right. **Note:** The plunger may come out when the bolt is jarred, so take care that it isn't lost.

12. If the retaining plunger didn't exit in the previous step, use a small tool to nudge it forward for removal from the extractor spring tunnel.

13. To remove the cleaning rod, push it toward the rear, tip it outward, and take it out toward the front. There is a muzzle cap with wrench flats that can be unscrewed, and the front sight base is retained by a roll cross pin and an Allen screw in its underside.

14. If the buttstock needs to be removed, it is retained internally by a large Allen-type screw that requires a long-shanked tool that will hold an Allen bit. For access to this, remove the single Phillips screw at the rear, and take off the buttplate. Disassembly of the action, however, does not require removal of the buttstock.

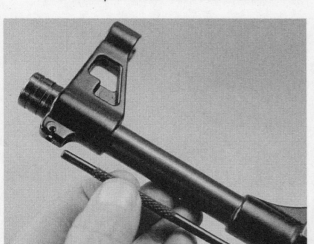

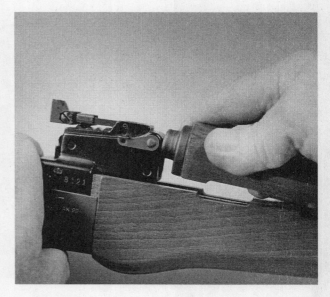

15. Use an Allen bit to remove the screw and washer that retain the handgrip, and take it off downward.

16. Push the upper handguard forward, against the tension of its spring, and tip it upward at the rear for removal.

17. The upper handguard spring is removable by turning it and pulling it out toward the rear. The handguard base can be taken off forward by removing the Allen screw in the sling loop.

18. Restrain the hammer, pull the trigger, and ease the hammer down to fired position. Drift out the trigger guard cross pin toward the left, and take off the trigger guard downward.

19. Move the forearm cap forward on the barrel.

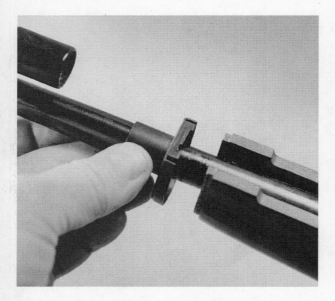

20. Move the forearm forward, and take it off downward.

21. Remove the screws on each side at the front of the receiver cover.

22. Remove the three screws on the left side of the receiver cover.

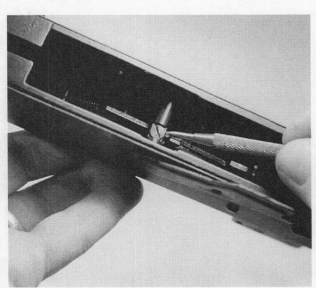

23. Remove the post screw in the safety cross-shaft.

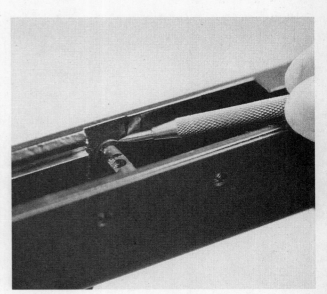

24. Remove the C-clip from the safety cross-shaft, inside the receiver on the right side. **Caution:** *Control the C-clip as it is taken off.* Exert inward pressure on the base of the safety-lever as the C-clip is taken off.

25. Remove the safety-lever toward the right.

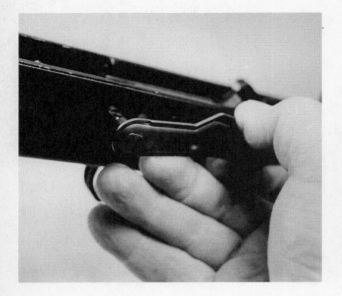

26. Remove the two screws on the right side at the rear of the receiver cover. Removal of the screws will release the sling loop on the left side.

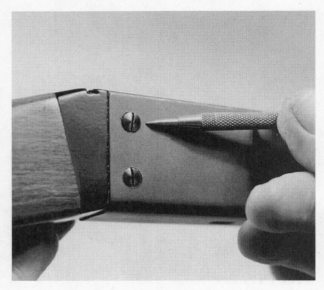

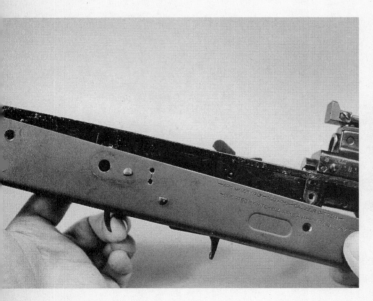

27. Remove the receiver cover downward. The cover will usually be tight, and it may require nudging with a nylon drift to start it. Pull the trigger to clear as the cover is moved downward.

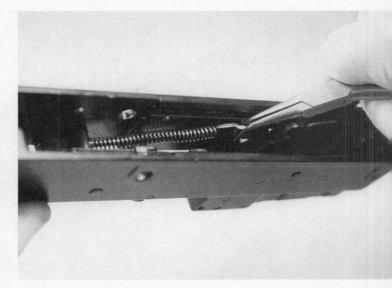

28. Use pliers to grip the hammer spring strut, and carefully disengage it from its recess in the back of the hammer. Tip it upward at the front for removal. **Caution:** *Control the strut and spring.*

29. Push out the hammer cross pin.

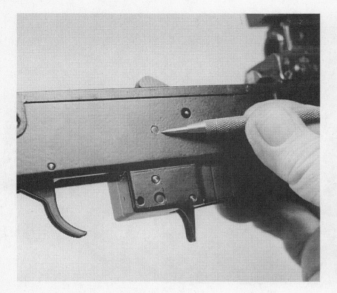

30. Remove the hammer upward.

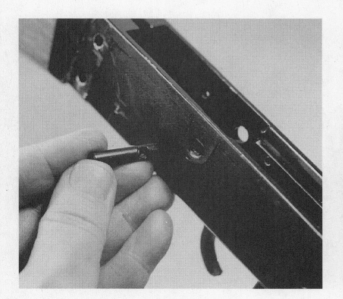

31. Remove the hammer spring base pin.

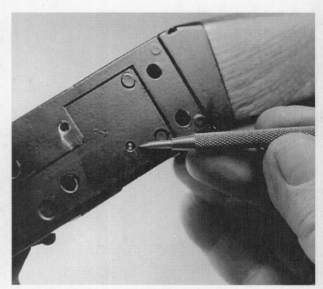

32. Remove the trigger spring cross pin.

33. Push out the trigger cross pin.

34. Remove the trigger assembly upward, moving it slightly rearward to clear it from the sear. The cross pin can be removed to separate the trigger bar from the trigger, and the spring is easily detached from the rear tip of the bar.

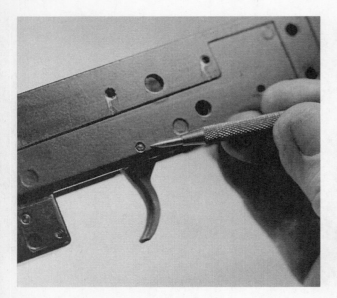

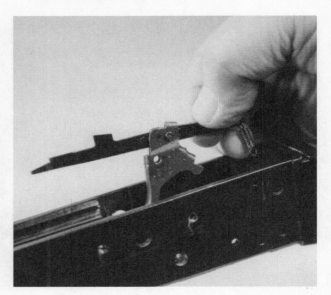

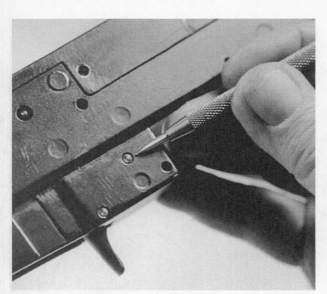

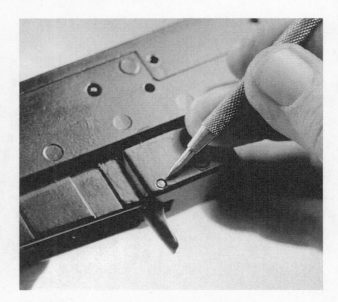

35. Drifting out this cross pin will allow removal of the sear and sear spring. Control the spring as the drift is taken out.

36. Drifting out this cross pin will free the magazine catch and its spring. Control the spring during removal.

37. The ejector and its spring are retained by a cross pin, and these parts are taken out upward.

38. If all parts have been taken off the barrel, and all parts removed from the receiver, removal of this Allen screw will allow the barrel to be driven out of the receiver toward the rear. In normal takedown, it is best left in place. The cleaning rod spring, visible at the front of the receiver, can be taken out of its well if necessary.

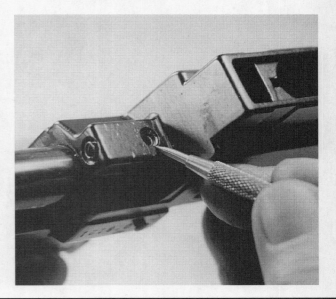

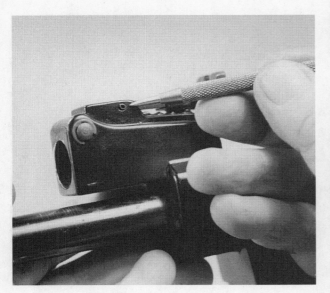

39. The rear sight is retained by a roll-type cross pin. The latch at the front of the sight base is a cosmetic part. If it needs to be removed, the C-clip on the left side is taken off, and the latch is removed toward the right.

Reassembly Tips:

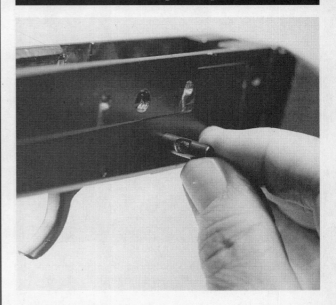

1. When installing the hammer spring base pin, be sure the recess in the pin is oriented toward the front, to accept the rear tip of the spring.

2. As the cross pins are replaced, be sure their ends are level with the side of the receiver, to avoid difficulty in replacing the cover.

3. As the cover is pushed back onto the receiver, hook the toe of the trigger in its opening, and depress the trigger as the cover is seated.

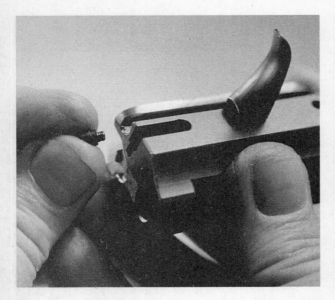

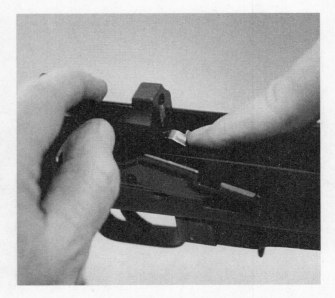

4. When installing the bolt handle retaining plunger, be sure its smaller tip is toward the rear, as shown.

5. As the bolt is pushed back toward the front, it will be necessary to depress the hammer for clearance.

Mossberg Model 44US

Data:	Mossberg Model 44US
Origin:	United States
Manufacturer:	O.F. Mossberg & Sons, Inc. North Haven, Connecticut
Cartridge:	22 Long Rifle
Magazine capacity:	7 rounds
Overall length:	$42^1/_2$ inches
Barrel length:	26 inches
Weight:	$7^1/_2$ pounds

A slight redesign of the earlier Model 44B, the 44US was primarily used for military marksmanship training during World War II. The one shown in the photos is marked "U.S. Property." Aside from its plain, military-style stock, it is similar to the other Mossberg bolt-action 22 rifles of this time period, and the instructions can be applied generally to most of these. The knowledgeable shooter can see which of our instruction steps apply to his gun. There are many variations of Mossberg mechanisms.

Disassembly:

1. Remove the magazine. Open the bolt, hold the trigger to the rear, and withdraw the bolt from the rear of the receiver. The aperture sight can be pivoted around to the side for clearance.

3. Grip the bolt and the rear domed end piece firmly and unscrew the end piece from the rear of the bolt. **Caution:** *The striker spring is under some tension, so keep the end piece under control.* After it is removed, the spring and guide are easily taken out.

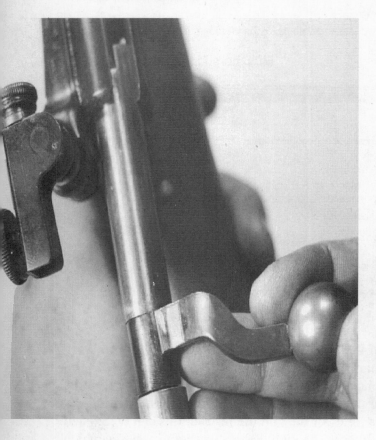

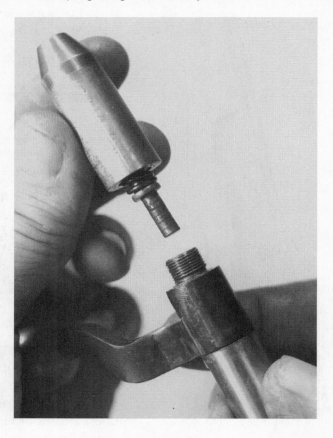

2. Turn the bolt handle clockwise (rear view) to allow the striker to move forward to the fired position.

4. Move the bolt handle sleeve toward the rear, the striker moving with it. When the sleeve has enough clearance, remove it toward the rear.

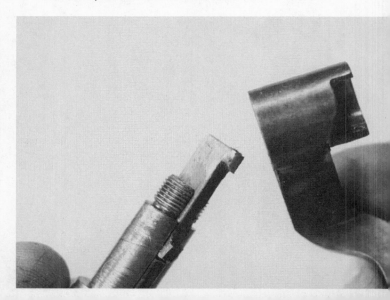

5. Remove the striker/firing pin unit from the bolt.

6. The twin extractors can be removed by inserting the tip of a small screwdriver between each extractor and its plunger, pushing the plunger toward the rear, and lifting the extractor out of its recess. **Caution:** *Take care the screwdriver doesn't slip during this operation, and ease the plungers and springs out for removal.*

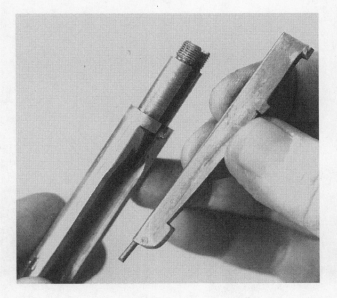

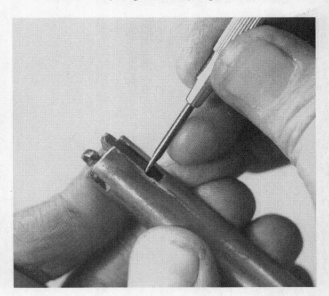

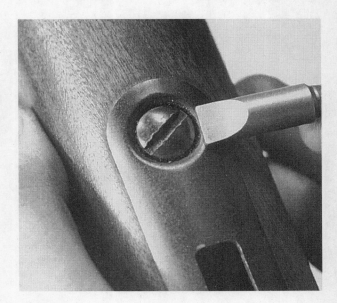

7. The rear sight is removable by taking out the two large screws on the left side, at the rear of the receiver. Further disassembly of the sight is not recommended.

8. Loosen the front sling loop screw and back out the sling loop. The rebated screw shaft will keep the unit on the stock. Back out the main stock mounting screw, located in the forward portion of the magazine plate on the underside, and separate the action from the stock. The barrel band can be taken off only after the front sight is drifted out of its dovetail.

9. Remove the screw at the front of the trigger bracket, on the underside of the receiver. Remove the screw at the rear of the trigger bracket. This screw also is the pivot for the safety-lever.

10. Remove the trigger bracket downward. The safety-lever is easily detached from the rear of the trigger bracket.

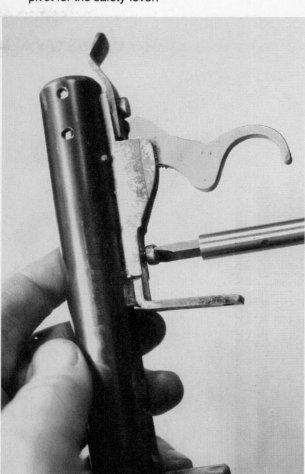

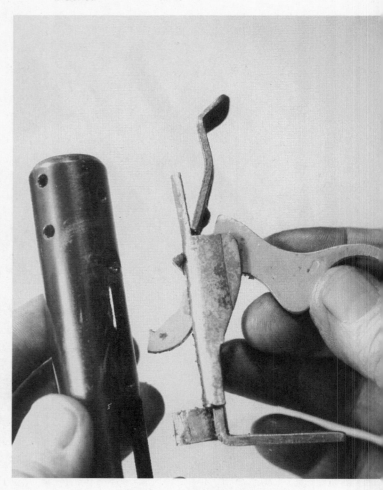

11. The trigger can now be moved forward, and then up out of its slot in the bracket. The cross pin at the top and the spring and plunger at the upper rear are easily detached from the trigger.

Reassembly Tips:

1. When replacing the trigger and safety system on the underside of the receiver, be sure the cross pin at the top of the trigger is positioned in its groove on the receiver, and install the front screw first. When inserting the safety-lever, use a small screwdriver to lift the trigger spring plunger onto the front tab of the safety-lever before installing the rear screw.

2. When replacing the action in the stock, the barrel ring, or band, must be oriented so its screw hole is at the bottom and aligned with the front sling loop screw.

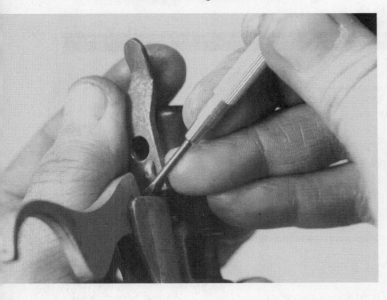

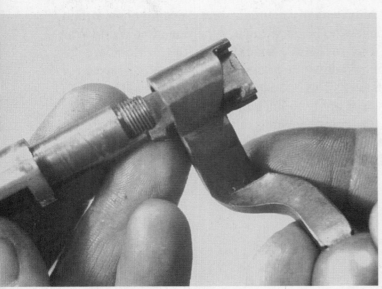

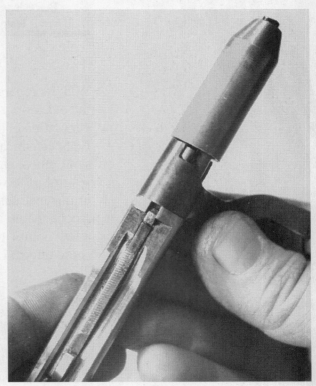

3. When replacing the striker and the bolt handle sleeve, note that the sleeve must be fitted onto the rear of the striker before the striker is fully inserted into the bolt.

4. Before the bolt is reinserted into the receiver, it must be recocked by firmly gripping the forward portion of the bolt and turning the bolt handle counterclockwise (rear view) until the striker lug is brought back to the cocked position, as shown.

Mossberg Model 151M

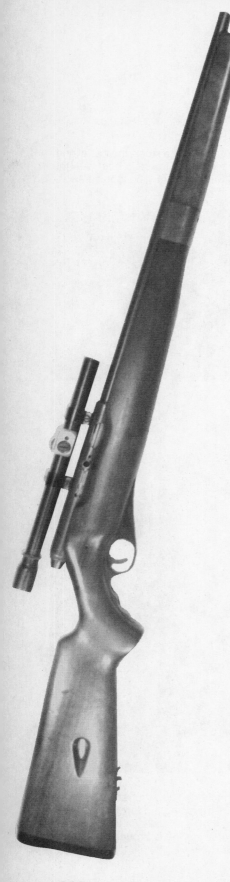

Data:	Mossberg Model 151M
Origin:	United States
Manufacturer:	O.F Mossberg & Sons
	North Haven, Connecticut
Cartridge:	22 Long Rifle
Magazine capacity:	15 rounds
Overall length:	40 inches
Barrel length:	20 inches
Weight:	7 pounds

With its separate front stock piece giving it a full "Mannlicher" look, the old Model 151M is instantly recognizable, especially to a certain generation of shooters who began using it in the year after World War II. Mechanically, the 151M is similar to the other Mossberg 22 semi-autos, and the takedown instructions can generally be used for several of those, as well. The knowledgeable shooter can see which of our instruction steps apply to his gun. There are many Mossberg mechanisms. The firing mechanism is relatively simple, but there are a few points in total disassembly and reassembly where the amateur could get into difficulty.

Disassembly:

1. Back out the screw on the underside of the front section of the stock, near the muzzle. The screw has a rebated shaft and will stay in the stock piece when it has cleared its threads in the barrel. Remove either of the two screws on the underside of the connector between the front section and the main stock, as shown, and remove the front section forward. The connector band will remain attached to either the stock or the front section, depending on which screw is removed. The upper sling swivel is normally on the band, but on the gun shown it is missing.

2. Back out the main stock mounting screw, on the underside of the stock, forward of the trigger guard, and separate the action from the stock.

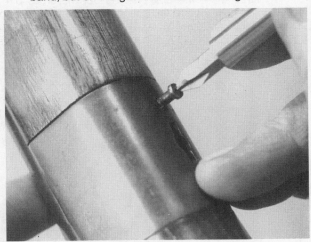

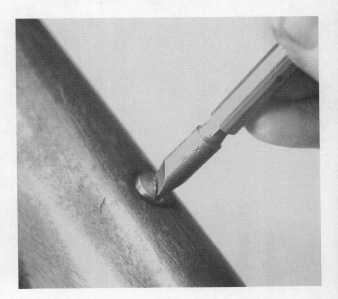

3. Being sure the striker is in fired position, unscrew the receiver end cap and remove it toward the rear.

4. Move the bolt toward the rear until the bolt handle aligns with the larger opening at the rear of its slot in the receiver, and remove the bolt handle toward the right.

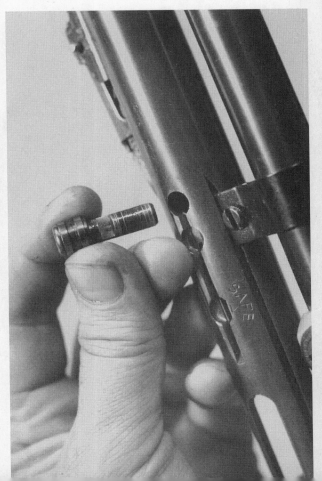

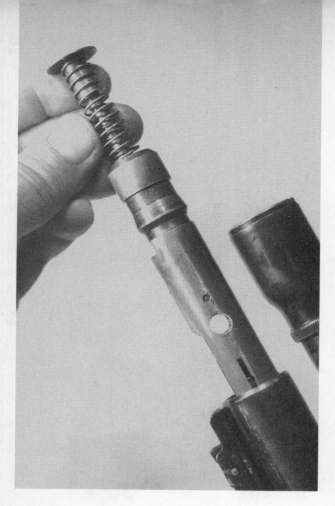

5. Remove the bolt assembly from the rear of the receiver.

6. Drifting out the cross pin in the bolt, just to the rear of the bolt handle hole, will release the striker and its spring, and the bolt spring and its guide, toward the rear. **Caution:** *Both of these springs are under tension, and this entire assembly will be instantly released when the drift pushing out the cross pin is withdrawn.* Retard the springs and let the tension off slowly.

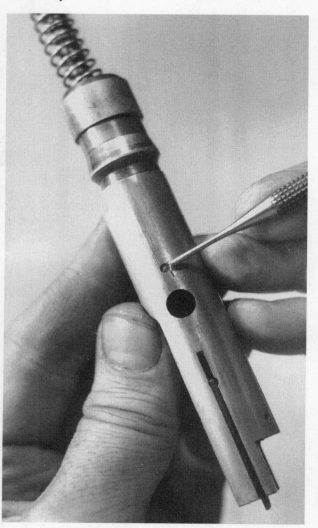

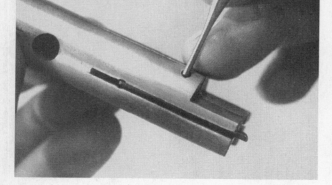

7. The extractor is retained by a vertical pin on the right side of the bolt near the front. After the pin is drifted out, the extractor and its coil spring are taken off toward the right.

8. The firing pin is retained in the top of the bolt by stake depressions (arrows) in the bolt above a notch near the rear of the firing pin. The stakes are usually not severe, and the firing pin can normally be driven out toward the front, swaging the stake marks as it passes them.

9. Support the disconnector mount on the underside of the receiver to avoid deformation, and drift out the cross pin in the disconnector. Remove the disconnector downward.

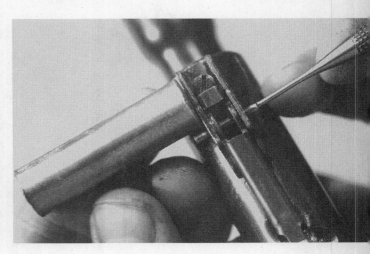

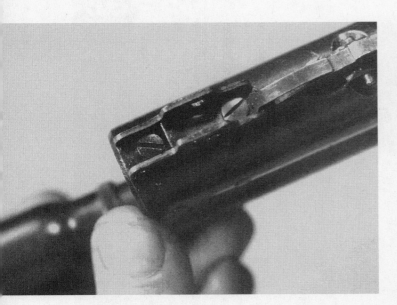

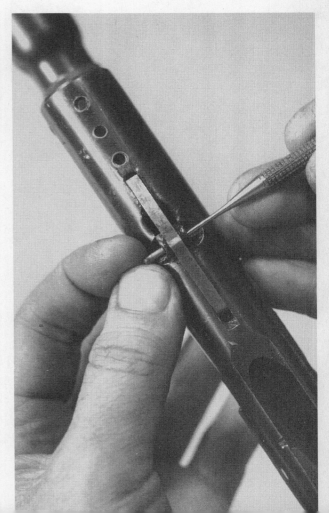

10. Take out the two screws in the disconnector mount. Remove the front screw first and take off the combination sear and disconnector spring. When both screws are removed take off the disconnector mount downward.

11. Push out the sear cross pin and remove the sear from the bottom of the receiver.

12. To remove the ejector, carefully pry its rear tail out the vertical recess on the outside left of the receiver, and move the ejector forward; then remove it toward the left.

13. Remove the inner magazine tube. Take out the outer magazine tube retaining spring by removing its screw, located inside the stock well forward of the end of the magazine tube.

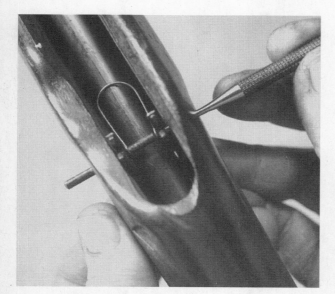

14. Push out the trigger pivot pin, which crosses the stock above the magazine tube, and remove the trigger spring upward.

15. The outer magazine tube assembly can now be moved up and forward, out of the stock, and the trigger taken out upward.

16. The cartridge stop (arrow) is normally powered and retained by a spring which is mounted on the outer magazine tube in the same manner as a pencil pocket clip. To release the cartridge stop, the tail of the spring must be gently pried out of its slot in the tube, and the spring slid back until it clears the stop. The stop is then slid downward off the tube. On the gun shown, an old repair has replaced the stop spring with a blade spring, screw-mounted in the stock well.

Reassembly Tips:

1. When replacing the bolt handle, align the handle hole in the bolt with the rear opening in the slot in the receiver, and be sure the handle is oriented so its cuts correspond with the narrow portion of the slot.

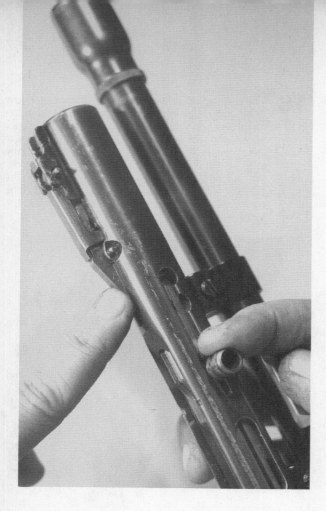

2. When moving the bolt forward, press in the front of the sear to allow the striker to pass, so there will be no tension on the spring.

3. When installing the trigger spring, put it in with its separate ends to the rear. This will allow easy insertion of the pin without tension. When the spring is mounted on the pin, swing each of the separate ends over forward to hook each one around the vertical extensions of the trigger.

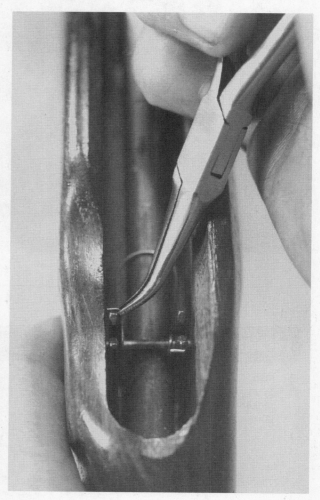

4. When replacing the action in the stock, pull the trigger very slightly to be sure its upper extensions properly engage the cross pin in the disconnector.

When replacing the outer magazine tube, be sure the angled tip of the retaining spring engages its recess on the underside of the magazine tube before tightening the spring mounting screw. When inserting the tube, use a tool to guide it at the rear, to ensure that it centers in its hole in the buttplate.

Avoid over-tightening the screw which retains the front section of the stock, as this screw has a tendency to break at the head.

Mossberg 640K

Similar/Identical Pattern Guns
The same basic assembly/disassembly steps for the Mossberg Model 640K also apply to the following guns.

Mossberg Model 640KS   **Mossberg Model 620K**

Data:	Mossberg 640K
Origin:	United States
Manufacturer:	O.F. Mossberg & Sons North Haven, Connecticut
Cartridge:	22 WMR (22 magnum)
Magazine capacity:	5 rounds
Overall length:	44$^3/_4$ inches
Barrel length:	24 inches
Weight:	6$^1/_4$ pounds

Marketed as the "Chuckster," the Model 640K was first offered in 1959, the same year the 22 WMR cartridge was introduced. Two other versions were offered, one with fancy wood and several gold-plated parts (the 640KS), and one in single shot only (the 620K). These two were discontinued in 1974, and the regular Model 640K was made until 1986. The instructions can be applied to all three versions.

Disassembly:

1. Remove the magazine, and back out the large screw on the underside in the front tip of the magazine plate. Separate the action from the stock. Removal of the small Phillips screw at the rear of the magazine plate, and at each end of the trigger guard, will allow these parts to be taken off downward.

2. Push the receiver endpiece latch downward, and remove the endpiece toward the rear.

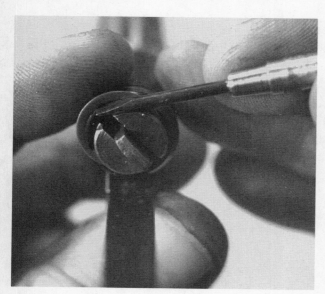

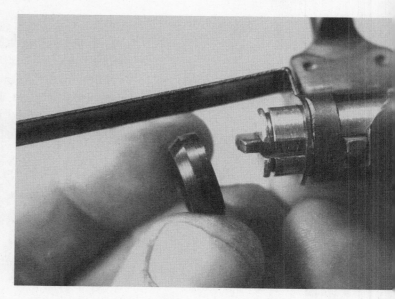

3. Open the bolt, and remove it toward the rear. Remove the C-clip (retaining ring) at the rear of the bolt.

4. Remove the bolt collar from the rear of the bolt.

5. Remove the bolt track cover plate from the rear of the bolt.

6. Remove the bolt handle assembly toward the rear, taking with it the firing pin. Turn the firing pin within the bolt handle until its lug is aligned with the groove inside the handle ring, tip the firing pin, and remove it toward the front.

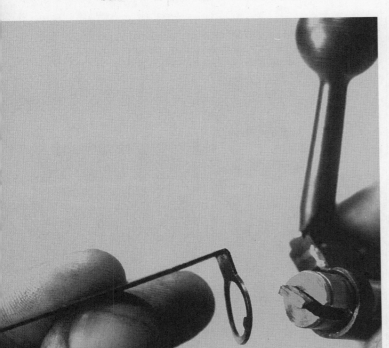

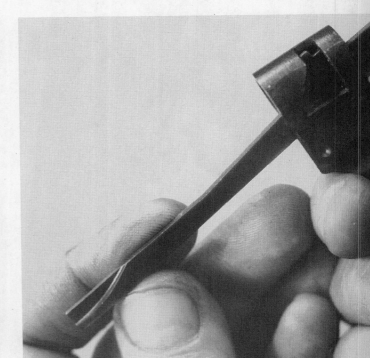

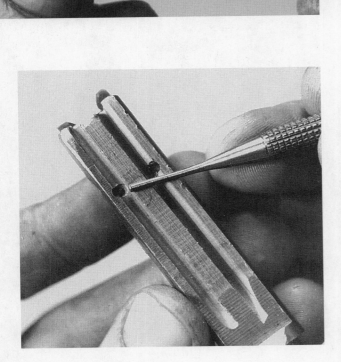

7. The extractors are retained by vertical pins on each side near the front of the bolt. The pins are drifted out upward to release the extractors and their small coil springs for removal toward each side.

8. Insert a tool inside the receiver to restrain the hammer, depress the sear lock on the right side, and pull the trigger. Ease the hammer down to the fired position. Push the hammer spring base out of its recesses in the front of the trigger housing, and remove the base and hammer spring assembly downward. The hammer spring assembly can be taken apart by removing the C-clip behind the base. **Caution:** *The spring is under compression. Control it, and ease it off.*

9. Unhook the rear arm of the sear lock spring from the right bar of the sear, and allow it to spring downward. Remove the spring from its groove in the tip of the hammer post.

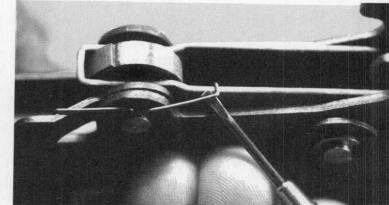

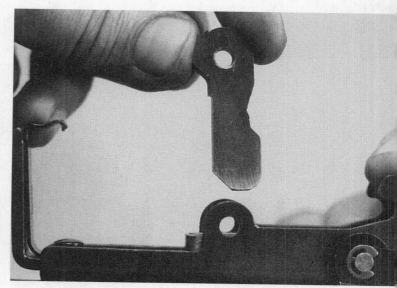

10. Push the hammer pivot pin toward the left. Remove the sear lock downward and toward the front.

11. Restrain the trigger, remove the hammer pivot pin toward the left, and take out the hammer downward. Release the trigger, and allow the sear and trigger assembly to pivot, relieving the spring tension.

12. Remove the C-clip from the cross pin in the top of the trigger, and take out the sear cross pin toward the right. Remove the sear toward the front. Allow the trigger to rotate further, completely easing the tension of its spring. Remove the C-clip from the tip of the trigger pin, take out the pin, and remove the trigger and its spring downward.

13. Remove the C-clip from the end of the safety pivot, and while doing this keep the right side of the gun upward. Push the safety pivot through to the inside, and remove it.

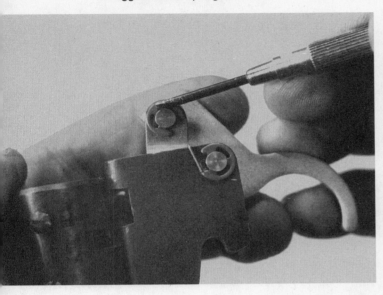

14. Take off the safety positioning spring. This will uncover the safety detent ball, lying in a hole in the safety-lever. Remove the ball, and take care that it isn't lost.

15. The safety-lever can't be taken off until the sub-frame (trigger housing) is removed. Remove the screw on the underside in the tail of the magazine guide bar and catch. Remove the magazine guide bar and catch downward.

16. The screw just removed also retains the ejector inside the receiver, and this part can now be removed.

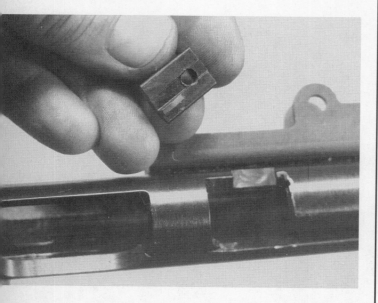

17. Remove the vertical screw on the inside of the sub-frame at the rear, and take off the sub-frame downward. The safety can now be removed from the top of the sub-frame.

Reassembly Tips:

When replacing the ejector in the receiver, note that the raised projection on the base must be on the left side of the gun. Use a fingertip to hold the ejector in place while installing the screw through the magazine catch and guide bar.

1. When replacing the trigger and its spring, note that the spring is positioned on the trigger as shown.

2. When inserting the sear for reattachment to the trigger at the rear, note that the front cross bar goes at the bottom, as shown, when viewed from the front. When the sub-frame is reassembled, the hammer must be recocked before the bolt can be put back into the receiver. Insert a tool through the bolt track, and push the hammer back to the fully cocked position.

3. When replacing the firing pin and the bolt handle, remember that the firing pin must be inserted into the handle ring before the two parts are put back on the bolt.

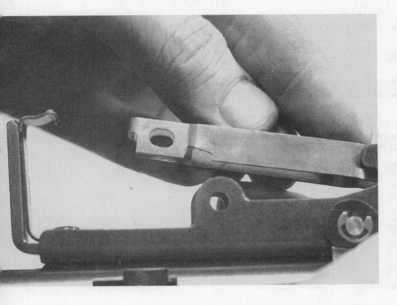

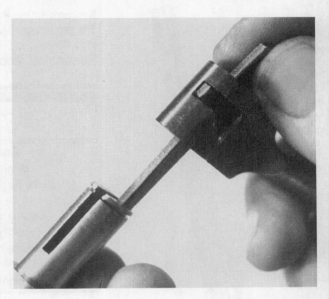

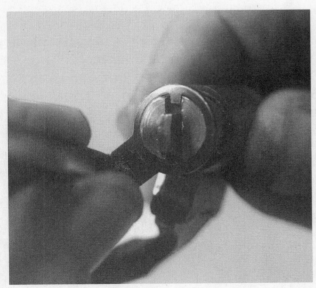

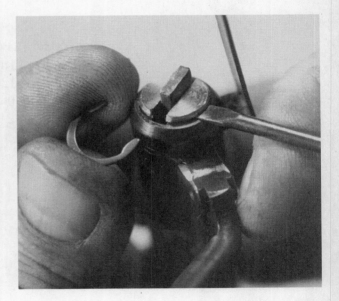

4. Note that the bolt track cover has an inner projection on its mounting ring that fits into the firing pin slot in the bolt, as shown.

5. When installing the C-clip on the rear of the bolt, use a small screwdriver to compress the cover ring. When installing the receiver end piece, have the bolt at the rear of the receiver, and lift the rear tip of the cover plate onto the end piece as it is moved into place.

Remington Model 121A

Similar/Identical Pattern Guns
The same basic assembly/disassembly steps for the Remington Model 121A also apply to the following guns:
Remington Model 121S   **Remington 121SB**

Data:	Remington Model 121A
Origin:	United States
Manufacturer:	Remington Arms Co. Illion, New York
Cartridge:	22 Long Rifle
Magazine capacity:	14 rounds
Overall length:	41 inches
Barrel length:	24 inches
Weight:	6 pounds

The Model 121A evolved from the earlier Model 12A, and while they are similar, there are numerous mechanical differences. There was also a Model 121S, chambered for the 22 WRF cartridge. A smoothbore version, the Model 121SB, was designed to use 22 shot rounds. The Model 121 guns were made from 1936 to 1954. They were marketed under the trade name "Fieldmaster."

Disassembly:

1. Remove the inner magazine tube and cycle the action to cock the hammer. Set the safety in the on-safe position. With a coin or a specially shaped screwdriver, loosen the takedown screw and pull it out until it stops.

2. Separate the buttstock and trigger group from the main receiver, toward the rear and downward.

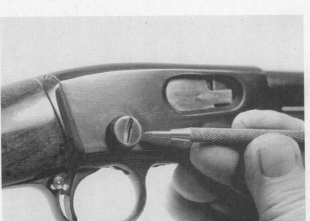

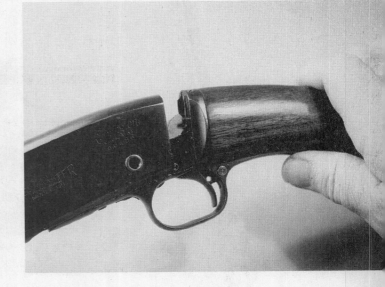

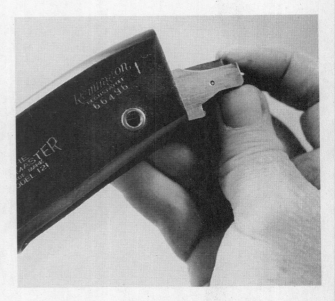

3. Move the action slide all the way to the rear, and tip the protruding rear of the bolt downward.

4. With the bolt held in that position, move the action slide back toward the front, and take out the bolt toward the rear.

5. Drift out the firing pin retaining cross pin.

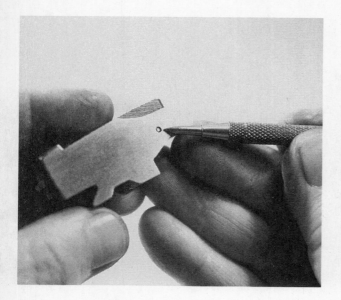

6. Remove the firing pin and its return spring toward the rear.

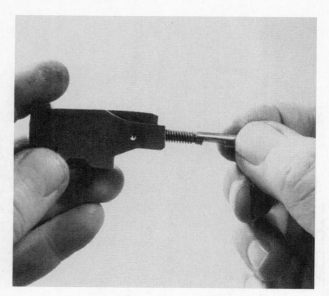

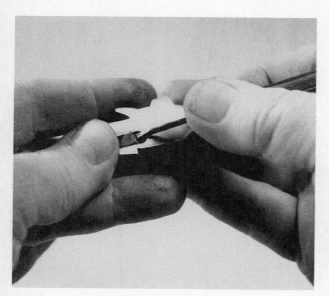

7. Insert a screwdriver between the extractor and its plunger. Depress the plunger rearward, and lever the extractor outward for removal. **Caution:** *Control the plunger and spring, and ease them out.*

8. Remove the screws on each side of the forend. Note that the screws are retained by lock screws, which must be removed first.

9. Move the forend forward until it is clear of the enlarged portion of the magazine housing.

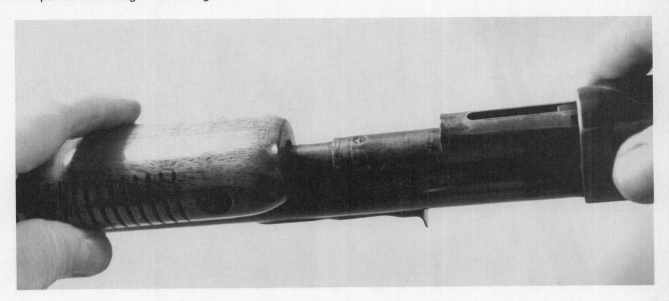

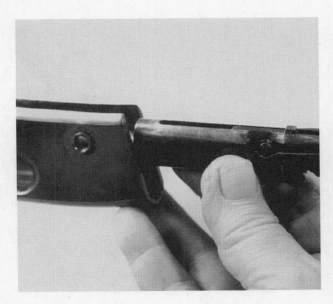

10. Remove the magazine housing toward the rear. The forend will be freed as the magazine housing clears it.

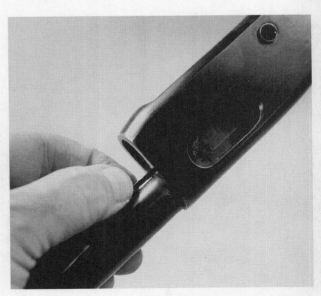

11. Lift the front portion of the cartridge guide and remove it toward the rear. **Caution:** *Lift it only enough to clear its retaining recess.*

12. To remove the magazine hanger, insert a tool or wooden dowel and unscrew it from the barrel.

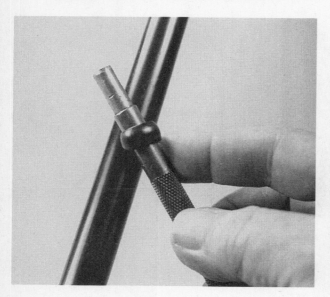

13. Remove the two wood screws that retain the stock buttplate and take it off. With a B-Square stock tool or a long screwdriver, remove the stock mounting bolt.

14. Remove the trigger group from the stock.

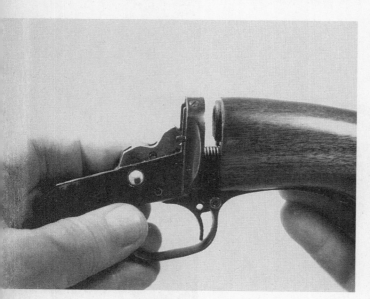

15. Move the safety to off-safe position. Insert a small tool or keeper pin in the cross hole in the hammer spring guide and pull the trigger, easing the hammer forward until the spring is trapped.

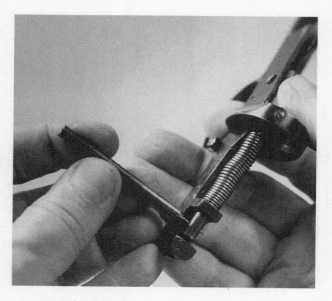

16. Use a large tapered drift to push out the hammer and carrier pivot sleeve.

17. Restrain the hammer and remove the tool or keeper pin from the guide. Ease the hammer assembly and carrier out toward the front and upward. **Caution:** *Control the spring.* The guide can be separated from the hammer by drifting out its cross pin, but this is usually staked in place, and it should be removed only if necessary for repair.

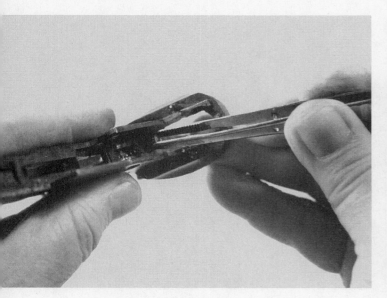

18. Remove the combination trigger and carrier spring and plunger from their well in the top of the trigger.

19. Drift out the trigger pin toward the right.

20. Remove the trigger upward.

21. Drift out the cross pin that retains the safety detent plunger and spring. **Caution:** *When the drift is withdrawn, the spring will be released, so control it.*

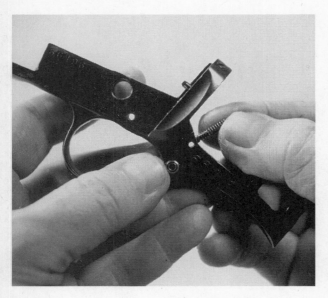

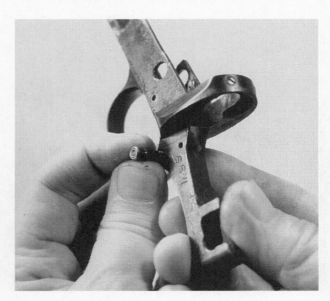

22. Remove the safety detent spring and plunger upward.

23. Remove the safety button toward either side.

24. Depress the carrier trip plunger, and the cartridge stop can be removed toward the rear.

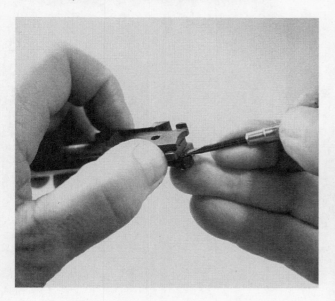

25. Removal of this screw, which retains the carrier trip plunger spring, will allow the spring and plunger to be taken out of the magazine housing.

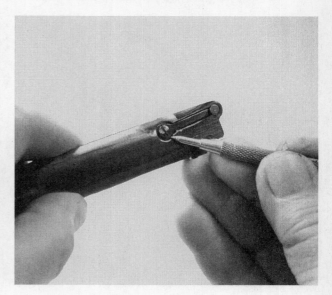

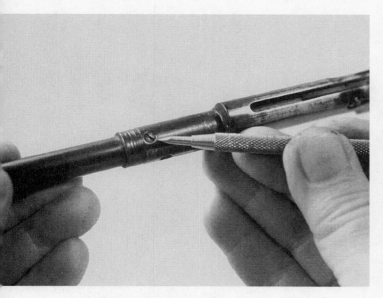

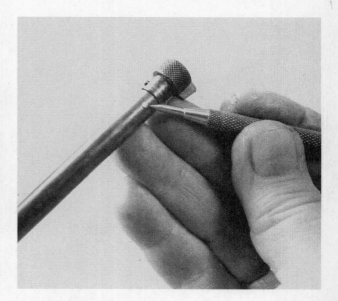

26. The outer magazine tube is screwed into the housing and is also retained by a lock screw. In normal takedown, this system should not be disturbed.

27. The inner magazine tube latch is pivoted and retained by a cross pin in the knob, inside the tube. For access, it is necessary to remove the knob by drifting out the lock pin. In normal takedown, this system is best left in place.

Reassembly Tips:

1. When installing the safety button, be sure the side with the recessed band is on the left, and that the square-cut recess is toward the trigger, as shown.

2. When installing the safety plunger and spring, insert a small tool to depress the spring as the cross pin is reinserted.

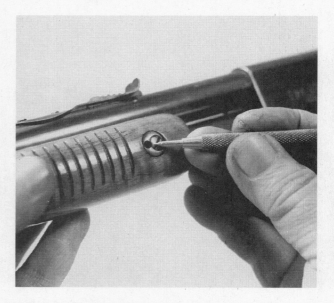

3. When installing the hammer and carrier system, be sure the rear tail of the carrier engages the plunger of the combination trigger and carrier spring. Use the pivot sleeve to hold the carrier in place while the hammer spring is compressed, and use the tool or keeper pin to hold it while the sleeve is removed and reinserted through the hammer and carrier.

4. When installing the forend screws, avoid over-tightening. Turn them until snug; then back them off slightly to install the lock screws.

Remington Model 341P

Similar/Identical Pattern Guns
The same basic assembly/disassembly steps for the Remington Model 341P also apply to following guns:

Remington Model 341A　　　　　　　　**Remington Model 341SB**

Data:	Remington Model 341P
Origin:	United States
Manufacturer:	Remington Arms Co. Bridgeport, Connecticut
Cartridge:	22 Short, Long, or Long Rifle
Magazine capacity:	22 Short, 17 Long, 15 Long Rifle
Overall length:	42$\frac{1}{4}$ inches
Barrel length:	24 inches
Weight:	6$\frac{1}{2}$ pounds

The Model 341 was made for a relatively short period, from 1936 to 1940, and the few examples that turn up occasionally on the market are snapped up by those who want an old-style bolt-action 22 with solid steel parts. The gun was offered in three versions: The 341A, with regular open rear sight, the 341P, with a receiver-mounted peep sight, and the 341SB, a smoothbore gun for use with 22 shotshells. The takedown and reassembly instructions apply to all three guns.

Disassembly:

1. If your gun is the Model 341P, with the peep sight, the sight must be either removed or swung up out of the way by taking out the rear mounting screw before the bolt can be taken out of the gun.

2. Open the bolt, hold the trigger pulled to the rear, and remove the bolt from the rear of the receiver.

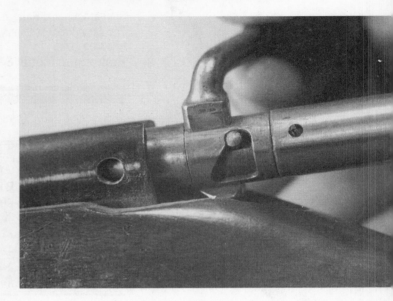

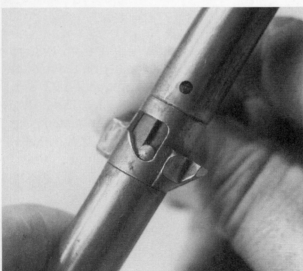

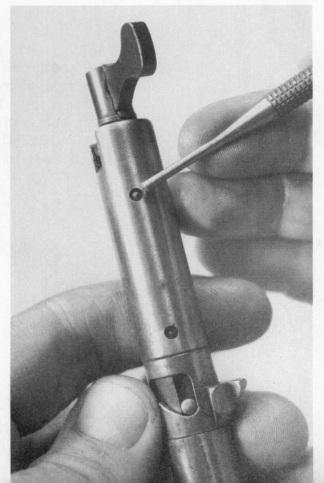

3. Grip the bolt firmly and turn the bolt handle clockwise (rear view) to allow the striker to move forward to the fired position, as shown.

4. Drift out the cross pin near the rear edge of the bolt end piece. **Caution:** *This will release the striker spring tension toward the rear, so control the parts and ease the tension slowly.*

5. Drift out the cross pin just to the rear of the bolt handle sleeve.

6. Push out the cocking cam pin.

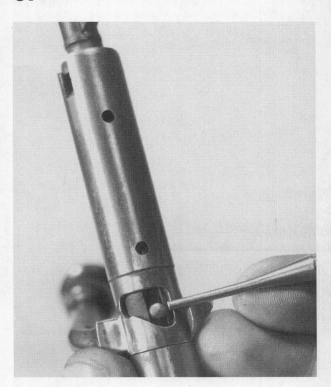

7. Remove the striker assembly toward the rear.

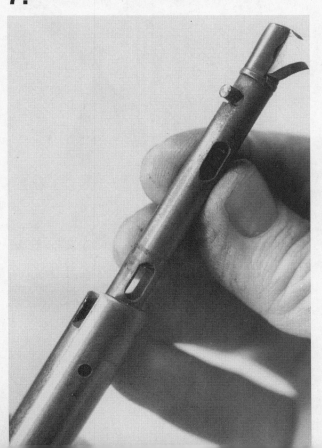

8. With the safety turned all the way to the left, insert a small diameter drift punch through the hole in the side of the striker and drive out the safety cam pin.

9. Remove the bolt sleeve toward the rear. Remove the bolt handle assembly toward the rear. Drift out the cross pin at the front of the bolt that retains the extractor.

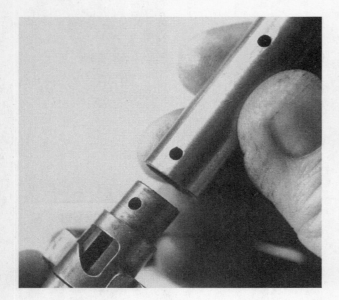

10. Restrain the extractor plunger and spring, and remove the extractor from its recess. Ease out the plunger and spring.

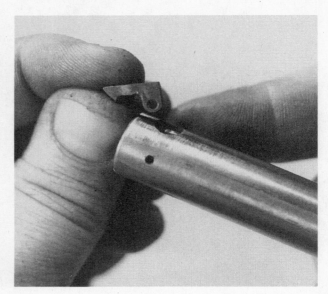

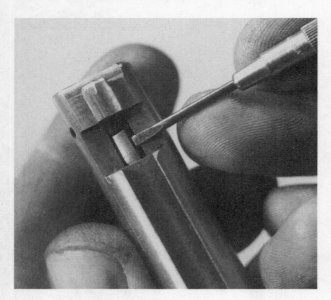

11. The ejector can now be moved toward the rear and then turned toward the side and removed from the interior of the bolt.

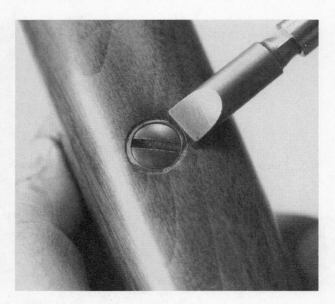

12. Remove the inner magazine tube and take out the large screw on the underside of the stock. Separate the action from the stock.

13. Drift out the sear cross pin on the side, near the center of the receiver.

14. This will release the trigger to swing forward, beyond its normal position, and the trigger spring and plunger can be moved from the upper rear of the trigger.

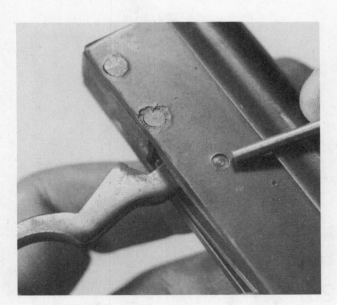

15. Drift out the trigger and carrier pivot cross pin.

16. Remove the trigger and the attached sear downward. The trigger and sear can be separated, if necessary, by drifting out the connecting cross pin.

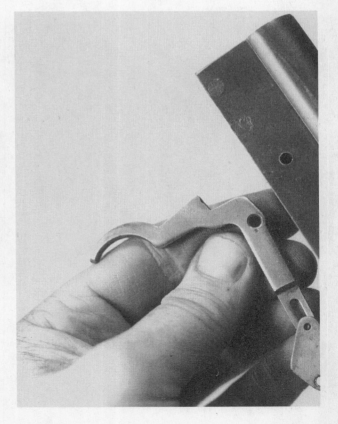

17. Remove the carrier toward the rear. **Caution:** *Take care to restrain the carrier tension plunger, spring and cup on the left side near the front as the carrier emerges from the receiver.*

18. Remove the tension plunger, spring and cup from the left side of the carrier.

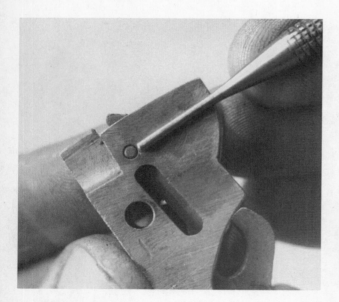

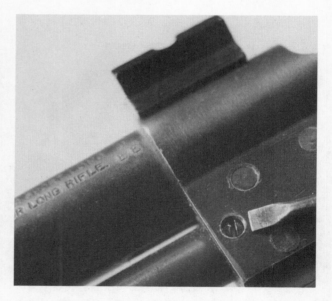

19. Drifting out the cross pin at the front of the carrier will free the cartridge stop for removal toward the front.

20. Backing out the small headless screw on the left side near the front of the receiver will release the outer magazine tube for removal toward the front. The magazine tube loop and spacer screw are both threaded into the underside of the barrel, and can be unscrewed for removal.

Reassembly Tips:

1. The cartridge slide, located inside the carrier, is riveted to a plate which is hooked into a slot in the bottom of the carrier. **Note:** The removal of this unit is definitely not recommended in normal takedown.

2. To avoid damage to the extractor when replacing the cross pin, insert a small drift punch from the other side to align the hole while driving the pin into place.

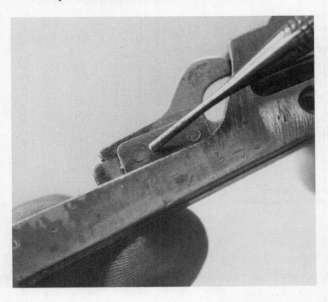

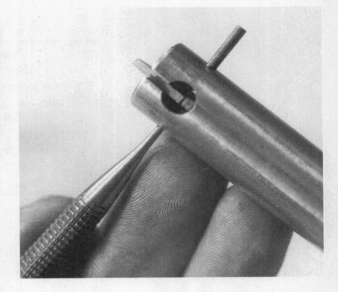

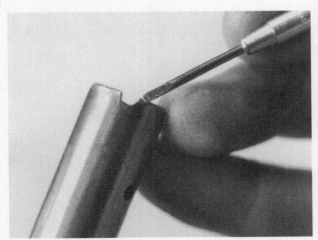

3. When replacing the bolt sleeve on the bolt, note that the small notch at the rear of the sleeve goes on the underside of the bolt.

4. When replacing the rear cross pin in the striker, use a screwdriver from the rear to depress the spring, and insert a drift punch to hold the spring while the pin is started into place. When driving in the two cross pins in the bolt sleeve that pass through the striker, take extreme care to ensure that all parts are in alignment, as it is possible to deform the pins or break the wings of the spring plunger if they are not.

Remington Model 522

Data:	Remington Model 522
Origin:	United States
Manufacturer:	Remington Arms Company Ilion, New York
Cartridge:	22 Long Rifle
Magazine capacity:	10 rounds
Overall length:	40 inches
Barrel length:	20 inches
Weight:	$4^5/_8$ pounds

Marketed as the "Viper," the Model 522 was introduced in 1993. With its mostly polymer construction, it fills the gap in the Remington line left by the discontinuance of the Nylon 66. Mechanically, it is more simple than that gun, but it has been designed so that several systems are not routinely dismountable. Operationally, though, it is an excellent and dependable gun.

Disassembly:

1. Remove the magazine, draw the bolt back, and push in the handle to lock the bolt open. Set the safety in on-safe position. Use a 1/8-inch Allen wrench or bit to remove the front action screw.

2. Remove the Allen screw at the rear of the trigger guard and take the action out of the stock.

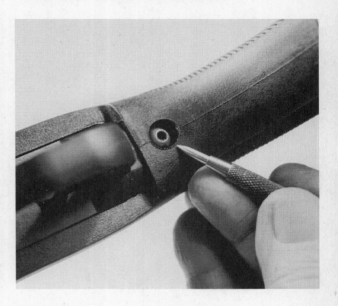

3. Pull the bolt handle outward and ease the bolt forward to closed position. Move the safety to off-safe position. Insert the magazine and pull the trigger to drop the striker to fired position. Remove the magazine. Push the barrel and receiver toward the rear and tip the lower housing downward at the front, as shown. Ease the housing off toward the rear, controlling the tension of the recoil spring and striker spring.

4. Remove the red-colored striker spring and guide toward the right.

5. Remove the recoil spring and its guide toward the left.

6. Move the bolt all the way to the rear and take out the striker assembly. The combination striker and firing pin unit is retained in the red polymer headpiece by a roll-type cross pin. Except for repair purposes, this system should be left in place.

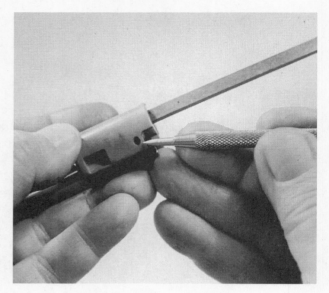

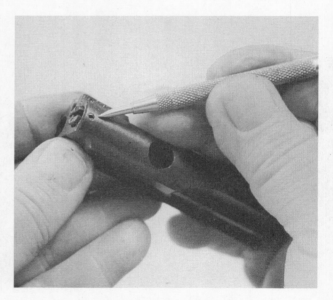

7. Align the bolt handle with its exit space in the track, and remove the handle toward the right.

8. Remove the bolt toward the rear. The striker rebound piece and its spring are retained at the right rear of the bolt by a roll-type cross pin. In normal takedown, this system is best left in place. If removal is necessary, restrain the rebound piece, as the spring is quite strong.

9. To remove the extractor, use a small tool to depress the plunger rearward, and lift out the extractor. **Caution:** *Control the plunger and spring and ease them out.*

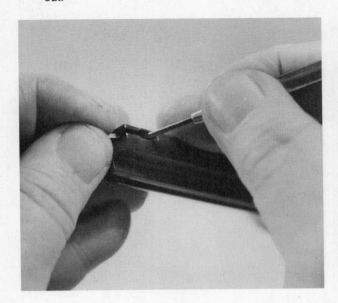

10. The twin sears are pivoted on a pin that goes across the bottom of the receiver. If the sears are to be removed for repair, note their relative positions for reassembly.

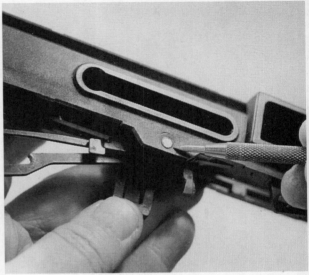

11. On the left side of the receiver, the sear pin is heat-sealed. For removal, the polymer must be softened with a small soldering iron. In normal takedown, this system should not be disturbed.

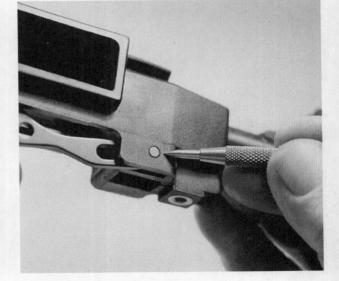

12. The bolt holdopen device and its spring can be removed by pushing the pin toward the left just far enough to clear the part.

13. If removal of the safety is necessary, insert a tool inside the lower housing to nudge the pin outward. **Caution:** *The safety detent spring and plunger will be released upward.* After the spring and plunger are removed, the safety can be pushed out of its cross-tunnel.

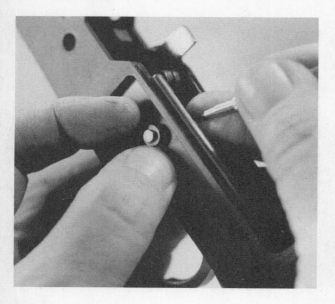

14. Pushing out this cross pin will release the trigger assembly and trigger spring for removal. **Caution:** *The spring will be freed, so control it.* The trigger must be turned during removal to withdraw its forward arm (the magazine safety) from beneath the bridge in the housing. The trigger bar is attached by a cross-screw. If the trigger assembly has been removed (it is still in place here), pushing out this cross pin will release the trigger bar spring for removal. **Caution:** *Control the spring.*

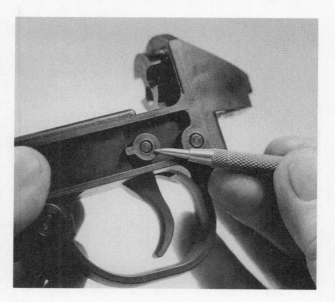

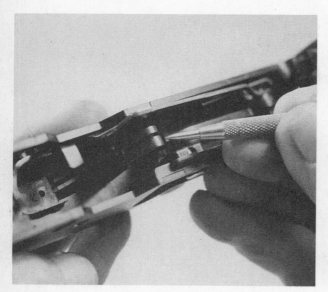

15. The blade-type springs that power the twin sears are heat-locked into a mount in the floor of the lower housing. They are not routinely removable.

16. This small screw secures a bracket plate and the combination ejector and magazine catch. Removal of the screw will free the plate, but because of the heat-sealed bridge, the ejector/magazine catch is not routinely removable.

17. The front sight is retained by a single screw. The rear sight base is retained by two screws. The adjustment slide must be moved for access to the rear one.

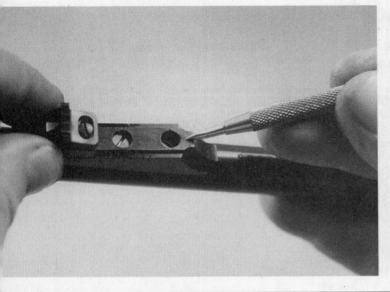

Reassembly Tips:

1. When installing the striker spring and the recoil spring, remember that the red-colored striker spring goes on the right, and the black-colored recoil spring guide goes on the left. To help with this, the guide heads are of different sizes.

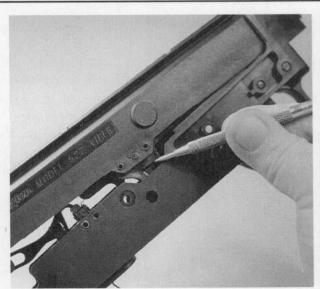

2. With the springs properly engaged, move the lower housing forward and upward until its latch at lower front engages. There is an assembly guide on the left side of the receiver that helps in proper placement.

3. Before the action is put back into the stock, lock the bolt in open position to keep tension on the housing latch. The safety must be in on-safe position when the action is put back in the stock.

Remington Model 550

Similar/Identical Pattern Guns

The same basic assembly/disassembly steps for the Remington Model 550 also apply to the following guns:

Remington Model 550P   **Remington Model 550-2G**

Remington Model 550A

Data:	Remington Model 550
Origin:	United States
Manufacturer:	Remington Arms Company
	Bridgeport, Connecticut
Cartridge:	22 Short, Long, or Long Rifle
Magazine capacity:	22 Shorts, 17 Longs, 15 Long Rifles
Overall length:	$43^1/_2$ inches
Barrel length:	24 inches
Weight:	$6^1/_4$ pounds

Introduced in 1941, the Model 550 was the first 22-caliber semi-auto to use all three 22 rimfire cartridges interchangeably. It accomplished this with a unique "floating chamber" which allowed the Short cartridge to deliver the same impact to the bolt as the longer rounds. During its time of production several sub-models were offered—the 550A, 550P, and so on, with different sight options. All of the 550 series guns are mechanically identical, and the same instructions will apply.

Disassembly:

1. Back out the stock mounting screw on the underside of the stock, and separate the action from the stock. If necessary, the stock screw can be removed by moving it out until its threads engage the threads in its escutcheon, and then unscrewing it.

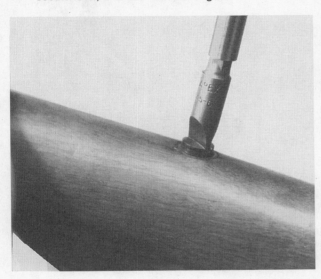

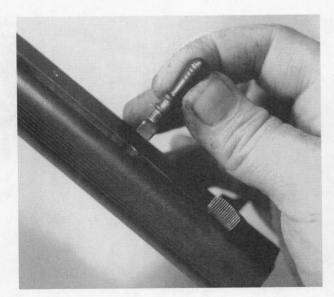

3. Move the bolt all the way to the rear, until the bolt handle aligns with the opening at the end of its track, and remove the bolt handle toward the right.

4. Use a small tool to push the bolt toward the rear, and remove it from the rear of the receiver.

2. Pull the trigger to release the striker, so it will be in the fired position, and unscrew the receiver end cap at the rear of the receiver. If the end cap has been over-tightened, there is a large coin slot at the rear of its dome to aid in starting it. Remove the end cap and its attached spring guide, and the bolt spring and striker spring and guide toward the rear. The springs are under some tension, but not so much that the end cap can't be easily controlled. The springs are easily removed from the guide on the end cap, but the hollow guide is not removable. Take care not to lose the collar at the front of the bolt spring.

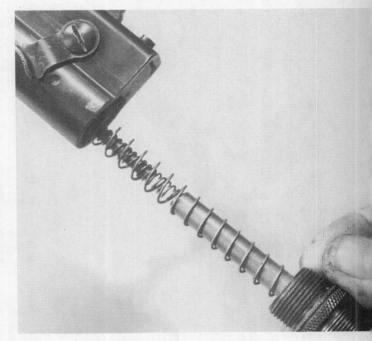

5. Remove the striker (firing pin) from the rear of the bolt.

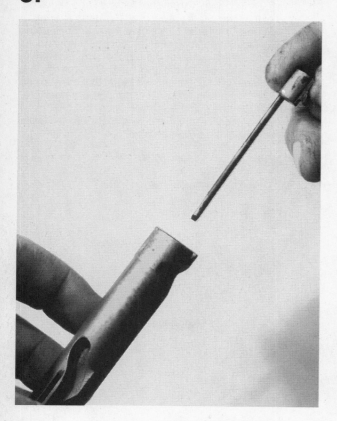

6. Use a small screwdriver to depress the extractor spring plunger, and lift the extractor out of its recess in the bolt. **Caution:** *Take care that the plunger and spring don't get away, as the compressed spring can propel the parts quite a distance.* They are very small and difficult to locate.

7. Remove the small screw and washer on the underside of the receiver near the rear edge, and take out the L-shaped end cap lockplate.

8. With the safety in the on-safe position, remove the safety screw and take off the safety-lever toward the right. The safety tumbler can then be moved inward and removed toward the rear. As the tumbler is moved inward, the trigger spring will move its plunger upward, so control it and ease its tension slowly. Next, drift out the trigger pin and the trigger limit pin. The trigger will be freed, but can't be removed at this point because of its attached disconnector assembly.

9. Drift out the cross pin in the forward section of the receiver, and remove the carrier assembly and its spring downward. The two leaves of the carrier, the spacer bushing, and the spring are easily separated. This pin also is the sear pivot, and the sear can now be moved forward and taken out downward.

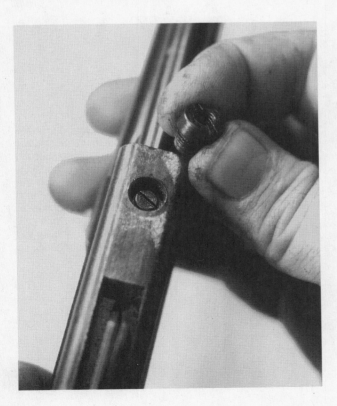

10. Remove the screw-slotted sear spring housing (looks like a large screw head) from the bottom center of the receiver, along with the sear spring it contains. The housing is often found staked in place, and some effort may be required to start it. **Caution:** *Never try to remove the housing while the sear is still in place on its cross pin, or the parts are likely to be damaged.* The trigger assembly may now be moved upward into the receiver, then forward, and out the carrier opening. The disconnector system may be separated from the trigger by drifting out the small cross pin, releasing the disconnector and its spring and plunger. However, the cross pin is usually riveted in place, and during routine disassembly it is best left undisturbed.

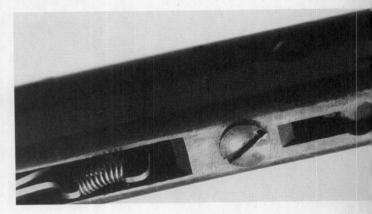

11. Removal of the stock mounting base at the lower front of the receiver will give access to a small screw beneath it. Taking out this screw will allow removal of the outer magazine tube toward the front. This will also release the receiver insert—the sub-frame which forms the cartridge guide—and allow it to be pushed out toward the rear. The insert is often tight, and may require the use of a hammer and nylon drift to start it. Take care that it is not deformed during removal. The ejector is staked in place in the left wall of the receiver, and no attempt to remove it should be made during normal disassembly.

Reassembly Tips:

1. When replacing the striker in the bolt, be sure its slim forward portion enters its tunnel in the bolt, and that the striker goes all the way forward. This can be checked on the underside of the bolt, as shown.

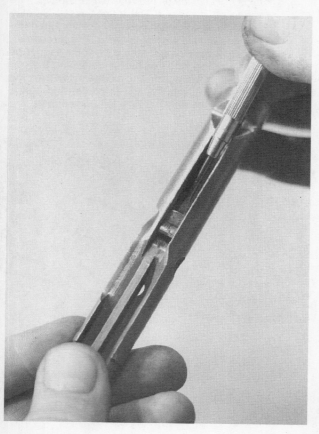

3. Before replacing the receiver end cap, be sure the springs are in the proper order, with the striker spring guide in the front of the spring, and the collar on the front of the bolt spring, as shown.

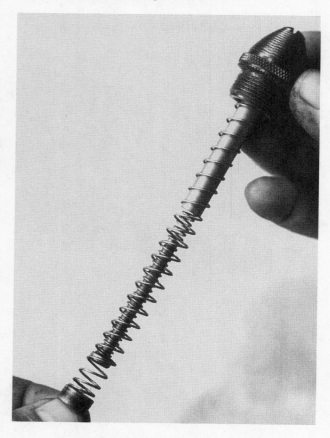

When installing the sear and sear spring system, put the sear and carrier system in place, and insert a smaller diameter rod or drift through the pin hole to keep them in general position. Then install the sear spring housing, being sure the top of the spring enters its recess in the underside of the sear. Next, move the sear downward and toward the rear, engaging its rear lobe with the collar on the housing. When it is in position, insert the cross pin, pushing out the smaller diameter rod or drift. This is the most difficult point in the reassembly of the Model 550.

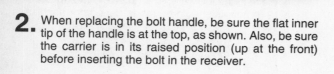

2. When replacing the bolt handle, be sure the flat inner tip of the handle is at the top, as shown. Also, be sure the carrier is in its raised position (up at the front) before inserting the bolt in the receiver.

Remington Model 552

Similar/Identical Pattern Guns

The same basic assembly/disassembly steps for the Remington Model 552 also apply to the following guns:

Remington Model 552C

Remington Model 552GS

Remington Model 552BDL

Data:	Remington Model 552
Origin:	United States
Manufacturer:	Remington Arms Company Bridgeport, Connecticut
Cartridge:	22 Short, Long or Long Rifle
Magazine capacity:	20 Short, 17 Long, 15 Long Rifle
Overall length:	42 inches
Barrel length:	25 inches
Weight:	$5^1/_2$ pounds

The Model 552 was intended to be the 22-caliber counterpart of the centerfire Model 742. It does have somewhat similar looks and handling qualities, though it's lighter, of course. Introduced in 1958, the 552 is still in production and is marketed under the name "Speedmaster," a name that was used earlier for the Model 241. The Model 552 has also been offered in a carbine version with a 21-inch barrel (552C), and a Gallery Special gun in 22 Short only chambering. The instructions apply to all of these.

Disassembly:

1. Remove the inner magazine tube and cycle the bolt to cock the hammer. With a non-marring tool such as a brass or bronze drift punch, push out the large cross pin at the rear of the receiver and the smaller cross pin at the center of the receiver. It may be necessary to tap the drift with a small hammer to start the pins out.

2. Remove the trigger group downward and toward the rear.

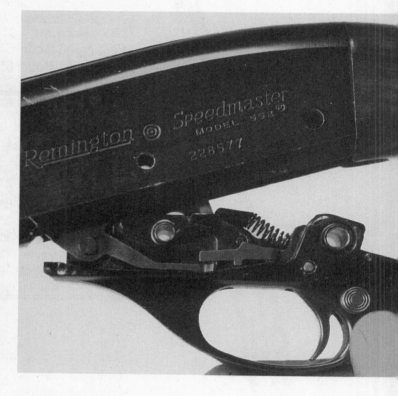

3. Restrain the hammer against the tension of its spring, pull the trigger, and ease the hammer down to the fired position. Remove the small spring clip from the right end of the front cross pin sleeve and push the sleeve out toward the left. This will free the carrier and its spring for removal from the right side of the group. **Caution:** *The carrier spring is strong and is under some tension, so restrain the carrier and ease it off.*

4. Pull the trigger and hold it back to relieve the tension on the rear cross pin sleeve; then push it out toward the left with its spring clip left in place.

5. Removal of the cross pin sleeve will allow the trigger top to move further to the rear, relieving the tension of the trigger/sear spring. Flex the spring away from its stud on the back of the sear and remove the spring upward.

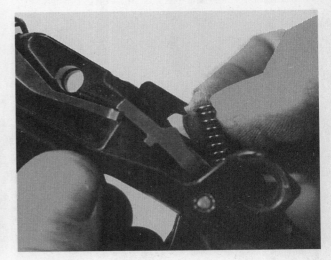

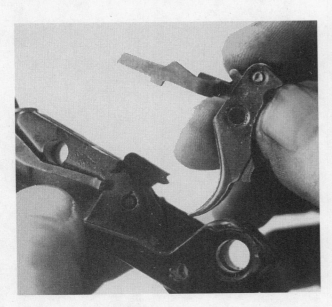

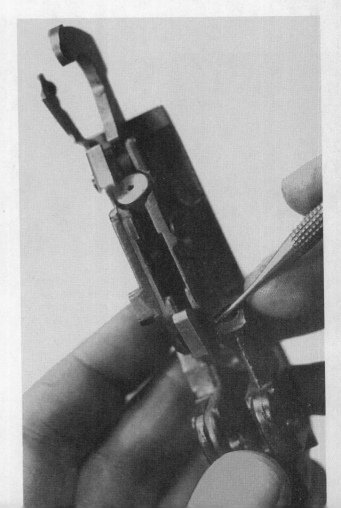

6. Drift out the trigger cross pin and remove the trigger, with its attached connector bar, upward. The two leaves of the connector are riveted at the top of the trigger and removal in normal takedown is not advisable.

7. Insert a small drift punch on the right side of the trigger group, as shown, and push out the sear pivot toward the left. The sear is then removed upward.

8. Push out the small cross pin at the extreme rear of the trigger group and remove the safety spring and ball upward. The safety can then be slid out toward either side. **Caution:** *The spring is under some tension, so hold a fingertip over the top of the hole when removing the drift punch to control it.* If the detent ball can't be shaken out the top after removal of the spring, wait until the safety is taken out, and then insert a small drift punch from the top and push it out into the safety channel. Take care that this small steel ball isn't lost.

9. A large cross pin with an enlarged head on the left side pivots and retains both the hammer and the disconnector, and the pin is riveted over a washer on the right side of the trigger group (illus.). Because of the riveting, a drift punch of smaller diameter than the pin body must be used. Be sure the disconnector is well supported when driving out the pin, to avoid damage. **Caution:** *Removal of the disconnector will also release the hammer spring and plunger, so take care to restrain them and ease them out.*

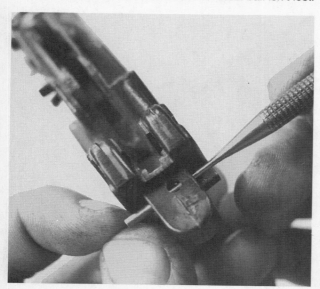

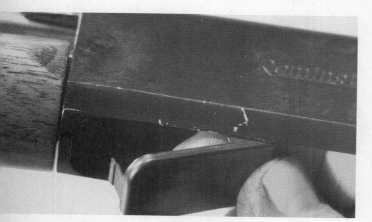

10. Slide the receiver coverplate on the underside about a quarter inch toward the rear, and insert a finger inside the receiver from the rear to tip its front end outward. Pivot it over toward the rear and remove it.

11. With a coin or a specially shaped screwdriver, remove the large screw on the underside of the forend. Move the rear of the forend slightly downward to clear the forward extension of the receiver, and slide the forend forward on the magazine tube. It is not removed at this point.

13. Restrain the tension of the bolt spring by holding onto the action bar, and carefully detach the rear vertical lug of the action bar from its recess in the side of the bolt. Remove the bolt toward the rear and ease the action bar forward, relieving the tension of the spring.

12. Move the barrel assembly forward out of the receiver.

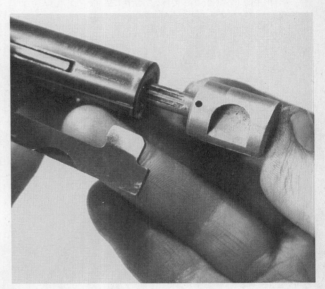

14. Remove the small screw on the underside of the front magazine tube hanger and slide the outer magazine tube out toward the front.

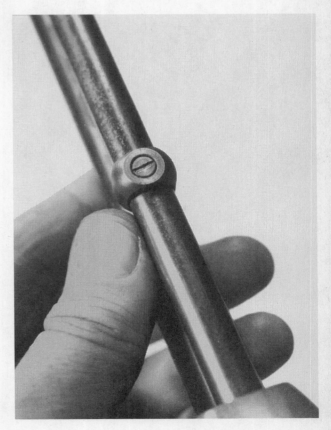

15. Removal of the magazine tube will release the forend piece, action bar and bolt spring to be taken off downward. The front magazine tube hanger has a threaded mounting post and is unscrewed from the underside of the barrel. The steel support piece at the front of the forend can be slid out forward.

16. The firing pin is retained by a small cross pin in the larger rear portion of the bolt, and after removal of the pin it can be taken off upward.

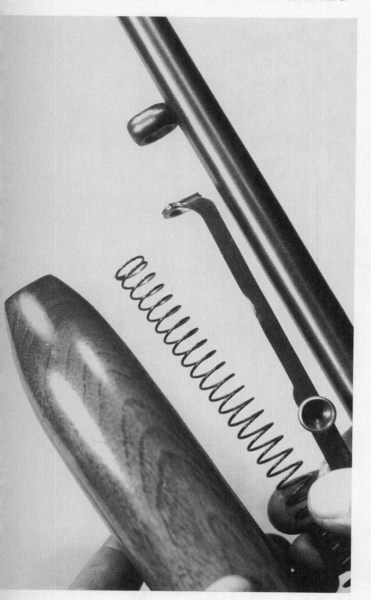

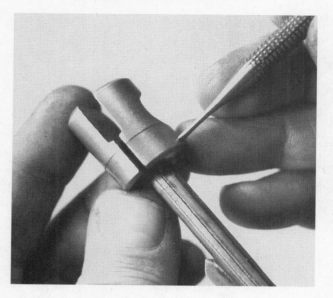

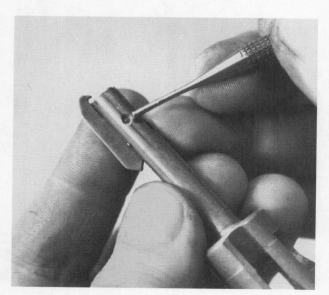

17. After the firing pin is removed, the very short vertical pin that retains the extractor can be driven out, and the extractor and its coil spring can then be taken off toward the right.

18. Inside the receiver at the rear is a steel bolt buffer and a rubber buffer pad. With the gun inverted, these can be pried upward out of their recess and removed. The stock is retained by a through-bolt from the rear, accessible by removing the buttplate.

19. To remove the ejector, insert a small screwdriver at its rear and move the ejector forward. When its front end can be grasped, tip it outward and remove it toward the left. The rear magazine tube hanger is removed in the same manner as the front one, by simply unscrewing it, and this will release the cartridge ramp that it retains.

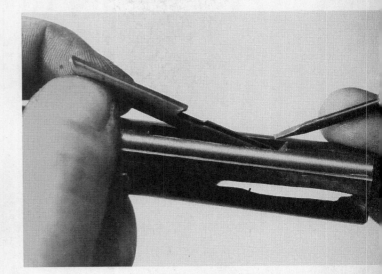

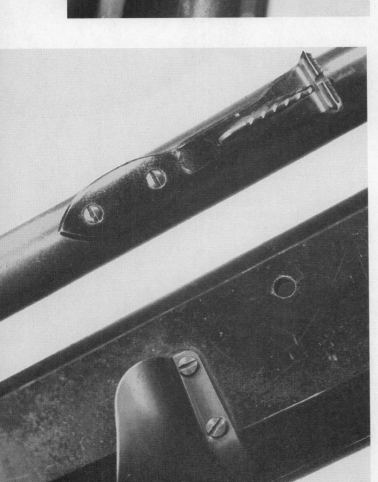

20. The rear sight and the shell deflector are each retained by two small screws. On some Model 552 rifles, the front sight is also retained by two screws. Others have a standard dovetail mount.

Reassembly Tips:

1. When replacing the extractor pivot pin in the slim forward section of the bolt, take care that it does not protrude into the firing pin recess at the top.

2. When replacing the safety in the trigger group, remember that the side with the red band goes on the left side. When replacing the trigger and its attached connector bars, note that the left connector arm must be installed *above* the rear tip of the disconnector, as shown.

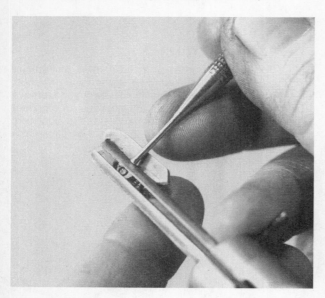

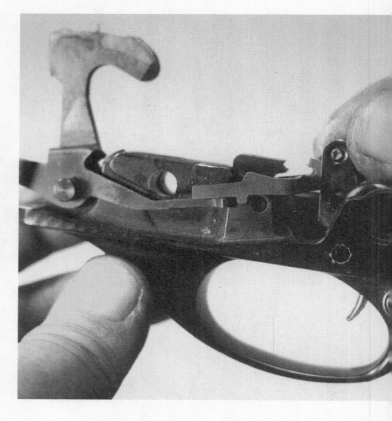

3. Before replacing the barrel assembly in the receiver, put all the components together prior to insertion. The photo shows the proper engagement of the action bar and the bolt. Take care that the lug of the action bar doesn't slip out of its recess in the bolt as the assembly is being slid back into the receiver.

4. To replace the receiver coverplate on the underside, invert the gun and start the plate with its inner surface facing outward. Press it inward, compressing its rear side wings; then swing it over forward until it can be snapped into its retaining grooves.

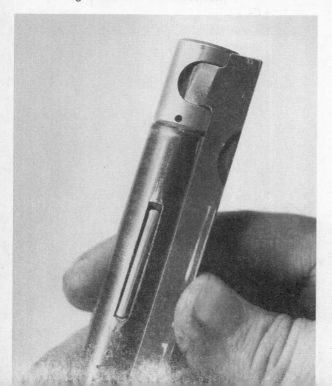

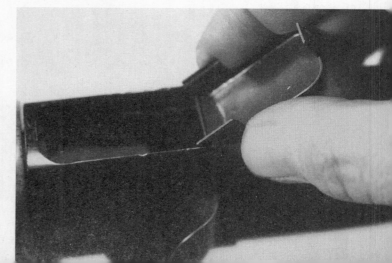

Remington
Model 581

Similar/Identical Pattern Guns
The same basic assembly/disassembly steps for the Remington Model 581 also apply to
the following gun:
Remington Model 581-S

Data:	Remington Model 581
Origin:	United States
Manufacturer:	Remington Arms Company
	Bridgeport, Connecticut
Cartridge:	22 Short, Long, or Long Rifle
Magazine capacity:	5 rounds
Overall length:	$42^3/_8$ inches
Barrel length:	24 inches
Weight:	$4^3/_4$ pounds

The Model 581 was introduced in 1967 and was made until 1984. For
many shooters it served the same purpose as the 512 and 513 for an
earlier generation. The 581 was supplied with a single shot adapter,
a useful accessory when teaching youngsters to shoot. It was also
available in a left-handed version, the mechanical details being the
same.

Disassembly:

1. Remove the magazine, and use a wide, thin-bladed screwdriver to back out the main stock mounting screw, on the underside just forward of the magazine well. Separate the action from the stock. To remove the bolt, open it and move it toward the rear while pushing the safety-lever forward, beyond its normal off-safe position. Withdraw the bolt from the rear of the receiver.

2. Grip the underlug of the striker head, at the rear of the bolt, in a sharp-edged bench vise, and be sure it is firmly held. Push forward on the bolt end piece, against the tension of the striker spring, and unscrew the forward portion of the bolt from the end piece. **Caution:** *The powerful spring is under heavy tension, so control the bolt as the threaded section is cleared.*

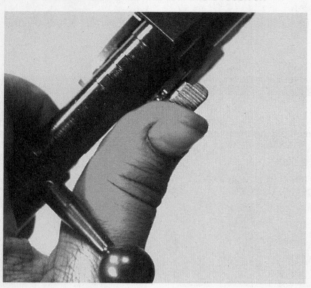

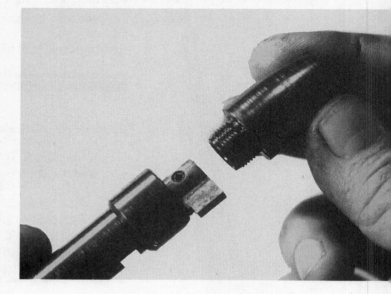

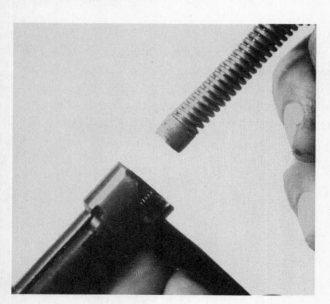

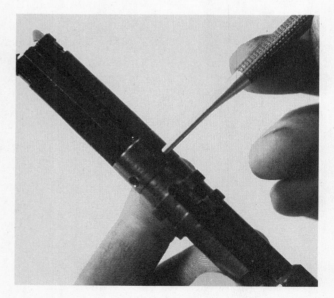

3. Remove the striker and its captive spring assembly from the rear of the bolt. The striker head may be separated from the front portion of the striker by drifting out the roll cross pin. This will release the striker spring with force, so proceed with caution. In normal disassembly, this unit is best left intact. If it is taken apart, take care not to lose the compression washer, located between the spring and the striker head.

4. A solid cross pin near the forward end of the bolt body retains the breechblock on the front of the bolt. Drifting out the cross pin will allow the breechblock to be taken off toward the front.

5. Use a small screwdriver to gently pry the left end of the semi-circular spring-clip at the front of the bolt upward. Flexing the left extractor very slightly outward will make insertion of the screwdriver tip easier. Take care to lift the clip only enough to slip it off, as it will break if flexed too far.

6. After the spring clip has been removed, the extractors are easily removed from their recesses on each side, and the firing pin can be taken out of its slot in the top. Note that the extractors are not identical, and each must be returned to the proper side in reassembly.

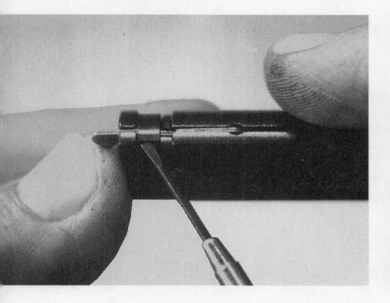

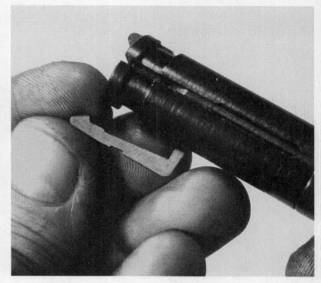

7. The safety-lever is mounted on the trigger housing by its pivot post at the rear and a guide post at the front, and these posts are retained on the left side of the housing by C-clips. Carefully remove the C-clips, guarding against their loss, and take out the two mounting posts toward the right.

8. Remove the safety-lever toward the right. **Caution:** *As the safety-lever is removed, the safety plunger and spring will be released from their cross-hole in the housing.* Control them during removal, and take them out of the housing. The safety plunger and spring will usually come out of the housing together. If not, it may be necessary to use a small screwdriver to lift out the spring.

9. The large pin at the upper rear of the trigger housing is the sear pivot pin. It is sometimes mistaken for the trigger group retaining pin, and is drifted out in error. This will release the sear within the housing, and the housing must then be removed to replace the sear and its spring in proper order.

10. The trigger housing retaining pin is a roll pin at the upper center of the housing. Drifting out this cross pin will allow the trigger housing to be taken off downward. When the housing is removed, the bolt stop and its spring can be lifted from their well in the top of the housing, and the sear is easily removed by drifting out its cross pin.

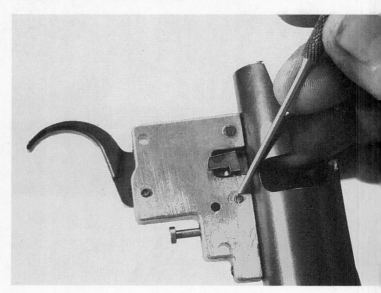

11. The trigger is retained by a roll cross pin at the lower edge of the housing, and is removed downward. The same coil spring powers both the sear and the trigger.

12. The housing tension screw at the extreme front edge of the housing can be backed out if the housing mounting pin is unusually tight, as this will ease tension on the cross pin.

13. Backing out the single screw at the rear of the magazine catch will allow removal of the magazine catch and magazine guide downward. The ejector is an integral part of the magazine guide.

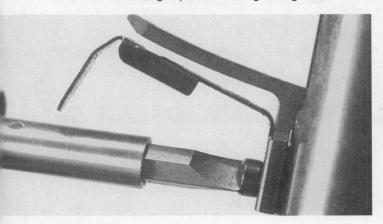

14. Removal of the large screw just forward of the rear sight will allow the sight and sight base to be taken off upward.

Reassembly Tips:

1. When replacing the safety-lever, seat the tip of the safety spring plunger in the larger, dished-out recess on the inside of the lever while pushing the safety into place. In this position, the plunger will be less likely to slip out during installation.

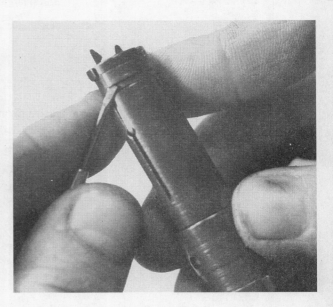

2. When replacing the semi-circular spring clip at the front of the bolt that retains and powers the extractors, note that the small central projection at its top must go toward the front, and its split wing toward the left. Use a small screwdriver to guide its lower end over the extractor as it is pushed into place.

When replacing the extractors, note that the one with the sharp break must be placed on the right.

Remington No. 4

Data:	Remington No. 4
Origin:	United States
Manufacturer:	Remington Arms Company Ilion, New York
Cartridge:	22 Long Rifle
Overall length:	37 inches
Barrel length:	$22^1/_2$ inches
Weight:	$4^1/_2$ pounds

One of the premium "boy's rifles" of earlier times, the No. 4 "rolling block" was made from 1890 to 1933. Up to 1901, the gun was a non-takedown design with a fixed barrel. From 1901 to 1926, the barrel was retained by a lever, as on the gun shown here. From 1926 to 1933, the lever was replaced by a large knurled screw with a coin slot.

Disassembly:

1. Turn the barrel latch lever over toward the front, and separate the barrel assembly from the action.

2. The forend is retained on the barrel by a single screw. The front and rear sights are dovetail-mounted.

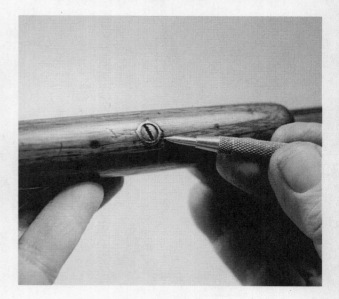

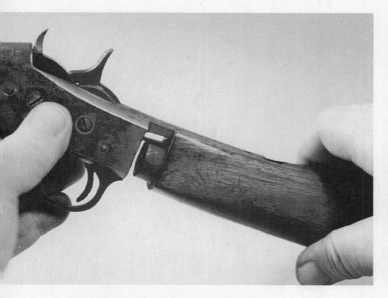

3. Remove the large screw at the end of the upper tang. Take off the buttstock toward the rear. The buttplate is retained by two wood screws.

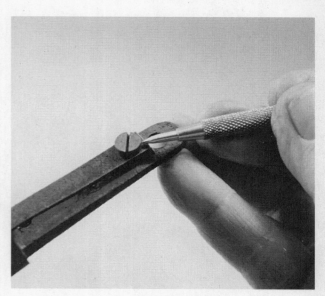

4. Remove the hammer spring screw and take out the hammer spring toward the rear.

5. Remove the hammer pivot screw. The hammer is not taken out at this time. Remove the breechblock pivot screw.

6. Tip the hammer to the rear and remove the breechblock upward. Remove the hammer upward.

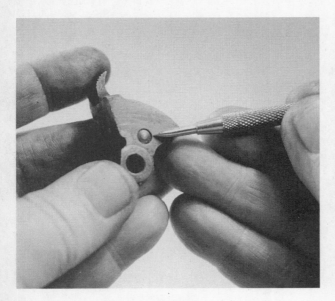

7. Drift out the firing pin cross pin. Remove the firing pin toward the rear.

8. Drift out the trigger cross pin and remove the trigger upward.

9. Drift out the ejector cross pin. Be sure the barrel latch lever is turned out of the way.

10. Remove the ejector upward.

11. Remove the screw inside, in the floor of the receiver, and take out the combination spring.

12. Drift out the barrel latch stop pin toward the right.

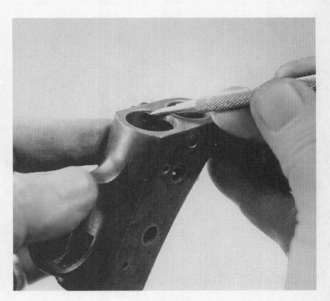

13. Unscrew the barrel latch from the receiver, turning it clockwise. Note that it has a reverse thread.

Reassembly Tips:

1. When installing the combination spring that bears on the trigger, ejector and breechblock, turn the screw about halfway in, and reserve tightening until the trigger and ejector are installed. This will make the alignment for cross pin insertion easier. Don't forget to tighten the screw after they are in place.

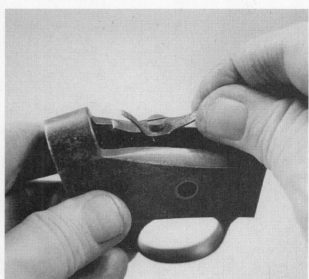

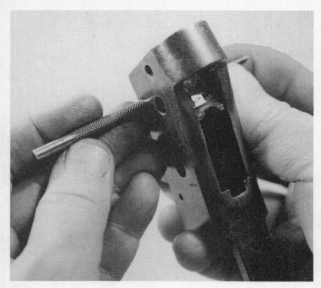

2. Insert a drift to position the trigger and ejector for insertion of the cross pins.

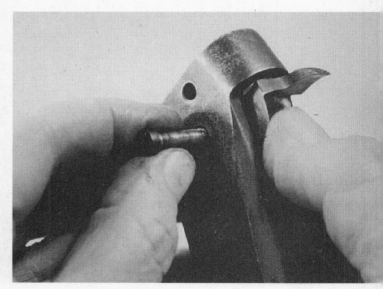

3. Remember that the hammer must be put back in the receiver before the breechblock can be installed. For insertion of the breechblock screw, the block must be pushed down and forward, against the tension of its bearing spring.

Remington Nylon 66

Similar/Identical Pattern Guns

The same basic assembly/disassembly steps for the Remington Nylon 66 also apply to the following guns:

F.I.E. Model GR-8	**Remington Nylon 66MB**
Magtech Model MT-66	**Remington Nylon 66 Bicentennial**
Remington Nylon 66GS	

Data:	Remington Nylon 66
Origin:	United States
Manufacturer:	Remington Arms Company Bridgeport, Connecticut
Cartridge:	22 Long Rifle
Magazine capacity:	14 rounds
Overall length:	$38^1/_2$ inches
Barrel length:	$19^5/_8$ inches
Weight:	4 pounds

Around 1959, when the Remington Nylon 66 first arrived on the scene, many firearms traditionalists sneered at its DuPont Zytel stock/receiver, stamped-steel parts and expansion-type springs. Over the years, though, they found that it works, and keeps working, uncleaned, mistreated, and abused—a tribute to Wayne Leek and the design team at Remington. For those not familiar with its mechanism, though, the Nylon 66 can be a disassembly/reassembly nightmare. The Nylon 66 was discontinued by Remington in 1988, but has been made in South America since then. This later version was marketed by Firearms Import & Export (F.I.E.) as the GR-8, and by Magtech Recreational Products as their MT-66.

Disassembly:

1. Remove the inner magazine tube from the stock. Grip the bolt handle firmly and pull it straight out toward the right.

2. Back out the two cross-screws, located near the lower edge of the receiver cover, and remove them toward the right.

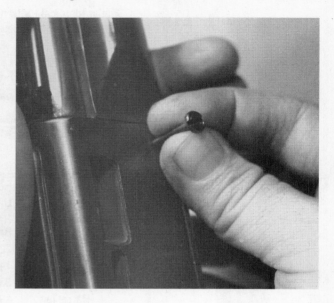

3. Remove the receiver cover assembly upward. The internal cartridge guide spring and the rear sight base are riveted on the cover, and removal is not advisable in normal disassembly.

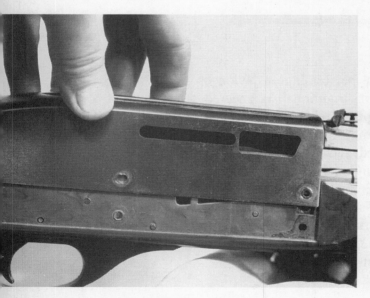

4. Remove the ejector from its recess in the left side of the receiver.

5. Loosen the large cross-slotted screw on the underside of the stock, just forward of the trigger guard; then push it upward to raise the barrel retaining piece until its upper cross bar clears its recess on top of the barrel. Slide the barrel out toward the front.

6. The front sight is retained on top of the barrel by two screws, one at each end.

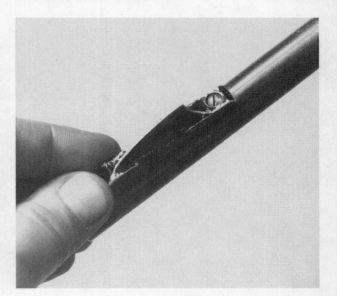

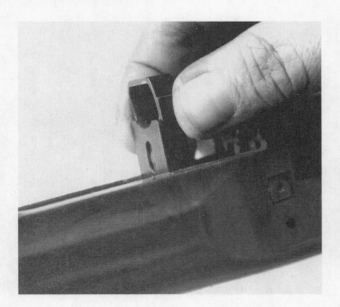

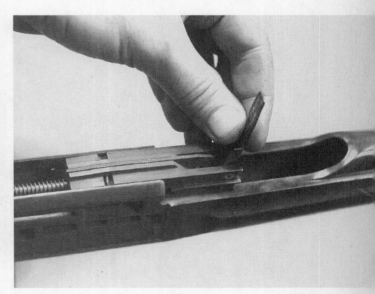

7. Take out the cross-slotted screw from the bottom of the stock, and lift the barrel retainer and its front plate out of their recess in the top of the stock.

8. Be sure the hammer is in its cocked position (at the rear), and the safety in the on-safe position. Grasp the cartridge guide, and move the bolt forward out of its tracks in the receiver. Remove the bolt spring and its guide toward the front.

9. Move the safety to the off-safe position, restrain the hammer against the tension of its spring, and pull the trigger to release the hammer. Ease the spring tension slowly, and move the hammer forward out of its tracks in the receiver. Remove the hammer spring and its guide.

10. Push out the cross pin located in the receiver just above the forward end of the trigger guard (arrow). Tip the trigger guard downward at the front, disengage its rear hook from inside the receiver, and remove the guard downward.

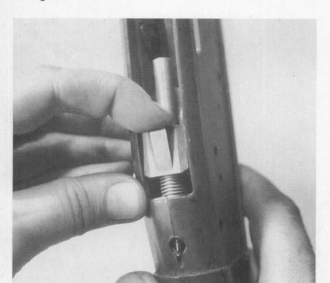

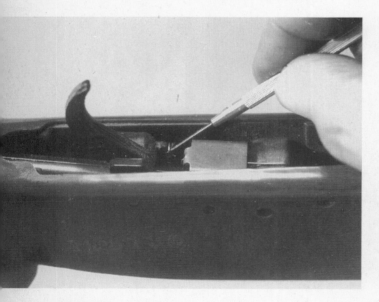

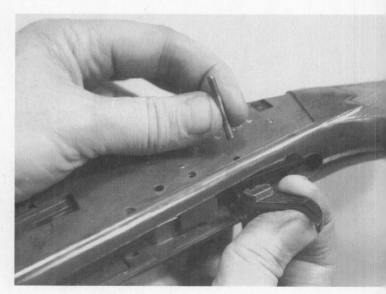

11. Use a small tool to unhook the trigger spring from its groove on the front of the trigger.

12. Push out the trigger cross pin, and remove the trigger downward.

13. Push out the cross pin just below the ejector recess (arrow), and remove the cartridge stop and its flat spring from the bottom of the receiver.

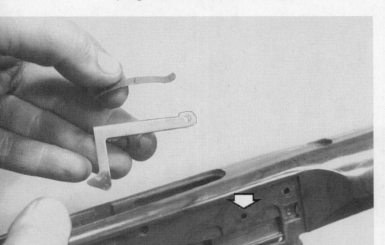

14. Use a tool to push the front of the cartridge feed throat (insert) downward, and tip it out of its recess for removal from the bottom of the receiver.

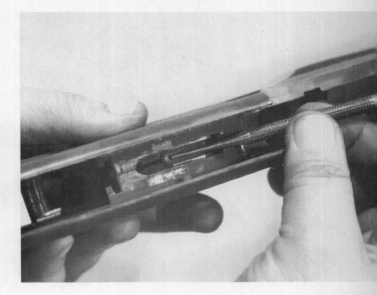

15. Use a small tool to lift the magazine tube retainer from its recess inside the receiver, and remove it from the top. Take out the magazine tube toward the rear.

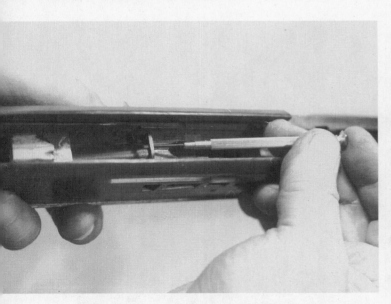

16. Restrain the sear at the top of the receiver against its spring tension, and push the disconnector pivot at the bottom of the receiver to release the sear. Allow the sear to pivot upward, slowly releasing the tension of its spring.

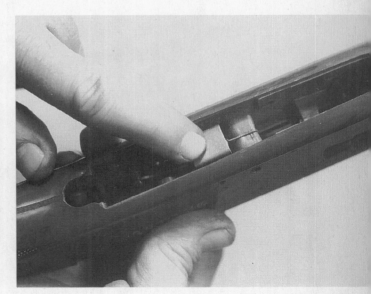

17. Use a tool to disengage the hook of the disconnector pivot spring from the receiver cross-piece at the bottom.

18. Push out the disconnector pivot points, one on each side of the receiver. After one has been removed, the other may be pushed out from the inside, using one of the other cross pins already removed or a drift punch.

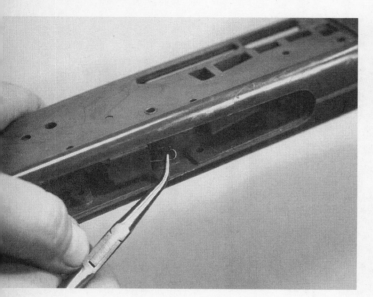

19. Depress the sear slightly to clear the rear arm of the disconnector, and remove the disconnector assembly from the top of the receiver. The disconnector is easily separated from its pivot by squeezing the sides of the pivot inward just enough to detach the lugs from the holes in the disconnector. The springs are also easily detached by turning their ends out of the holes in the parts.

20. Push out the sear pivot pin, and remove the sear and its spring from the top of the receiver (actually, the spring will usually fall from the bottom as the pin is taken out).

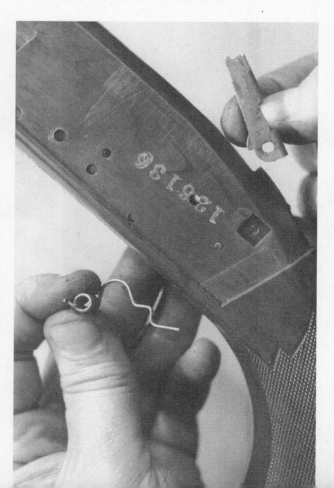

21. Push out the safety-lever cam pin, the last cross pin at the rear of the receiver. This will allow the safety-lever to drop, and the safety and its attached lever can then be removed upward.

22. Use a fingernail or a small tool to move the safety detent spring retaining pin out toward the rear. The pin has a groove at its rear tip to aid removal. The detent spring is not under heavy tension, but it can flip the pin as it is removed, so restrain it with a fingertip during removal. Take out the detent spring and the ball bearing from their hole in the top of the receiver, and take care that the bearing isn't lost.

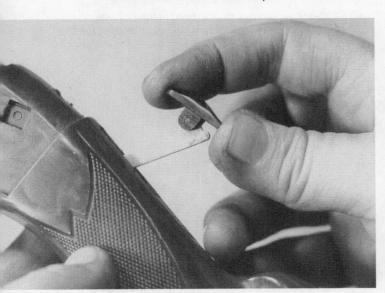

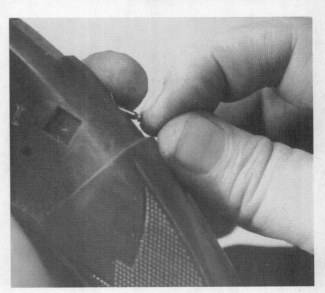

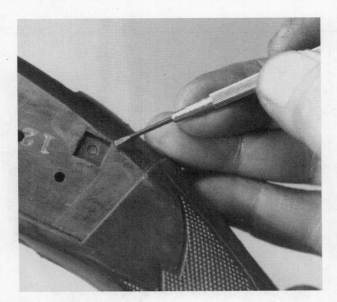

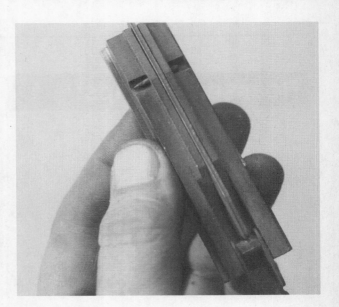

23. The two internal cross screws with square nuts on the left side do not retain parts, and their removal is neither necessary nor advisable during normal takedown.

24. The firing pin is retained in the bolt by a cross pin on top, near the rear of the bolt. The retaining pin is bent down on each side to lock it in place, and one end must be pried upward before the pin is drifted out. The firing pin is then removed toward the rear.

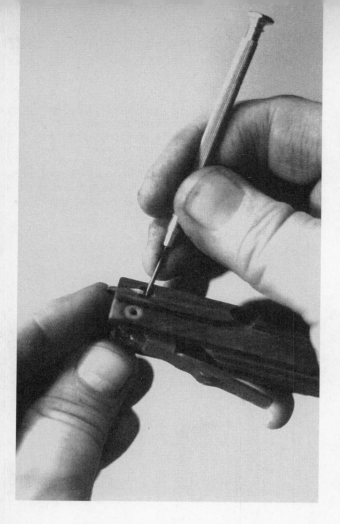

25. Insert a small screwdriver between the rear of the extractor and its plunger, and depress the plunger while lifting the extractor out of its recess. **Caution:** *The spring is under compression, so take care it doesn't get away.* Ease it out, and remove the plunger and spring.

26. A roll pin across the top front of the bolt retains the cartridge guide. Drifting out the pin will release the guide for removal. Be sure to use a roll pin punch to avoid deforming the pin.

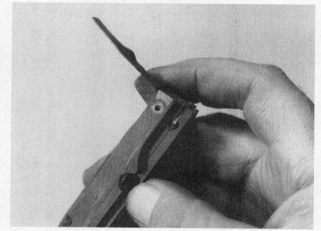

Reassembly Tips:

1. When replacing the disconnector assembly, remember that the sear (arrow) must be tipped forward to allow the rear arm of the disconnector to go behind the sear.

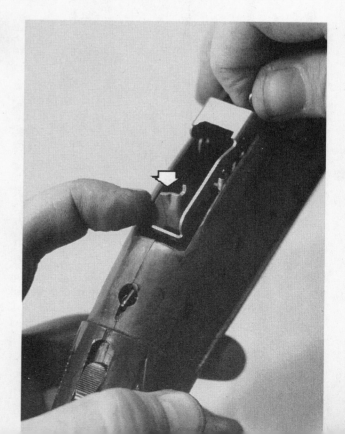

2. Remember that the cartridge feed throat ("cartridge insert") must be put in from below. Insert its rear tip first; then swing its front wings upward into the recesses while holding the rear tip in place with a tool, as shown. When the cartridge feed throat is in place, invert the gun so the feed throat will not fall back into the stock before installation of the cartridge stop (the front tip of the stop spring holds the feed throat in place). Installation of the cartridge feed throat is the single most difficult point in the reassembly of the Nylon 66.

3. Do not attempt to install the cartridge stop and its flat spring at the same time. Install the stop, then insert the spring, with its forward end going under the pin (remember, the gun is inverted), and push the spring forward until its indented catch locks on the front edge of the cartridge stop.

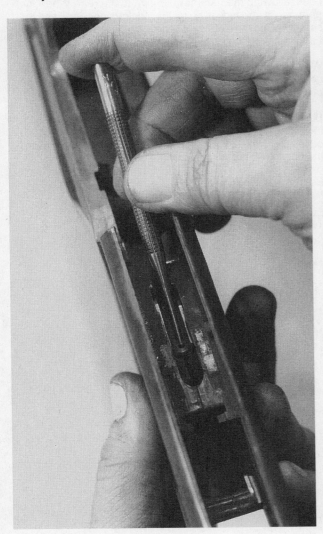

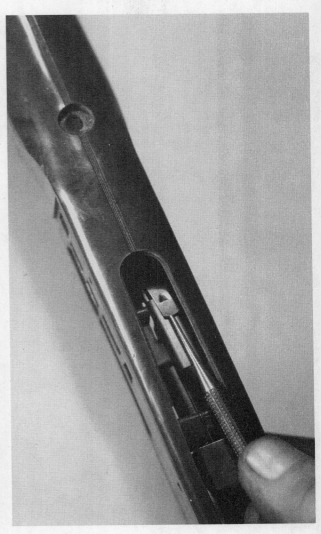

4. When properly installed, the front lip of the sear (arrow) should be under the front cross-piece of the disconnector, as shown.

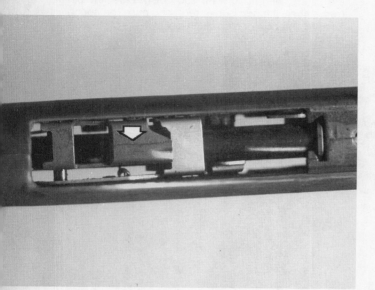

When reinstalling the hammer assembly, it is necessary to use a small tool to depress the sear while holding the trigger back, allowing the hammer to move to the rear. When the hammer is moved back to the cocked position, set the safety in the on-safe position to prevent release of the hammer while the bolt is installed.

When installing the barrel retainer, note that the front plate goes at the front of the retainer, and that the plate has an oblong slot which mates with a stud on the retainer.

Before replacing the receiver cover, be sure the ejector is in place in its recess on the left side. This part is often left out during reassembly, or drops off if the gun is tilted toward the left during replacement of the cover.

Before replacing the cover, be sure the cartridge guide is flipped over forward, to lie on top of the barrel.

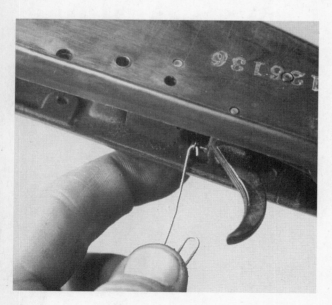

5. It is very difficult to reattach the trigger spring to the front of the trigger without a small hooked tool. The one shown was made from an opened paper clip.

Ruger 10/22

Similar/Identical Pattern Guns

The same basic assembly/disassembly steps for the Ruger 10/22 also apply to the following guns:

Ruger 10/22 Sporter

Ruger 10/22 International

Ruger 10/22 Deluxe Sporter

AMT Lightning 25/22

AMT Lightning Small Game

Data:	Ruger 10/22
Origin:	United States
Manufacturer:	Sturm, Ruger & Company Southport, Connecticut
Cartridge:	22 Long Rifle
Magazine capacity:	10 rounds
Overall length:	$36^3/_4$ inches
Barrel length:	$18^1/_2$ inches
Weight:	$5^3/_4$ pounds

Since its introduction in 1964, the Model 10/22 has established an enviable record of reliability. Over the past fifteen years, I have repaired only one of these guns, and that one had been altered by its owner. Originally offered in Carbine, Sporter and International models, the latter with a full Mannlicher-style stock was discontinued for many years. The gun is again available in all three styles, however, the only differences being in the stock and barrel band. The instructions will generally apply to any of the 10/22 guns.

Disassembly:

1. Loosen or remove the cross-screw at the lower end of the barrel band, and take off the barrel band toward the front. If the band is tight, applying slight downward pressure on the barrel will make it move off more easily.

2. Remove the magazine, and cycle the action to cock the internal hammer. Back out the main stock screw, located on the underside just forward of the magazine well.

3. Center the safety halfway between its right and left positions so it will clear the stock on each side, and move the action upward out of the stock.

4. When the action is removed from the stock, the bolt stop pin, the large cross pin at the rear of the receiver, will probably be loose and can be easily taken out at this time.

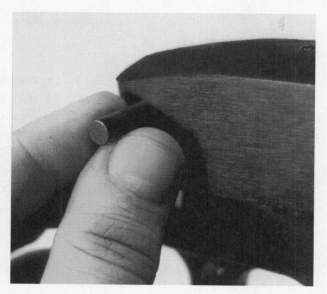

5. Drift out the front and rear cross pins (arrows) that hold the trigger group on the receiver. Then remove the trigger group downward.

6. If the bolt stop pin was not taken out earlier, it must be removed now. With the gun inverted, move the bolt all the way to the rear and tip the front of the bolt outward, away from the inside roof of the receiver. **Caution:** *Keep a firm grip on the bolt handle, as the bolt spring is fully compressed.* Ease the bolt handle forward, slowly relieving the spring tension, and remove the bolt from the underside of the receiver. Remove the bolt handle and its attached spring and guide rod from the ejection port.

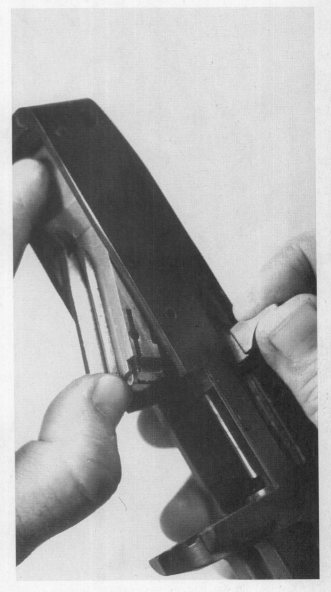

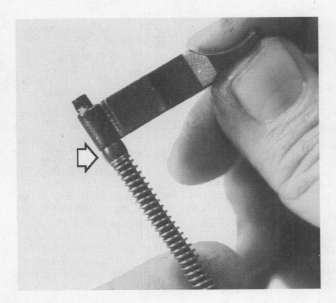

7. The bolt spring guide rod is staked at the forward end, ahead of the bolt handle, and if the stake lumps are filed off for disassembly, a new guide rod may be required. In normal disassembly, this unit is best left intact. If it is taken apart, be careful not to lose the small spacer (arrow) between the spring and the handle at the forward end.

8. The firing pin is retained by a roll cross pin at the upper rear of the bolt. Use a roll-pin punch to drift out the cross pin, and remove the firing pin and its return spring toward the rear.

9. To remove the extractor, insert a small screwdriver to depress the extractor spring plunger, and hold it in while the extractor is lifted out of its recess. **Caution:** *Take care that the screwdriver doesn't slip, as the plunger and spring can travel far if suddenly released.* Ease them out slowly, and remove them from the bolt.

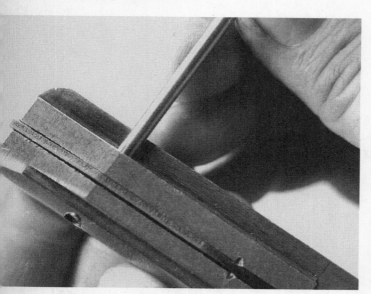

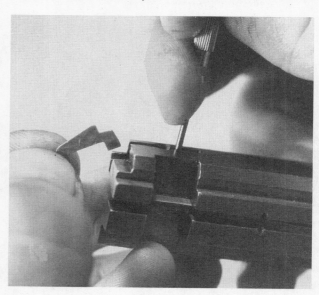

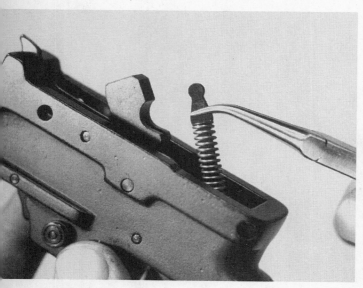

10. Restrain the hammer against the tension of its spring, pull the trigger, and ease the hammer forward beyond its normal fired position. The hammer spring assembly can now be moved forward and upward, out of the trigger group. The hammer spring assembly can be taken apart by compressing the spring and sliding the slotted washer off the lower end of the guide. Proceed with caution, as the spring is under tension.

11. Before going any further with disassembly of the trigger group, carefully note the relationship of all parts and springs, to aid in reassembly. Tip the front of the ejector out of its slot in the front of the trigger group, push out the cross pin at the rear of the ejector, and remove the ejector upward. Note that removal of the cross pin will also release the upper arm of the bolt latch spring.

12. A cross pin at the lower front of the trigger group pivots and retains the bolt latch and the magazine catch lever. The bolt latch is removed upward. Restrain the magazine catch plunger with a fingertip, remove the catch lever downward, and ease the plunger and its spring out toward the front.

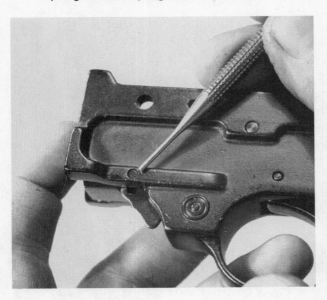

13. Hold the trigger back to remove sear tension from the hammer, and push out the hammer pivot cross pin. Remove the hammer assembly upward. The bolt latch spring encircles the hammer bushing on the right side, and the two hammer pivot bushings are easily removed from the hammer.

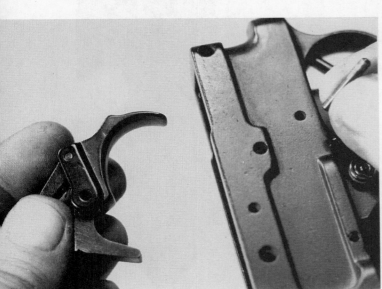

14. Note the position of the sear and disconnector in the top of the trigger before disassembly. Push out the trigger pivot cross pin, and remove the trigger/sear/disconnector assembly upward. As the trigger is moved upward, the trigger spring and plunger will be released at the rear of the trigger guard. Ease them out, and remove them downward and toward the front.

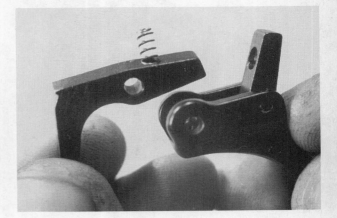

15. The sear is removed from the trigger toward the front, along with the combination sear and disconnector spring. Drifting out the cross pin at the upper rear of the trigger will release the disconnector for removal.

16. Grip the safety firmly with a thumb and finger at each end, and give it a one-quarter turn toward the front; then push it out toward the left. **Caution:** *Insert a fingertip inside the trigger group, above the safety, to arrest the safety plunger and spring, as they will be released as the safety is moved out.*

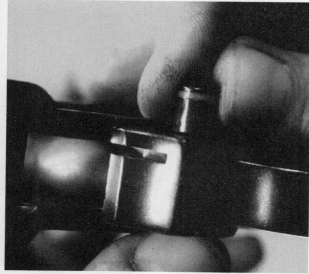

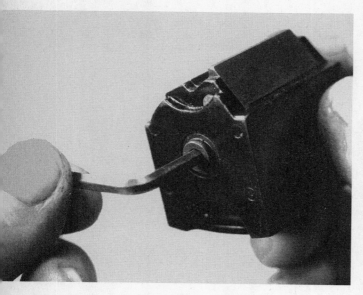

17. In normal takedown, removal of the barrel is not advisable. If necessary, however, use an Allen wrench to back out the two large screws that secure the barrel retainer block and take out the barrel toward the front. If the barrel is tight, grip the barrel in a padded vise and use a nylon hammer to tap the receiver off toward the rear.

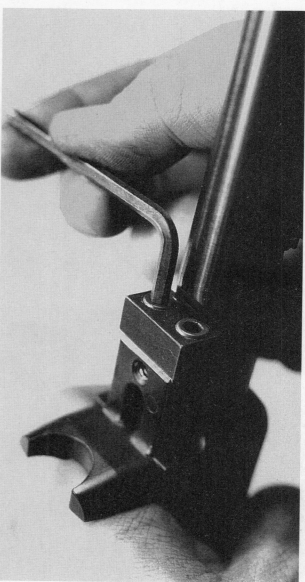

18. Magazine disassembly is not recommended in normal takedown. If it becomes necessary, removal of the screw at the front of the magazine will allow the backplate to be taken off, and the internal parts can then be taken out toward the rear. **Caution:**—*Don't remove the spring from the rotor.* Carefully note the relationship of all parts to aid in reassembly.

Reassembly Tips:

1. When replacing the trigger/sear/disconnector assembly in the trigger group, use a slave pin to hold the three parts and the spring in position for reinsertion. The photo shows the parts in place and the slave pin in the pivot hole.

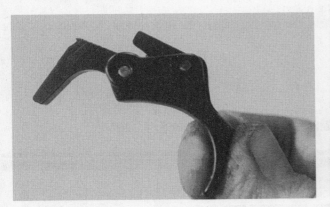

2. When replacing the hammer, its pivot bushings and the bolt latch spring, note that the spring must be on the right side of the hammer, as shown. Be sure the lower arm of the spring engages its notch in the cross-piece of the bolt latch. The upper arm of the spring goes below the cross pin that retains the ejector.

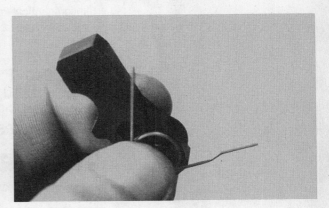

3. When replacing the magazine catch system, remember that the bolt latch must be in place before the catch lever, plunger, and spring are installed. Insert the magazine catch plunger and spring first; then put in the catch lever from below. The upper arm of the lever will hold the plunger and spring in place while the cross pin is inserted. Be sure the cross pin passes through the bolt latch and the magazine catch.

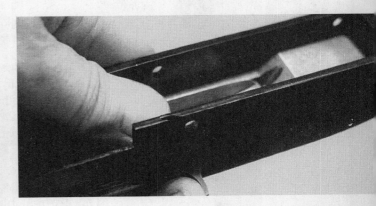

4. When replacing the bolt in the receiver, remember that the bolt handle must be fully to the rear, with the spring compressed, before the bolt can be tipped back into engagement with the handle at the front.

When replacing the action in the stock, be sure the safety is again set between its right and left positions to clear the interior as the action is moved into place.

If the magazine has been disassembled, insert the screw in the magazine body and place the rotor and spring on the screw, with the longer hub of the rotor toward the front. Replace the feed throat, being sure the larger end stud enters its recess at the front. Put the backplate back on the magazine body and hold it in place. Insert the front of the hexagonal-headed magazine nut into the rear of the spring, and be sure the hooked tip of the spring engages the hole in the nut. Turn the nut clockwise (rear view) until the rotor stops turning; then give it an additional $1\frac{1}{4}$ turns to properly tension the spring. Move the nut into its recess and tighten the magazine screw, taking care not to over-tighten.

Ruger Model 77/22

Similar/Identical Pattern Guns

The same basic assembly/disassembly steps for the Ruger Model 77/22 also apply to the following guns:

Ruger 77/22R	**Ruger 77/22RS**
Ruger 77/22RP	**Ruger 77/22RSP**
Ruger 77/22RM	**Ruger 77/22RSM**
Ruger K77/22RP	**Ruger K77/22RSP**
Ruger K77/22RSMP	**Ruger K77/22RMP**

Data:	Ruger Model 77/22
Origin:	United States
Manufacturer:	Sturm, Ruger & Company Southport, Connecticut
Cartridge:	22 Long Rifle
Magazine capacity:	10 rounds
Overall length:	39³/₄ inches
Barrel length:	20 inches
Weight:	5³/₄ pounds

The original blued-steel and wood-stocked version of the Model 77/22 was introduced in 1983. Six years later, in 1989, the gun was offered in stainless steel with an optional synthetic stock, and also in a 22 WMR version. A beautifully-engineered bolt action, the Model 77/22 uses the same magazine and barrel-mounting system as the Ruger 10/22 autoloader.

Disassembly:

1. Remove the magazine and open the bolt. Depress the bolt stop, located at the left rear of the receiver, and remove the bolt toward the rear.

2. Insert a drift through the hole in the underlug of the striker end piece and turn the bolt headpiece to the position shown.

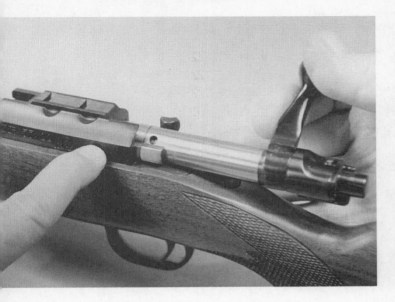

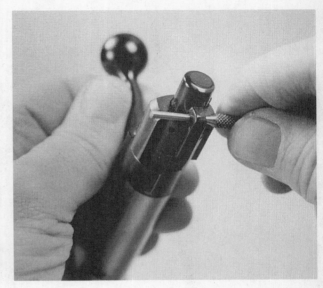

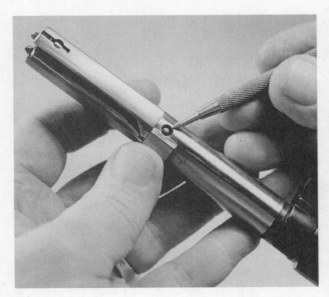

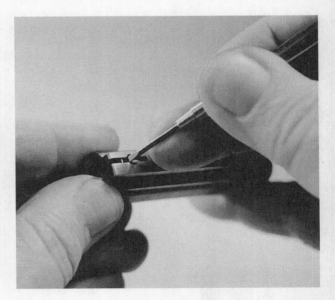

3. After the headpiece is turned, the head of the breechblock pin will be visible in this opening. Use a drift in the aperture on the other side, and push the breechblock pin out. Remove the breechblock toward the front.

4. The extractors can be removed by using a small tool to push their plungers toward the rear. **Caution:** *Control the plunger and spring on each side, and ease them out.* Keep the extractors separate—they are not interchangeable.

5. Using the drift in the hole in the striker underlug, unscrew the striker assembly from the bolt body. Remove the assembly toward the rear. Note that the firing pin can be detached from its hook at the front of the shaft as it emerges.

6. While it is possible to use a vise and special jigs to further disassemble the striker system, the factory advises against this. In normal takedown, it is best left intact.

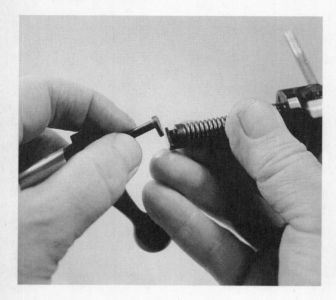

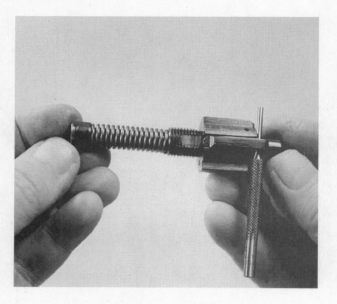

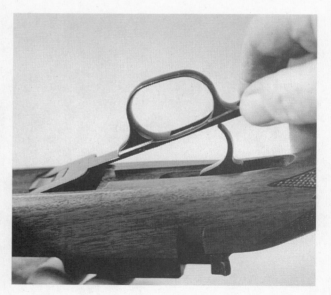

7. Remove the large screw in front of the magazine opening and take off the forward plate.

8. Remove the large screw behind the trigger guard. Tip the trigger guard unit outward to unhook it from the receiver and remove it. Carefully lift the action out of the stock.

9. Restrain the magazine catch plunger and push out the catch lever cross pin.

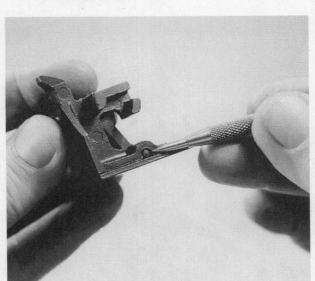

10. Remove the catch lever downward.

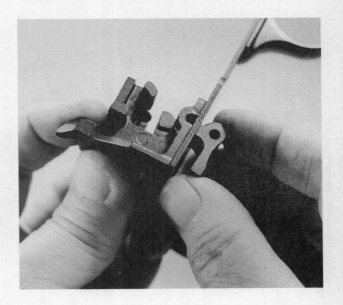

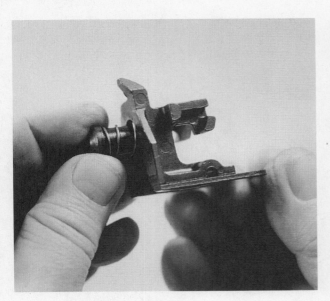

11. Ease the spring tension and remove the plunger and spring toward the front.

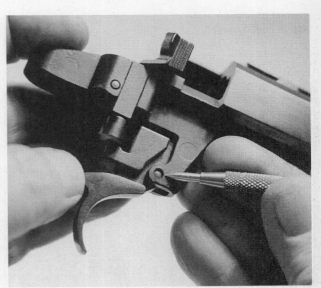

12. Restrain the trigger and push out the trigger cross pin.

13. Remove the trigger downward, along with its spring.

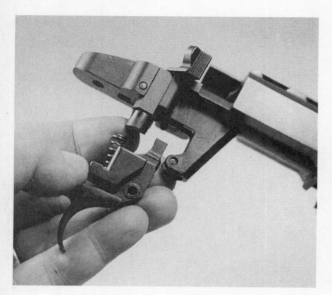

14. Push out the sear cross pin.

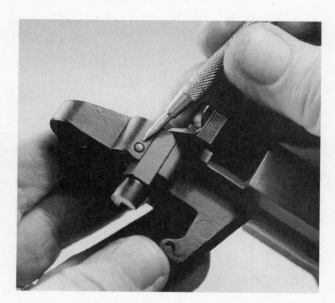

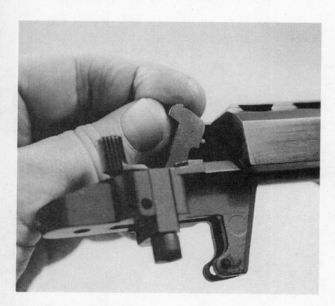

15. Move the sear forward and take it out upward.

16. Turn the safety-lever until it is in the position shown, over the bolt track.

17. Holding the safety in place at top and bottom, push the safety housing upward. **Caution:** *Keep control of the safety, as the detent plunger and spring will force it outward.*

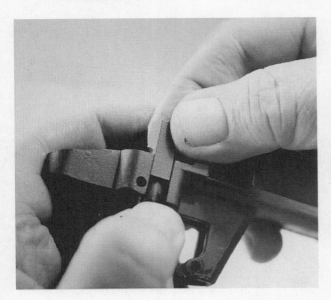

18. Ease the spring tension slowly and remove the safety toward the right.

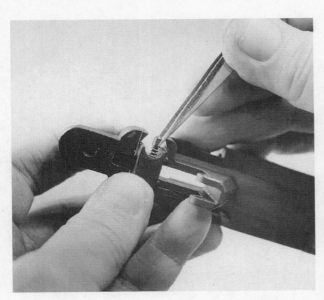

19. Remove the safety plunger and spring.

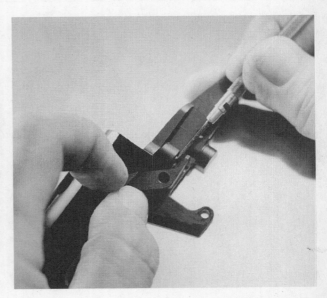

20. To remove the bolt stop, use a tool to depress the plunger and spring upward and take off the bolt stop toward the left. **Caution:** *Keep the plunger and spring under control, and ease them out.*

21. If barrel removal is necessary, remove the two Allen screws at the front of the receiver, take off the block and remove the barrel toward the front. The front and rear sights are dovetail-mounted.

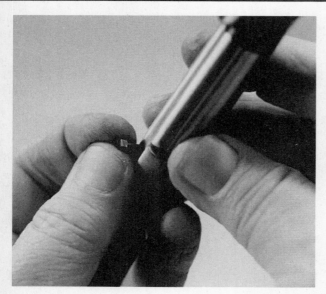

2. When installing the breechblock pin, note that the flats on its head must be oriented to front and rear. Properly installed, the head of the pin must be recessed below the outer surface of the bolt body.

Reassembly Tips:

1. When installing the safety housing, be sure the recess for the sear cross pin is at the rear, as shown.

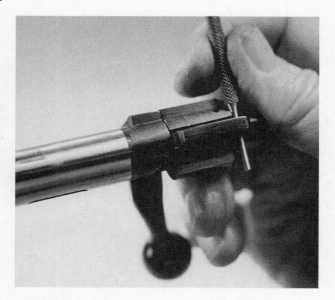

3. Remember to turn the bolt head back to cocked position, as shown, before the bolt is reinserted in the receiver.

Savage Model 63

Similar/Identical Pattern Guns
The same basic assembly/disassembly steps for the Savage Model 63 also apply to the following guns:

Savage Model 63M

Savage Model 63KM

Savage Model 73

Savage Model 73Y

Data:	Savage Model 63
Origin:	United States
Manufacturer:	Savage Arms Company
	Westfield, Massachusetts
Cartridge:	22 Short, Long, or Long Rifle
Overall length:	36 inches
Barrel length:	18 inches
Weight:	4 pounds

Made between 1964 and 1974, the Model 63 was also offered as the Model 63M, chambered for the 22 WMR round. Another version soon followed, the Model 73, which differed only in having a half-stock rather than the full Mannlicher style of the 63 and 63M. Both guns were offered concurrently during their time of production, and since they are mechanically identical, the takedown and reassembly instructions can be applied to both models, with the exception of details involving the stock of the Model 63.

Disassembly:

1. On the underside of the stock near the muzzle is a small, headless screw in the center of a slotted nut. The inner tip of the screw retains the front sight, and the nut secures the unit to the stock. The nut can be removed with a twin-pointed tool, and the screw will often turn out with it. Or, the nut can be immobilized and the small screw aligned with the slot in the nut, and a wide, thin-bladed screwdriver can be used to back out both at once.

2. Back out the main stock mounting screw, located on the underside of the stock, just forward of the trigger guard, and remove the action from the stock.

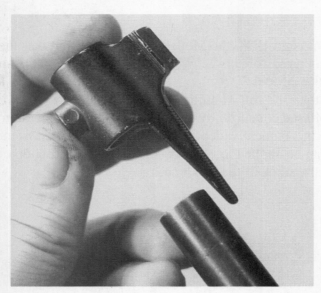

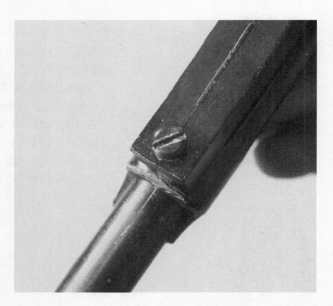

3. When the action is out of the stock, the front sight is easily slid off toward the front.

4. Cycle the bolt to cock the internal hammer and remove the vertical screw at the front of the trigger group.

5. Remove the vertical screw at the rear of the trigger group. The head of this screw is not directly accessible, being in a recess at the rear of the guard unit, so it is necessary to use an offset screwdriver, or one with an angled tip, as shown, to remove it.

6. Remove the trigger group downward.

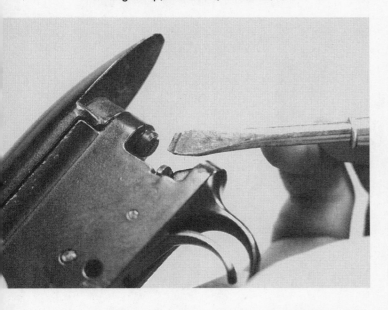

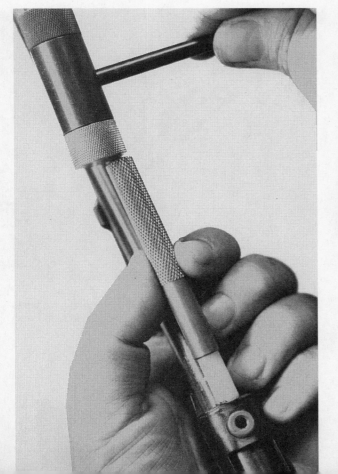

7. Removal of the front trigger group screw will have released the barrel for removal from the receiver, as the tip of this screw enters a recess on the underside of the barrel. Grip the barrel in a padded vise, and use a hammer and nylon drift to gently tap the receiver off the barrel toward the rear.

8. When the receiver has moved a certain distance off the rear of the barrel, it will be possible to lift the bolt assembly out of the underside of the receiver. If only bolt removal is desired, and barrel removal is not necessary, the receiver need not be drifted completely off the barrel.

9. The extractor is retained on the front of the bolt because it acts like a spring clip, its opposed gripping arms riding in a groove around the front of the bolt. To remove the extractor, push against the opposed arms of its spring clip, snapping it off toward the side. It is pushed, of course, from the open side of its clip. Be sure to apply pressure only to its mounting clip, not to its long front arm or tail. Usually, this can be done without tools.

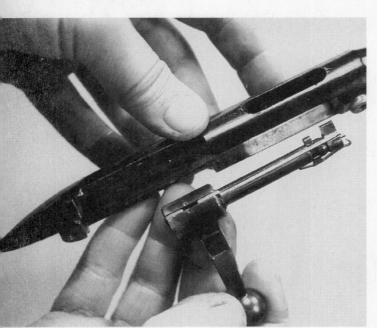

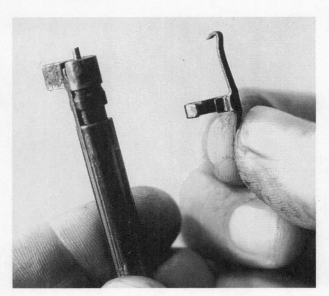

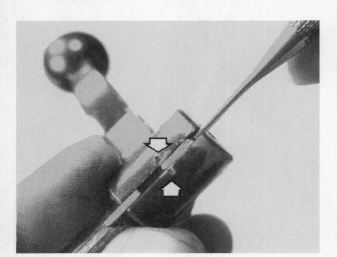

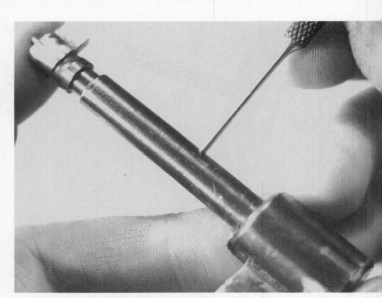

10. The firing pin is retained in its channel in the top of the bolt by stake marks (arrows) in the channel edges over a rectangular recess in the top of the firing pin. The firing pin may be drifted out forward and upward, or out toward the rear, swaging the stake marks aside as it passes.

11. The ejector and its spring are retained by a small roll cross pin at the center of the bolt and are taken out toward the rear.

12. The safety-lever and the bolt safety trip at the front are retained on the right side of the trigger group by separate screws, and are taken off toward the right. Removal of these parts will also release the round spring-wire connector between the levers.

13. The bolt bearing screw is accessible through the main stock screw hole in the underside of the guard unit, and is removed downward.

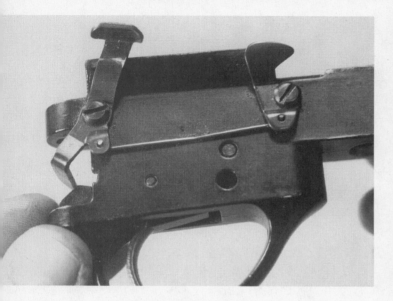

14. Restrain the hammer against the tension of its spring, pull the trigger, and ease the hammer down to the fired position. Drift out the hammer pivot, the larger of the two cross pins, and remove the hammer and the combination hammer and trigger spring upward. Drift out the trigger pivot, the smaller cross pin, and remove the trigger upward, along with the sear, which is mounted in the top of the trigger and pivots on the same pin.

Reassembly Tips:

1. As the receiver is tapped back onto the rear of the barrel, remember that the bolt must be inserted before the barrel and receiver are moved fully into place. The photo shows the optimum position for insertion of the bolt.

2. When replacing the trigger group on the underside of the receiver, be sure the front screw, the one with the extended tip, is put back in front, and see that the barrel is oriented so the screw tip will enter the recess in the underside of the barrel, locking it in place.

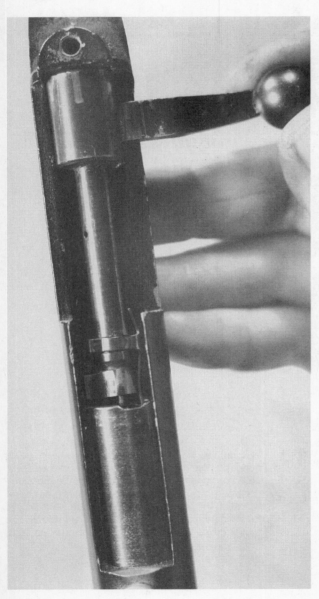

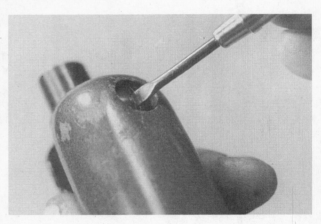

3. When replacing the action in the stock, note that the front sight must be slid onto the muzzle before the action is seated, so the protrusion on its underside will enter its well in the stock. The sight screw and nut may be turned into place together; then the small center screw may be turned separately for any adjustment necessary to snug the unit in place.

When replacing the sear and trigger assembly, be sure both the sear and trigger are properly aligned with the cross-hole in the trigger group before inserting and driving in the cross pin. If there is difficulty, a slave pin can be used.

When replacing the extractor on the bolt, note that it is snapped into its groove upward, so the operating arm of the extractor will lie on the right side when the bolt is in the receiver.

Savage/ Anschutz Model 54

Similar/Identical Pattern Guns
The same basic assembly/disassembly steps for the Savage/Anschutz Model 54 also apply to the following gun:
Savage/Anschutz Model 54M

Data:	Savage/Anschutz Model 54
Origin:	Germany
Manufacturer:	J.G. Anschutz Gmbh, Ulm/Donau (Imported by Savage Arms, Westfield Massachusetts)
Cartridge:	22 Long Rifle
Magazine capacity:	5 rounds
Overall length:	$41^7/_8$ inches
Barrel length:	$22^1/_2$ inches
Weight:	$6^3/_4$ pounds

The Anschutz family has been making fine guns in Germany since 1793, and the J.G. Anschutz firm was established in Zella-Mehlis about 1922. In the post-war years, the factory was relocated to Ulm/Donau. From 1966 to 1981, Savage Arms imported an elegant little Anschutz rifle, the Model 54. It cost somewhat more than contemporary guns of its type, but many discriminating shooters felt that the quality was worth the price. The Model 54M is the same, except it's chambered for the 22 WMR cartridge.

Disassembly:

1. Remove the magazine and back out the screw on the underside, at the rear of the trigger guard. When the screw is out, flex the trigger guard very slightly to free it from its recess in the stock at the rear, and swing the guard out to the side to give access to the rear vertical screw in the trigger plate. Back out the rear trigger plate screw.

2. Remove the main action screw, located at the center of the trigger plate, just forward of the guard, and separate the action from the stock. The smaller screw at the front of the trigger plate is a wood screw that retains the trigger plate on the stock. With the plate removed, it is possible to take off the guard, if necessary, by turning off its nut on the inside of the plate.

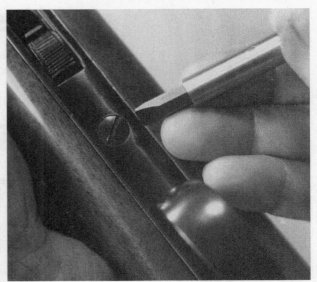

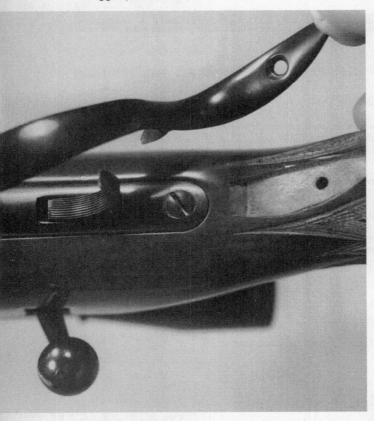

3. To remove the bolt, open it and move it toward the rear while depressing the bolt stop, located on the left side of the receiver, and withdraw the bolt toward the rear. Note that the safety must be in the horizontal off-safe position before the bolt can be opened.

4. Grip the front section of the bolt and turn the safety-lever counterclockwise (rear view) until the striker drops to the fired position. Continue turning the safety until it stops; it can then be taken off toward the rear.

5. The cocking indicator and its spring are held inside the safety dome by an enlarged coil at the rear end of the indicator spring, and the indicator and spring are easily removed by pushing them out toward the front.

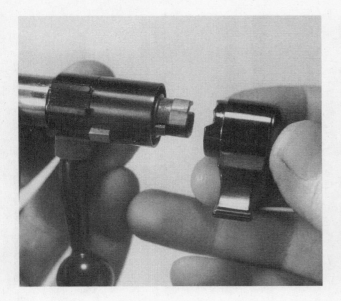

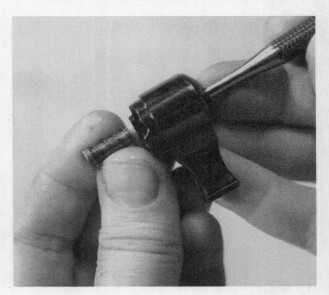

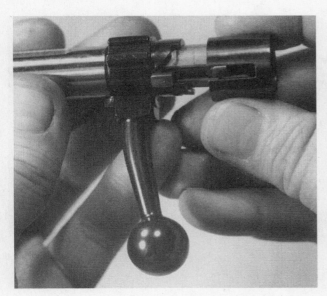

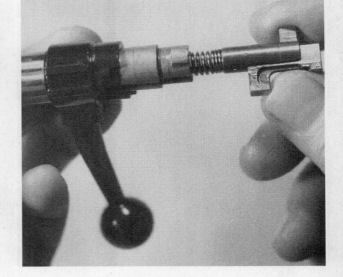

6. Remove the safety sleeve toward the rear.

7. Remove the striker assembly toward the rear.

8. To disassemble the striker assembly, grip the rear of the striker with a strong hand or a padded vise, and push the ridged collar at the front of the spring very slightly toward the rear. Give it a half turn and ease it off toward the front, slowly releasing the tension of the spring. **Caution:** *Control the striker spring.* Remove the collar, spring, and rear spring guide from the striker/firing pin toward the front.

9. After the striker assembly is removed, take off the bolt handle toward the rear.

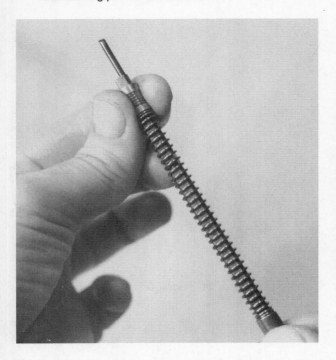

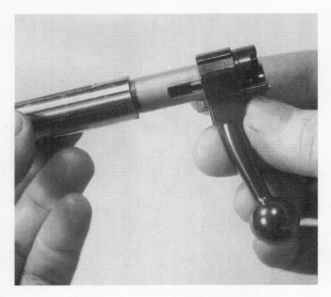

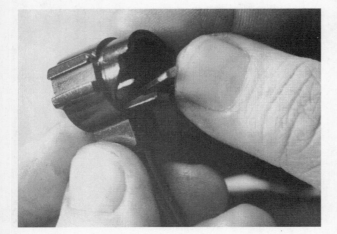

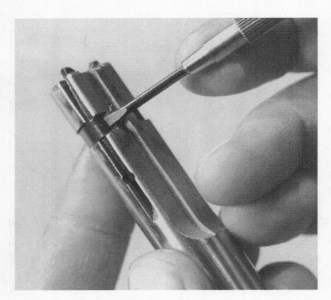

10. To remove the bolt handle positioning plunger and its spring, push the plunger toward the rear and tip its flat rear end inward; then move the part out toward the front of the handle sleeve. Take care not to lose the small coil spring.

11. The extractors are retained on the front of the bolt by a semi-circular spring clip. Use a small screwdriver to pry either end of the clip outward, and ease it off the top of the bolt. The extractors are then easily removed toward each side. Take care to pry the clip only enough to clear the bolt body during removal, as it also is the spring for the extractors, and must not be weakened.

12. The trigger mount is secured at the rear of the receiver by a single vertical screw, and access to the screw head is limited by a rear projection of the mount. An offset or angle-tip screwdriver must be used. Take care not to lose the lock washer under the screw head. Note that it is possible to remove the entire trigger assembly without disturbing the adjustment settings of the trigger spring screw and sear engagement screw. If necessary, these are also easily removed. The nut must be loosened to take out the sear engagement screw at the front. The cross pin can also be driven out, separating the trigger from the mount, but this is usually staked at the ends, so take care not to deform the upper arms of the trigger during removal of the pin. In normal takedown, the assembly is best left intact.

13. The sear is retained on the underside of the receiver by a cross pin and is removed downward, along with its spring, after the pin is drifted out.

14. The bolt stop is retained on the left side of the receiver by a vertical pin. After the pin is drifted out, the bolt stop and its coil spring are removed toward the left.

15. The magazine housing and catch assembly is retained on the underside of the receiver by two large screws at its front and rear. The rear screw is a limited access type and will require the use of an angled-tip screwdriver for removal. The rear screw also secures the internal rear magazine guide and the bolt guide within the receiver. After removal of the screws, the magazine housing and guide are taken off downward, and the bolt guide can be removed from inside the receiver.

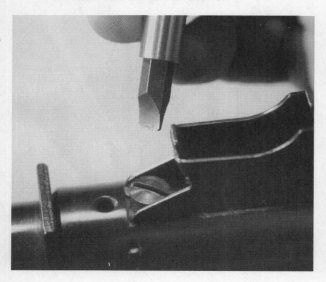

16. The magazine catch and its spring are mounted on a cross pin in the rear of the magazine housing, and the cross pin is usually semi-riveted at the ends. Care must be taken when drifting it out to avoid deformation of the magazine housing and the catch. If the catch and spring don't need repair, they are best left on the housing.

Reassembly Tips:

1. Before the reassembled bolt can be put back into the receiver, it must be recocked. Grip the forward portion of the bolt in a padded vise, and move the bolt handle counterclockwise (rear view) until the striker lug on the underside is in the position shown, and the striker indicator is protruding from the rear of the safety dome. Note that the safety-lever must be in its off-safe position before the bolt handle can be moved.

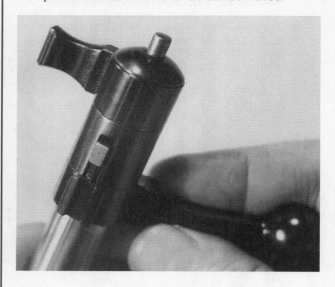

Savage Model 72

Similar/Identical Pattern Guns

The same basic assembly/disassembly steps for the Savage Model 72 also apply to the following gun:

Savage-Stevens Model 74

Data:	Savage Model 72
Origin:	United States
Manufacturer:	Savage Arms Company Westfield, Massachusetts
Cartridge:	22 Long Rifle
Overall length:	37 inches
Barrel length:	22 inches
Weight:	4½ pounds

The Model 72 was marketed as the "Crackshot." There was an earlier Stevens gun with that name, but this little rifle is not similar. Actually, it is an updated version of the popular "Favorite." Briefly, there was a Model 71, which differed in some mechanical details. The Model 74, made from 1972 to 1974, was a lower-priced version with a round barrel. The Model 72 was produced from 1972 to 1987.

Disassembly:

1. Remove the two buttplate screws and take off the stock buttplate. Use a B-Square stock tool or a long screwdriver to unscrew the stock mounting bolt and remove the stock from the receiver.

2. Remove the forend screw and take off the forend.

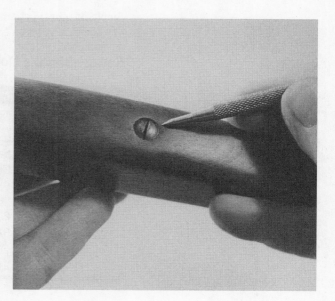

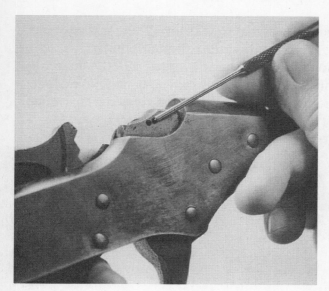

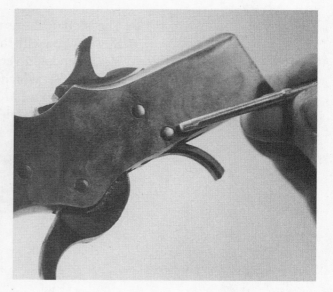

3. If only the firing pin needs to be removed for repair purposes, it can be taken out, along with its return spring, by drifting out the roll-type cross pin in the breechblock.

4. Open the action and drift out the trigger cross pin toward the right. On these large pins, use a bronze drift of suitable size to avoid marring the heads of the pins.

5. Remove the trigger and its spring downward, detaching the trigger from the hammer block loop, which will be stopped by its cross-piece. Take out the hammer block upward.

6. The hammer block and trigger spring are shown in their relative positions here.

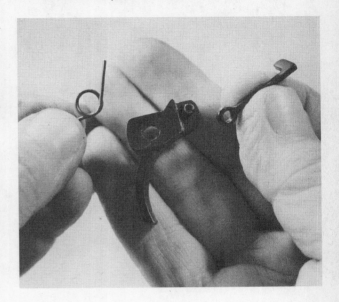

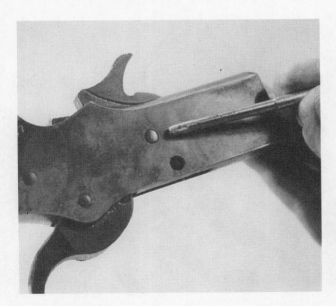

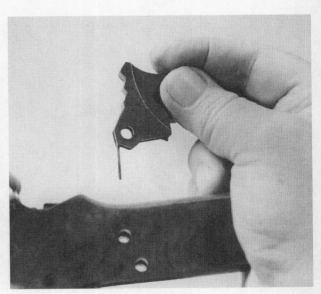

7. Removal of the trigger pin will have released the tension of the hammer spring. Drift out the hammer cross pin toward the right.

8. Remove the hammer and its spring upward. Note that the spring may fall out the lower opening as the hammer is removed.

9. Drift out the lever pivot cross pin.

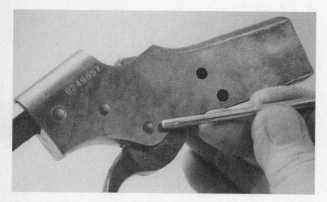

10. Drift out the breechblock pivot pin.

11. Remove the lever and breechblock assembly downward.

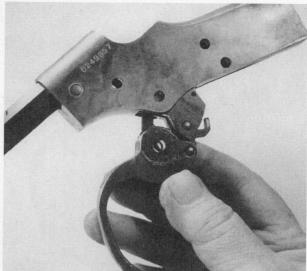

12. Remove the ejector from the front of the lever.

13. Drift out the breechblock link pin and separate the breechblock and link. If the firing pin has not been previously removed, drift out its roll-type pin and remove the firing pin and its spring toward the rear.

14. The link can be removed from the lever by drifting out this cross pin. **Caution:** *In Model 72 and Model 74 guns, there is a link tension plunger and spring in the lever under the link, and these will be released when the pin is removed, so control them.*

15. The barrel is retained by a large cross pin that is drifted out toward the right. The receiver is then driven off the barrel shank, using a hardwood buffer to prevent marring. In normal takedown, the barrel is left in place. The sights are drifted out of their dovetails toward the right.

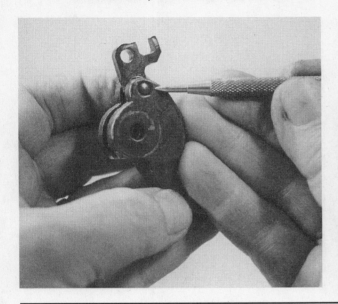

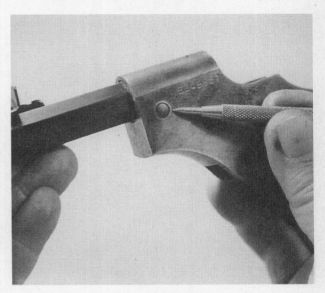

Reassembly Tips:

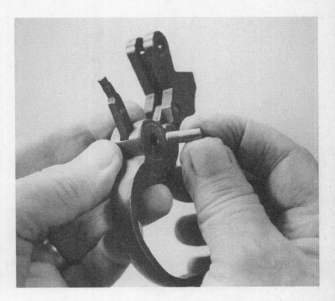

1. When installing the breechblock and lever assembly, be sure the ejector is replaced in the front of the lever in the proper orientation, as shown. Also, be sure the top of the ejector engages its recess below the chamber.

2. Use a slave pin to keep the ejector in position in the lever during reassembly.

3. Insert the breechblock pivot pin first; then move the lever into position for insertion of its cross pin.

4. When installing the trigger spring, note that the longer arm of the spring goes toward the front, as shown.

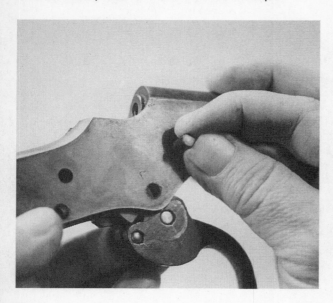

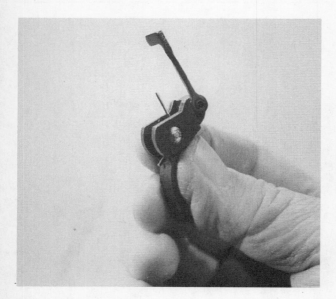

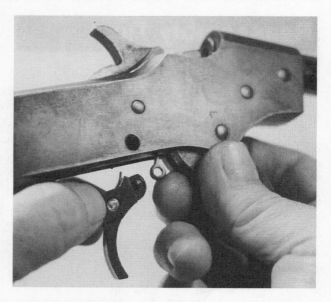

5. Use a slave pin to retain the trigger spring during reassembly and be sure the loop of the hammer block engages the post on the trigger.

6. With the hammer pulled back, the hammer block is inserted at the top, its cross-piece lying in the "hook" at the back of the link. Its lower loop will protrude as shown to engage the post on the trigger.

Sears Model 25

Data:	Sears Model 25
Origin:	United States
Manufacturer:	High Standard Firearms Hamden, Connecticut
Cartridge:	22 Short, Long, Long Rifle
Magazine capacity:	22 Short, 17 Long, 15 Long Rifle
Overall length:	43$^3/_4$ inches
Barrel length:	22$^1/_4$ inches
Weight:	5$^5/_8$ pounds

Made for Sears, Roebuck & Company by High Standard, this gun was also marketed by High Standard under their own name as the "Sport King" Model A-102. The sear/disconnector system has elements of the old Savage Model 6 and Stevens Model 87, with the bolt staying open between shots until the trigger is released. The gun was discontinued around 1976, but apparently a lot of them were sold, by both Sears and High Standard, because they are frequently seen.

Disassembly:

1. Remove the inner magazine tube and back out the stock mounting screw, located on the underside of the stock. Separate the action from the stock.

2. Pull the trigger to drop the hammer to the fired position and unscrew the receiver end piece, taking it off toward the rear.

3. Move the bolt to the rear, and remove the hammer assembly from the rear of the receiver. This includes the hammer and the captive hammer and bolt springs and their guide rod. This unit can be disassembled, but the guide rod ends are riveted to contain the unit, and disassembly might require that a new guide and rod be made.

4. Align the bolt handle with the opening at the rear of its track in the receiver, and remove the handle toward the right.

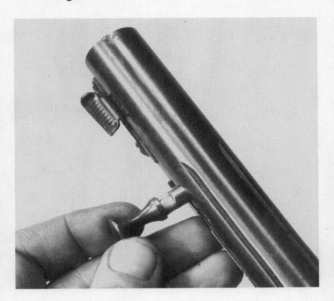

5. Use a small tool to push the bolt toward the rear until it can be grasped and taken out of the receiver.

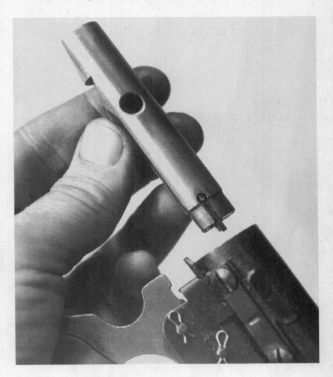

6. Lift the firing pin straight up out of its slot in the top of the bolt.

7. To remove the twin extractors, insert a small screwdriver to depress the plunger, and lift each extractor out of its recess toward the side. **Caution:** *Take care that the screwdriver doesn't slip, as the compressed springs can drive the plungers quite a distance. Ease them out.*

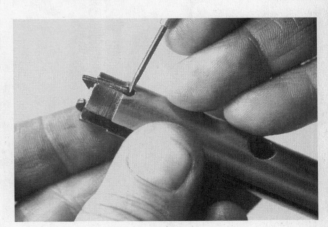

8. Use a small screwdriver to detach the rear hooks of the carrier spring from their notches on the front of the sub-frame. Move the rear arms of the spring outward, and allow them to move toward the rear, partially relieving the tension.

9. Detach the carrier spring from the ends of the carrier pivot on each side and remove the spring.

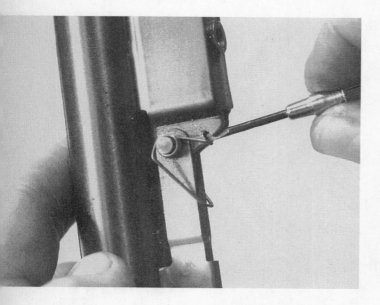

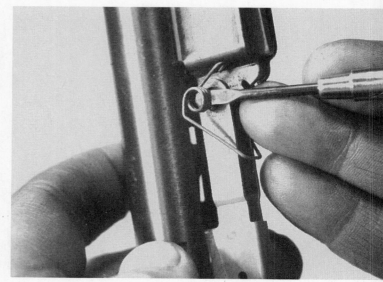

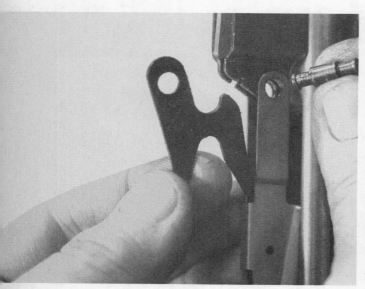

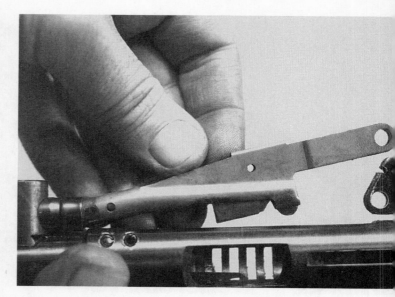

10. Remove the carrier pivot and take out the carrier downward.

11. The cartridge feed throat can now be moved toward the rear, tilted downward at the rear, and taken off.

12. The safety catch and its positioning spring are retained on the right rear of the receiver by two post screws, and these are taken out to allow removal of the spring and safety toward the right.

13. Take off the spring clip on the tip of the trigger pivot, and push the pin out toward the opposite side.

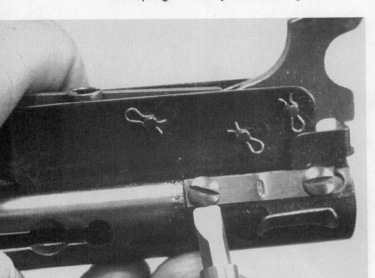

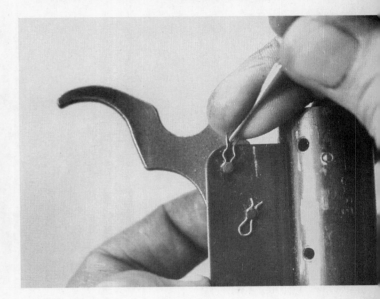

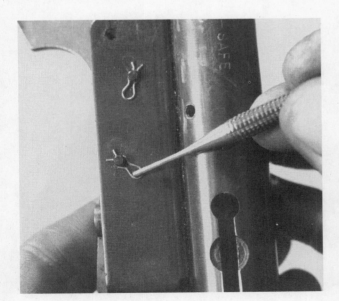

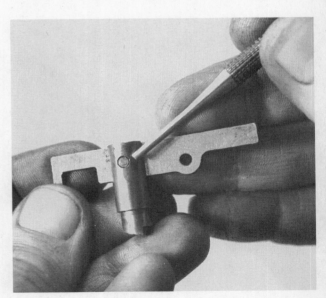

14. Take off the spring clip on the tip of the trigger bar pivot, and take out the pin toward the opposite side. **Caution:** *Keep pressure on the underside of the bar while removing the pin, to control the pressure of the springs, and ease it out.* Remove the bar and disconnector assembly downward.

15. Drifting out the cross pin in the disconnector will allow it to be separated from the bar. **Caution:** *There is a strong coil spring mounted inside the part, so control it when drifting out the pin.*

16. Remove the trigger and sear assembly downward. Note that the other cross pin retained by a spring clip is a stop pin for the trigger and does not have to be removed.

17. Drifting out the cross pin at the front of the trigger will allow separation of the sear from the trigger. **Caution:** *Ease out the compressed spring mounted inside the sear. Also, take care that the front wings of the trigger are not deformed during removal of the pin.*

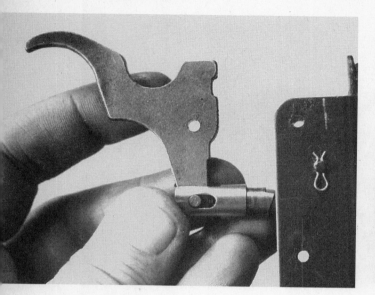

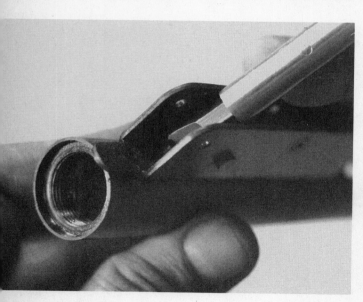

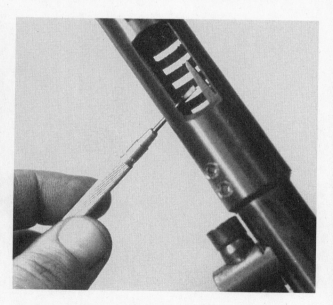

18. The sub-frame, the trigger and sear housing, is retained on the underside of the receiver by two vertical screws; when these are taken out it is removed downward.

19. The cartridge guide, mounted inside and above the chamber, is removable only when the barrel is taken out. There is also a small coil spring mounted in a recess in the roof of the receiver, above the guide.

20. The barrel is retained by two large roll cross pins. Use a roll pin punch to drift these out; then grip the barrel in a padded vise and use a non-marring punch to drive the receiver off the barrel toward the rear. The outer magazine tube is staked in place inside the rear loop (the stock mounting stud), and removal is not recommended except for replacement of a damaged unit. If necessary, the tube can be driven out toward the front using a large wooden dowel as a drift to avoid damaging the tube mouth.

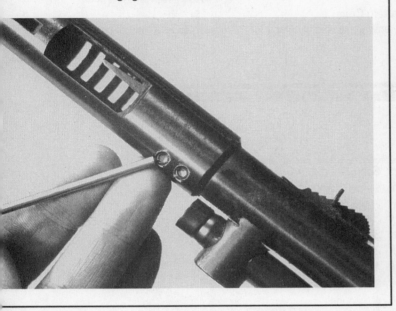

Reassembly Tips:

1. When replacing the carrier spring, use small sharp-nosed pliers to grasp the rear arms of the spring and guide them into their notches in the sub-frame.

2. When replacing the bolt, pull the trigger to ease insertion in the receiver. Also, when replacing the hammer assembly, pull the trigger to allow the hammer to move forward to fired position to facilitate replacement of the receiver end piece.

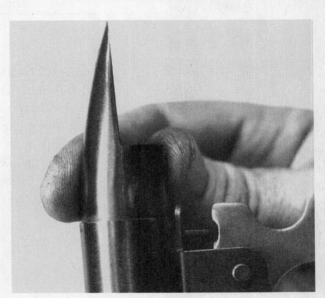

3. When replacing the end piece, tighten it by hand only, no tools; then back it off until it is in the position shown to mate with the stock.

When replacing the barrel in the receiver, take care that the small spring above the cartridge guide is not deformed as the barrel and attached guide are slid into place.

Sears Model 31

Similar/Identical Pattern Guns
The same basic assembly/disassembly steps for the Sears Model 31 also apply to the following gun:
Sears Model 34

Data:	Sears Model 31
Origin:	United States
Manufacturer:	High Standard
	Hamden, Connecticut
Cartridge:	22 Short, 22 Long Rifle
Magazine capacity:	25 Shorts, 17 Long Rifles
Overall length:	$41^{3}/_{4}$ inches
Barrel length:	$23^{1}/_{4}$ inches
Weight:	$5^{1}/_{2}$ pounds

Made for Sears, Roebuck & Company by High Standard, the Model 31 was marketed under the "J.C. Higgins" brand name. Its appearance was unusual in one area—long, slim panels extended from the forend back along each side of the receiver. As an option, the gun could be supplied with a tape-measure-style nylon web sling which was mounted inside the buttstock. The gun was later redesigned to become the Model 34, but the internal mechanism was essentially the same, and the instructions generally can be used for either gun.

Disassembly:

1. Remove the inner magazine tube, cycle the bolt to cock the hammer, and set the safety in the on-safe position. Remove the cross screw located near the rear tip of the wooden side panels which cover the receiver.

2. Pull the rear of the trigger group downward, move the unit slightly toward the rear, and remove it downward.

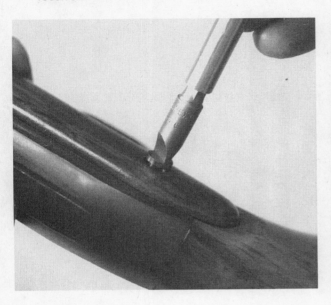

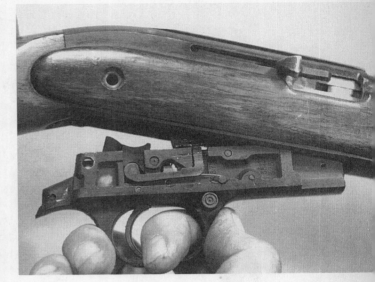

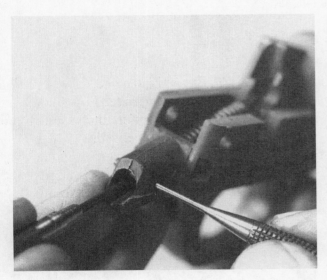

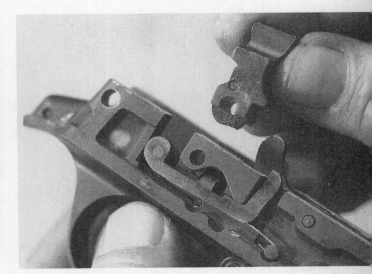

3. Release the safety, restrain the hammer against the tension of its spring, and pull the trigger. Ease the hammer down to the fired position. Use a small drift punch to push out the small cross pin at the extreme rear of the trigger group, and remove the hammer spring and its guide toward the rear. **Caution:** *The spring is under tension, even with the hammer at rest.* Removal of the pin will be easier if a small screwdriver is inserted at the rear to exert pressure on the spring, and this will also help in easing it out.

4. Push out the hammer pivot pin and remove the hammer from the top of the trigger group.

5. Disengage the disconnector spring from its groove in the bottom front of the disconnector and remove the disconnector toward the right. The spring is mounted on a cross pin, and the pin and spring are easily removed toward the right.

6. Drifting out the sear pivot pin toward either side will allow removal of the sear and its spring upward. Before removal, note the relationship of the sear and its spring to aid reassembly.

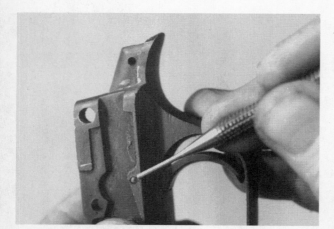

7. Drift out the trigger cross pin and remove the trigger and its spring upward.

8. Insert a drift punch of very small diameter, or an opened paper clip, into the tiny hole in the underside of the safety cross-piece on the left side to depress the safety positioning and retaining plunger and spring. While holding the plunger in, use the drift to turn the safety slightly (about a quarter turn) in either direction, and remove the safety toward the left. When the safety clears the plunger and spring they will be released, so restrain them and ease them out.

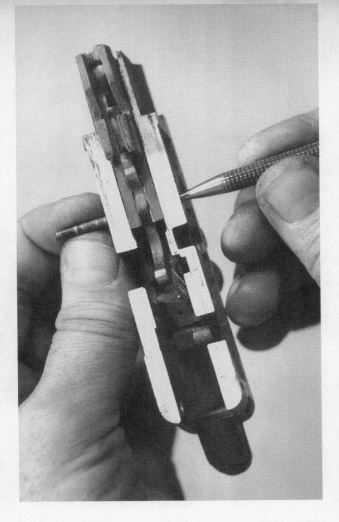

9. Push out the carrier pivot pin toward either side and remove the carrier upward. The carrier is under some tension from the spring below it, but not so much that it can't be easily controlled.

10. Use a roll-pin punch to drift out the small cross pin at the front of the trigger group and remove the two sides of the cartridge guide upward.

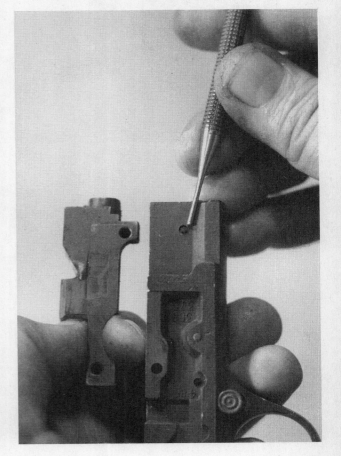

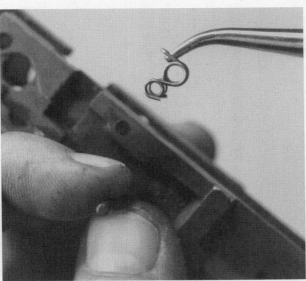

11. Push out the cross pin at the lower edge of the trigger group, just forward of the guard, and remove the carrier spring upward. Before removal, note the way the spring is installed on the pin, to aid reassembly.

12. Invert the gun and retract the bolt all the way to the rear to clear the ejector. Lift the front of the bolt away from the inside top of the receiver, and slide the cocking handle forward; then remove it from the ejection port.

13. Continue tipping the front of the bolt outward until it clears the inner edge of the receiver; then ease it out, releasing the spring tension slowly. Take out the bolt spring and its guide.

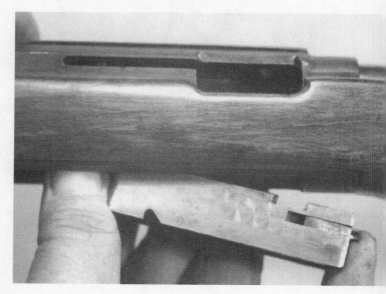

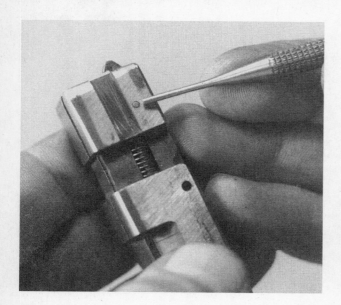

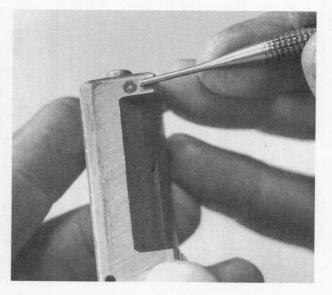

14. The extractor and its coil spring are retained by a vertical pin at the right front of the bolt. Remove the pin by drifting it out toward the top, and take out the extractor and its spring toward the right.

15. The firing pin is retained by a vertical pin at the left rear of the bolt, and this pin must be removed upward. The firing pin and its spring are then taken out toward the rear.

Reassembly Tips:

1. The most difficult reassembly operation is replacement of the carrier spring and carrier. In this photo they are shown assembled outside the trigger group to show the proper relationship of the carrier spring and the small notch on the underside of the carrier. When replacing the carrier, be sure the cross bar of the spring is at the top. Insert the carrier pin through one side of the trigger group wall and one side of the cartridge guide, up to the carrier space. Be sure the small notch in the underside of the carrier engages the cross bar of the spring. Push the carrier down and forward, slightly compressing the spring, until the pivot pin can be pushed through the hole in the carrier and on to the other side. When properly installed, the carrier should move with an audible snap between its raised and lowered positions.

16. The ejector is staked in place inside the left wall of the receiver and should not be removed except for replacement of a broken part. If this is necessary, it can be drifted out downward, alternating the drift point to each end of the ejector as it is struck. Backing out the large screw on the underside of the forend will allow the forend and its integral side panels to be taken off downward. The magazine tube is retained by a cross pin through the tube hanger, and the tube is taken out toward the front. The buttstock is attached by a through-bolt at the rear, accessible after removal of the buttplate. If the gun has the reel-type sling, the reel must be lifted out to give access to the stock bolt.

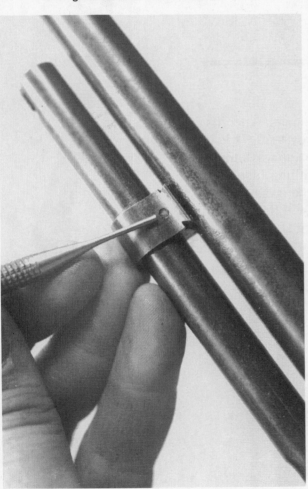

Install the sear, hammer and disconnector in that order, to ensure that the inner arm of the disconnector is in proper engagement with the side tab of the sear. When installing the sear, be sure the right-angled tip of the forward arm of the sear spring engages properly with its shelf on the inside right wall of the trigger group.

Stevens Favorite

Data:	Stevens Favorite
Origin:	United States
Manufacturer:	J. Stevens Arms & Tool Company Chicopee Falls, Massachusetts
Cartridge:	22 Long Rifle
Overall length:	36$\frac{1}{2}$ inches
Barrel length:	22 inches
Weight:	4 pounds

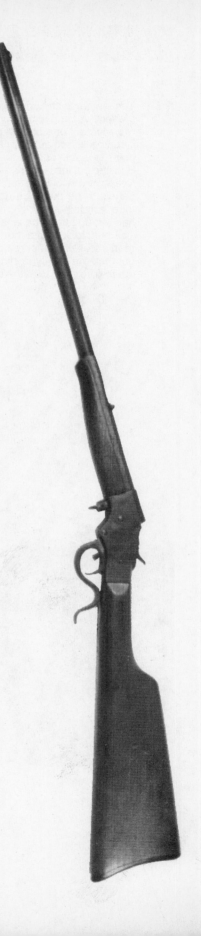

The little Stevens Favorite was certainly well-named. After its introduction in 1889, it became the most popular "boy's rifle" of all time, and lasted through 46 years of production. The gun was simple and reliable, a single shot with a lever-actuated falling block. In 1915 it was redesigned, the most notable internal changes being in the ejector and hammer spring. These differences will be noted in the instructions. The gun covered here is the early model, made prior to 1915.

Disassembly:

1. Back out the barrel retaining screw, located just forward of the lever on the underside of the gun. On guns made after 1915, the head of the screw will be a knurled piece, rather than a ring.

2. Remove the barrel and forend assembly forward.

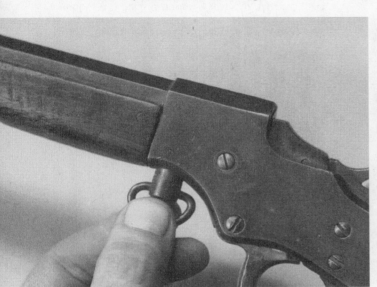

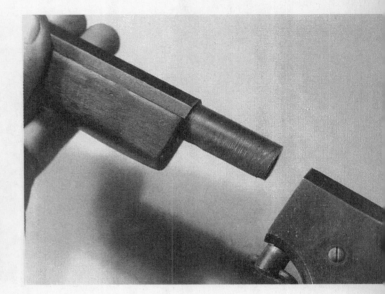

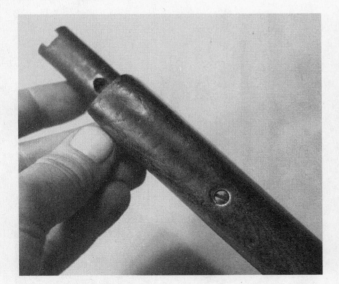

3. The forend is held on the underside of the barrel by a single screw.

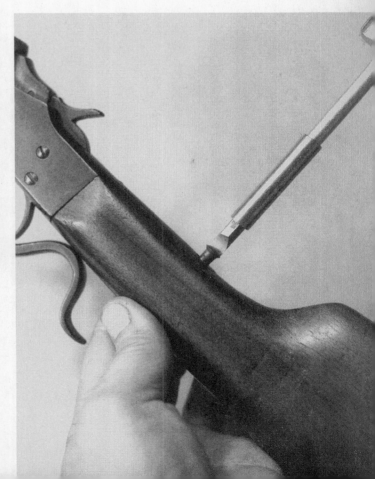

4. Remove the screws at the rear tip of the upper and lower receiver tangs to release the stock for removal. Remove the stock toward the rear. If the stock is very tightly fitted, it may be necessary to bump the front of the comb with the heel of the hand or with a soft rubber hammer.

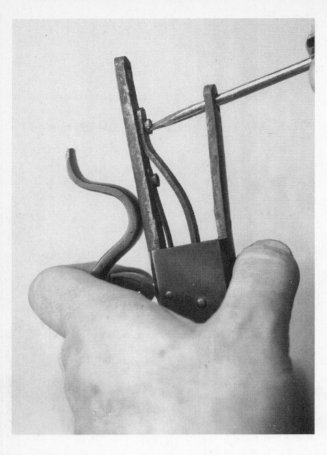

5. The screw that retains the hammer spring can be reached through the stock screw hole in the upper tang. Remove the hammer spring screw and take out the spring toward the rear. On the post-1915 guns, the hammer spring will be a heavy coil with an internal hammer strut and a base sleeve at the rear which bears on a groove in the head of a large screw in the lower tang. On these guns, grip the sleeve firmly with pliers and move it forward, and then upward to clear the base screw. After the hammer spring is removed, in both models, the screw which retains the trigger spring will be accessible. For this screw, use either an offset screwdriver or a screwdriver with the tip cut to an angle.

6. Taking out the hammer and trigger pivot screws will release the hammer for removal upward and the trigger for removal downward.

7. Remove the lever pivot screw, located at the lower edge of the receiver.

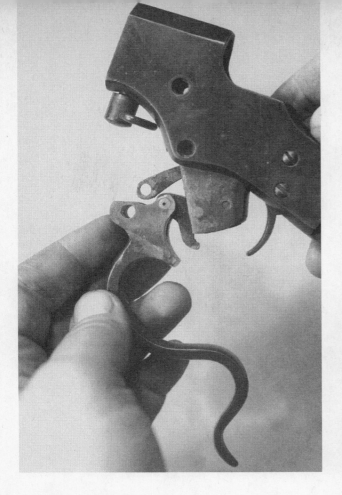

8. Remove the breechblock pivot screw.

9. Remove the lever and breechblock assembly downward. The ejector, which is retained by the lever pivot screw, will also come out at this time.

10. The ejector on the later model guns is different from the one shown. On the post-1915 guns, it has a front lobe which contains a plunger and spring, the plunger bearing on the breechblock pivot. The plunger is staked in place, and removal in routine disassembly is not advisable. Drifting out the upper cross pin in the breechblock will release the firing pin for removal toward the rear. The lower cross pin holds the link to the breechblock, and the pin at the top of the lever retains the lever on the link.

Reassembly Tips:

1. When replacing the lever and breechblock assembly in the receiver, be sure the ejector is in the position shown, with its cartridge rim recess and firing pin groove toward the rear. Also, be sure the link is in the position shown, with its hooked beak downward and pointing toward the rear.

When replacing the lever and breechblock assembly in the receiver, the forward arms of the breechblock should be inserted into the bottom of the receiver first; then the breechblock is tipped into position.

On both models, insert the breechblock pivot screw first; then insert the lever pivot screw, being sure it passes through the lower loop of the ejector. On the later guns, it will be necessary to use a small tool to center the ejector loop while inserting the screw, holding it against the tension of its plunger and spring.

Stevens-Springfield Model 53A

Similar/Identical Pattern Guns

The same basic assembly/disassembly steps for the Stevens-Springfield Model 53A also apply to the following guns:

Stevens-Springfield Model 53   **Stevens-Springfield Model 053**

Data:	Stevens-Springfield Model 53A
Origin:	United States
Manufacturer:	Savage Arms Company Chicopee Falls, Massachusetts
Cartridge:	22 Long Rifle
Overall length:	38¼ inches
Barrel length:	21 inches
Weight:	4 pounds

Savage Arms completed a purchase of the old Stevens firm in 1936, and Stevens continued to make guns in the original Chicopee Falls factory as a subsidiary of Savage. The "Springfield" brand name should not be confused with the U.S. Springfield Armory. The Model 53, 53A, and 053 differed only in sight options and stock configurations. The guns were made from 1935 to 1948.

Disassembly:

1. Hold the trigger to the rear, open the bolt and remove the bolt toward the rear.

2. Back out or remove the action mounting screw located on the underside of the forend. Remove the action from the stock.

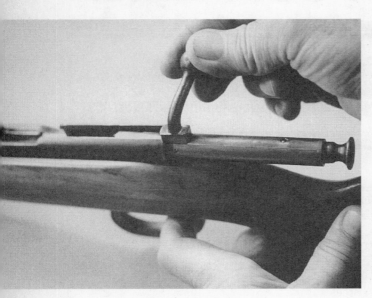

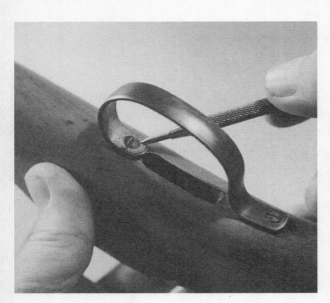

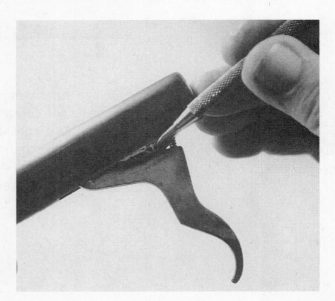

3. Two wood screws retain the trigger guard on the stock. An angled or offset screwdriver will be necessary for the screw at the front, inside the guard. The stock buttplate is also retained by two wood screws.

4. The trigger is retained by a cross pin. Drift out the pin and remove the trigger downward. The coil trigger spring can then be removed from its well at the rear of the trigger.

5. Unscrew and remove the knob at the rear of the bolt.

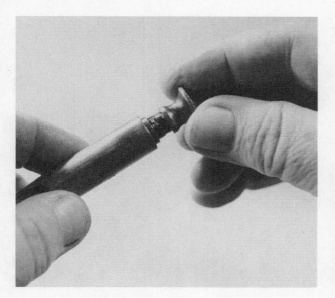

6. The striker rebound spring will likely come off with the cocking knob. If not, it is retrieved from inside the bolt.

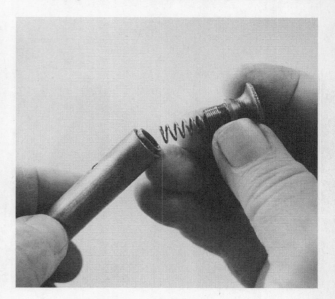

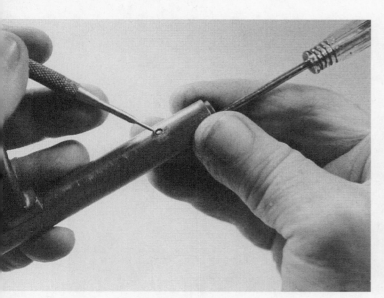

7. Insert a screwdriver at the rear to slightly depress the striker spring, and push or drift out the retaining cross pin. Take care that the pin is not canted during removal.

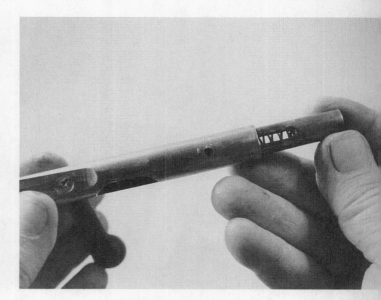

8. Remove the striker assembly toward the rear. The spring is easily removed from inside the striker.

9. Drift out the firing pin retaining pin located just below the bolt handle. Remove the firing pin and its return spring toward the rear. **Caution:** *The spring is under tension.*

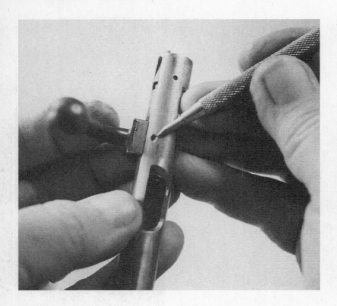

10. Drift out the extractor cross pin and remove the extractor and its plunger and spring. **Caution:** *The spring is under tension, so restrain the extractor as the drift is removed.*

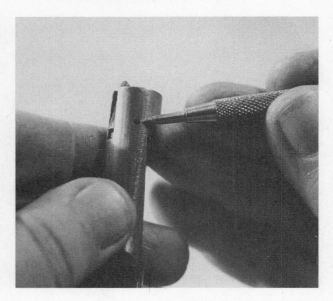

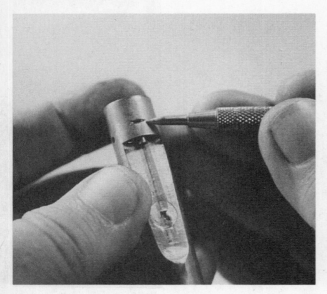

11. The ejector is retained by a recess in its shaft and a stake mark on the underside of the bolt. If removal is necessary, the part is driven out, ironing the stake mark. In normal takedown, it is best left in place.

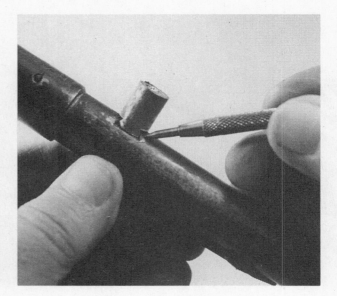

12. The stock mounting post and the front and rear sights are dovetail-mounted on the barrel. If removal is necessary, they are driven out toward the right.

13. The barrel is retained in the receiver by a cross pin. In normal takedown, this is left in place. If barrel removal is necessary, drift out the pin and use a wood block to move the receiver off the barrel.

1. When replacing the striker in the bolt, be sure the sear contact notch is on the underside, as shown.

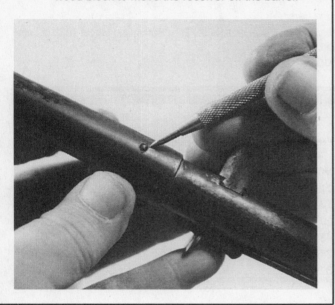

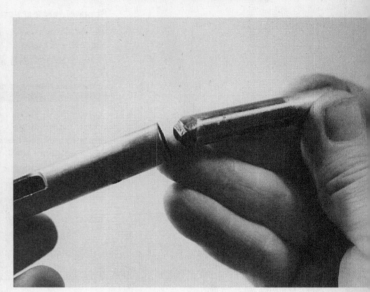

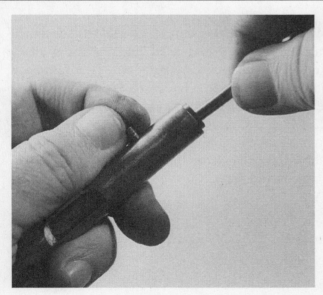

2. When replacing the striker assembly cross pin, insert a tool at the rear to compress the spring, keeping its rearmost coil in front of the pin.

U.S. Springfield Model 1922 M2

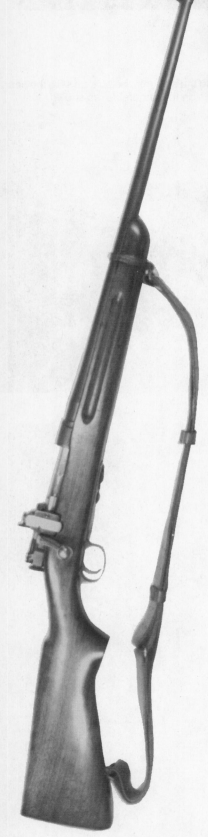

Similar/Identical Pattern Guns
The same basic assembly/disassembly steps for the U.S. Springfield Model 1922 M2 also apply to the following gun:
U.S. Springfield Model 1922 M1

Data:	U.S. Springfield Model 1922 M2
Origin:	United States
Manufacturer:	Springfield Armory
Cartridge:	22 Long Rifle
Magazine capacity:	10 rounds
Overall length:	43.7 inches
Barrel length:	24 inches
Weight:	8.90 pounds

The Model 1922 M2 was the final version of a target rifle designed and made at Springfield Armory and used initially for military marksmanship training. A number of these guns were later furnished to educational institutions and sold to NRA members in cooperation with the DCM. The original 1922 rifle was modified to produce the 1922 M1 and 1922 M2 guns, and the earlier guns were usually changed by the Armory as they came in for repair. The earlier guns are different mechanically, especially in the bolt assembly. The final M2 version is the one covered here.

Disassembly:

1. Remove the magazine. Set the bolt stop lever, located at the left rear of the receiver, on its central position, just a few degrees above horizontal. Withdraw the bolt toward the rear.

2. Drift out the cross pin in the stock, just forward of the barrel band.

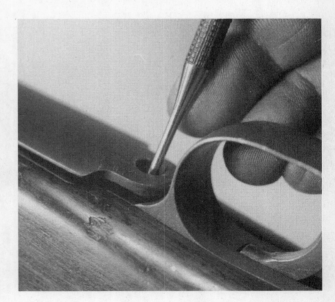

3. Remove the cross-screw at the bottom of the barrel band and take off the sling loop downward. The band can now be moved off toward the front.

4. Use a drift punch tip to depress the magazine floor-plate latch, accessible in a hole at the rear of the plate. While holding the catch in, move the plate toward the rear; then take it off downward.

5. Remove the vertical screw on the underside at the front of the trigger guard unit. Remove the vertical screw on the underside at the rear of the trigger guard and separate the action from the stock. The trigger guard unit can now be taken off downward. The floorplate latch and its spring are retained on the inside of the guard unit by a cross pin and are removed upward.

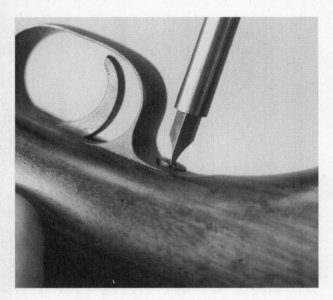

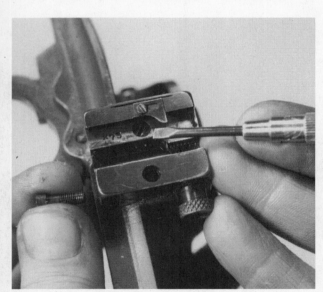

7. Remove both of the mounting screws, the short one inside the slide track, and the longer one in the forward portion of the sight, and take off the sight base toward the right. Further disassembly of the rear sight is not recommended in normal takedown.

6. To remove the rear sight, first turn out the knurled knob on the right side at the front of the sight until it stops; then push it toward the rear and hold it there while sliding the sight upward out of its base. It can be taken completely off, or just moved until it exposes the screw covered by the sight slide, near the scale marker.

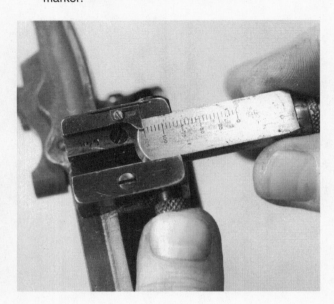

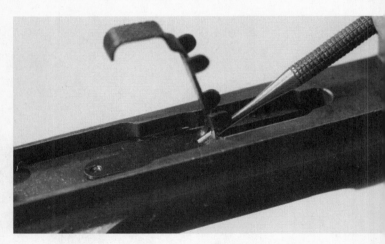

8. The magazine catch is tempered to be its own spring, and is mounted on the underside of the receiver by two forward side projections which are slid into recesses on each side. To remove it, use a small screwdriver to very slightly lift its rear tail, to clear the locking dimple from its recess, and place a drift punch against the end of the slot in the front of its base, next to the receiver. Tap the unit toward the rear until its side projections clear their slots in the receiver, and remove the magazine catch. **Caution:** *Apply pressure **only** to the mounting base plate, and **not** to the lower extension of the catch, or it may be deformed or broken.*

9. Push out the sear pivot pin toward the left, the side on which it has a large, nail-like head.

10. Remove the sear and the attached trigger downward, along with the coil spring mounted in the front of the sear. Drifting out the cross pin in the sear will allow separation of the trigger from the sear.

11. To remove the bolt stop, first back out the small screw in the serrated outer edge of the stop lever. After the screw is removed, withdraw the bolt stop pin toward the rear, using a fingernail or tool in the cannelure provided at its rear tip. During this operation, have the bolt stop turned up to the locked position, and exert slight downward pressure on it to restrain the plunger and spring mounted inside the stop lever. When the pin is out, the bolt stop can be taken off toward the left. Take care not to lose the small spring and plunger.

12. Grip the bolt firmly and pull back the striker knob until the safety can be turned up to vertical position, halfway between the on-safe and off-safe positions. This is more easily done before taking the bolt out of the receiver. Press the bolt sleeve lock inward, hold it in, and turn the rear section of the bolt counterclockwise (rear view), unscrewing the rear portion from the bolt body.

13. When the middle lug on the bolt body has turned sufficiently to clear the lug on the bolt head from its internal recess, the bolt head can be taken off toward the front.

14. Continue turning the rear section until its threads clear the bolt body, and withdraw the rear assembly from the body of the bolt. During this operation, take care not to disturb the safety-lever, as it is holding the lower lug of the cocking piece out of engagement with the rear of the bolt body.

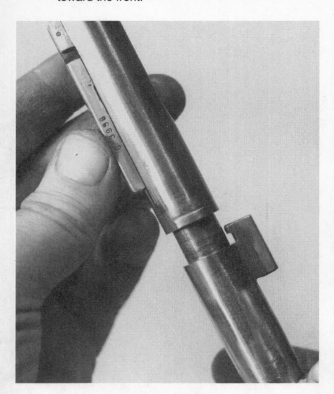

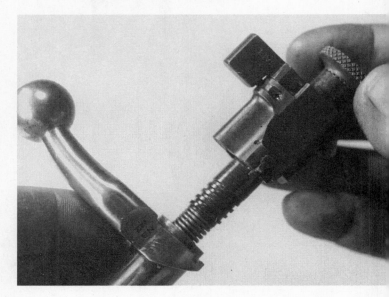

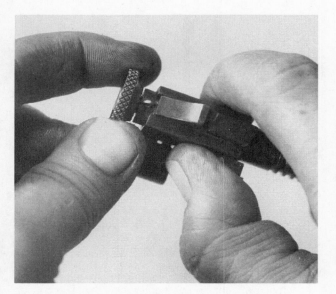

15. Grip the firing pin section of the striker in a padded vise, taking care to exert no side pressure that might break it. While holding the bolt sleeve against the tension of the striker spring, release the safety and keep the sleeve pressed down, away from the striker knob. Slowly release the tension, allowing the sleeve to move back against the knob, as shown.

16. With the front section still gripped in a padded vise, exert downward pressure on the bolt sleeve, slightly compressing the striker spring, and unscrew the cocking knob ("firing pin nut") from the rear tip of the striker shaft. **Caution:** *Keep the bolt sleeve under control, against the compressed spring. When the knob is off, slowly allow the sleeve to move off, releasing the tension of the spring.*

17. Remove the bolt sleeve and the striker spring from the rear of the striker shaft.

18. Remove the cocking piece from the rear of the bolt sleeve. The round-wire nut tension spring is mounted in the rear of the cocking piece and is easily taken out toward the rear.

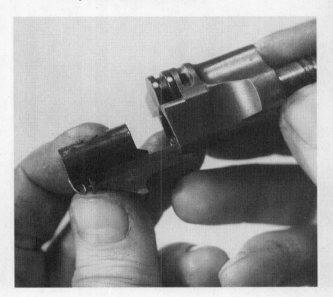

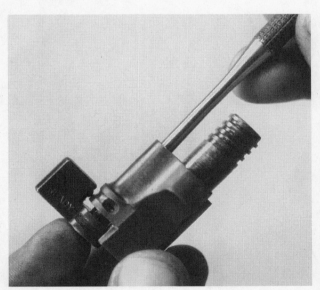

19. To remove the safety from the bolt sleeve, turn the lever up to central position and use a drift punch against the front tip of its pivot shaft, as shown, to nudge it out toward the rear. **Caution:** *As the small plunger and spring inside the safety-lever clear the rear top of the sleeve, they will be released downward. Restrain them, and take care they aren't lost.*

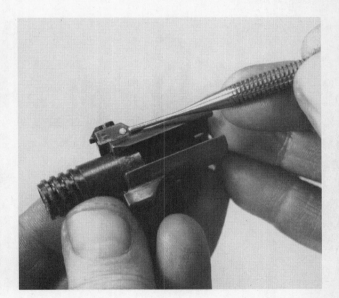

20. A vertical pin on the left side of the bolt sleeve retains the lock plunger and its spring. The pin is drifted out upward, and the plunger and spring are taken off toward the left.

21. The ejector is retained on the left side of the bolt head by a very small vertical pin, requiring a small diameter drift punch. When drifting out the pin, keep a fingertip over the hole at the front of the ejector, to restrain the coil spring housed inside it, as this will be released as the ejector is removed.

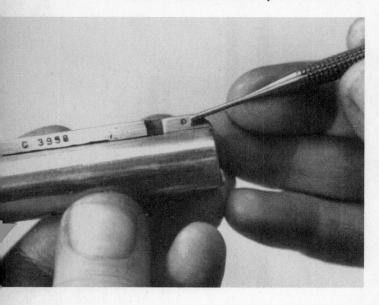

22. The extractor is its own spring. Insert a small screwdriver under its forward beak, and very carefully lift it just enough to clear its underlug from its well in the bolt head; then move it toward the front and off. Use extreme care, as replacement parts for this gun are virtually impossible to find.

Reassembly Tips:

1. When replacing the extractor in the bolt head, place it in position over its recess and press it inward and toward the rear, with a fingertip centered on the arch of its back. This can usually be done without tools.

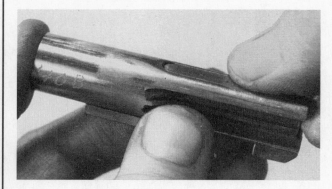

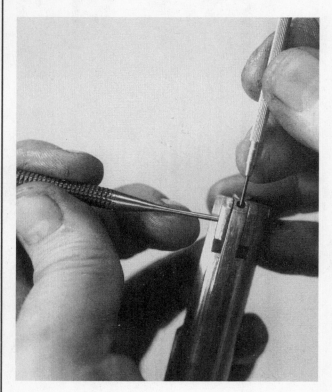

2. When replacing the ejector in the bolt head, use a very small screwdriver to depress the internal spring while the pin is driven back into place, to avoid possible damage to the spring.

3. When replacing the bolt head, remember that this must be done before the final turn of the bolt sleeve at the rear. Place the bolt head in position; then complete the turn of the bolt sleeve and allow the bolt lock to snap into its notch.

4. When the bolt is inserted into the receiver, the bolt stop must be in its open position and the bolt lug must be at the top. Once the front section is inserted, the lug is easily oriented by just turning the bolt handle.

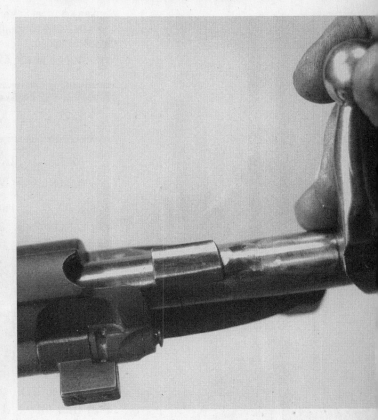

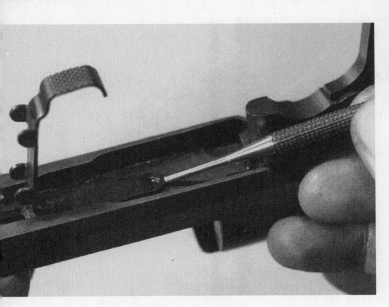

5. When replacing the magazine catch, start it into its side tracks; then use a drift against its rear tail, next to the underside of the receiver, to tap it into place. *Do not exert any pressure on the lower extension of the catch, or it may be deformed or broken.*

Weatherby Mark XXII

Similar/Identical Pattern Guns

The same basic assembly/disassembly steps for the Weatherby Mark XXII also apply to the following gun:

Weatherby Mark XXII Tube Magazine

Data:	Weatherby Mark XXII
Origin:	United States
Manufacturer:	Weatherby, Inc. South Gate, California (Made under contract in Japan)
Cartridge:	22 Long Rifle
Magazine capacity:	5 and 10 rounds in box magazines, 15 rounds in tubular magazine model
Overall length:	$42^1/_4$ inches
Barrel length:	24 inches
Weight:	6 pounds

The Mark XXII had the classic Weatherby look and, in addition to its fine fit and finish, it had several unique features. One was a selector lever that allowed the gun to be used as a single shot, with the bolt remaining open after firing until released by the lever. With the lever in its other position, the gun would function as a normal semi-auto. There were two versions of the Mark XXII, the only difference being in the magazine systems—one had a tubular magazine, and the other, shown here, had a detachable box type. The Mark XXII was made from 1963 to 1989.

Disassembly:

1. Remove the main stock mounting screw, located on the underside, forward of the magazine well. Remove the screw at the rear of the trigger guard on the underside and lift the action straight up out of the stock. It should be noted that it is possible to take off the barrel and receiver unit alone by pushing out the large takedown pin at the rear of the receiver toward the left, and moving the barrel/receiver unit forward and upward, but this will leave the trigger group sub-frame in the stock. After the two screws are taken out, the trigger guard unit can be taken off downward.

2. Push out the cross pin at the rear of the receiver toward the left and remove it.

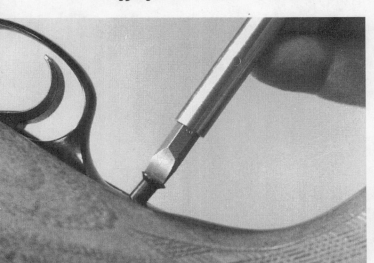

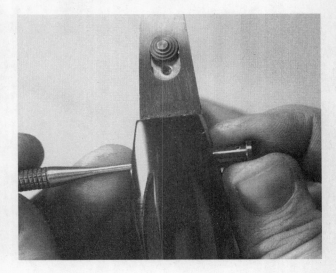

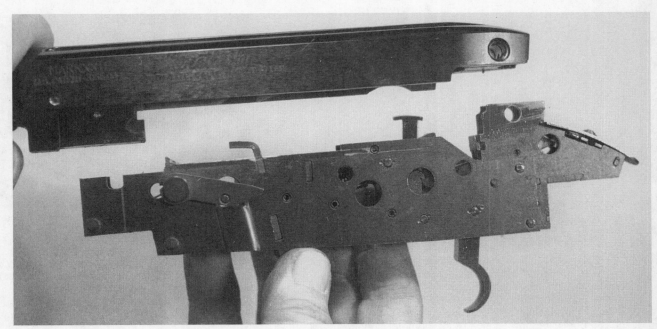

3. Move the trigger group about $1/8$-inch toward the rear and remove it downward.

4. Before any disassembly of the trigger group, hold the hammer against its spring tension, pull the trigger and ease the hammer down to the fired position. The selector lever on the right side of the group is retained by a large C-shaped spring clip. Carefully slide the clip off downward and remove the selector lever toward the right.

5. The pivot and mounting stud for the single shot bolt-catch is retained inside the group by a C-clip. Use a small screwdriver to slide the clip off upward, and take care that it isn't lost. There is an access hole on the left side through which the clip can be reached. The bolt-catch piece is then removed toward the right, along with its pivot-post, unhooking its spring at the front. The torsion spring is held in the group by a roll cross pin.

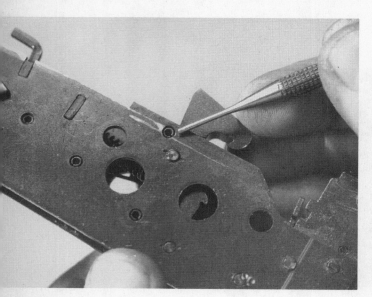

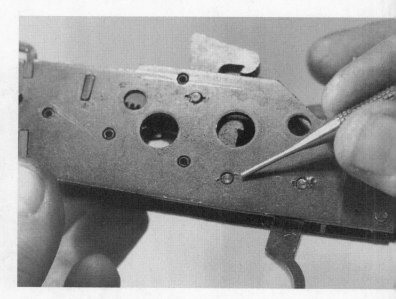

6. Set the hammer on its first step, and drift out the roll cross pin just forward of the hammer at the top edge of the group. Restrain the hammer, pull the trigger to release it and let it go forward beyond its normal down position, relieving the tension of the hammer spring. Drifting out the solid pin just below the roll pin, the hammer pivot, will allow removal of the hammer and its spring and guide upward.

7. The sear is retained by a solid pin near the lower edge of the receiver. Drifting out this pin will allow removal of the sear and its spring downward.

8. The trigger is retained by a cross pin just to the rear of the sear pin. The trigger and its attached sear bar and spring are removed downward. The coil trigger spring will be released as it clears its plate at the rear of the trigger, so restrain it and take care that it isn't lost.

9. Drifting out a small roll pin at the rear of the trigger group will allow removal of the safety bar toward the front. **Caution:** *The safety bar plunger and spring will be released upward as the bar is moved out, so restrain them against loss.* The rear portion of the safety, the button and indicator plate, are not easily removable, as this would require taking off the staked tang plate. This is not advisable in normal takedown.

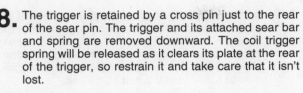
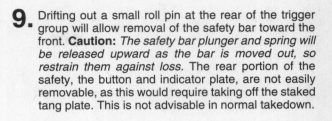

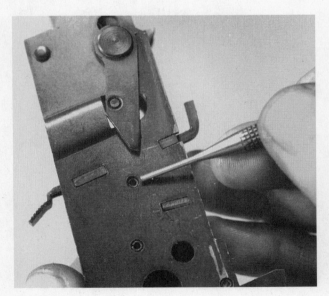
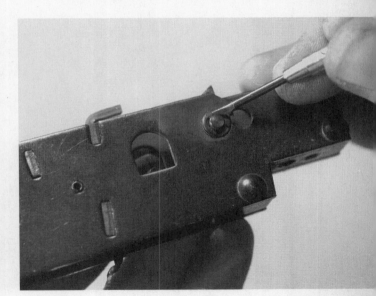

10. The magazine catch and its spring are retained by a roll cross pin. Note the relationship of the spring and the catch before removal, to aid reassembly. The catch and spring are removed downward. The ejector is staked in place between the riveted side-plates of the trigger group and is not removable in normal takedown.

11. The bolt hold open device is retained by a C-clip on the right side of the group, the clip gripping the end of its cross-shaft. Note that there is also a small washer under the C-clip, and take care that it isn't lost. The hold open is removed toward the left.

12. Firmly grasp the bolt handle and pull it straight out toward the right.

13. Invert the gun and move the bolt slowly toward the rear. Lift the front of the bolt enough to clear the receiver, and ease the bolt out forward, slowly relieving the tension of the bolt spring. **Caution:** *Control the compressed spring.* Remove the spring and its guide from the rear of the bolt.

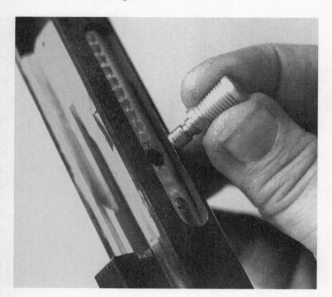

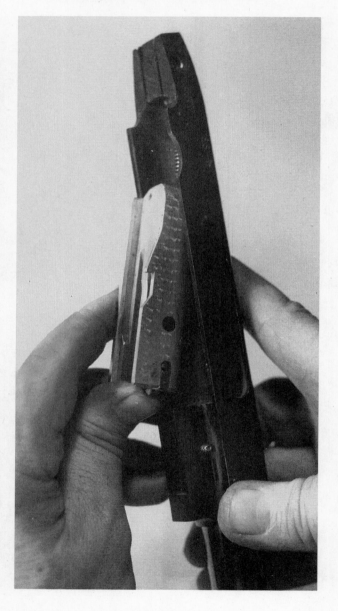

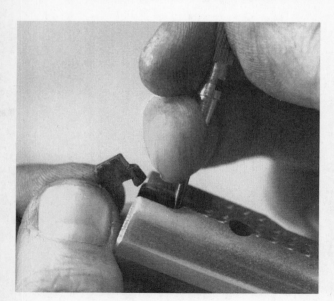

14. Use a small screwdriver to depress the extractor spring plunger, and lift the extractor out of its recess at the right front of the bolt. **Caution:** *Do not allow the screwdriver to slip, as the small plunger and spring will travel quite a distance if suddenly released.*

15. The firing pin is retained by a vertical roll pin located at the left rear of the bolt, and the firing pin and its return spring are removed toward the rear.

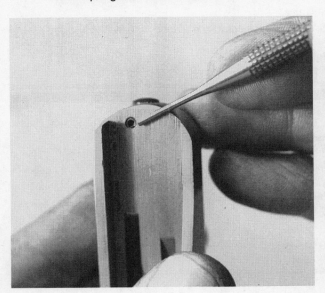

Reassembly Tips:

1. When replacing the single shot bolt-catch on the right side of the trigger group, remember to hook the torsion spring under its forward end. The spring may be installed first, and then its end moved out, downward and up to hook it under the part.

When replacing the large takedown cross pin at the rear of the receiver, be sure it is inserted from left to right. Otherwise, the stock will block its removal when the rifle is fully reassembled.

Winchester Low Wall

Data:	Winchester Low Wall
Origin:	United States
Manufacturer:	Winchester Repeating Arms Co. New Haven, Connecticut
Cartridge:	22 Long Rifle
Overall length:	42 inches
Barrel length:	26 inches
Weight:	8 pounds

Designed by John Moses Browning, the Winchester single shot rifle was made from 1885 to 1920. It was chambered for a long list of cartridges, both rimfire and centerfire. The heavier rounds were in the version popularly called the "High Wall," with the receiver fully enclosing the breechblock. A later takedown version of the gun had a torsion-type spring on the hammer axis, but was otherwise mechanically the same.

Disassembly:

1. Remove the rear wood screw from the lower tang. Remove the stock retaining screw from the upper tang. Remove the buttstock toward the rear.

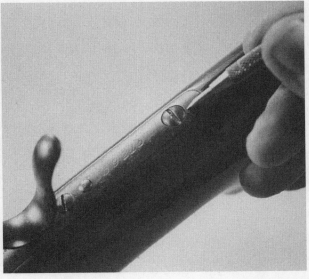

2. Remove the forend retaining screw. Remove the forend downward and toward the front.

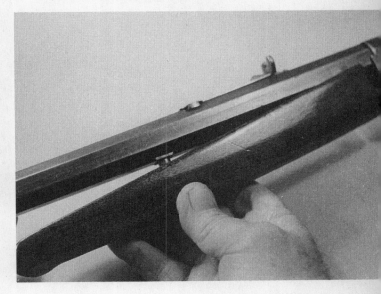

3. Remove the hammer spring retaining screw. **Note:** In the gun shown, the spring and screw are non-original replacements. The spring is normally longer and heavier and is attached to a dovetail-mounted base. Remove the hammer spring toward the front.

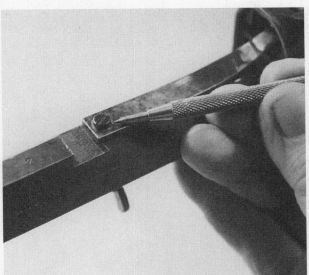

4. Remove the lever pivot lock screw.

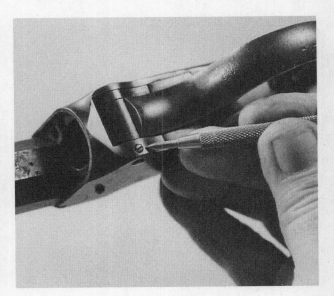

5. Push or drift out the lever pivot toward the right.

6. Remove the breechblock and lever assembly downward. The ejector will fall free as the assembly clears the receiver.

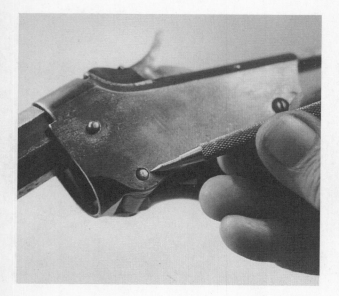

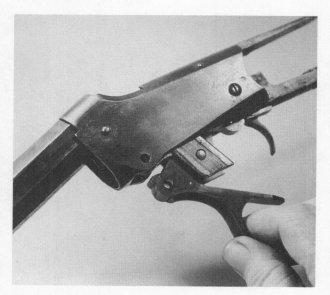

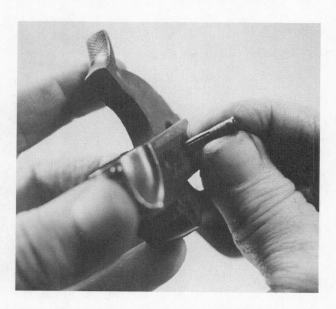

7. The hammer pivot is locked by a tempered split end that resembles a screw slot. This must be driven out toward the side that has the solid end of the pin. A regular drift may start it out, but if not, it may be necessary to make a V-tip tool to compress the ends of the pin.

8. After the tip of the pin is compressed and freed, drift out the hammer pivot. This will allow the hammer to be removed from the breechblock.

9. Push out the lever pin and separate the lever from the breechblock.

10. Push out the lever link pin and remove the link.

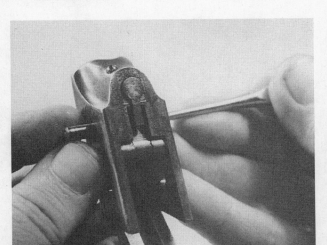

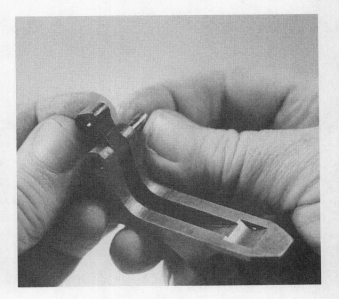

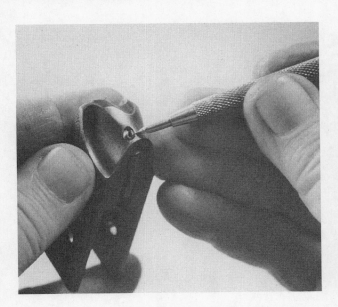

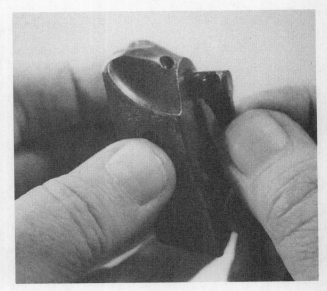

11. Remove the firing pin retaining screw. **Note:** In the High Wall version, the firing pin is retained in the breechblock by a cross pin.

12. Remove the firing pin toward the rear.

13. Remove the screws on each side of the receiver that retain the lower tang unit. **Note:** Keep these in order, right and left, and they will fit better on reassembly.

14. Remove the lower tang assembly toward the rear. This unit will likely be tight and may require a nudge with a nylon drift. If so, be sure the drift is against a shoulder of the tang, and not the trigger, or the trigger pivot could be bent.

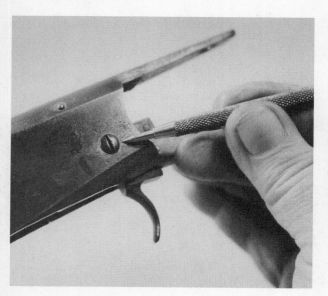

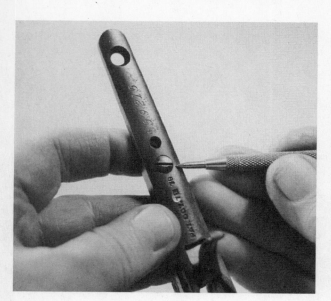

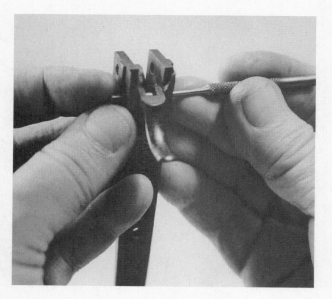

15. Remove the sear knock-off spring retaining screw and take out the spring.

16. Push out the trigger pin and remove the trigger downward.

17. Push out the sear knock-off pin and remove the sear knock-off. When the sear knock-off is taken out, take care that the trigger contact pin is not lost, as it is often loose. The lower pin in the tang unit is the trigger stop pin, and it is not removed in normal takedown.

18. In most guns, the sear spring will be retained by a screw in this location. The gun shown has a filler screw at this point.

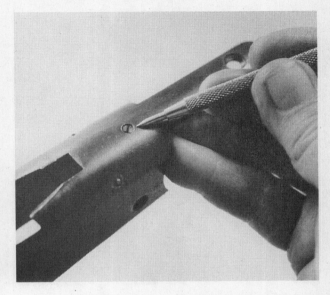

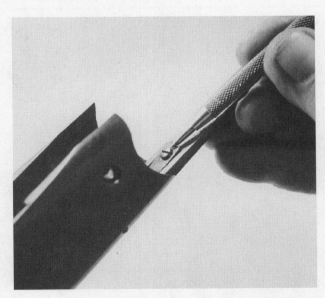

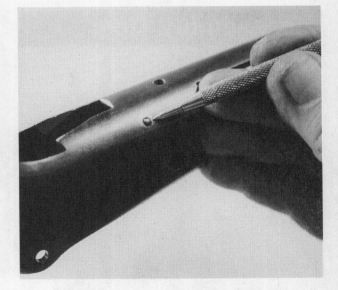

19. In our subject gun, the sear spring screw is located inside the upper tang. Remove the screw and take out the sear spring.

20. Drift out the sear cross pin. Take care not to mar the curved top of the receiver.

21. Removal of the pin will free the sear to be taken out downward.

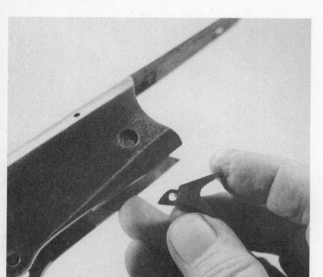

22. The barrel is threaded into the receiver and is also secured by a large cross pin. In normal takedown, this is left in place.

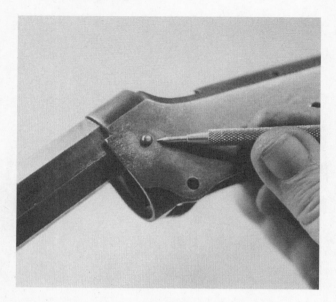

Reassembly Tips:

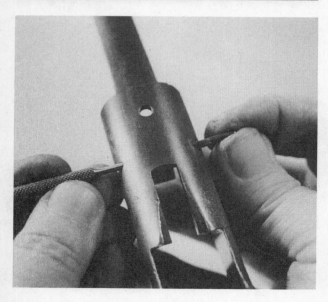

1. When replacing the sear, be sure it is properly oriented with the crescent-shaped surface toward the front (see step 21 in takedown). Insert a drift to hold the sear in position while the cross pin is started.

2. When replacing the sear knock-off spring, be sure its front tip goes under both of the cross pins, as shown.

3. As the tang is pushed into place, use a finger inside the receiver to depress the sear to clear the sear knock-off. Be sure the tang is positioned properly for entry of the two screws. If the first screw does not go in and engage easily, adjust the tang position.

4. If the link has been removed from the lever, be sure it is installed with its lobe toward the rear, as shown.

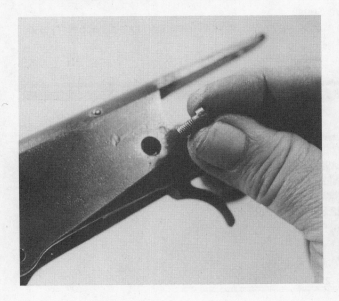

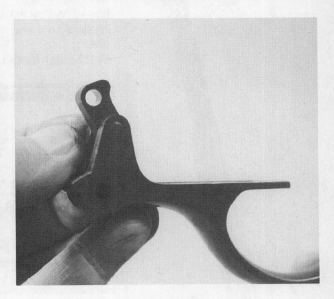

5. To restart the split-end hammer pivot, squeeze the end with pliers as it is inserted.

6. Before the breechblock and lever assembly is reinserted, place the ejector in position in the receiver, as shown.

Winchester Model 61

Similar/Identical Pattern Guns

The same basic assembly/disassembly steps for the Winchester Model 61 also apply to the following gun:

Winchester Model 61 Magnum

Data:	Winchester Model 61
Origin:	United States
Manufacturer:	Winchester Repeating Arms New Haven, Connecticut
Cartridge:	22 Short, Long, or Long Rifle
Magazine capacity:	20 Short, 16 Long, 14 Long Rifle
Overall length:	41 inches
Barrel length:	24 inches
Weight:	5½ pounds

A sleek little slide-action "hammerless" gun, the Model 61 had a virtually infallible feed system, with the cartridge rim firmly guided up a T-slot in the bolt face from the moment of leaving the magazine. This system was also used in the Model 9422 lever-action rifle. Made from 1932 to 1963, the Model 61 was also offered in 22 WRF chambering, and for a short time, just before it was discontinued, in 22 WMR. Internal mechanisms are the same, and the instructions will apply to any of these.

Disassembly:

1. Remove the inner magazine tube and cycle the action to cock the internal hammer. Use a coin or a specially shaped screwdriver to back out the takedown screw, located at the rear of the receiver on the left side.

2. When the takedown screw has moved a short distance to the left, clearing its seat in the receiver wall, separate the front and rear sections of the gun, moving the rear section toward the rear and downward.

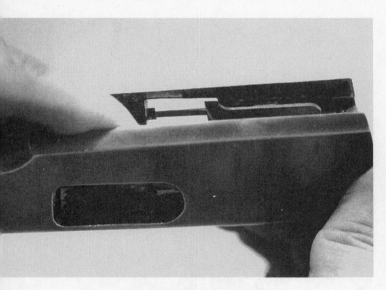

3. With the front section of the gun inverted, move the breechblock (bolt) all the way to the rear and depress the retaining spring, located in a slot inside the right wall of the receiver. Move the bolt forward and upward, disengaging its side lug from the action slide bar; then move the bolt toward the rear.

4. Remove the bolt from the rear of the receiver.

5. To begin disassembly of the bolt, drift out the vertical pin in the left lower front that retains the feed extractor and its transverse coil spring. The pin should be driven out downward using a very small diameter drift punch to start it. Its upper end is within a recess on the bolt, so it can't be drifted straight out. After starting, it usually comes out easily.

6. The ejector and its spring are retained on the left side of the bolt by a vertical pin which is driven out upward, its lower end being within the same recess as the one described in step 5. The ejector and its spring are moved out forward. Note that the ejector must be removed before the firing pin can be taken out.

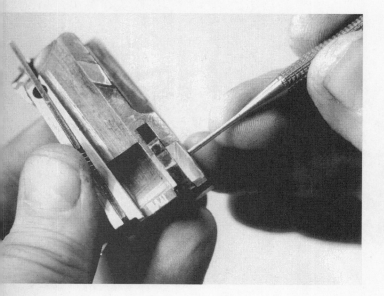

7. The firing pin is retained by a cross pin at the upper rear of the bolt, and the pin is also the compressor for the firing pin return spring on the right side. The pin is fixed into the body of the firing pin itself, rather than into the bolt. After the ejector is removed, the firing pin cross pin is driven out toward the left, and the firing pin and its spring are removed toward the rear.

8. To remove the extractor, use a small screwdriver to depress and hold the extractor spring plunger, and lift the extractor out of its recess toward the right. **Caution:** *Take care that the tool holding the plunger doesn't slip, and ease out the plunger and its spring.*

9. The carrier plunger and its spring are retained on the right side of the bolt by a lengthwise pin which is drifted out toward the front. **Caution:** *As the pin clears the coil spring housed within the plunger, the spring will be released, so restrain it and ease it out.* The plunger is easily moved out of its recess toward the right.

10. Drift out the cross pin in the rear magazine tube hanger loop and remove the outer magazine tube toward the front.

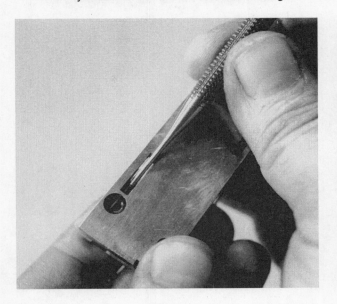

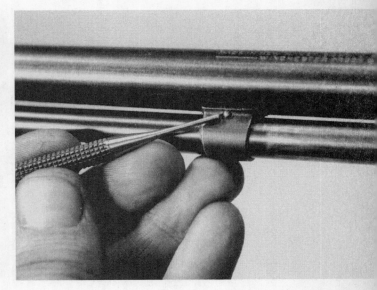

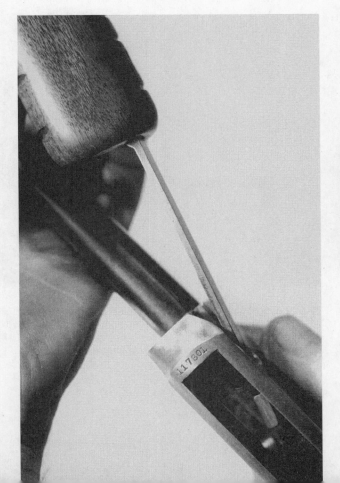

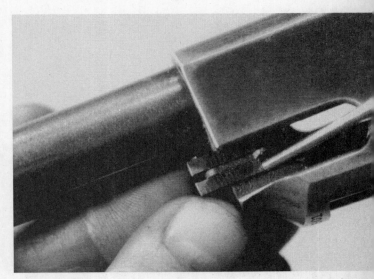

12. Push the cartridge stop housing out of the receiver toward the front.

11. With the magazine tube removed, the action slide bar and its handle are easily tilted out toward the side and detached from the receiver. Removal of the screws on each side of the handle will allow separation of the handle from the action slide piece.

13. The cartridge stop is retained in the housing by a vertical pin, but this should not be removed in normal disassembly. If it is absolutely necessary for repair, take care when drifting out the pin that the side block of the housing is well supported, or it can be deformed.

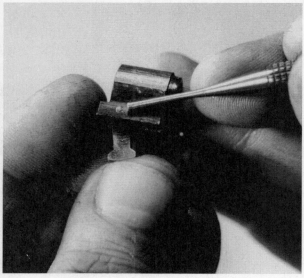

14. Remove the buttplate and use a B-Square stock tool or a long screwdriver to take out the stock mounting bolt. Take off the stock toward the rear.

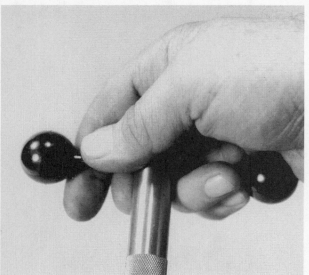

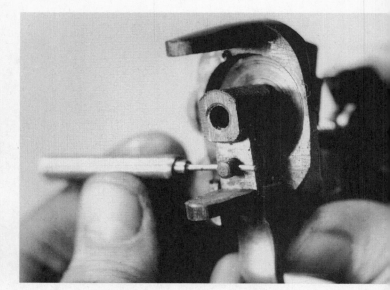

15. If removal of the takedown cross-screw becomes necessary, use a very slim drift punch to drive out the small cross pin that transverses its shaft on the right side, just at the edge of the threaded section.

16. With the hammer in the cocked position, insert a small pin or drift punch tip through the transverse hole in the rear tip of the hammer spring guide. Restrain the hammer, pull the trigger and ease the hammer forward until the pin or drift rests against the rear of the frame, trapping the spring.

17. Depress the action slide lock to clear the left end of the hammer pivot and drift out the hammer pivot pin. This pin is also the pivot for the carrier. Note the relationship of these parts before removal.

18. Restrain the hammer against the tension of its spring and carefully remove the pin or drift from the hole in the rear tip of the spring guide. Ease the hammer off forward and upward, along with its guide and spring. The spring is easily removable from the guide, but the cross pin that attaches the guide to the back of the hammer is usually riveted in place, and in normal takedown it is best left on the hammer.

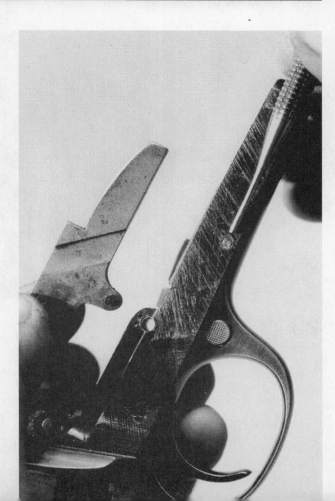

19. Remove the carrier upward and toward the rear, disengaging the tip of its frame-mounted torsion spring from the slot and cross pin in the lower lobe of the carrier. Do not lift the carrier straight up or move it forward during removal, or the spring will be deformed. The spring is retained in the frame by a cross pin, located just forward of the guard. Note its position inside the frame before removal.

20. Drift out the trigger cross pin, move the trigger toward the rear to clear the inner projection of the slide latch, and remove the trigger upward.

21. Removal of the trigger pin will also free the hammer catch/slide latch lever, and it can be tipped down at the front, moved toward the rear, and taken out the rear opening of the frame. The clearances here are close, and some maneuvering of the part will be required.

22. The slide lock can now be moved off its post toward the left, then moved out toward the front. Take care not to lose the round-wire spring mounted in a vertical hole in its underside.

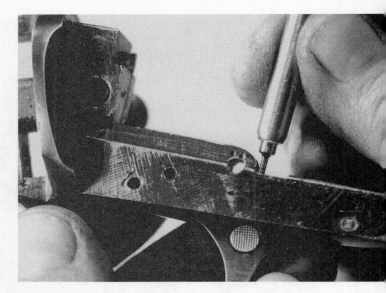

23. With the safety in off-safe position, insert a very small drift into the hole in its top, inside the frame, and tip the drift punch over toward the front of the unit, turning the safety to disengage its positioning plunger from the detent cuts on the underside of the safety. The safety can now be tapped out toward the left side. **Caution:** *As the safety clears the plunger and spring mounted below it, they will be released.* Restrain them, and ease them out.

Reassembly Tips:

1. When replacing the trigger, slide latch lever/hammer catch, and slide latch system, insert the latch lever first, then the trigger and its spring, and push the trigger pin only halfway across the frame. With the latch lever/hammer catch still loose, move the slide latch in toward the rear, being sure the rear tip of its spring goes *beneath* the side stud on the latch lever, and the rear tip of the latch *above* the stud. When the latch is back on its stud, the lever can be moved into alignment, and the trigger cross pin driven into place.

2. When installing the carrier, grip the rear arm of the carrier spring with sharp-nosed pliers, and hold it in raised position while fitting it into the slot in the lower lobe of the carrier, on top of the cross pin. The carrier is then moved forward and downward until its pivot hole is aligned with the cross pin hole in the frame, and the tension of the spring will hold it in place until insertion of the hammer.

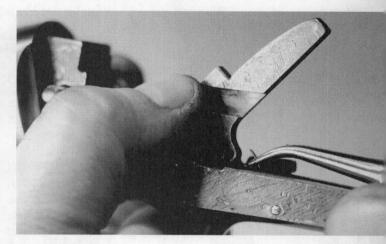

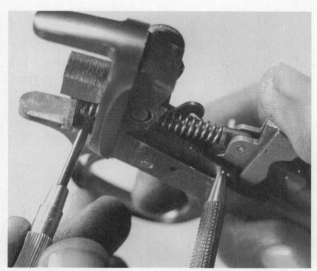

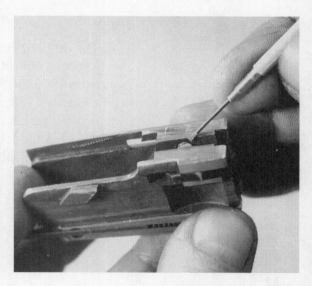

3. Place the hammer in general alignment with the cross pin hole, and insert a drift punch of smaller diameter than the pin, just to hold the hammer in place while aligning the rear tip of the guide and the spring with the hole at the rear of the frame in the vertical spring baseplate. When the tip of the guide rod can be inserted through the hole in the plate, put a pin or drift tip through the transverse hole in the guide, just as in takedown, to trap the spring while the hammer pivot pin is driven through the hammer and carrier.

4. When replacing the carrier plunger, note that the rounded portion of its inner tip must be oriented toward the bottom of the bolt, as shown.

Winchester Model 63

Similar/Identical Pattern Guns

The same basic assembly/disassembly steps for the Winchester Model 63 also apply to the following gun:

Winchester Model 1903

Data:	Winchester Model 63
Origin:	United States
Manufacturer:	Winchester Repeating Arms Co.
	New Haven, Connecticut
Cartridge:	22 Long Rifle
Magazine capacity:	10 rounds
Overall length:	$39^1/_2$ inches
Barrel length:	20 and 23 inches
Weight:	$5^1/_2$ pounds

The original gun of this design, the Model 1903, was chambered for a special cartridge, the 22 Winchester Auto. It was made in this form from 1903 to 1932. The Model 63, in 22 Long Rifle, was made from 1933 to 1958. Very early guns will have the 20-inch barrel and pedal-type latch on the takedown knob that were carried over from the 1903 model. Otherwise, mechanically, the two models are practically identical.

Disassembly:

1. Use a coin or a specially shaped screwdriver to loosen the takedown screw at the rear of the receiver. After it is freed, the serrated knob is easily turned by hand. Back it out until it is stopped by its internal pin. **Note:** If you have a Model 1903, or a very early Model 63, the knob will have a pedal-type latch below it which must be depressed to allow turning.

2. Separate the buttstock and trigger group assembly from the receiver, moving the assembly straight toward the rear. Tight fitting may require the use of a rubber mallet for initial separation.

3. Remove the two screws, one on each side, that retain the forend cap. Remove the forend cap and cocking plunger assembly toward the front. The plunger spring is easily removed from inside the plunger. The knob is retained on the plunger by a cross pin.

4. Keep the forend snugged to the rear to avoid damaging it and carefully drift the forend cap base out of its dovetail toward the right. Use a brass or nylon drift to avoid damaging the screw-hole threads. Remove the forend toward the front.

5. Unscrew and remove the recoil spring guide rod. **Caution:** *Restrain the spring as the rod is taken out.*

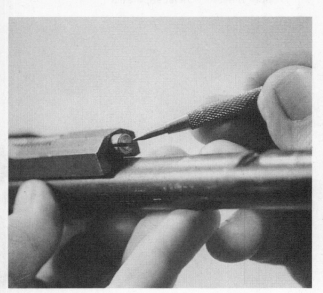

6. One method of controlling the spring during removal of the guide rod is shown here.

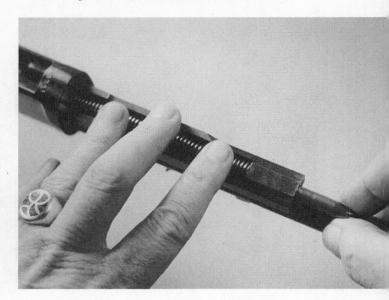

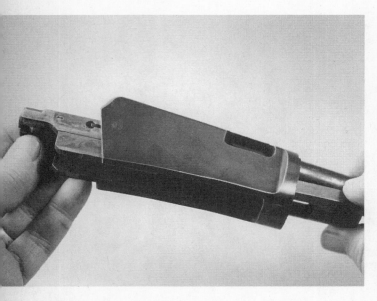

7. Move the bolt assembly rearward and take it out of the receiver.

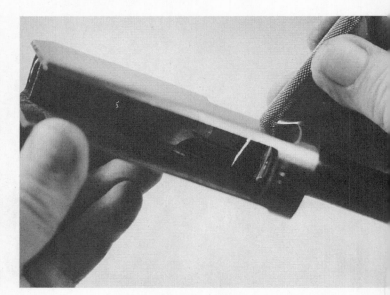

8. The ejector is retained by a single screw inside the left wall of the receiver, and the screw is accessible through the ejection port. In normal takedown, this is best left in place.

9. Restrain the firing pin and push out the firing pin retaining cross pin.

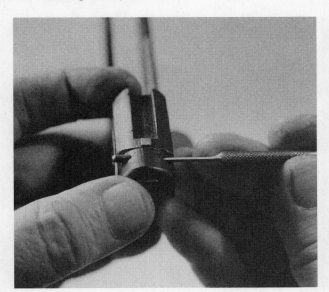

10. Remove the firing pin and its rebound spring toward the rear.

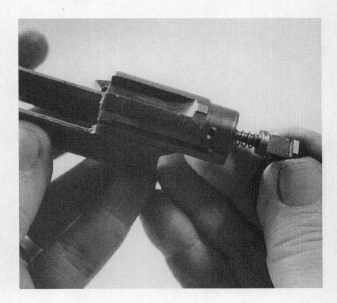

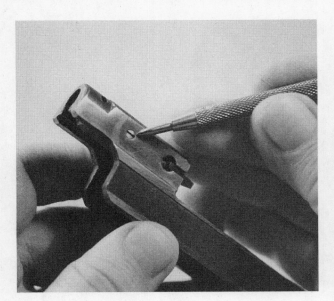

11. Remove the extractor plunger stop screw.

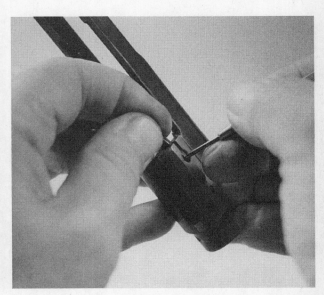

12. Insert a small tool between the extractor and its plunger, and depress the plunger toward the rear. Lift out the extractor. **Caution:** *Control the plunger and its compressed spring.*

13. Remove the inner magazine tube. Take out the two buttplate screws and remove the buttplate.

14. The best way to remove the stock mounting nut is to alter a $5/8$-inch deep socket, cutting away its edge to leave two projections that will engage the slots in the nut. Removal can also be done this way: Use an angled drift punch to break the nut loose.

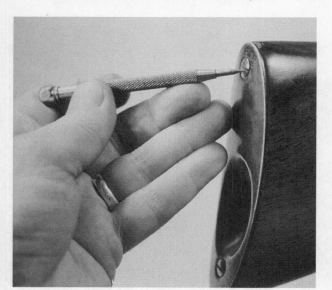

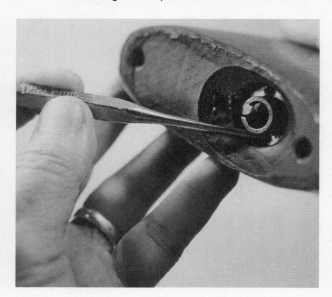

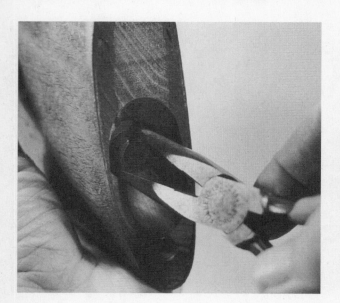

15. Once the nut is freed, an opened sharp-nosed plier can be used to unscrew it.

16. Remove the stock mounting nut and its washer toward the rear.

17. Remove the buttstock toward the rear.

18. Remove the safety detent plunger and spring toward the rear.

19. Retract the hammer slightly until the cross-hole near the tip of the spring guide is accessible, and insert a small pin to trap the hammer spring. Ease the hammer back forward.

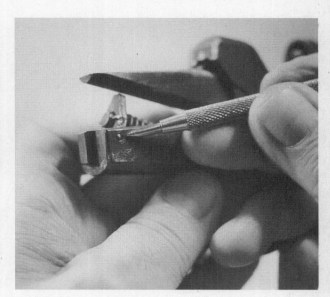

20. Drift out the hammer spring base lock pin.

21. Tip the hammer spring base to the side until its upper portion stops against the frame. This will free it from its recess.

22. Drift out the hammer pivot pin.

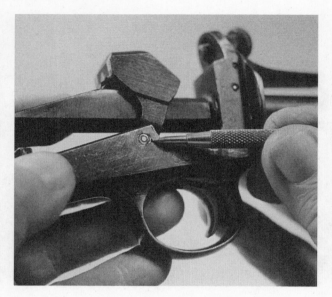

23. Remove the hammer and spring assembly toward the front. Pressing the spring base against a slightly opened vise and removing the keeper pin will allow the base and spring to be taken off the guide. **Caution:** *The spring is under tension.* The guide pivot pin can also be removed to take the guide off the hammer.

24. Drift out the trigger cross pin.

25. Take out the sear and its spring from inside the trigger group.

26. Turn the trigger downward into the guard for removal.

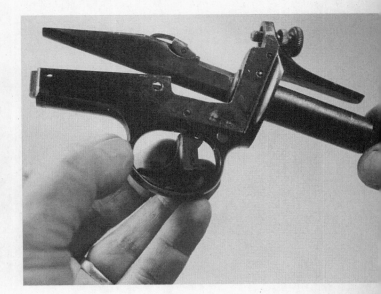

27. Use a tool to push the trigger spring out toward the front, into the receiver, for removal. **Caution:** *Lay a shop cloth over the lower receiver to arrest the spring as it is freed.*

28. Remove the safety button toward either side.

29. If removal of the takedown screw is necessary, determine the smaller end of the cross pin in its tip, and drift that end to push it out. The knob/screw can then be taken off rearward.

30. If you have removed the takedown screw, then drifting out this pin will release the takedown screw lock plunger and its spring for removal upward. **Caution:** *The spring is under tension.*

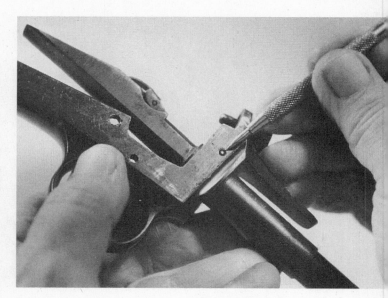

31. The cartridge stop and its spring can be removed from the magazine housing by pushing out this cross pin. Take care that the small coil spring is not lost.

32. In normal takedown, the magazine housing is best left in place. However, if removal is necessary, this cross pin retains it in the lower receiver. After the pin is drifted out, the housing is moved forward out of the lower receiver. In removal of the magazine housing, there is always the possibility of damage.

Reassembly Tips:

1. When reinstalling the safety, remember that the flat recess goes toward the front and also that the shorter of its two ends goes toward the right side, as shown.

2. The trigger spring must be inserted through the trigger guard, and a tool is used to push it back into its tunnel. The proper orientation is shown. You will know it is properly in place when its rear bends are visible at the back of the lower receiver (see step 27).

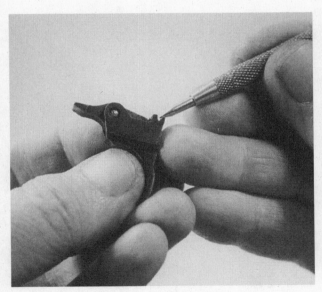

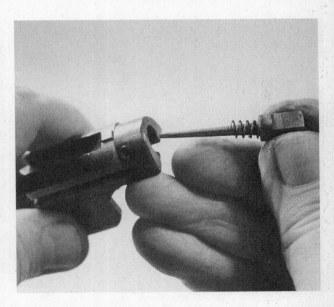

3. When installing the trigger and sear, and the sear spring, it is best to use a short slave pin to pre-assemble them, as shown. The slave pin is pushed out as the trigger pin is inserted. As the assembly is put in place, be sure the recess at the rear of the trigger engages the trigger spring.

4. Be sure the firing pin is installed in the orientation shown, with the long flat on top.

5. In rifles that have seen a lot of use, the firing pin retaining pin may be a loose fit. After it is reinstalled, it is best to stake the pin lightly on each side, as shown.

6. When replacing the recoil spring and its guide, start the spring onto the rod as the rod is pushed toward the rear, moving it in small increments. As the end is neared, use a tool to compress the spring forward while the threads are engaged.

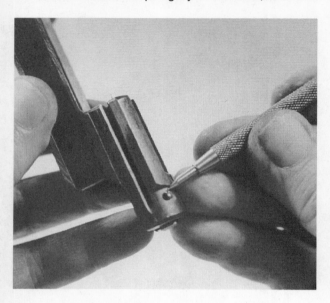

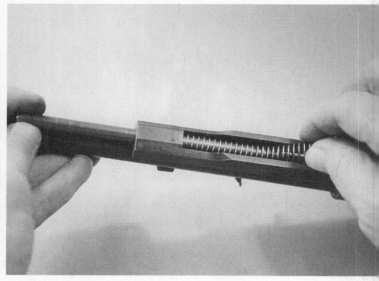

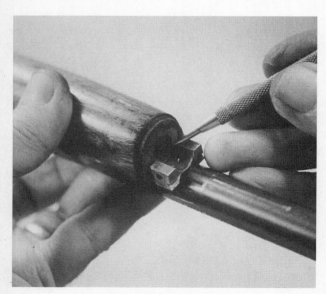

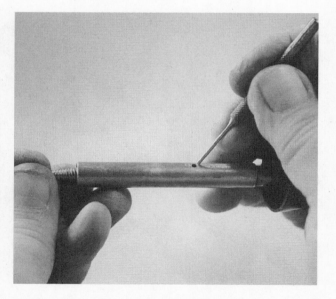

7. When installing the forend cap base, be sure it is perfectly centered to align with the opening in the forend. Also, be sure it is put back in the same orientation, as the screw holes are not always centered in the base.

8. Use a tool to compress the cocking plunger spring, and insert a small tool in the hole provided to trap the spring. When the plunger has engaged the end of the recoil spring guide rod, and just before the forend cap is pushed into place, the tool is removed to release the spring.

Winchester Model 67A

Similar/Identical Pattern Guns

The same basic assembly/disassembly steps for the Winchester Model 67A also apply to the following guns:

Winchester Model 67 Boy's Rifle   **Winchester Model 677**

Data:	Winchester Model 67A
Origin:	United States
Manufacturer:	Winchester Repeating Arms Co., New Haven, Connecticut
Cartridge:	22 Long Rifle
Overall length:	43 inches
Barrel length:	27 inches
Weight:	5 pounds

The Model 67 had a relatively long period of production, from 1934 to 1963. There was also a "boy's rifle," the Model 67BR, with a 20-inch barrel and a shorter stock. From 1937 to 1939, the Model 677 variation was made, with no sights, designed for use with a scope. All of the variations were the same, mechanically.

Disassembly:

1. Hold the trigger to the rear, open the bolt and remove the bolt toward the rear. Drift out the bolt cross pin.

2. Remove the striker assembly toward the rear.

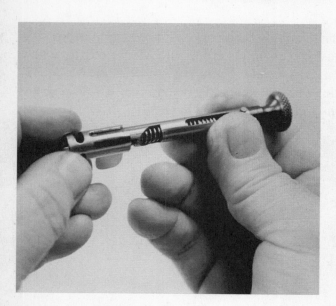

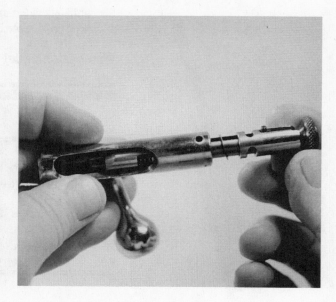

3. Remove the safety spring-washer toward the front. Remove the safety sleeve toward the front.

4. Drift out the striker knob pin. **Caution:** *Restrain the knob as the drift is removed, as the springs are under tension.* Ease the spring tension slowly, and remove the striker knob toward the rear. The rebound spring is easily removed from inside the striker knob shaft. Remove the striker spring and plunger from inside the striker.

5. Use a specially shaped screwdriver bit or a coin to back out the action mounting screw. This is a captive screw, and it will stay in its escutcheon in the stock. Remove the action from the stock.

6. The trigger guard is retained by two wood screws. An offset or angle-tip screwdriver will be necessary for the screw inside the guard.

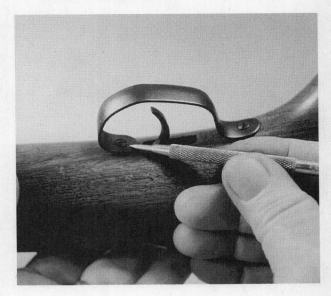

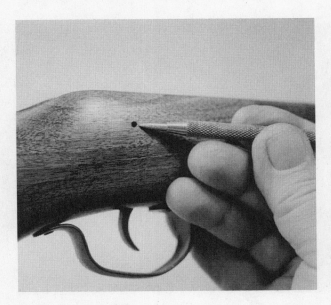

7. Push out the trigger cross pin. Use extreme care to avoid marring the stock. It is not necessary to remove the pin—just push it far enough to clear the trigger.

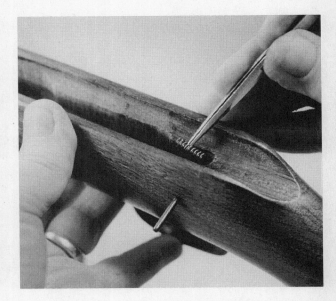

8. Remove the trigger upward. Remove the trigger spring from its well in the stock.

9. Slide the combination sear and ejector to the rear.

10. Pull the rear of the sear/ejector downward, just far enough to clear its rear upper projection, and remove it toward the rear.

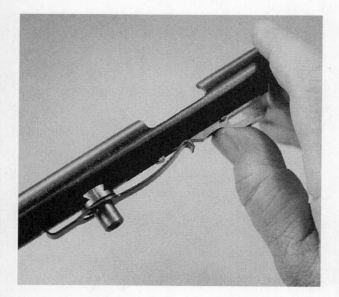

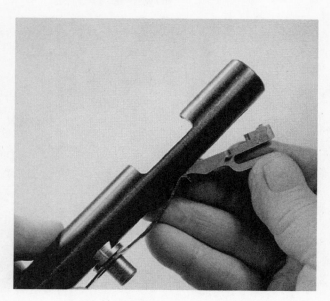

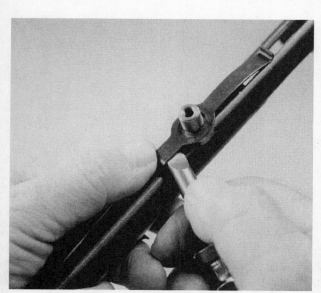

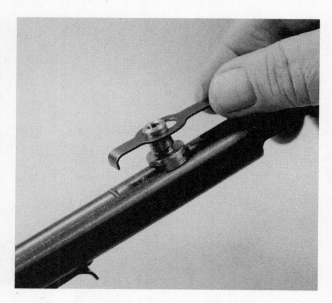

11. Lift the front of the sear spring just enough to clear its notch and push it rearward to align its exit hole with the post.

12. Remove the sear spring. If necessary, the post can be driven out of its dovetail toward the right. The front and rear sights are also dovetail-mounted, and are drifted out toward the right.

Reassembly Tips:

1. After the sear is reinstalled, push it back to the front, as shown.

2. When installing the trigger, drift the cross pin just far enough that the trigger can be put on it. Then, drift the pin into place. Again, take care not to mar the stock.

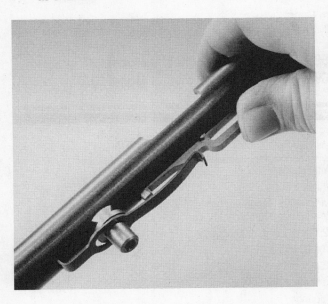

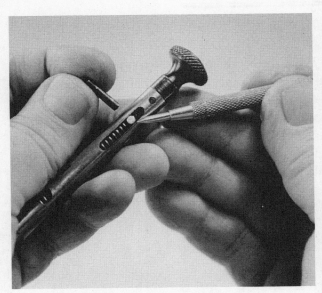

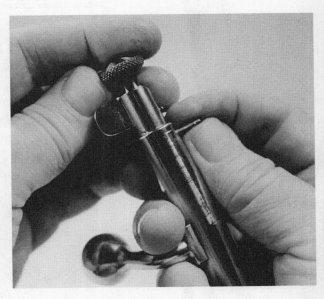

3. Use a slave pin to separate the rebound spring from the head of the striker spring plunger, as shown.

4. Viewed through the hole in the bolt body, use the slave pin as a guide to position the striker assembly for insertion of the bolt cross pin. The parts are shown here at the proper depth, but the slave pin head is a more precise guide.

Winchester Model 69

Similar/Identical Pattern Guns

The same basic assembly/disassembly steps for the Winchester Model 69 also apply to the following guns:

Winchester Model 69T

Winchester Model 69M

Winchester Model 697

Winchester Model 69A

Data:	Winchester Model 69
Origin:	United States
Manufacturer:	Winchester Repeating Arms New Haven, Connecticut
Cartridge:	22 Short, Long, or Long Rifle
Magazine capacity:	5 or 10 rounds
Overall length:	42 inches
Barrel length:	25 inches
Weight:	5 pounds

Made from 1935 to 1963, the Model 69 was also offered in target and match versions, the only difference in these being the addition of standard sling swivels and two different sights. Since they are mechanically the same, these instructions apply to all guns in the 69 series including the Model 697, except for removal of sights. The basic magazine was a 5-shot detachable box type, but a 10-shot version was available as an optional accessory.

Disassembly:

1. Remove the magazine and back out the main stock screw on the underside of the stock, forward of the magazine plate. Remove the action from the stock.

2. To remove the bolt, hold the trigger in the pulled position while opening the bolt and moving it out the rear of the receiver.

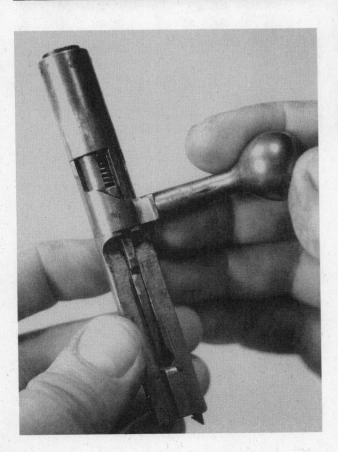

3. Grip the front portion of the bolt in a padded vise and turn the bolt handle to allow the striker to move forward to the fired position, partially easing the tension of its spring. The photo shows the bolt after the handle is turned, with the striker forward.

4. The screw-slotted end piece at the rear of the bolt is *not* a screw. The slot is there to aid reassembly. With the bolt still gripped in a padded vise, exert slight pressure on the end piece to control the tension of the striker spring, and push out the cross pin at the rear of the bolt. **Caution:** *The striker spring is under some tension, even when at rest, so control it and ease out the end piece.*

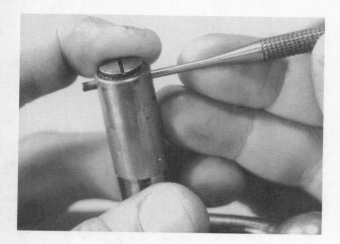

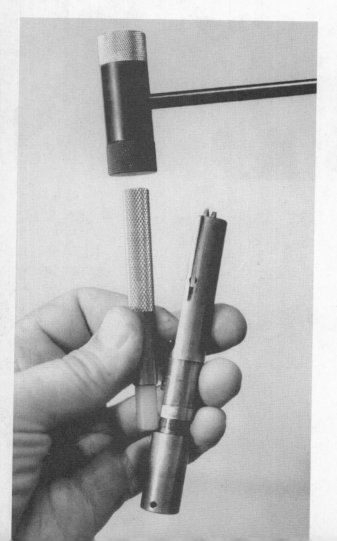

5. Remove the bolt end piece and the striker spring toward the rear.

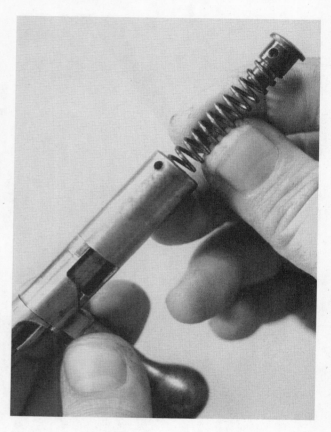

6. Remove the bolt sleeve toward the rear. The sleeve is often tightly fitted, and may require a few nudges with a nylon drift and hammer to start it off.

7. Move the bolt handle sleeve slightly toward the rear until the firing pin (striker) retaining cross pin is exposed and drift out the cross pin.

8. Move the bolt handle sleeve back forward, against its shoulder on the bolt, and turn it until the widest part of its internal opening is aligned with the firing pin on the underside of the bolt. Then, move the firing pin all the way to the rear, tip its rear end downward and remove it from the bolt. The clearances are very close here, so proceed with care.

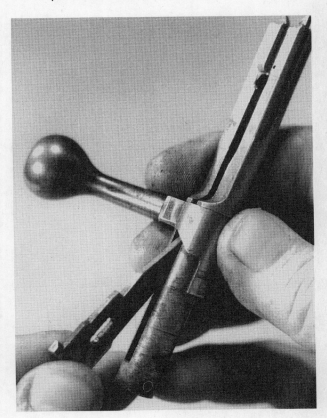

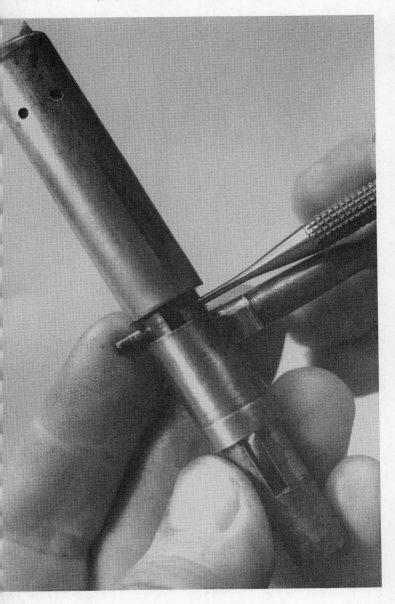

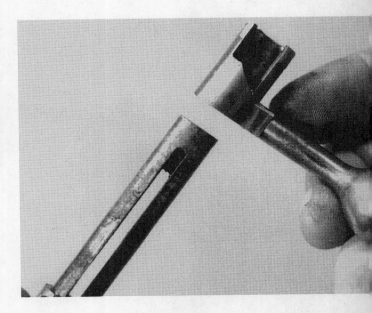

9. Remove the bolt handle sleeve toward the rear.

10. A drift punch of very small diameter is required to remove the vertical pins at the front of the bolt which retain the two extractors. The punch shown was made in the shop for this purpose. The pins must be driven out upward, and the extractors and their small coil springs are taken off from each side.

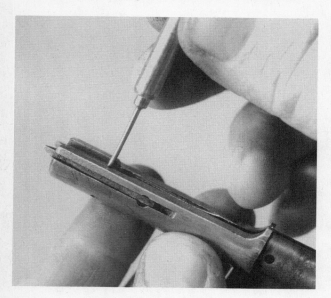

11. The formed steel that is the magazine catch is secured on the right side of the magazine housing by a single screw.

12. Remove the front magazine housing screw.

13. Remove the rear screw from the magazine housing and remove the magazine housing downward.

14. The magazine housing can be taken off without disturbing the trigger spring adjustment screw, but it is best to at least back it off to relieve the spring tension. If this is done, note its depth if the same weight of pull is desired on reassembly.

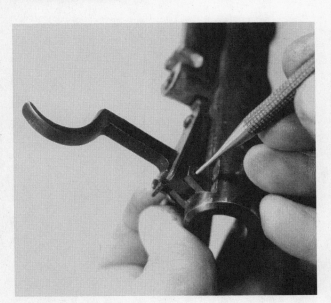

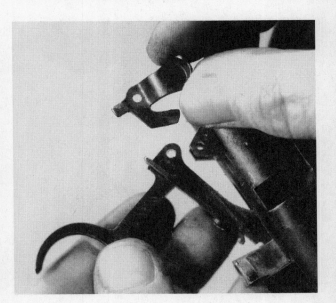

15. Drift out the cross pin that retains the trigger.

16. Remove the trigger and safety-lever downward.

17. Remove the screw on the underside of the front arm of the trigger, and slide the safety plate off toward the front. **Caution:** *Removal of the safety plate will release the safety positioning plunger and spring, so control them as the plate is taken off to prevent loss.*

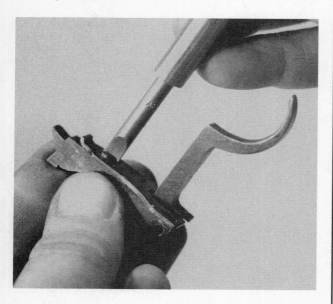

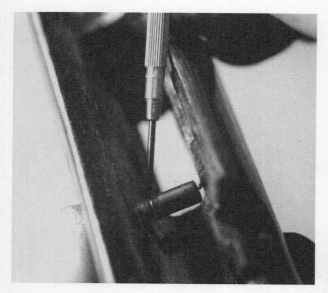

18. The magazine catch release button is retained in the left side of the stock by a circular spring clip which rests in a groove on the button shaft. Push the button in to give access to the clip, move it out of its groove and slide it off the shaft toward the right. The button and its coil spring can then be taken off toward the left.

Reassembly Tips:

1. When replacing the trigger and safety-lever, be sure the upper front arm of the lever goes into its slot in the receiver, and that the lower arm of the lever enters its slot in the safety plate on the trigger. Be sure the holes in the trigger and lever are aligned with the holes in the mount on the receiver before driving in the cross pin.

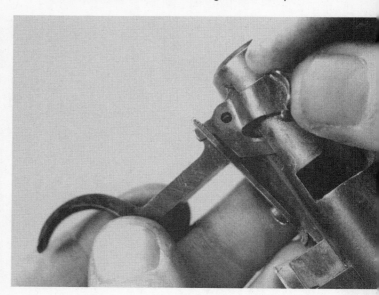

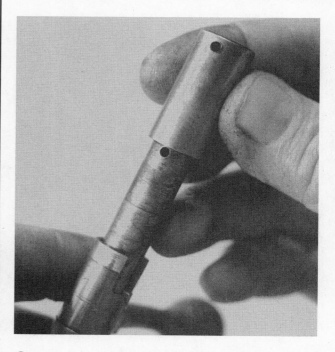

2. When replacing the bolt sleeve, be sure the cross pin holes at the rear are as closely aligned as possible with the holes in the bolt body before tapping the sleeve into place. When the sleeve is fully forward, insert a small drift punch through the holes to complete the alignment.

3. To reinstall the bolt end piece, grip the front portion of the bolt in a padded vise and push the end piece into place, holding it against the tension of the striker spring. Be sure the striker is in the fired position. Use a wide-bladed screwdriver to turn the end piece until the cross pin hole is in alignment with the holes in the bolt sleeve and body, and insert a drift punch to hold the end piece in place while driving in the cross pin.

4. Before the bolt is reinserted in the receiver, the striker must be in cocked position. With the bolt still gripped in the padded vise, turn the bolt handle to cock the striker. The photo shows the striker in the cocked position.

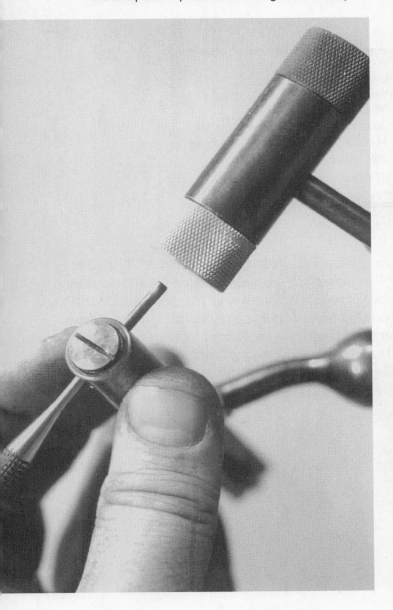

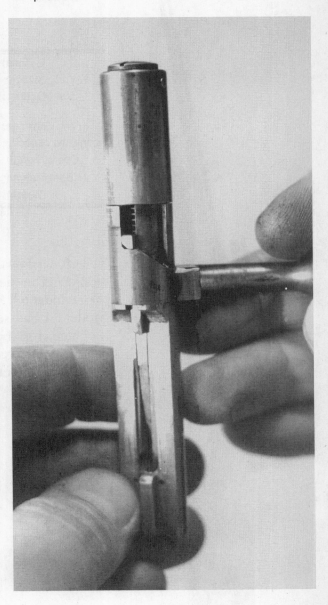

Winchester Model 74

Data:	Winchester Model 74
Origin:	United States
Manufacturer:	Winchester Repeating Arms Company New Haven, Connecticut
Cartridge:	22 Long Rifle, 22 Short (separate guns)
Magazine capacity:	14 in Long Rifle model, 20 in Short model
Overall length:	43¾ inches
Barrel length:	22 inches
Weight:	6¼ pounds

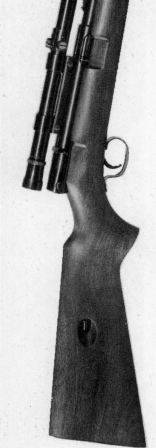

The Model 74 was originally intended to be an "economy" 22-caliber autoloader in the Winchester line, costing about one-third less than their Model 63. Made from just before World War II until 1955, the Model 74 had several unusual features. Among these were a top-mounted cross-bolt safety and a bolt and firing mechanism that could easily be removed as a unit, without taking the rifle action out of the stock. The Model 74 was a simple and reliable gun, and many of them are still in use.

Disassembly:

1. Remove the magazine tube from the rear of the stock. Back out the large screw on the underside of the stock, and separate the action from the stock.

2. Press in the rear of the disconnector on the underside of the receiver to drop the striker to fired position (the safety must be on the "F" mark, of course). Then, push the takedown latch (at the left rear of the receiver) toward the right until its right end clears its recess in the receiver.

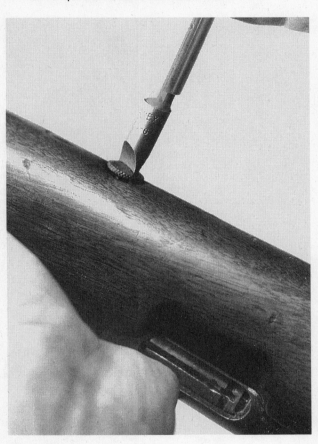

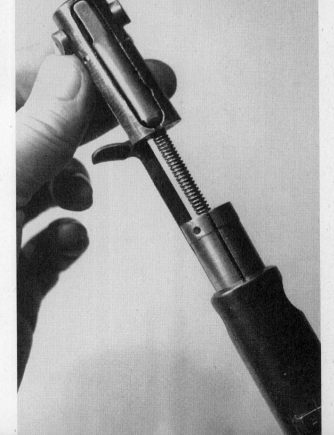

3. While holding the latch to the right, withdraw the bolt and firing mechanism assembly from the rear of the receiver.

4. Bring the bolt and sear housing (end piece) together until they meet to cock the striker. With a firm grip on the bolt and end piece, push out the cocking handle retaining pin, located at the right rear of the bolt. **Caution:** *Control the compressed bolt spring, and let the tension off slowly as you move the bolt and end piece apart.* Removal of the cocking handle will instantly release the two parts, so be prepared for it.

5. Remove the bolt spring and its guide from the bolt and end piece. At this point, the striker is still held in place by the sear. Grip the striker firmly, and release the sear by pressing its rear tab inward. **Caution:** *Keep the striker and end piece under control, and ease out the striker and its spring slowly.*

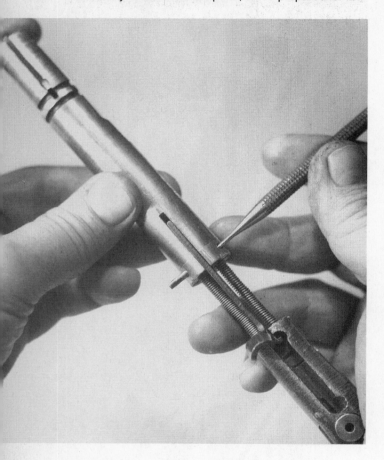

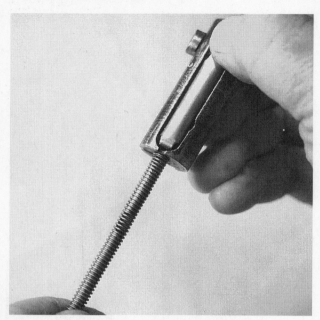

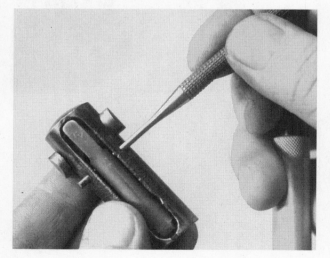

6. Drifting out the cross pin at the top of the end piece will release the sear for removal upward. Take the sear spring out of its well at the rear.

7. Partially depress the takedown latch until the hole in its upper surface aligns with a small hole inside the end piece, and use a very slim drift punch to drive out the retaining pin downward. **Caution:** *Be sure a punch of very small diameter is used, to avoid damaging the parts.* The punch shown was especially made in the shop for this purpose. When the pin is partially out, the small coil spring inside the latch will be released toward the right, so keep a fingertip over the hole in the right end of the latch to catch it. When the pin is out, the latch can be removed.

8. The extractor is retained by a vertical pin at the front of the bolt, accessible at the extreme rear of the open firing pin groove in the top of the bolt. The pin is driven out toward the bottom of the bolt. Here, again, use a very slim drift punch. When the pin is out, the extractor and its spring are removed toward the right.

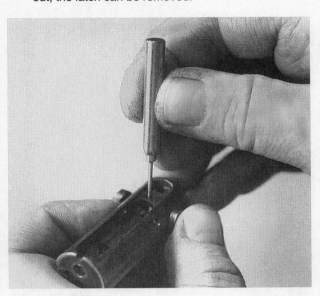

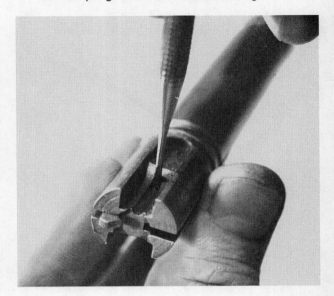

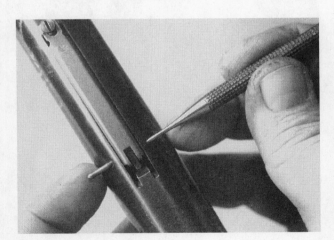

9. The disconnector is retained by a cross pin on the underside of the receiver.

10. When the cross pin is pushed out, the front end of the disconnector will be pulled into the receiver by its spring. Use a small tool to lift it slightly; then move it forward until its rear yoke clears the screw/post at the rear and remove the disconnector from the receiver. **Caution:** *Take care to lift the part only enough to ease it off. If you raise it too far, the spring may break.*

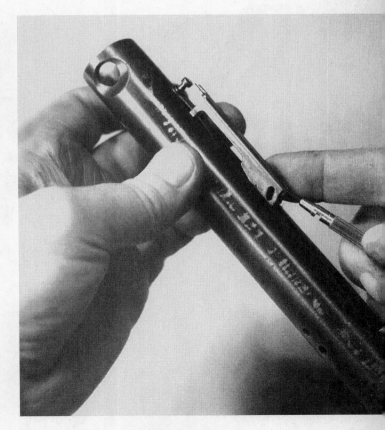

11. Backing out the screw/post at the rear of the disconnector slot will allow removal of the curved flat spring.

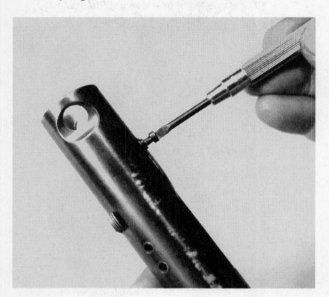

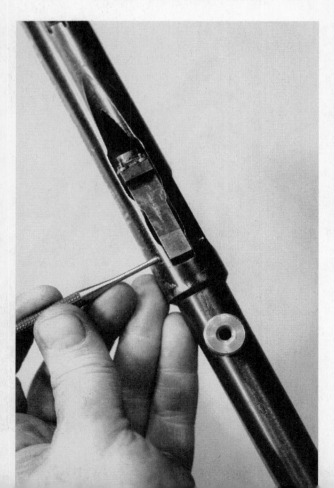

12. While observing the underside of the safety catch through the disconnector slot, insert a small tool from the rear of the receiver and carefully lift the tip of the safety spring just enough to allow the safety to be slid out of the top of the receiver. The spring is staked in place, and removal is not recommended except for replacement of a broken spring.

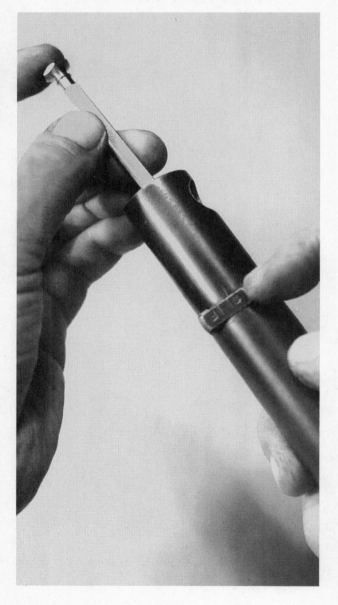

13. The cartridge feed guide is retained by a single cross pin on the underside of the receiver. After the feed guide is removed, the twin cartridge stops are easily detachable from it by swinging them outward on their fixed pins and removing them toward the rear.

14. The top cartridge guide is retained by a cross pin at the top front of the receiver, and is removed toward the rear and downward. The ejector is staked in place in the left wall of the receiver, and should not be disturbed in normal takedown.

15. Drift out the cross pin that passes through the stock above the trigger to free the trigger and its spring. The trigger is removed upward, but only after removal of the magazine tube.

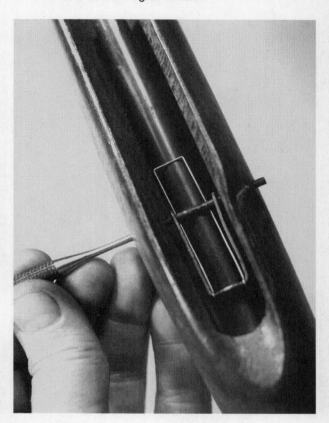

16. To remove the outer magazine tube, remove the buttplate screws and take out the buttplate and the attached magazine tube toward the rear. When the tube is slid out, the magazine tube tension spring will be released at the front. Restrain it and remove it from its well in the stock. The trigger can now be removed from the stock.

Reassembly Tips:

1. When replacing the magazine tube and buttplate assembly, use a tool to depress the magazine tube tension spring while sliding the magazine tube into place. Remember that the trigger must be put back in the stock before insertion of the magazine tube.

2. When replacing the takedown latch retaining pin, use a small screwdriver or drift to depress the internal spring beyond the pin location. Take care that the pin does not hit the spring and deform it.

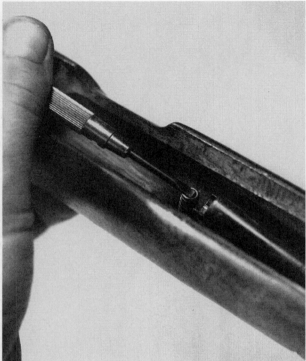

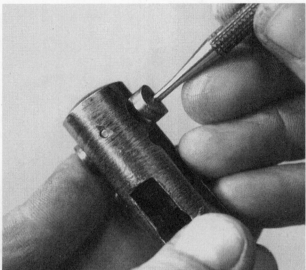

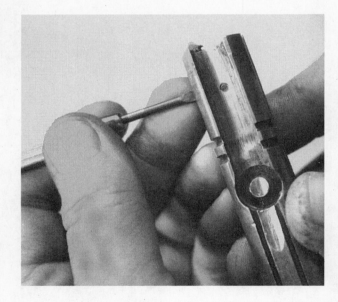

3. When replacing the extractor pivot pin, be sure the hole in the extractor lobe is exactly in alignment with the pin hole to avoid damage to the pin or the extractor. The pin must be driven in from the underside of the bolt, toward the top. Be sure the pin does not protrude into the firing pin groove.

4. When replacing the disconnector, lift the spring with a small tool and be sure the tip of the spring enters the opening at the front of the disconnector.

5. After hooking the front tip of the spring into the disconnector, insert a small screwdriver under the tip of the spring to hold it in place while sliding the disconnector forward, and then back to fit its rear yoke around the neck of the screw/post.

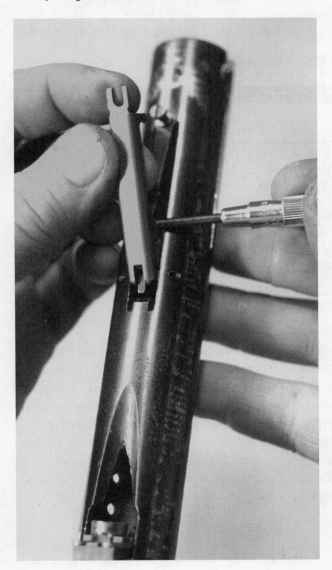

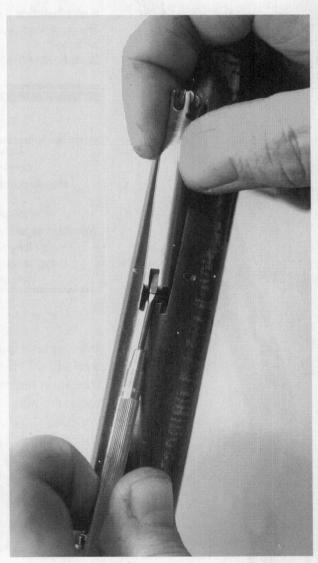

Winchester Model 77

Similar/Identical Pattern Guns
The same basic assembly/disassembly steps for the Winchester Model 77 also apply to the following gun:
Winchester Model 77 Box Magazine

Data:	Winchester Model 77
Origin:	United States
Manufacturer:	Winchester Repeating Arms New Haven, Connecticut
Cartridge:	22 Long Rifle
Magazine capacity:	15 rounds
Overall length:	40 inches
Barrel length:	22 inches
Weight:	$5^{1}/_{2}$ pounds

In comparison to other Winchester rifles, the Model 77 was made for a relatively brief period—from 1955 to 1963. In a way, it was like a transition between the old and the new, with its beautiful solid steel receiver and a nylon/plastic trigger guard. The gun was made in two versions, box magazine and tube magazine, and the latter gun is covered here. Except for the difference in feed systems, the instructions can apply to either version. There are one or two very tricky points in the takedown/reassembly of the Model 77, and these are noted in the instructions.

Disassembly:

1. Remove the inner magazine tube and back out the screw on the underside of the stock, forward of the trigger guard. Back out the screw at the rear of the trigger guard and remove the action upward.

2. If the trigger guard is to be removed, take out the screw at the front of the guard. Note that this screw has a nut on the inside of the stock which may have to be held while removing the screw.

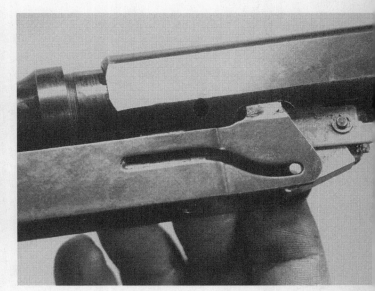

3. Pull the trigger to drop the striker to the fired position and push out the barrel retaining pin, which crosses the underside of the receiver below the chamber area.

4. Move the barrel and bolt assembly forward until the upper rear arms of the operating slide are aligned with the exit cuts in the underside of the receiver. Spread the rear arms of the slide into the cuts to free the feed throat and carrier assembly.

5. Moving the rear arms of the slide into the exit cuts will free the side studs on the carrier assembly from the open tracks in the arms, and the carrier and feed throat can then be removed downward and toward the rear.

6. The carrier and feed throat assembly can be taken apart by careful removal of the C-clips from the ends of the cross pin on each side. When the carrier is removed from the feed throat, the feed platform and its spring will also be released from inside the carrier, so restrain these parts and ease them out. The cam pin across the front can also be removed.

7. Restrain the action slide against the tension of the recoil spring, and disengage the rear upper arms of the action slide from their recesses in the underside of the bolt. Allow the action slide to move forward, relieving the tension of the spring.

8. Remove the barrel from the receiver.

9. Remove the action slide and recoil spring from the rear of the magazine tube.

10. The outer magazine tube may be removed by drifting out the small cross pin in the tube hanger loop. Move the tube out toward the front.

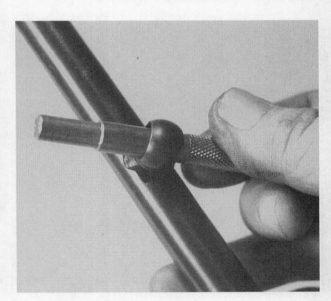

11. The hanger loop appears to be dovetail-mounted. Actually, it is keyed into a circular recess, and the loop is turned at a right angle to its normal position for removal.

12. Remove the bolt assembly toward the front.

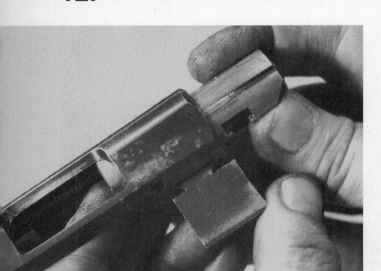

13. Retract the timing rod spring and its collar from the rear tip of the rod, and remove the C-clip from the groove at the tip. Slowly release the tension of the spring, and remove the collar and spring toward the rear. Take out the timing rod toward the front.

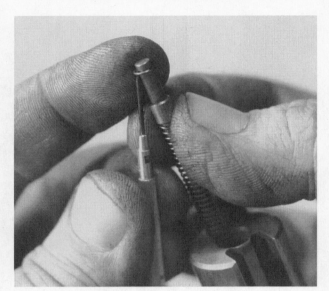

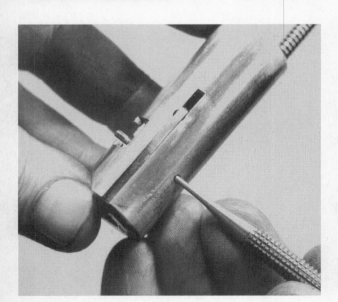

14. Drift out the vertical pin on the right side of the bolt, freeing the extractor, its spring and the firing pin inside the bolt.

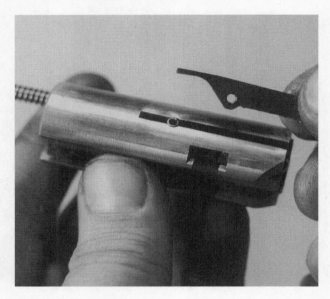

15. Remove the extractor and its spring toward the right.

16. Removal of the extractor will release the firing pin assembly, and this can now be taken out toward the rear. If the return spring is not on the front of the firing pin, remove it from the firing pin tunnel and take care not to confuse it with the extractor spring, as they are not interchangeable.

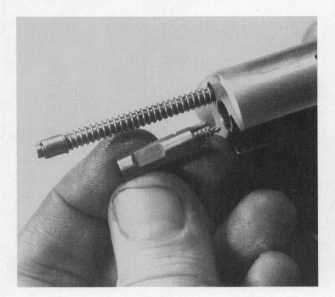

17. The ejector is mounted inside the firing pin, along with its spring, and they are retained by a cross pin at the rear of the firing pin. Push out the pin, while restraining the spring, and remove the ejector and spring toward the rear.

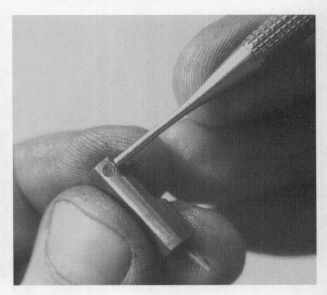

18. Remove the striker and its spring from inside the receiver. If they do not come out easily, pulling the trigger to relieve the sear tension should release them.

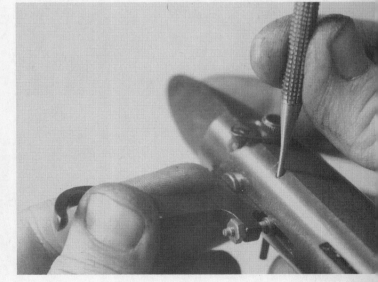

19. Restrain the trigger against the tension of the trigger and sear springs and push out the trigger cross pin.

20. Remove the trigger downward, slowly relieving the tension of its spring. It is not necessary to disturb the trigger adjustment screw.

21. Remove the sear and disconnector assembly downward.

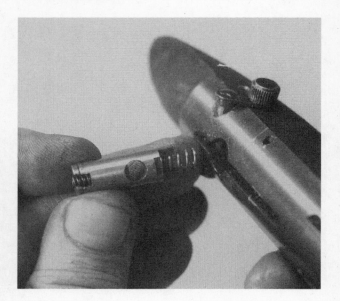

22. The sear, disconnector, and their attendant springs are easily separated.

23. The safety is retained by a C-clip on the end of its cross-shaft, on the left side of the receiver. Carefully remove the C-clip, restraining the safety spring and removing it from the end of the cross-shaft.

Winchester Model 77 : **455**

24. Remove the safety-lever toward the right.

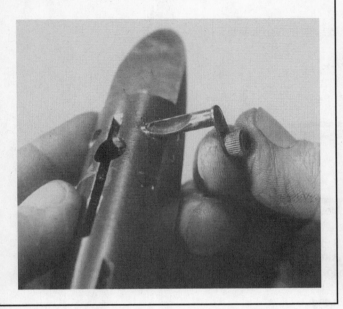

1. When replacing the firing pin in the bolt, insert a small screwdriver beside its cross pin at the rear to orient the firing pin within the bolt for mating with the pin lobe of the extractor.

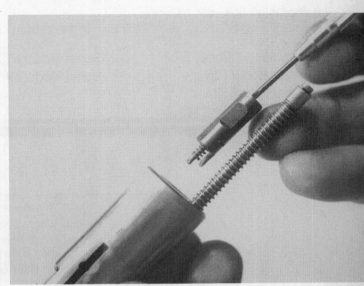

2. When replacing the sear/disconnector assembly in the receiver, note that the larger hole in the disconnector goes toward the rear, and that the shelf on the top of the sear goes toward the rear. This is an important point, as it is possible to reassemble them in reverse.

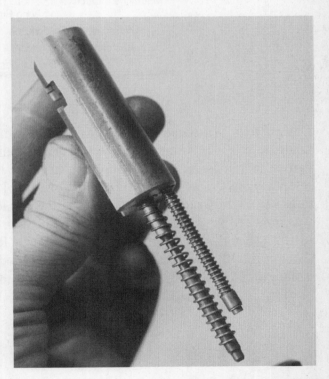

3. Replacement of the striker and its spring will be easier if they are placed in their hole in the rear of the bolt and inserted with the bolt.

Winchester Model 90

Similar/Identical Pattern Guns

The same basic assembly/disassembly steps for the Winchester Model 90 also apply to the following guns:

Winchester Model 1906   **Rossi Model 62SAC**
Rossi Model 62SA   **Rossi Model 59**
Rossi Model 62A

Data:	Winchester Model 90
Origin:	United States
Manufacturer:	Winchester Repeating Arms New Haven, Connecticut
Cartridge:	22 Short, Long, Long Rifle or WRF (separate guns)
Magazine capacity:	15 Short, 12 Long 11 Long Rifle, 10 WRF
Overall length:	40 inches
Barrel length:	24 inches
Weight:	5^1/$_2$ pounds

Designed for Winchester by John M. Browning, the Model 1890 was made until 1932. Along the way, in 1906, a part was added to the carrier to allow the use of Short, Long, and Long Rifle rounds interchangeably, and that gun became the Model 1906. In 1932, the gun was slightly redesigned to become the Model 62, and this one was replaced very soon by the Model 62A, with production ending in 1959. The design returned in 1973, made by Rossi in Brazil, and the gun is still available. Except for the true Model 62, which has a different bolt/action slide system, the instructions will apply to any of the guns mentioned above.

Disassembly:

1. Back out the thumbscrew at the left rear of the receiver, and when its threads are clear, the screw will move slightly toward the left, out of its recess in the left side of the receiver, but will stay on the gun. If the screw is tight, a coin slot is provided to aid in starting it.

2. Set the hammer on the safety step, and move the rear portion of the gun off toward the rear.

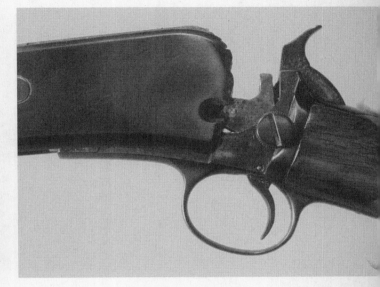

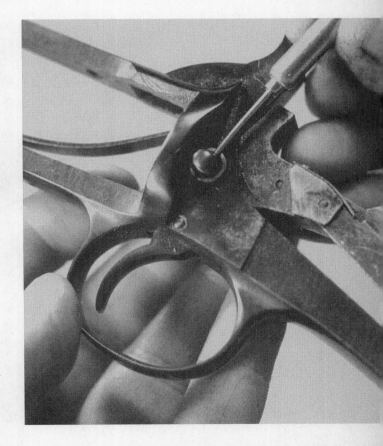

3. Remove the stock mounting screw, located at the rear tip of the upper tang, and take off the stock toward the rear. If the stock is very tight, it may be necessary to bump the front of the comb with the heel of your hand to start it.

4. To remove the takedown cross screw, use a very small diameter drift punch to drive out the transverse pin near its left tip. To make the pin accessible, the takedown screw must be moved as far toward the right as it will go. After removal of the pin, the screw is removed toward the left.

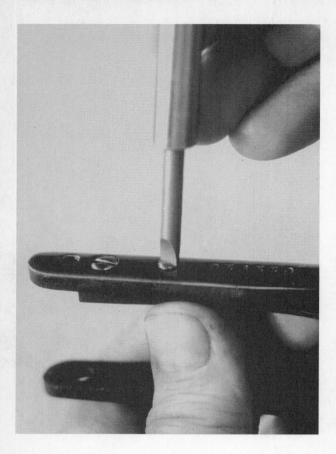

5. With the hammer lowered to the fired position, remove the hammer spring screw, the larger of the two screws at the rear of the lower tang. Removal will be made easier by first backing out the hammer spring tension screw, the smaller screw just forward of the other one.

6. Disengage the hammer spring hooks from the hammer stirrup, and remove the hammer spring toward the rear.

7. With a large diameter non-marring drift punch, push out the hollow hammer/carrier pivot toward the right.

8. Remove the carrier toward the front and upward.

9. The carrier lever spring is retained on the right side of the carrier by a vertical screw. Remove the screw and the spring upward.

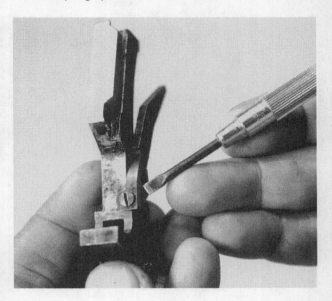

10. The carrier lever is retained on the carrier by a cross pin. When drifting out the pin, take care not to pinch the lever slot on the right side. After the pin is taken out, the lever is removed toward the front. The cross pin at the rear of the carrier is a limit pin that retains no part, and is not removed in normal takedown.

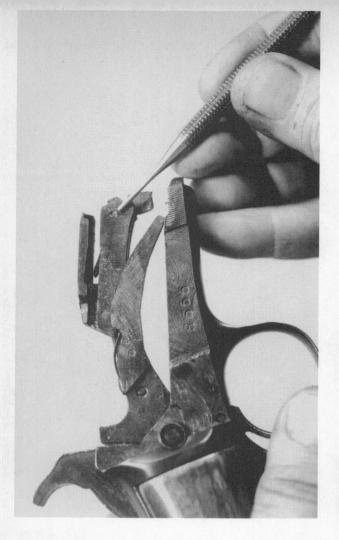

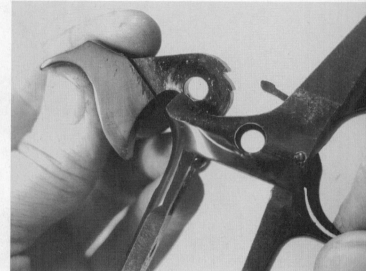

11. On the later models, after 1906-08, and including the Model 62A, there is a pivoting cartridge stop in the lower front projection of the carrier. Drifting out its cross pin will allow removal of the cartridge stop toward the front.

12. The previous removal of the hollow cross-piece has also released the hammer. Pull the trigger to clear its sear arm from the front, and remove the hammer upward.

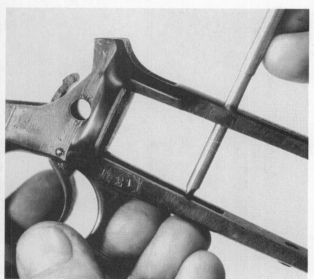

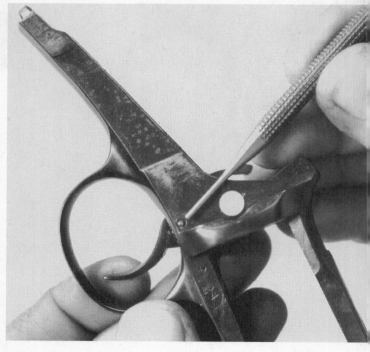

13. The trigger spring is retained by a vertical screw inside the lower tang. This screw can be removed by an offset or angled-tip screwdriver, or a small filler screw can be taken out of the upper tang, allowing a screwdriver with a very thin shaft to reach the screw from above, as shown. The screwdriver in the photo was specially made for this purpose.

14. Drifting out the trigger cross pin will allow the trigger to be removed upward. The sear is an integral part of the upper projection of the trigger.

15. Remove the slide coverplate screw, located on the left side of the receiver at the lower edge of the coverplate, and slide the coverplate off toward the front. Exerting slight inward pressure on the slide bar will make removal of the plate easier.

16. Use a non-marring tool to prop the slide bar out to the left, being sure its rear lug clears its track in the lower lobe of the breechblock. Depress the firing pin and hold it in while lifting the front of the breechblock upward, out of its locking recess in the receiver. Remove the breechblock toward the rear.

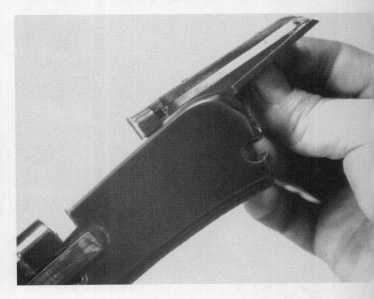

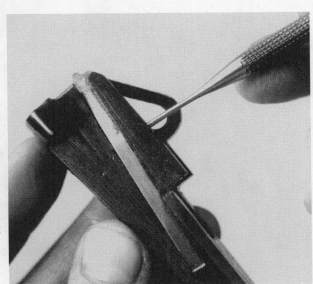

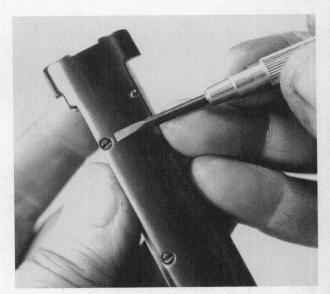

17. The extractor is retained on the right side of the breechblock by a vertical pin. Drift the pin out toward the top, and remove the extractor toward the right. The extractor is tempered to be its own spring. Note that the pin is installed at a right angle to the extractor, but not in relation to the other surfaces of the breechblock. In relation to these, it is slanted.

18. Removal of the two small vertical screws on top of the breechblock will release the firing pin retaining block, located on the left side.

19. After the screws are taken out, move the firing pin retaining block out toward the rear. **Caution:** *Do not try to remove the block toward the left, and especially avoid any leftward pressure on the rear tip of the block, as this will break the slim block at the rear screw hole.*

20. After the retaining block is removed, take out the firing pin and its coil return spring toward the rear.

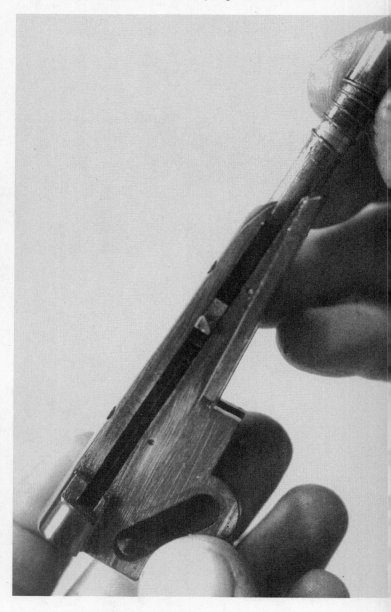

21. Remove the inner magazine tube, and drift out the cross pin in the rear magazine tube hanger loop. This will allow removal of the outer magazine tube toward the front, and the action slide and its handle can then be easily detached from the receiver. Removing the screws on each side of the handle will allow the action slide to be separated from the handle. On early guns, the magazine hangers are rotated to free them from the underside of the barrel. On later models, they are driven out of their dovetails toward the right.

22. The rear sight is secured at the front by a screw which enters a retainer in a dovetail cut. As the screw is turned, the sight base will climb off the top of the headless screw. Take care that the small screw and its base are not lost.

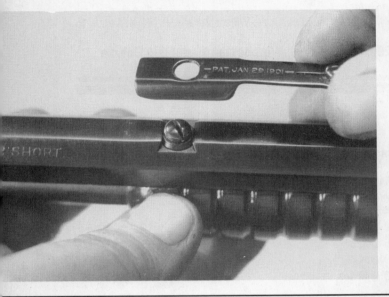

Reassembly Tips:

1. When replacing the screws that retain the firing pin block, insert a small diameter drift punch in one of the screw holes to hold the block in place while putting in the first screw.

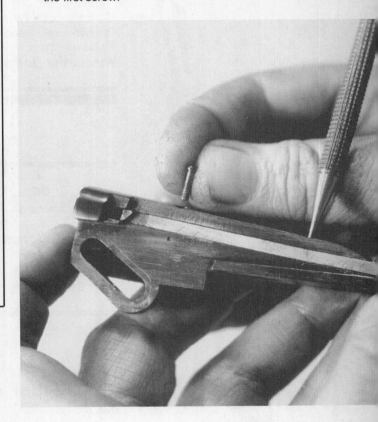

2. When replacing the pin that retains the takedown screw, note that the pin is slightly smaller at one end, and be sure that this end is inserted in the hole. Grip the pin with sharp-nosed pliers to start it; then tap it into place with a small drift punch and hammer. Remember that the pin must have equal projection on each side of the takedown screw, to allow the screw to move toward the left during takedown and reassembly.

Winchester Model 190

Similar/Identical Pattern Guns

The same basic assembly/disassembly steps for the Winchester Model 190 also apply to the following guns:

Winchester Model 290   **Winchester Model 290 Deluxe**

Data:	Winchester Model 190
Origin:	United States
Manufacturer:	Winchester Repeating Arms Company New Haven, Connecticut
Cartridge:	22 Long Rifle
Magazine capacity:	15 rounds
Overall length:	39 inches
Barrel length:	20$\frac{1}{2}$ inches
Weight:	5 pounds

Introduced as the Model 290 in 1964, and in a "deluxe" version, this gun was offered in an economy style in 1974 as the Model 190. In this designation, it was made until 1980. Some very early guns will be found to have a plastic rear sight and a combination front sight and magazine tube hanger of the same material, and some elements of takedown involving those parts will be slightly different. However, the instructions will apply to either model.

Disassembly:

1. Cycle the bolt to cock the hammer and move the safety to the on-safe position. Remove the magazine tube and push out the large plastic cross pin located in the receiver just above the trigger. The pin can be pushed out toward either side.

2. Tip the trigger housing down at the rear and move it slightly toward the rear to disengage its forward stud from its recess inside the receiver. Remove the trigger group downward.

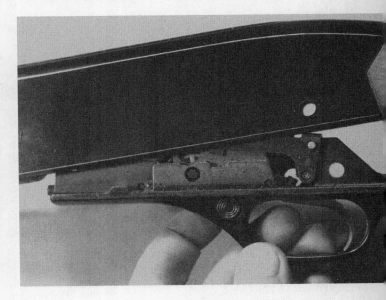

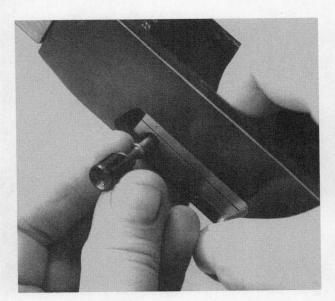

3. With the gun inverted, retract the bolt slightly and use a finger or tool to hold it inside the receiver. Lift the front of the bolt, and remove the bolt handle from its hole in the bolt.

4. Move the bolt toward the rear to clear its forward end from the barrel throat and tip the front of the bolt upward (the gun is still inverted) until it can be removed from the receiver. **Caution:** *The bolt spring is under tension. Ease it out.*

5. Remove the bolt spring and its nylon guide from the receiver.

6. Removal of the buttstock requires a special socket wrench with a very deep end. It is possible to alter an ordinary socket for this, but in normal disassembly it is best to leave the stock in place. If the stock is removed, and the headless mounting bolt taken out, the recoil plate inside the receiver will be released for removal.

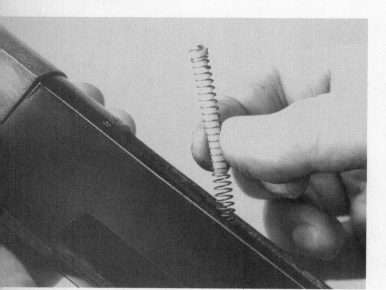

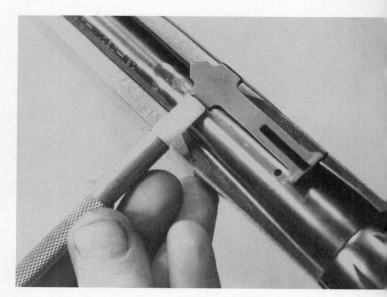

7. Drifting out the small, short cross pin in the magazine tube hanger near the muzzle will release the outer magazine tube for removal toward the front. This will allow the forend to be taken off downward. After removal of the forend, the nylon forend mount is easily slid out of its dovetail toward either side.

8. Flex the rear sight very slightly upward, and take out the sight elevator. Drifting out the rear sight toward the right will release the barrel collar cover for removal upward, giving access to the barrel collar.

9. With the proper wrench (available from Brownells) turn the barrel collar counterclockwise (front view) until it is out of the receiver. Remove the barrel toward the front. **Note:** Because of the permanently attached magazine tube hanger, the barrel collar is not removable from the barrel.

10. If the barrel is very tight in the receiver, grip the barrel in a padded vise and tap the front of the receiver with a wood, leather or nylon hammer, moving the receiver off the rear of the barrel. **Caution:** *Take care not to deform the lower front of the receiver.*

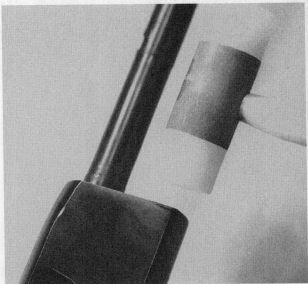

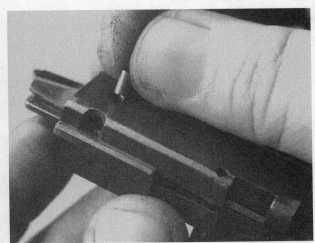

11. Drift out the vertical pin on the left side of the bolt to allow the firing pin to be moved toward the rear, easing the tension of the combination firing pin spring and extractor spring. **Note:** There is a steel ball bearing at each end of the spring. Take care that these are not lost. Remove the extractor pivot pin from its hole in the top front of the bolt. With the spring tension relieved, the pin should come out when the bolt is inverted and tapped with a light hammer. If the pin is tight, it can be nudged out by using a pointed tool in the stake mark on the underside of the bolt. Take care that this very small pin isn't lost.

12. Remove the extractor from the right side of the bolt, taking it out forward and toward the right.

13. Move the firing pin forward to nudge the spring out of its tunnel in the bolt and remove the spring and the two ball bearings from the extractor recess. Again, take care that the ball bearings aren't lost.

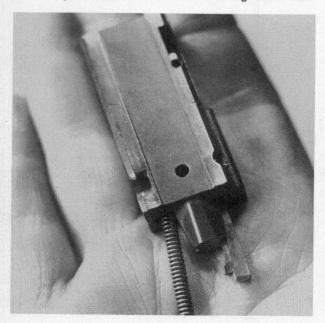

14. Move the firing pin toward the center of the bolt and remove the firing pin toward the rear.

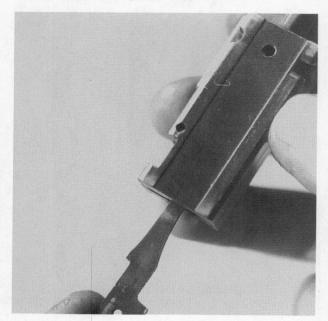

15. Move the safety to the off-safe position, restrain the hammer and pull the trigger, lowering the hammer to the fired position. Restrain the sear/disconnector assembly and remove its pivot pin toward the right.

16. Remove the sear/disconnector assembly upward. The sear and its spring are a permanent assembly inside the disconnector, the pivot pin being riveted in place at the factory. Routine removal is unwise in normal disassembly.

17. Push the hammer pivot out toward either side (left) and remove the hammer assembly upward (right). The hammer spring and its two nylon support pieces are easily removed from the hammer.

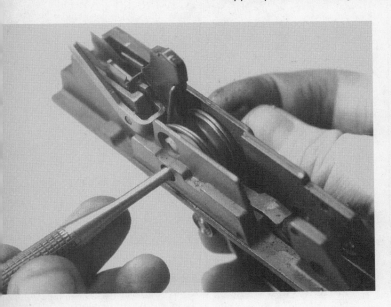

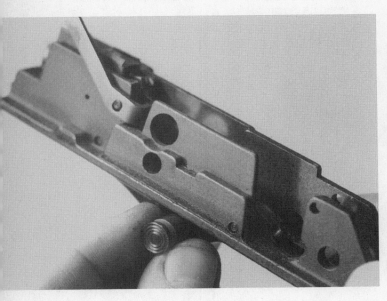

18. The right rear tail of the hammer spring retains the safety, and the safety can now be turned slightly and removed toward the left.

19. Push out the trigger pivot pin and remove the trigger from the top of the trigger housing. The sear contact stud on the trigger is factory-staked at the proper level, and it should not be disturbed.

20. The feed system is retained by three cross pins. The large pin at the rear (upper right in the photo) retains the carrier lever. When drifting it out, restrain the carrier, as its spring is under tension. Moving the carrier out to the rear will release the spring and its plunger, so proceed with caution. The cartridge feed guide is retained by a tiny roll pin near its center and by a larger pin near the lower edge of the housing. When these are removed, the guide can be taken out toward the top.

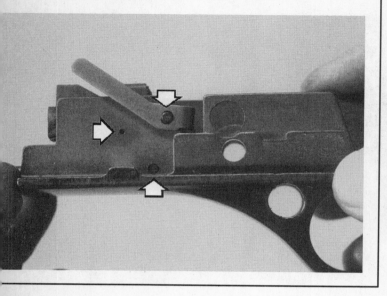

When replacing the safety in the trigger housing, remember that the end with the red ring goes toward the left, and be sure that the positioning recesses on the right side are at the top.

Note that the hammer pivot has one flat side, and be sure both of the nylon hammer spring supports are oriented so that their inside flats will align with the flat on the pin. If not, the support bushings may be damaged as the pin is pushed into place.

When driving in the firing pin stop pin on the left side of the bolt, insert the bolt handle temporarily to prevent the loss of the extractor pivot pin.

When replacing the bolt spring and guide, use a small screwdriver to push in the spring, a few coils at a time, while keeping pressure on the guide toward the rear. When the rear tip of the guide is in the spring hole, restrain the guide and spring with a tool or fingertip while inserting the bolt and bolt handle. Then, move the bolt back, being sure that the head of the guide engages its recess on the rear of the bolt.

When replacing the hammer assembly in the trigger housing, be sure the right lower tail of the hammer spring enters its recess inside the housing, so it will contact the positioning grooves in the safety. Be sure the left tail of the spring lies on its shelf in the housing, or it may bind the trigger.

Reassembly Tips:

1. When replacing the sear/disconnector assembly, be sure the lower end of the sear spring goes toward the rear, down the slope of the trigger.

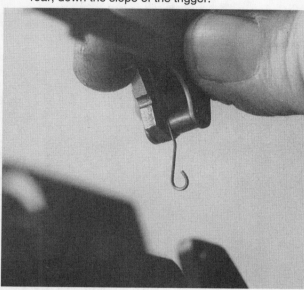

2. When installing the outer magazine tube, be sure it is fully to the rear and the groove in its upper flange is aligned with the cross pin hole in the hanger before inserting the cross pin.

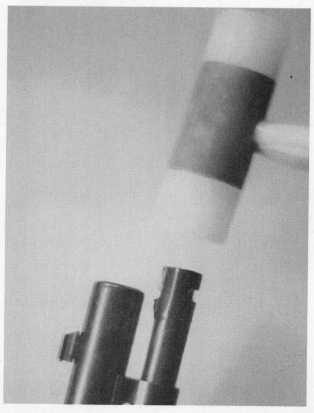

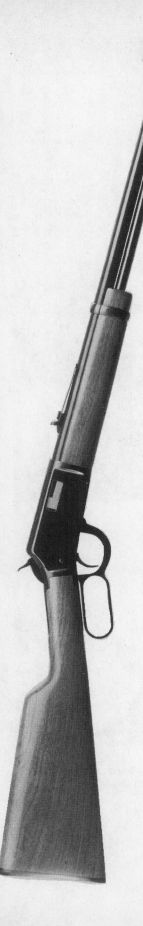

Winchester Model 9422

Similar/Identical Pattern Guns

The same basic assembly/disassembly steps for the Winchester Model 9422 also apply to the following guns:

Winchester Model 9422 XTR **Winchester Model 9422 XTR Classic**

Winchester Model 9422M XTR **Winchester Model 9422M**

Data:	Winchester Model 9422
Origin:	United States
Manufacturer:	Winchester Repeating Arms Co. New Haven, Connecticut
Cartridge:	22 Short, Long, Long Rifle
Magazine capacity:	21 Shorts, 17 Longs, 15 Long Rifles
Overall length:	37$^{1}/_{8}$ inches
Barrel length:	20$^{1}/_{2}$ inches
Weight:	6$^{1}/_{2}$ pounds

Introduced in 1972, the Model 9422 is the 22-caliber counterpart of the popular Model 94 centerfire gun. Externally it is very much like the Model 94, but the internal mechanism is quite different. The feed system is similar to the one used in the Model 61, making malfunctions extremely unlikely. The Model 9422 is fairly simple for a lever action, and with the exception of the cartridge stop and its spring, takedown and reassembly are relatively easy.

Disassembly:

1. Remove the magazine tube and take out the large coin-slotted cross screw at the rear of the receiver. A nickel fits the slot best. Separate the two sections of the gun, moving the rear portion down and toward the rear.

2. Remove the bolt assembly from the receiver toward the rear.

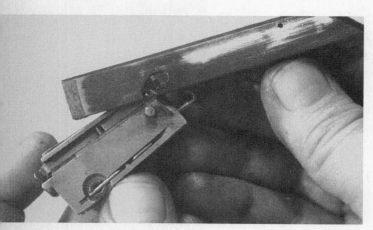

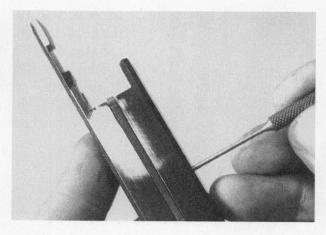

3. Separate the bolt from the bolt slide and take out the bolt cam pin which crosses the bolt at the rear. The cam pin does not fit tightly and can fall out, so take care that it isn't lost during disassembly.

4. Use a roll pin punch to drift out the cross pin in the bolt slide and remove the firing pin striker upward.

5. The firing pin is retained in the bolt by a roll pin across the upper rear, and the firing pin and its return spring are removed toward the rear.

6. A vertical pin on the left side of the bolt retains three parts—the left extractor, the ejector, and the carrier pawl retainer. The extractor and pawl retainer are removed toward the left, and the ejector is moved out toward the rear. Take care that the small coil springs with the ejector and inside the carrier pawl are not lost.

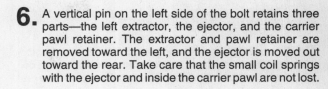

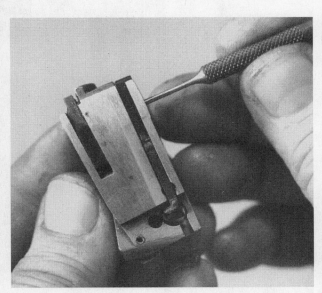

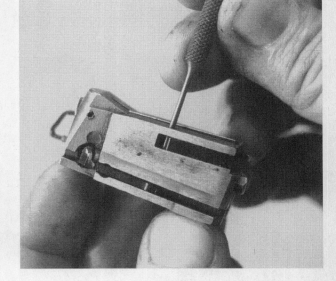

7. The right extractor is retained by a vertical roll pin on the right side of the bolt. The pin is accessible through a hole in the bottom right of the bolt, and is driven out upward. The extractor and its coil spring are taken off toward the right.

8. The lower extractor, part of the feed system, is retained by a vertical roll pin, accessible through a hole in the top of the bolt on the right side, and the pin is driven out downward. The lower extractor and its spring are then removed toward the right. Keep the spring with the lower extractor, and don't get it confused with the upper one, as they are not interchangeable.

9. Remove the buttplate, and use a B-Square stock bolt tool, or a long screwdriver, to take out the stock retaining bolt. When the bolt is out, take off the buttstock toward the rear.

10. Before removing the carrier and cartridge stop, carefully note the position and relationship of the combination spring which powers these parts, to aid in reassembly. Push out the cross pin which pivots and retains the cartridge stop, carrier, and the spring. All are removed upward, but the cartridge stop must be moved slightly forward before being lifted out. **Caution:** *The spring is under some tension, so keep the parts under control when pushing out the cross pin.*

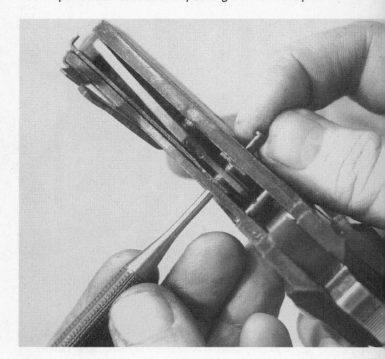

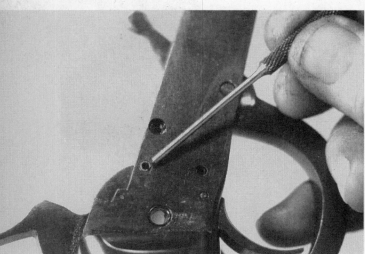

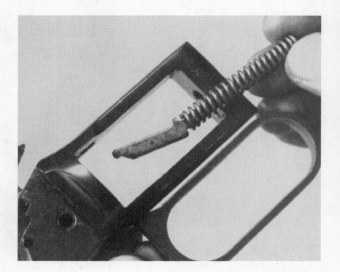

11. Use a roll pin punch to drift out the hammer stop pin, located just forward of the hammer. Set the hammer on its safety step while the stop pin is drifted out.

12. Restrain the hammer against its spring tension, pull the trigger to release it, and ease the hammer forward, past its normal down position. This will relieve the tension of the hammer spring, and the spring and its guide strut can then be removed from the rear, toward either side.

13. The hollow hammer pivot is now easily pushed out toward either side, and the hammer is removed upward. If the hammer pivot is tight, use a non-marring tool as large as its diameter, and take care not to deform its end edges.

14. With an Allen wrench of the proper size, take out the screw that retains the lever tension spring and its plate, and remove the plate and spring upward.

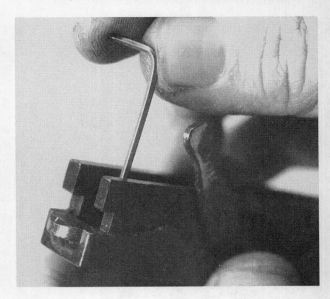

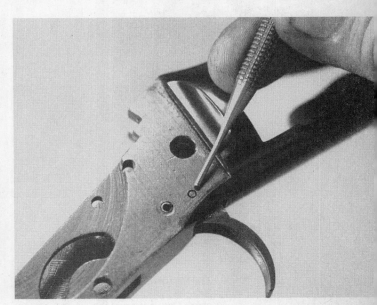

15. Push out the lever pivot pin toward the left, and remove the lever downward. Tip the upper lever arm toward the left as it is lifted out of its semi-circular opening and remove it.

16. Drifting out the solid cross pin above the trigger will release the trigger downward. The trigger spring is retained by a roll pin, just forward of the trigger pin.

17. Remove the cross screw in the rear barrel band, and slide the band off toward the front. If the band is very tight, it will be necessary to nudge it with a nylon drift and hammer. Nudge it equally, on alternate sides, to avoid binding.

18. Remove the cross screw from the front barrel band, and slide the outer magazine tube out toward the front. Remove the forend forward and downward.

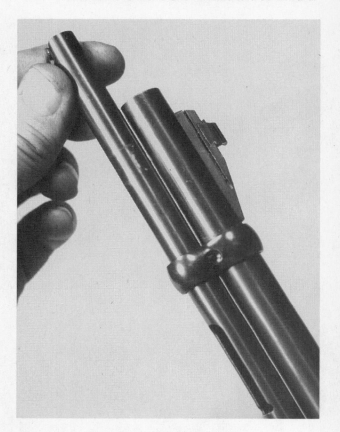

19. The barrel is retained in the receiver by a cross pin that is riveted on the right side. The pin must be driven out toward the left. The barrel can then be gripped in a padded vise and the receiver driven off with a wood or nylon mallet. In normal disassembly, however, the barrel is best left in place.

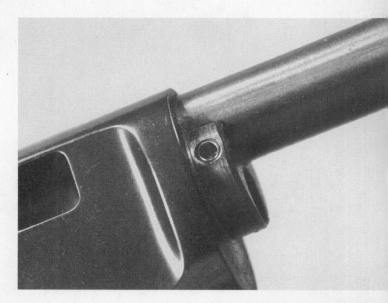

Reassembly Tips:

1. When replacing the outer magazine tube, be sure it is installed to its proper depth, and that the shallow groove in its top is aligned with the cross screw hole in the front barrel band.

2. To install the carrier, cartridge stop, and combination spring without great difficulty will require the use of a slave pin, a short length of rod stock to hold the parts together while they are positioned for insertion of the cross pin. The photo shows the proper arrangement of the parts and the spring, with the slave pin in place. The longer left arm of the spring goes below the hammer stop pin.

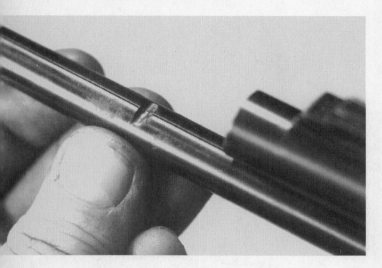

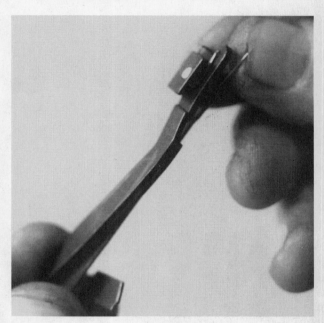

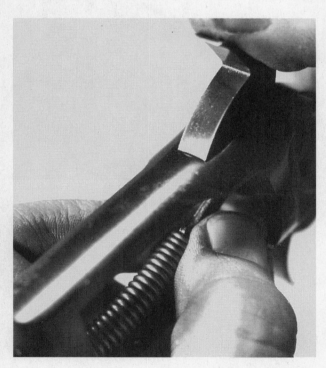

3. When replacing the hammer strut and spring, guide the spring at the rear to position the rear tip of the strut in alignment with its hole in the rear vertical bar of the trigger group. Be sure the front tip of the strut enters its recess on the rear of the hammer as the hammer is drawn back to the safety step.

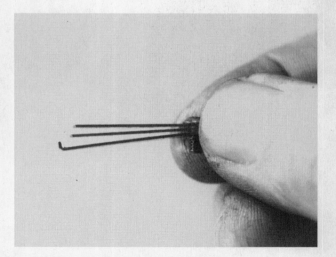

4. When replacing the lever tension system in the front of the trigger group, note that the single or double spring leaves go on top, and the L-shaped plate on the bottom, with the short arm of the "L" upward.

5. When replacing the lever, note that the upper arm of the lever must be in position in the trigger group before the lever is moved into place.

6. When replacing the bolt assembly in the receiver, the bolt and bolt slide should be engaged as shown, with the bolt in the unlocked position, as the assembly is moved into the rear of the receiver.

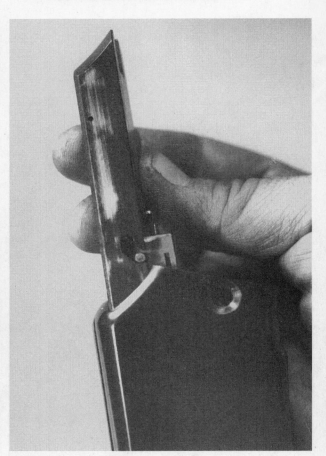

Index/Cross Reference